The Astrology Guide

Understanding Your Signs, Your Gifts, and Yourself

Claudia Trivelas

ABOUT THE AUTHOR

Claudia Trivelas provides an eclectic synthesis of a broad body of knowledge from many spiritual, esoteric, and metaphysical traditions. Graduating from Boston University with a degree in psychology and mathematics prepared her well to become an astrologer. She was mentored by astrology luminaries who include Isabel Hickey and Charles Emerson, a cosmobiologist and founder of the Uranian Society. She has touched the lives of many thousands of clients both in the United States and abroad with her insights and unique perspective that cultivate self-awareness and are ultimately self-empowering. You can find her New Moon and Full Moon updates on social media and online at www.DiscoverYourImprint.com. She does monthly predictions on the High Road to Humanity channel. Trivelas lives in North Kingstown, Rhode Island.

The Astrology Guide

UNDERSTANDING YOUR SIGNS, YOUR GIFTS, AND YOURSELF

CLAUDIA TRIVELAS

DETROIT

ALSO FROM VISIBLE INK PRESS

Ancient Gods: Lost Histories, Hidden Truths, and the Conspiracy of Silence
by Jim Willis
ISBN: 978-1-57859-614-0

Angels A to Z, 2nd edition
by Evelyn Dorothy Oliver and James R. Lewis
ISBN: 978-1-57859-212-8

Armageddon Now: The End of the World A to Z
by Jim Willis and Barbara Willis
ISBN: 978-1-57859-168-8

Censoring God: The History of the Lost Books (and other Excluded Scriptures)
by Jim Willis
ISBN: 978-1-57859-732-1

Demons, the Devil, and Fallen Angels
by Marie D. Jones and Larry Flaxman
ISBN: 978-1-57859-613-3

The Dream Encyclopedia, 2nd edition
by James R. Lewis and Evelyn Dorothy Oliver
ISBN: 978-1-57859-216-6

The Dream Interpretation Dictionary: Symbols, Signs and Meanings
by J. M. DeBord
ISBN: 978-1-57859-637-9

Earth Magic: Your Complete Guide to Natural Spells, Potions, Plants, Herbs, Witchcraft, and More
by Marie D. Jones
ISBN: 978-1-57859-697-3

The Encyclopedia of Religious Phenomena
by J. Gordon Melton, Ph.D.
ISBN: 978-1-57859-209-8

The Fortune-Telling Book: The Encyclopedia of Divination and Soothsaying
by Raymond Buckland
ISBN: 978-1-57859-147-3

The Handy Bible Answer Book
by Jennifer R. Prince
ISBN: 978-1-57859-478-8

The Handy Christianity Answer Book
by Stephen A. Werner, Ph.D.
ISBN: 978-1-57859-686-7

The Handy Islam Answer Book
by John Renard, Ph.D.
ISBN: 978-1-57859-510-5

The Handy Mythology Answer Book
by David Leeming, Ph.D.
ISBN: 978-1-57859-475-7

The Handy Religion Answer Book, 2nd edition
by John Renard, Ph.D.
ISBN: 978-1-57859-379-8

The New Witch: Your Guide to Modern Witchcraft, Wicca, Spells, Potions, Magic, and More
by Marie D. Jones
ISBN: 978-1-57859-716-1

Nightmares: Your Guide to Interpreting Your Darkest Dreams
by J. M. DeBord
ISBN: 978-1-57859-758-1

Real Miracles, Divine Intervention, and Feats of Incredible Survival
by Brad Steiger and Sherry Hansen Steiger
ISBN: 978-1-57859-214-2

Real Visitors, Voices from Beyond, and Parallel Dimensions
by Brad Steiger and Sherry Hansen Steiger
ISBN: 978-1-57859-541-9

The Religion Book: Places, Prophets, Saints, and Seers
by Jim Willis
ISBN: 978-1-57859-151-0

The Spirit Book: The Encyclopedia of Clairvoyance, Channeling, and Spirit Communication
by Raymond Buckland
ISBN: 978-1-57859-790-1

Supernatural Gods: Spiritual Mysteries, Psychic Experiences, and Scientific Truths
by Jim Willis
ISBN: 978-1-57859-660-7

Time Travel: The Science and Science Fiction
by Nick Redfern
ISBN: 978-1-57859-723-9

The Vampire Almanac: The Complete History
by J. Gordon Melton, Ph.D.
ISBN: 978-1-57859-719-2

The Witch Book: The Encyclopedia of Witchcraft, Wicca, and Neo-paganism
by Raymond Buckland
ISBN: 978-1-57859-114-5

The Witches Almanac: Sorcerers, Witches and Magic from Ancient Rome to the Digital Age
by Charles Christian
ISBN: 978-1-57859-760-4

Please visit us at visibleinkpress.com

THE ASTROLOGY GUIDE

Visible Ink Press®
43311 Joy Rd., #414
Canton, MI 48187-2075

Visible Ink Press is a registered trademark of Visible Ink Press LLC.

Most Visible Ink Press books are available at special quantity discounts when purchased in bulk by corporations, organizations, or groups. Customized printings, special imprints, messages, and excerpts can be produced to meet your needs. For more information, contact Special Markets Director, Visible Ink Press, www.visibleinkpress.com, or 734-667-3211.

Managing Editor: Kevin S. Hile
Cover Design: Graphikitchen, LLC
Page Design: Alessandro Cinelli, Cinelli Design
Typesetting: Marco Divita, Graphix Group
Proofreaders: Christa Gainer and Shoshana Hurwitz
Indexer: Larry Baker
Cover images: Shutterstock.

Paperback ISBN: 978-1-57859-738-3
Hardcover ISBN: 978-1-57859-819-9
eBook ISBN: 978-1-57859-820-5

Cataloging-in-Publication data is on file at the Library of Congress.

Printed in the United States of America.

10 9 8 7 6 5 4 3 2 1

DEDICATION

I dedicate this book to my grandchildren: Harrison, Eleanor, Max and Willa and to the spirit of Jack, who came close to his sojourn on Earth. May they discover their unique path in life and never lose track of who they are, regardless of the challenges and the influences they encounter.

I would like to credit a close family member, Dr. Louis D'Amario, who has briefed me on interesting facts about the planets. He worked at the NASA Jet Propulsion Laboratory for 35 years designing and navigating robotic solar system exploration missions.

CONTENTS

Photo Sources

Osama Shukir Muhammed Amin: p. 64.

Petrus Apianus: p. 278.

Annibale Carracci: p. 317.

Daderot (Wikicommons): p. 188.

Warren K. Leffler: p. 205.

Mentnafunangann (Wikicommons): p. 316.

Museo del Prado: p. 302.

National Museum of Finland: p. 311.

Shutterstock: pp. 3, 6, 10, 11, 13, 15, 17, 20, 22, 24, 26, 29, 32, 34, 39, 42, 44, 46, 48, 51, 53, 56, 58, 60, 62, 68, 70, 73, 74, 77, 79, 82, 84, 87, 89, 92, 94, 97, 99, 102, 104, 107, 108, 111, 114, 118, 120, 123, 124, 127, 130, 132, 134, 137, 140, 142, 144, 147, 149, 152, 154, 156, 160, 162, 164, 167, 169, 171, 174, 176, 178, 181, 183, 190, 192, 194, 198, 199, 201, 205, 208, 213, 215, 217, 220, 222, 224, 227, 230, 232, 235, 237, 238, 241, 243, 245, 248, 252, 255, 257, 259, 262, 264, 266, 269, 271, 274, 281, 283, 285, 288, 291, 293, 296, 300, 304, 307, 310, 313.

Lucien Waléry: p. 210.

Public Domain: p. 35.

FOREWORD

The Astrology Guide is the perfect title for this highly informative book by longtime astrologer Claudia Trivelas. It takes you on a guided tour of all aspects of this ancient art, allowing the reader to either search out bits of astrological wisdom that are of specific interest or to acquire the kind of wide-ranging knowledge that leads to expertise.

I have known Claudia since before we both began our astrological studies with the iconic and beloved astrologer Isabel Hickey of Boston in the late Sixties. And from the time I met her, I was impressed by Claudia's ability to zero in on and synthesize information of all kinds. If I wanted to catch up on just about anything, Claudia would be the one to ask. She was amazingly *au courant* and aware, and she brings this special talent to astrology in her own inimitable way.

Her succinct descriptions of the planets—astrology's alphabet—and their placements in each astrological sign are wonderfully accurate and enlightening. Her approach is also multifaceted because, while giving us the positive attributes of the signs and aspects, what she describes as our "gifts," she also provides the "shadow" side. This term is used very much in the Jungian sense as the part of oneself that isn't seen or acknowledged but that can create chaos and difficulties because it isn't apparent to its owner.

Every possible planetary placement and combination is covered in this book, clearly and concisely. Nothing is left out, so the kind of information it offers is never one-sided. Claudia also includes the dwarf planets and asteroids in insightful detail, enabling us to grasp their significance and put this information to work. Her knowledge and wisdom lend her descriptions of every facet of the astrological view a depth that goes well beyond what is generally available.

Astrology has many facets and comes in a bewildering number of forms. To be involved in it is a constant learning experience. Claudia's ability to absorb and integrate a vast array of information comes across in this wide-ranging book. It is a treat to delve into such a rich source, and anyone who does so will come away with an expanded understanding that informs their life and personal growth.

—Katharine Merlin (*Town & Country* astrologer and author of three books on astrology)

INTRODUCTION

Astrology is a wonderful tool for understanding personal growth. We can look to our own birth chart to discover ways to feel more in alignment with our highest potential and to live from a place of deep authenticity. As we develop and grow, an awareness of our innate, unique gifts helps direct us to areas of life where we can gain satisfaction and fulfillment. This, in turn, generates confidence and self-empowerment. Furthermore, we develop resilience to life's cycles and outer influences, based upon a strong foundation of who we are.

We all have different learning styles and absorb information and process experiences differently. This astrology guide is meant to provide insight and trigger "a-ha!" moments in terms of identifying the potential of your personal gifts as they relate to both the planetary energies and the placement in your birth chart.

We partner with the planets! I believe that it is a misnomer to look at the planets and planetary bodies as if they are doing something to us and we are their victims. If we can connect with the totality of the energy of planetary influence, then we can dance with their energies and exist in harmony with them.

This astrology guide points out the many sides of planets, luminaries, and important asteroids so we can welcome them into our consciousness and embrace each energy to its fullest. We can learn the gifts and challenges that the planetary energies offer.

We are all human, and our paths can vary. Some have more twists and turns, as we all learn differently. Learning lessons of life, the proverbial "hard way" can have a deepening value and serve a purpose in the journey. We are not apt to forget those experiences in a hurry! Astrology is a great tool for assisting us on our path.

The "shadow" is a concept first coined by Swiss psychiatrist Carl Jung that describes those aspects of the personality that we choose to reject and repress. We all have parts of ourselves that we don't like—or that we think society won't like—so we push those parts down into our unconscious psyches. As a result, these unconscious parts of ourselves can subtly influence our behavior and result in uncomfortable and unfulfilling results. As we become more consciously aware of our sub-conscious or unconscious patterns, we can choose how we want to respond to life and the situations that come before us.

With Jungian shadow work, you liberate a tremendous reservoir of energy that you were unconsciously investing in protecting yourself. This can improve your physical, mental, and emotional health. Shadow work can bring you inner strength and a greater sense of balance, making you better equipped to take on life's challenges.

To successfully embrace our destiny, we must first face our shadow, which includes the limiting beliefs we might have. Letting go of false and limiting beliefs that have defined our lives is often challenging and downright difficult. It can challenge us to our core, and yet it can empower us in ways we can't even imagine.

In the pages that follow, you will find the gift as well as the shadow side of each planetary combination to provide a deeper understanding of how the planetary energies are expressed.

Embracing the shadow manifestation of either a planet or a combination of planetary energies is the first step toward receiving its inherent gift. It is the dance with the devil we know that strengthens our resolve and puts fear in its proper perspective. A high price is paid for giving in to fear. Fear stifles creativity, prevents us from taking risks, and interferes with relationship fulfillment.

The shadow and the gift are but two sides of a double-edged sword. The sword is a tool that can cut through illusions that are reinforced by the pervasive and penetrating aura of the collective unconscious. Freedom and liberation are the results of knowing all aspects of who we are at our core.

> The purpose of Shadow work is to see and engage it within yourself, so that everything about your life becomes a richer, more wondrous experience—for everybody.
>
> —Caroline Myss

The insights provided in this astrology guide are meant to offer you fragments of information that serve as a starting point for you to contemplate what is possible. Each piece of information has to be put into the context of the rest of the astrology chart. Your own personal interpretation will add to the gestalt of your unique imprint. Stephen Forrest noted in his book *The Inner Sky*, "A fair criticism of most astrology is that 'it puts people in little boxes.'"

The art of chart interpretation develops over time and includes learning the planetary energies and how these planetary dynamics interact with each other as well as a great deal of contemplation and admiration for the uniqueness of every chart.

Aptly put in an excerpt from *The Art of Contemplation* by Richard Rudd:

> The core message that contemplation teaches us is that feeling fear is safe. That is, fear does not feel safe, but it is safe to feel it. Similarly, as we approach pain of any sort, instead of flinching, through contemplation we soften into it. When someone is physically wounded, our immediate instinct is to behave gently and calmly around them. Contemplation applies this same wisdom inwardly. We all carry tender emotional wounds of one sort or another. The touch of contemplation is the gentlest, most all-forgiving touch. When you feel any level of pain, this is the spirit in which you need to approach yourself.
>
> At the center of your being you have the answer; you know who you are and you know what you want.
>
> —Lao Tzu

The Basics

BASIC INFORMATION ABOUT SIGNS

Signs are grouped into arrangements determined by the geometric layout of the Zodiac. Triplicities deal with the tendencies of temperament, and quadruplicities influence the basic mode of functioning.

THE FOUR ELEMENTS

The four basic elements—Fire, Earth, Air, and Water—belong to one of the four triplicities, meaning that each of the four elements have three signs.

THE FIRE TRIPLICITY: ARIES, LEO, SAGITTARIUS

Fire sign people are inspirational and often uplifting. Energy exudes from their faces, especially when they have a Fire sign as their Sun, Moon, or Ascendant sign or a preponderance of planets in Fire signs.

These individuals are positive, ardent, energetic, and creative in their expression. They often display leadership in a way that resonates with each sign: an Aries may initiate with their decisiveness; a Leo may hold the gavel as a central figure in an organization; or a Sagittarius can act as a spiritual or philosophic leader in areas related to law, higher education, or spirituality.

THE EARTH TRIPLICITY: TAURUS, VIRGO, CAPRICORN

When several planets are in Earth signs, especially when the Sun, Moon, or Ascendant is in an Earth sign, a vibration of solidity occurs. These people are practical, grounded, display common sense, and have a general sensibility of structural or material integrity. Taureans resonate with Earth and value the resources and comforts that Earth offers. Virgos are adept at creating and maintaining the order necessary for everyday functioning. Capricorns can offer the ability to structure and organize business and economic affairs in order to bring practical and efficient solutions.

THE AIR TRIPLICITY:
GEMINI, LIBRA, AQUARIUS

Air signs bring a lightness of being that contributes to social interaction and social relationships. When Air signs are dominant in a chart as the Sun, Moon, or Ascendant or when several planets are in Air signs, an ease in both social and intellectual atmospheres occurs. Air signs often display a strong interest in mental activities and different types of social interactions that resonate to their particular sign. Gemini has a desire to acquire, digest, and communicate information that has been gleaned. Diplomacy is key with dominant planets in Libra along with a strong sense of social justice and fairness. A concern for the well-being of humanity along with an intuitive grasp of universal principles can be common with Aquarians.

THE WATER TRIPLICITY:
CANCER, SCORPIO, PISCES

When the Sun, Moon, or Ascendant are in a Water sign or when several planets are in Water signs, an attunement with the realm of emotion and feeling occurs. These signs do well in situations that call for sensitivity, intuition, and the deeper psychic aspects of life. Cancers have sensitivity and strong feelings for those close to them, and they do well at nurturing and taking care of others. Cancer aligns to soul urges. A Scorpio can rally to the fore in any critical or life-or-death situation. Scorpio aligns to what is not obvious. Pisces attune to those both near and far with their acute sensitivity and desire to be helpful. Pisces aligns to spirit.

THE THREE SIGN MODALITIES

The quadruplicities are groupings of four signs each that deal with modes of activity and with adaptability to circumstances. These groupings of signs are called Cardinal, Fixed, and Mutable signs.

CARDINAL:
ARIES, CANCER, LIBRA, CAPRICORN

The Cardinal modality is an active one, one that requires taking direct and decisive action in the present circumstance. It is not uncommon for an individual with several planets in Cardinal signs to make corrections to the action that was taken. Their main impulse is to "do something" initially. It is easy for them to take the initiative and make their intentions and desires known.

FIXED:
TAURUS, LEO, SCORPIO, AQUARIUS

Fixed signs have staying power. They are slow to change and have difficulty changing direction when something new is needed. These signs are more apt to achieve results through determination. Their success comes through unwavering persistence over an extended period of time. It may appear to an outsider that nothing is happening in regards to a stated goal; however, much is taking place beneath view, and they are on top of it. These folks are constant and reliable in their convictions; however, they can lean toward rigidity and stubbornness.

MUTABLE:
GEMINI, VIRGO, SAGITTARIUS, PISCES

Mutable signs are flexible and easily adjust to changing circumstances. They adapt

The Zodiac's 12 signs fall into four divisions, grouped naturally by the four elements—Fire, Earth, Air, and Water—each holding a triplicity of three signs.

themselves to the exigencies of life and, like chameleons, are able to meld into their circumstances and surroundings. This ability comes from previous experience in similar circumstances. If you want a spur-of-the-moment companion for any reason, ask a Mutable sign or someone with several planets in Mutable signs, and they are likely to come along. These individuals can be resourceful, although they may be prone to worry and nervousness.

YIN- AND YANG-ORIENTED SIGNS

Signs are grouped as being either Yin oriented or Yang oriented, indicating the sign's orientation to the world. In traditional astrology, signs were classified as masculine and feminine and oftentimes as positive and negative signs even though this classification did not refer to physical gender or an attitudinal slant.

Fire and Air signs are Yang, and Earth and Water signs are Yin. Basically, the odd-numbered signs, beginning with Aries, are Yang, and the even-numbered signs, beginning with Taurus, are Yin.

Yang-oriented signs: Aries, Gemini, Leo, Libra, Sagittarius, Aquarius

Yin-oriented signs: Taurus, Cancer, Virgo, Scorpio, Capricorn, Pisces

Those born under Yang signs are self-initiating. Those born under Yin signs are more apt to wait for things to come to them. Yang signs prefer to seize the moment, make things happen, and change what doesn't suit them with their actions and choices. Yin signs take a more subtle, passive approach when dealing with challenge or working for change.

Several planets in Yang signs can indicate a self-propelling person who is comfortable taking the initiative. Similarly, a strong preponderance of planets in Yin signs can indicate a person who can possess great strength in terms of passive endurance.

How Planetary Bodies Interact

Every planetary combination offers its gift when the energies are used in alignment with our true self and do no harm to others.

Planets rotate at different speeds around the Sun in somewhat the same plane in space. Most planets spin as though they were a coin spun on its edge, flicked counterclockwise, with a few exceptions. Of course, maverick Uranus spins like a bead rolled along the ground instead of spinning vertically. Surprisingly, Venus—the planet of balance, as her manifestation is in Libra—is even odder and spins clockwise.

It is the gravity of the Sun that keeps planets in their orbits. The Moon orbits Earth because of the pull of Earth's gravity, and Earth orbits the Sun because of the pull of the Sun's gravity.

An astrology chart is an attempt to represent the planets on a flat plane. An astrology chart is a circle that contains 360 degrees. Geometrically, the way planets combine is based upon their relationship to each other within the circle. Various angles, measured in degrees, minutes, and seconds, are formed between the planets as seen from Earth. These angular relationships are called aspects.

THE MAJOR ASPECTS

Certain degrees of angularity are important to astrology. Traditional astrology identifies as major aspects the connections between planets that result from dividing the chart circle in half, thirds, fourths, and sixths, which correspond to divisions based upon 0, 60, 90, 120, and 180 degrees. These aspects are called the Conjunction, Sextile, Square, Trine, and Opposition, respectively.

Conjunction: A conjunction is when planetary bodies are generally between 0 and 8 degrees of each other. A larger orb, 10 degrees, is used for the Sun and Moon, and a smaller orb, 6 degrees, is used when

Trines generally occur when planets are in the same element triplicity: Fire, Air, Earth, or Water. A natural flow occurs between these planetary energies. Trines are considered fortunate. It is easier to see where the energy is coming from.

Opposition: Planetary bodies are in an Opposition aspect, or 180 degrees apart, when a circle is divided in half. Similar to a Conjunction, an orb of 0–8 degrees is used, with a smaller orb for outer planets connecting to each other and a larger orb, up to 10 degrees, for aspects to the Sun, Moon, or Ascendant. Oppositions between planets can generate tension since each planet body is in a sign that manifests energy differently. However, when the planets can compromise and blend the difference between the signs, then the innate conflict between them can be used positively. Oppositions often manifest through other people, as the name implies. We can be blindsided when the conflict lies right in front of us.

Conjunctions—connections of celestial bodies within a small arc, as seen in this photo of Saturn in close approach to Jupiter—mark a strong focalized potential for expression.

outer planets connect to each other. Conjunctions (glyphs) are the dynamic aspects between planetary bodies and mark a strong focalized potential for expression.

Sextile: When the circle is divided by 6, planetary bodies are in a Sextile aspect, or 60 degrees apart.

Square: A Square aspect occurs between planetary bodies when they are 90 degrees apart or when the planets are in the same modality—Cardinal, Fixed, or Mutable—but in different elements. An orb of 0–6 degrees is used between the planetary bodies, except for the Sun and Moon, where an 8-degree orb can have an influence.

Trine: Dividing a circle by three, where the planets are 120 degrees apart from each other within an orb of 0–6 degrees, is called a Trine. A larger orb, up to 8 degrees, applies for the Sun and Moon.

When you make a 90-degree turn on the road, you have to look both ways before turning. Some effort is involved since a blind spot can occur. When a gentle, 120-degree or 60-degree curve occurs in the road, it is easier and smoother to navigate. Similarly, with Opposition, you may not always see something or someone headed straight at you, especially if you are not expecting it.

From the perspective of this planetary guide, an individual is more likely to initially manifest the shadow side of a planetary combination when the planets combine in Squares, Oppositions, and sometimes Conjunctions. Observation, conscious awareness of the planetary energies when they interact, will eventually lead to finding that gift, which leads to self-empowerment.

THE MINOR ASPECTS

The 360-degree circle that represents an astrology chart can be further divided into 5, 7, 8, 9, 10, and 12 parts. These further subdivisions of a chart are called minor aspects. These aspects can provide additional insights when interpreting a chart. Typically, an orb of 2 degrees is used for connections between most planets, except for the Sun and Moon, where an orb of 3 degrees is within the range of influence of each planet receiving energy from another planetary body.

Semi-Sextile (30 degrees): A Semi-Sextile is half of a Sextile. Gifts can be gleaned from a Semi-Sextile aspect, especially when applying conscious attention and a little extra work for the gift to manifest. The glyph for Semi-Sextile is ⊻.

Semi-Square (45 degrees): A Semi-Square is half of a Square. This aspect can indicate buried shadow traits that are not dominant in one's conscious awareness. The glyph for Semi-Square is ∠.

Sesquiquadrate (135 degrees): A Sesquiquadrate is a Square (90 degrees) plus a Semi-Square. With a Sesquiquadrate, shadows not only lurk around the corner, but they are not easily in view after turning the corner. One of the gifts of astrology is that we can see the aspects between planetary energies in the birth chart and then become further aware of their influence. The glyph for Sesquiquadrate is ⊡.

Quintile (72 degrees): Dividing a circle by 5 yields the Quintile, which can indicate a talent that can be developed. Gifts are easily recognized based upon the combination of the planetary energies. Quintiles are creative aspects that show our uniqueness as human beings. It is the energy of self-realization and personal power. The Quintile is a dynamic force and has an intensity similar to a Conjunction. The individual will be innovative, and their gifts can be used to turn something old into something new. The glyph for Quintile is the letter Q.

Bi-Quintile (144 degrees): The Bi-Quintile has double the degrees of the Quintile and is based upon dividing the circle by 5. Like the Quintile, this aspect indicates gifts and creative talents based upon the combination of the planetary energies involved. The glyph for Bi-Quintile is the letters bQ.

Quincunx (150 degrees): The Quincunx is also called an Inconjunct and is formed when two planets are five signs apart. The signs of the planets differ by both element and modality, making it difficult for the planets to operate well together. A Quincunx will add a touch of drama and conflict but is also solution oriented. A Quincunx is a 150-degree aspect, so it's made of a Square (90 degrees) and a Sextile (60 degrees). The best way to gain from a Quincunx is to first deal with the tension, or shadow side, of the Square. Then, once the tension is recognized, the opportunity of the Sextile comes, along with the gift from working with the shadow of the Square. Inner tension is felt in both areas of life where these planets are placed. Understanding the shadow side of both planetary energies will help to bring forward the gifts from each of the planets and thereby reduce the potential stress between these two planetary bodies. The Quincunx is an important aspect in medical astrology, as the aspect made by the planets has a Sixth House connotation. The glyph for Quincunx or Inconjunct is ⚻.

Septile (51 degrees, 26 minutes): The Septile results from dividing a circle by 7. Septiles reflect an element of the infinite since dividing 360 degrees by 7 does not yield a round number but rather a number that continues on endlessly (51.42857143…). Septiles are considered to be philosophical and wisdom seeking and offer gifts for attaining wisdom based upon the planetary energies themselves as well as in the areas indicated in the chart. Individuals with dominant Septiles can be inventive and may have abilities to comprehend esoteric realms.

Novile (40 degrees): The Novile aspect occurs when the circle is divided into 9 equal parts. Vedic astrologers focus to a great extent on the Ninth Harmonic chart, or the Navamsha chart, for information on where one is headed and one's goals. This aspect indicates gifts that we want to develop for our personal evolution.

Astrologers typically assign negative attributes to some planetary combinations, including Squares, Semi-Squares, Oppositions, Quincunxes or Inconjuncts, and sometimes Conjunctions. These planetary combinations have traditionally been considered difficult and challenging. I have found in my practice that challenging planetary combinations can yield beautiful gifts and insights for many of my clients. Much depth and wisdom can be learned from delving into challenges and unfulfilled expectations when managing a constant itch or irritation.

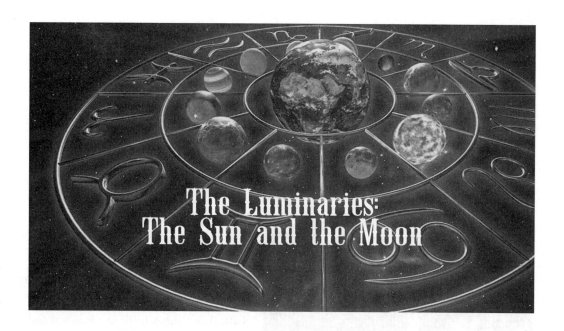

The Luminaries:
The Sun and the Moon

The Sun and the Moon are not planets. They are traditionally called luminaries.

THE SUN

The Sun, in all of its glory, brings us light and warmth. As the Sun moves around the constellations in the sky, the quality of its light and warmth changes for those of us here on Earth. The light may have a bluish or greenish, more subtle hue, or, perhaps, it is brighter and appears to have an orange hue. Similarly, sometimes the Sun's rays are hotter and burn us, and other times it brings delicious inner warmth.

Each of the subtle hues is a gift, as are increments of warmth, whether it is a frosty morning or warm midday. The Sun is what we are here to give to the world. The Sun is how we express ourselves. The strength of the Sun can indicate how easily you shine in your life. The Sun represents your will and purpose, your vitality. The Sun also reflects a deeper sense of our indi-viduality, which seeks acknowledgment and expression in our lives.

It is no accident that a newly sprouted seed resembles the Aries symbol: the horns of a ram. It is also amazing how much power a new seed exerts in pushing through the soil to the surface. Here again is the solar vitality of the Aries-exalted Sun that attracts the blind seed's pushing toward the light through the lunar-textured earth. All life, biological and spiritual, is drawn to the outer or inner Sun.

Libra, the polar opposite of Aries, represents the harvest as completed and weighed on Libra's Scales, then bartered, transacted, or traded.

Combining the Sun in its respective sign and house placement along with other planetary energies that the Sun interacts with can provide a view into that individual's soul's purpose in this life as well as possible core issues that could prevent a

The Sun in all of its glory brings us light and warmth. All life, biological and spiritual, is drawn to the outer or inner Sun.

manifestation of the soul's intent. An astrology chart is a blueprint of the soul and can provide insight into the gifts and challenges inherent in the soul's journey.

THE SUN IN THE SIGNS

Sun in Aries

As the first sign of the Zodiac, Aries is the sign of new beginnings. The Sun is well placed in Mars-ruled Aries, and the Sun is considered exalted as the first Fire sign of the Zodiac wheel.

Aries is the "I am" principle, the idea that in the beginning was a first impulse, and that first impulse was me! As a self-oriented sign, Aries exemplifies the right to behave autonomously, to set boundaries and defend them. As a Cardinal sign, Aries

is action oriented and believes that it is best to start somewhere.

Aries are direct and aggressive in expressing themselves. They are enthusiastic, courageous, energetic, and competitive. Aries rules the head, and as a result, they can be characterized as headstrong. The symbol for Aries is the Ram; a ram charges forward head-on with gusto, undeterred in their goal.

Aries, the first sign of the Zodiac, has a natural resonance with the First House.

Keywords for Aries and the First House: What do I have to do to become more fully me?

Gift: Aries brings forth inspirational and instinctive energy. Their keywords are "I can," "I am brave," "I am courageous." Aries is an infectious Sun sign and can inspire a lover or a crowd with their charm. Aries brings an aura of freshness and renewal. Aries thrive on adventure, competition, a worthy challenge, and lighting up a room. They are brave, generous, passionate, and driven.

Shadow: Impatient, self-centered, impulsive, headstrong, Aries can lack discernment in their action-oriented approach. Aries also indicates rashness and a willingness to rush in where angels fear to tread. The opposite sign to Mars-ruled Aries is Venus-ruled Libra. Blending compromise, balance, and diplomacy can serve an Arian native well in personal and social relationships. Aries can miss the nuances in personal interactions and social activities.

The Sun is in Aries from around March 20 until April 20. The dates for Aries change every year, so check an ephemeris if you're on the cusp.

Sun in Taurus

As a Fixed Earth sign, Taurus harnesses and grounds the fiery energy of Aries with its "don't rush me into anything unless I am ready for it" orientation. Sensual Taureans know how to relax and simplify the task at hand, but watch out: when they are ready to move forward, they are persistent and unstoppable. As a Venus-ruled sign, Taurus can be calm and pleasant until they are not. Practicality and plain old common sense are attributes you can count on with a Taurus. Taureans revel in the pleasures of life and enjoy the comforts of their familiar environments. As the first Earth sign, they are tuned in to the growth process in a very basic way. They understand that all living things are entitled to the dignity of their life cycle. Survival is important to Taureans from a very practical standpoint.

Taureans have a knack for effusing a calm, settled vibe, but can be inert and stubborn when they don't want to be moved.

Sun in Taurus individuals are generally calm, artistic, pleasure-oriented, possessive, and traditional. Taureans have an innate sensibility regarding business.

Taurus is the largest and most populated constellation in the Zodiac. It is also the sign that is most often mentioned in history and mythology. For example, many peoples throughout the world commenced their planting when the Pleiades, in Taurus, were rising. Taurus attracts what it needs and hangs on to it.

Keywords for Taurus and the Second House: Is it worth my time and resources?

Gift: Taurus folks have a knack for effusing a calm, settled vibe. Whether it is their patient and down-to-earth approach or a steadiness that you can count on, Taureans are good to have around when you need support or need to stop and smell the roses. Their advice is always guided by common sense and basic practicality. Taurus rules the throat, and Taureans are bestowed with a beautiful voice for speaking and singing. They exhibit great stamina and have a fixed purpose in their endeavors.

Shadow: Like their symbol, the Bull, Taureans can be inert and stubborn when they don't want to be moved. Possessions can take on unwarranted importance, whereas close family and friends can feel undervalued. Too much relaxation and sensual indulgence can lead to unfulfilled ambitions and a narrow-minded approach to life.

The Sun is in Taurus from around April 20 until May 20. The dates for Taurus can change every year, so check an ephemeris if you're on the cusp.

Sun in Gemini

Mercury-ruled Gemini is the first of the dual signs. The Gemini glyph is represented by the Roman number II, signifying the sign's dual nature. The two parallel vertical lines are joined by two crescents. One cannot exist without the other. Yin cannot exist without Yang. Yang cannot exist without Yin. Light cannot exist without shadow. We define our life on Earth by such polarities as dark–light, up–down, in–out, good–evil, or male–female. Gemini exemplifies that duality is the essence of third-dimensional humanity.

This Gemini duality is resolved through communications between both of their parts, and thus, Geminis are naturally good communicators. In the study of esoteric astrology, however, Gemini is ruled by Venus because the highest form of communication is love.

Gemini is a sign of relationships, of interplays between discrete objects, people, or ideas. Their path to unity is through the awareness of dualities. An innate playfulness evolves. The world becomes a kaleidoscope of input and a treasure chest of playthings. For Gemini, variety is truly the spice of life. As the symbol of the Twins implies, a Gemini likes someone or something to relate to, whether it's speaking, laughing, writing, or using their hands to create.

Mercury-ruled Gemini likes to disseminate information. They like fresh knowledge in order to keep their curious minds content.

As the winged messenger, Mercury plays the intermediary, the mediator. Gemini is a playful, curious child at heart, reminding everyone not to take themselves too seriously.

Gemini rules the lungs, where we exchange air between inner and outer worlds.

Keywords for Gemini and the Third House: What information can I communicate and disseminate?

Gift: Lively and versatile, a Gemini can lighten up an otherwise tense encounter. Motivated by their desire to communicate, a Gemini can put others at ease by being present and by showing interest in others. Onlookers can be in awe of a Gemini as they skillfully accomplish several activities in a day, often keeping several balls in the air at one time. In its constant focus on making connections, Gemini has perhaps the greatest opportunity of any sign to be an effective force for uplifting others. Gemini is truly versatile and multitalented. Like Libra, Gemini is a sign of relationships, of finding something in common and establishing a dialogue that leads to understanding and friendship.

> As the symbol of the Twins implies, a Gemini likes someone or something to relate to, whether it's speaking, laughing, writing, or using their hands to create.

Shadow: The Gemini's need for stimulation can create chaos and undermine progress when a situation calls for a steady hand, giving the impression of avoiding hard things. A too-friendly disposition can display a lack of seriousness and depth, not to mention those unfinished projects that result from being scatterbrained and having a monkey mind. Doubt, confusion, and undirected restlessness can make the Gemini mind a very tricky and destructive place when it is not balanced with reality and the perspective of the higher mind. The formless nature of Mercury, the ruler of Gemini, contributes to scattered or disorganized thoughts if the Mercurial process isn't grounded and formed.

The Sun is in Gemini from around May 21 until June 21. The dates for Gemini can change every year, so check an ephemeris if you're on the cusp.

Sun in Cancer

Cancer is a Cardinal Water sign ruled by the Moon. As the Moon guides us in the night with her waxing and waning light, Cancers navigate us through the watery depths of emotion and the dark unconscious. Cancers feel at home with cycles and fluctuations and can change their mood accordingly, the same way that the Moon changes signs every two to two and a half days. Cancer Sun people are meant to remind us not to look on the surface but to dive deep, where the waters are calm and life is sustainable. They remind us of the importance of deep connections, either through their caring disposition or their responsiveness to the slightest offhand remark. They tend to focus on those aspects of their lives that are near and dear: family, home life, close friends, businesses, or whatever else they feel is part of their stable and intimate base. Cancer is concerned about all the things in life that bring them comfort and generate a feeling of safety. Think of the glyph that is used for Cancer, the Crab. The Crab carries around its home on its back, its shell, which provides safety and protection.

As a Water sign, Cancer is associated with liquids: the amniotic sac, which nurtures an unborn child; the lymphatic system of the body, which supports cells; tears, which cleanse the soul; and the stomach, where digestive fluids break down food in order to prepare for the absorption of nutrients.

Those born under the sign of Cancer are deep, sensitive, protective, sensual, and

Sensitive and emotional, Cancers have a nurturing impulse to help others feel safe and secure. But they can be accused of extreme emotional fluctuations, moodiness, and overpersonalizing the slightest inference.

emotional. Cancer rules the mother; everyone was birthed by a mother, and many have been a mother. Cancer represents universal energy. The nurturing, protective Cancerean impulse is universal to both men and women.

The Cancer vibration that is capable of surrendering itself in order to give to another is exemplified when a mother nurtures their baby in the womb.

Keywords for Cancer and the Fourth House: I care for whatever is important to me.

Gift: Cancers bring the gift of caring. How did they even remember something I barely mentioned a month ago? They warm the heart and touch the soul. Cancers' nurturing impulses help others to feel safe and secure. With the keywords "I feel," Cancers remind us not to stay in our heads and overthink every little thing when the way we feel can get down to the nitty-gritty more acutely. We need Cancers as a balance, especially in today's world, where what we think can receive more credence than how we feel. A Cancer understands empathy and can go with the flow when others need assistance.

Shadow: Sensitive and emotional, Cancers can be accused of extreme emotional fluctuations, moodiness, and overpersonalizing the slightest inference. As the symbol of the Crab implies, Cancers can hide in their shells and withdraw in a defensive stance when they are not comfortable. An over-expression of emotion can make it difficult to count on a Cancer when efficiency is at play; however, once they know that you need them, they will drop the emotional indulgence and be right there for you. Cancers can cling to the past at the expense of moving forward. Oversentimentality can lead to excess clutter and hoarding, which can include holding on to relationships past the point of growth for both parties.

The Sun is in Cancer from around June 21 until July 22. The dates for Cancer can change every year, so check an ephemeris if you're on the cusp.

Sun in Leo

Like the Sun, a Leo loves to shine. The Sun is life, vitality, and light. The Sun is at the center of our solar system, around which all planets revolve. In like fashion, Leo types will ideally be found in the center of every circle either through magnetism or, less ideally, through self-asser-

tion. The developed Leo type will radiate like the Sun, attracting attention rather than forcing it.

Leos have an innate ability to see their role based on how they can best shine in any situation. Leo is the most regal and creative Sun sign. Represented by the Lion, Leos are courageous, stately, fiercely loyal, confident, and passionate and conduct themselves with pride.

Keywords for Leo and the Fifth House: How can I bring my love and light to the world?

Gift: Leo stands for unique individuality. Leo represents qualities that only you have, and if you choose to share and radiate those qualities, you will make the world a better place. The gift of Leo is a connection to their core self and how they can best express their core self. Leos are natural leaders. In a quote from Warren G. Bennis, author of *On Becoming a Leader*, "Becoming a leader is synonymous with becoming yourself. It is precisely that simple, and it is also that difficult." Leos emanate radiance, courage, and vitality. They are nourished by the Sun and like to burn brightly.

Shadow: Leos can become too fixed on their objects of affection. Their strong egos can get involved as a result of their passion and need for attention. It benefits a Leo to elevate their gaze to the realm of limitless compassion and emanate love. When they rule from their hearts, unobstructed by their egos and selfish pursuits, they truly shine. A Leo knows how to roar, and they add a dramatic flair to any situ-

> Leos have an innate ability to see their role based on how they can best shine in any situation.

ation. Sometimes, their chest-thumping and grandiose gestures come purely from ego and as ways to blow off steam rather than as serious assertions of who they are. Nonetheless, these radical assertions can be overbearing for the faint of heart when witnessed in an inappropriate setting.

The Sun is in Leo from around July 23 until August 23. The dates for Leo can change every year, so check an ephemeris if you're on the cusp.

Sun in Virgo

Virgo, as a Mutable Earth sign ruled by Mercury, wants to make sense out of the world and bring order to chaos and common sense to confusion.

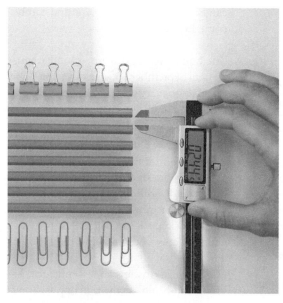

Virgo is impeccably discerning, an ardent perfectionist, and can be a purist, but should remember to look at the whole picture and not lose track of the forest for the trees.

Virgo is often symbolized by a female archetype. In ancient times, she was known as a goddess by many of her names: Isis, Nut, Ceres, Demeter, Kwan Yin, or Green or White Tara. She represents purity, quiet power, and the nurturing and caring qualities of Virgo.

Strong analytical abilities and attention to detail, coupled with a desire for perfection, gives Virgo an edge in areas that involve observation, research, problem solving, and analysis. Virgos excel in finding workable options for improving things.

Unless otherwise indicated in the birth chart, Virgos are dedicated to service rather than to power, and they will often prefer to work behind the scenes.

Virgo is a sign related to physical health, ruling the lower intestines, where nutrients are sorted out and then used by the body.

Keywords for Virgo and the Sixth House: How can I make my day-to-day life more functional?

Gift: Virgos are impeccably discerning, ardent perfectionists and can be purists. Virgos can diligently break down plans and projects into manageable tasks, then approach each task step by step. Virgos are gifted critics and rarely let any detail escape them. Their dry and descriptive take on situations give them a comedic edge that Virgos will display sometimes when least expected. Virgos are realists. They are willing to recognize and work with what exists. You can count on them for a no-nonsense evaluation.

Shadow: The Virgo addiction to perfection can be a problem at times. It behooves a Virgo to look at the whole picture and not lose track of the forest for the trees. Virgos can alienate others and be a hindrance to themselves until they learn to use their amazing powers of discernment and attention to detail in order to be critical of problems and not of people. Virgos can be obsessed with hygiene and can become hypochondriacs.

The Sun is in Virgo from around August 23 until September 23. The dates for Virgo can change every year, so check an ephemeris if you're on the cusp.

Sun in Libra

Venus-ruled Libra is the sign of relationships. It is the sign that teaches us how to understand another's perspective and, subsequently, harmonize with them. As a Cardinal Air sign, a Libra will initiate activities and seek cooperation from others.

Healthy relationships are essential to a Libran's well-being. As the sign opposite self-oriented Aries, they realize that who we are is only half of the story. For them to become whole, they need to integrate the other. The key to their ultimate relationship fulfillment is being able to integrate the "other" while maintaining one's center, or "self." This is the balance that is key to the sign of Libra. It is not surprising that the symbol most often used for Libra is the Scales.

The symbol of the Scales also represents the strong sense of justice and fair play that is so important to a Libra. They demand the same high standard of fairness and cooperation from others that they are willing to put forth themselves.

As part of the Air sign triplicity, those born under the sign of Libra are intellectual and actively seek knowledge, new ideas, and mental stimulation. They share an interest in relating, as do the other Air signs. The difference is that Gemini rules more casual acquaintances, or people we come into contact with based upon circumstances. Aquarius governs friendships and people we choose because we share a common ideal or a common interest. Libra rules personal and business partnerships.

A Libran relationship requires more participation than other types of relationships if one is to gain fulfillment from the connection. This can explain why Saturn, the planet of responsibility, is exalted in Libra. Finding wholeness with another while maintaining authenticity of one's self is a serious endeavor, especially when it requires leaving an unhealthy ego at the door.

Keywords for Libra and the Seventh House: How can I create balance in my life?

Gift: With an abundance of relational intelligence, Libras can put themselves in another person's shoes and negotiate from that positioning. They are diplomatic and can be natural peacemakers. They choose their words carefully and aim to find common ground. A Libra is in their element in almost any social gathering. They make charming hosts and hostesses when they entertain, especially in their tasteful and visually pleasing homes. Charm and grace are Libran qualities. Ruled by Venus, they love beauty and have a well-developed aesthetic sensibility that can create ambience in almost every environment.

Shadow: Making others' needs more important than their own is a pitfall for a Libra to avoid in their quest for a fulfilling relationship. They have to remember that they can't please absolutely everyone all of the time without eroding their own authenticity and sense of self. Libras' love of balance has been known to get in their way. As a result, they can get caught up in weighing the pros and cons of the smallest and most mundane decisions. Libras can be overly preoccupied with presentation, whether it be appearance or environmental aesthetics, which can be interpreted as vain or superficial by some.

The Sun is in Libra from around September 23 until October 23. The dates for Libra can change every year, so check an ephemeris if you're on the cusp.

Sun in Scorpio

Transformational Scorpios possess qualities of the psychologist, the shaman, and the mystic. Scorpios learn to master the art of letting go. They help us heal our deepest wounds by holding our hand as we face and release our shadows. They bring a new understanding to crisis situations with their depth of perception and their ability to be truly present.

Those born with their Sun in Scorpio can be understood by looking at their opposite sign, Taurus. A Taurus has what they have generally as a result of their own effort. Scorpios, on the other hand, have what they have as a result of merging with others. The place of merging is dark and scary; it is filled with mystery, secrets, and danger. It is also the place where real intimacy happens and where true connections are formed.

A Scorpio may appear at times to have a hard shell. They are not ones to show their vulnerabilities, except to a few people who have earned their trust. Nonetheless, they are highly sensitive beneath their secretive, mysterious outer appearance. A Scorpio cares deeply and passionately. Their emotions are intense. Deep within them is an intense power that understands pain and suffering. They understand the struggle of being trapped in a state of darkness. They also understand how to pick themselves back up and start anew. Transformation and the process of death and rebirth is understood, if not consciously, then instinctively.

Scorpios' understanding of struggle gives them the ability to successfully help others. But emotional involvement in close relationships can get out of their control, leading to obsessive and controlling behavior.

Scorpios can soar high, although they know the darkness of lows. Hence, the sign of Scorpio is symbolized by both the Serpent and the Eagle. The Eagle representation is the transformed Scorpio that has let go of blame, grudges, and retribution. The Eagle represents the shamanic renewal that can use its journey through the darkness to heal those in transit through darkness or overshadowed by their circumstances.

Keywords for Scorpio and the Eighth House: How can I transform and renew my desires?

Gift: Scorpios can easily see through the façade of illusions that people portray or that are eluded by circumstances. Ferreting out the truth is definitely one of their abilities. Their depth of perception makes them excellent detectives and sleuths. Like a cat with nine lives, a Scorpio has the inner strength to pick themselves back up in spite of pain and suffering they may have endured. Their understanding of struggle gives them the ability to successfully help others. If you want to get to the heart of a matter, ask a Scorpio to get an honest answer.

Shadow: Scorpios' lives are apt to be a constant struggle to control and conquer their intense and passionate desires through their wills. Since this sign is strongly related to the desire principle and the sex drive, a huge emotional involvement can occur in close relationships. When this is out of their control, it can lead to obsessive and controlling behavior, possessiveness, and jealousy. A false sense of power and a fascination with the dark side, or where others may fear to tread, can ultimately bring them pain and suffering.

The Sun is in Scorpio from around October 23 until November 22. The dates for Scorpio can change every year, so check an ephemeris if you're on the cusp.

Sun in Sagittarius

The glyph for Sagittarius is an arrow pointing toward the sky. It is about freedom, inspiration, faith, and perspective. The expansive, Jupiter-ruled Sagittarian energy revels in getting beyond humdrum pettiness and soaring to heights where the big picture is obvious. Like the Archer, Sagittarians aim for the highest, most lofty vision they can. It is that vision and perspective that elevates their spirit.

Sagittarians typically enjoy broadening their environment through travel and broadening their mind through knowledge and philosophy. It is easy to see why these individuals require both mental and physical freedom to attain their mission, and as a Mutable Fire sign, they innately have the flexibility and impulse needed to explore the higher realms of the mind and spirituality.

Sagittarius is a sign of law and order, justice, truth, integrity, higher values, higher education, travel, dreams, and visions.

Keywords for Sagittarius and the Ninth House: How can I bring my love and light to the world?

> Sagittarians can place too much emphasis on the future and forget to live life in the present moment.

Gift: Sagittarians elevate the vibrations around them with their "glass half full" optimism and undaunted faith. They often use humor to shift energy when it gets intense. Their gifts manifest by bringing a larger perspective to the problems, snags, and issues they encounter. Their love for expanding their knowledge and experiences give them a propensity to avail to new adventures, if not in actuality, then in spirit. They are enthusiastic travelers, interested in foreign cultures, and are open to exploring different states of consciousness, including the dream state.

Shadow: Overexpansion and idealism can lead a Sagittarian to becoming out of touch with the reality that is in front of them and forgetting the "one step at a time" approach. They can gloss over the necessary stages required to get them to their final goal. Overattachment to their belief systems can also lead to fanaticism.

In their religious zeal, they may, at times, overlook the personal side of life. Sagittarians can place too much emphasis on the future and forget to live life in the present moment.

The Sun is in Sagittarius from around November 23 until December 21. The dates for Sagittarius can change every year, so check an ephemeris if you're on the cusp.

Sun in Capricorn

Capricorn is often depicted as a goat climbing up a mountain, which describes their incredible perseverance and the ambition that this action-oriented, Cardinal Earth sign can draw upon. Furthermore, Capricorn represents reaching the mountaintop.

The symbolism of the mountain goat in reality is a chimeric sea goat: half goat, half sea creature. The mountaintop, in reality, represents the attainment of enlightenment, rising above the concrete levels of earthly existence.

Capricorn is ruled by Saturn, representing maturity, limits, and hard work. A Capricorn wants to do what it can to make the most of their time here on Earth. According to astrologer Malvin Artley in his Capricorn_22 letter, "Capricorn represents all that is best and worst in humanity. It represents the depths of materialism and the heights of spiritual attainment."

Capricorn has a natural resonance with the Tenth House, and thus, it correlates with our relationship to the outer world, which includes society, government, public institutions, and deeply held traditions as well as fashion. Capricorns care about making an impression, not flamboyantly, but with an air of traditional diplomacy. Reputation is important to a Capricorn. They work hard to preserve it. Capricorns

can often reinforce a cautious, play-by-the-rules approach. Capricorn is about duty. It is about self-respect and the integrity that sustains it.

As the sign opposite Cancer, which is concerned with distributing resources and nurturance, Capricorn cares about the management of resources and the material needs necessary for sustainability.

Keywords for Capricorn and the Tenth House: I can use this and make it better and more efficient.

Gift: Capricorns are successful in positions that require taking charge and getting the job done. Efficient and practical, they have the muscle needed to get to the top of the mountain, regardless of the impediments on the way. These traits contribute to Capricorns being master builders and implementors, moving forward one step at a time. Their patience pays off and sets an example to those around them. Their ability to engage in life and not get easily deterred bestows upon them a certain earthly wisdom, and when their opposite sign of Cancer is incorporated into their being, they can become the wise grandmother archetype.

Shadow: The Saturn rulership of Capricorn, which on one hand gives staying power at any cost, can crystalize to the point where they can lack empathy and consideration of basic human conditions. This can lead to tendencies that become dominating, critical, and cold-hearted. Due to the Saturn influence, these natives have a tendency to be melancholic, especially when they are not appreciated even though they don't often show that they need appreciation.

The Sun is in Capricorn from around December 22 until January 19. The dates for

Friendship and companionship are important to an Aquarian, who tend to be loyal friends. Eccentricity for the sake of being different can be counterproductive, but they can offer more by focusing on how they express their unique gifts.

Capricorn can change every year, so check an ephemeris if you're on the cusp.

Sun in Aquarius

Aquarius is the sign of universal brotherhood. The symbol for Aquarius is the humanitarian Water-Bearer, and it is she who pours out to mankind spiritual energy and life force. The stars surrounding the Water-Bearer inspire new ideas and new technologies that serve society as a whole.

Uranus-ruled Aquarius is the sign of the rebel. Aquarius rules our uniqueness and what makes us different from everyone else. Aquarians have a theme of individuality, whereby they know and recognize the unique gifts of themselves and of others that can then be offered to humanity.

As a Fixed Air Sign, Aquarians can have fixed ideas. It is therefore not surprising that the keywords for Aquarius are "I know."

Truth is important to them, and they have little tolerance for lying and hypocrisy. The Fixity of Aquarius demands commitment to higher aspirations. These natives aim for a lifestyle characterized by freedom and altruism. They value diversity and believe in sharing with all members of the community.

Aquarius represents large organizations and networks of people. It represents your hopes and dreams. It is how we share ideas and information and make the world a better place.

Keywords for Aquarius and the Eleventh House: I know.

Gift: Aquarians operate as equals among equals without affectation and snobbery. Friendship and companionship are important to an Aquarian, and they tend to be loyal friends, as they incorporate the characteristics of their opposite sign, Leo. They are independent, humanitarian, and kind. They respect others for their individuality and the uniqueness they bring.

Shadow: Eccentricity for the sake of being different can be counterproductive. They can garner more fulfillment and offer more to society by bringing their unique gifts forth in a way in which what they have to offer can be more easily received. Selfishly motivated group and organizational work can replace the altruistic sharing of the Aquarian Water-Bearer, who pours forth generously in world service. The Uranian rulership of Aquarius can trigger an oversensitive nervous system since Uranus rules electricity and the nervous system carries electrical impulses to the brain. These natives can be prone to anxiety and restlessness.

The Sun is in Aquarius from around January 20 until February 19. The dates for

Aquarius can change every year, so check an ephemeris if you're on the cusp.

Sun in Pisces

As the last sign in the Zodiac, Pisces has seen it all and done it all. Pisces understands it all. Pisces understands fate better than any other sign. Pisces knows when to surrender. Neptune-ruled Pisces is the sign of universality, and these natives innately understand that we are all here on the same planet and that in tough times, we can all stew in the same soup. Deep compassion is the by-product of this instinctive, multifaceted understanding.

As a Mutable Water sign, Pisces knows how to flow like no other sign. Pisces is supersensitive, highly intuitive, often psychic, creative, dreamy, and mysterious. They have well-developed imaginations as a result of tuning in to other realms.

Keywords for Pisces and the Twelfth House: I understand.

Gift: Pisces home in to oceanic depths, and they can feel what lies beneath the surface. They excel at reading people and situations. A Pisces native can elevate those they contact by tuning in to and acknowledging their best qualities. They speak to the higher selves of others, triggering them to respond accordingly. These natives are natural healers who can easily put themselves in the shoes of others, and they offer solace and compassion that can help ease their suffering. The Piscean energy is subtle and refined, and these natives often excel in the arts and make excellent cooks, with their penchant for subtlety in flavors.

> The Piscean energy is subtle and refined, and these natives often excel in the arts and make excellent cooks, with their penchant for subtlety in flavors.

Shadow: Pisces can become escapists as a result of tuning in to the best and the worst in people and in their surroundings. They are vibrational sponges, and they can absorb and take on negativity if they do not consistently reinforce their sense of self and maintain strong boundaries when dealing with those who are less fortunate. It is easy for them to identify strongly with others and lose their sense of self. They can be fatalistic and resort to martyrdom.

The Sun is in Pisces from around February 20 until March 20. The dates for Pisces can change every year, so check an ephemeris if you're on the cusp.

THE SUN IN THE HOUSES

The placement of the Sun in each of the 12 houses of the natal chart represents the department of life most strongly affected by the expression of the individual's drive for significance and their power potential. It shows how and where they can shine through the application of their will.

Sun in the First House

The First House rules appearance, health, general temperament, and sense of self. The First House defines you and the image you project to others.

The First House is naturally ruled by Aries and the "I am" principle. The Sun is exalted in Aries, and the drive for significance is easily expressed in this area of the chart. Expect these individuals to be energetic, expressive, daring, courageous, and self-oriented. Their determination to choose their own course in life is strong and dominates their attention. Their focus is on ac-

The Second House represents the value we give to ourselves and, in turn, that which we possess. These natives are highly resourceful, talented, and creative, and quality of life is important to them.

Sun in the Second House

The Second House is connected with finances, values, material possessions, talents, and resources. The Second House represents the value we give to ourselves and, in turn, that which we possess.

The Sun in the Second House of talents, resources, values, self-worth, and earnings gives the individual staying power and a strong desire for long-term security. Many concentrate on proving their worth through their strong value system, and others are interested in proving their worth through the acquisition of wealth and material resources.

Gift: These natives are highly resourceful, talented, and creative. They seek security through a practical approach to life. Often successful in business, they instinctively know how to provide value for their products and services. The quality of their lives is important to them, and they will go the extra mile for a stress-free and comfortable lifestyle. They appreciate high quality and sustainable possessions. These natives can have pleasant voices.

Shadow: The shadow side of this placement is an individual who is a show-off who flaunts their wealth and acquisitions. Too much emphasis on material possessions and material resources can lead to the exclusion of spiritual development and heart-oriented pursuits. Their self-worth can become overly dependent on their apparent wealth, which can leave them feeling underappreciated and unloved by those who are less materially inclined. These natives can overindulge and become complacent at the expense of expanding their horizons.

Sun in the Third House

The Third House is connected with ideas, communication, siblings, neighbors, and short journeys.

tivities that further self-discovery in order to strengthen their personal identity.

Gift: A First-House placement of the Sun gives abundant vitality and a good dose of self-awareness. This position carries the potential for leadership since these individuals are not easily swayed by the opinions and desires of others. They are willing to do what it takes to gain personal distinction and esteem in the eyes of those around them. Their sheer energy and vitality provide an edge in overcoming physical ailments and afflictions.

Shadow: A fiery combination of the Sun in Aries's home, these natives have to be conscious of burning out before they manifest their desires and intentions. They can become overshadowed by their egotism to the exclusion of others' needs. They can also miss out on the support provided by partners and teammates.

The Third House describes all forms of communication, including speaking and writing; local interactions, including neighbors and acquaintances; siblings, particularly the oldest sibling; and short trips. A drive to achieve recognition through mental accomplishments is present. A natural curiosity for gathering information aligns with Mercury-ruled Gemini, being the natural owner of the Third House.

Gift: A mental agility and ease of communication occurs with this placement of the Sun. These individuals can excel at various forms of communication, and they especially love to learn and then communicate their knowledge. They adapt easily to different and varied environments and love to explore their local surroundings. A road trip to ease any chance of boredom is always on the agenda.

Shadow: These natives can lack focus and scatter their energy when overstimulated. They can lose their humanity by placing too much importance on knowledge, whereby they become intellectual snobs and try to force their knowledge on others. Sibling rivalry can be a thorn in their sides.

Sun in the Fourth House

The Fourth House is about the home, family, genetic inheritance, foundational stability, innermost feelings, later life, and the end of matters.

The urge for security and fulfillment through the home and family life are highlighted with the Sun's placement in the Fourth House, the domain ruled by Cancer. The Fourth House is the house of nurturing, protecting, and sustaining, and these individuals derive satisfaction from being supportive to others.

Gift: These individuals naturally tune in to the emotional needs of those around

them. They are proud of their family heritage and may have an aristocratic outlook. An increase in prosperity and security may occur in the latter part of life, given that the Fourth House rules the end of matters.

Shadow: Excessive family pride, a tendency to want to dominate the family scene, and difficulty getting along with parents and close family members can emerge in the shadow with this placement. Past experiences, unresolved karmic family relationships, and genetic mutations can color the native's drive for significance and ability to find a meaningful purpose in life.

Sun in the Fifth House

The Fifth House rules creative self-expression, children, love, passion, romance, playfulness, and joy.

Natives with this placement are dramatic, creative, self-confident, and assertive. They like to be the center of attention with their happy, sunny dispositions, resulting from the Fifth House's natural association with Leo. They are courageous, romantic, and competitive and are well inclined toward sports, music, theater, and other artistic pursuits.

Gift: The Sun is well placed in the Fifth House, the house associated with Sun-ruled Leo. These natives are likely to keep their creative juices flowing in a variety of ways not limited to but including traditional artistic milieus. Naturally attuned to children and pets, they are playful and are fond of spending time with both. These individuals love to have fun, and the resulting love of life becomes a gift to those around them.

Shadow: The challenge with this placement is not to be overly demanding, naively childish, arrogant, or egotistical. They can lack maturity and subtlety, and their behavior can be blatant and overly

With a knack for establishing harmony in relationships, natives of the Seventh House attract strong, loyal partnerships but need to establish boundaries to avoid putting their own needs on the back burner.

Gift: These natives are generally excellent workers because they take pride in their work and their dedication to service. They intuitively know how to care for themselves and others. They appreciate dedication from others and do well working alongside others who share their desire for craftsmanship and perfection.

Shadow: These natives can become overly dependent on the appreciation they receive from others. Their self-esteem and dignity can be easily threatened by outside influences, which inadvertently affects their health. Individuals with this position of the Sun can be demanding and authoritarian toward those they employ. On the other hand, individuals who do jobs for others will demand many rights and privileges and will expect to be noticed and appreciated.

Sun in the Seventh House

The Seventh House rules close personal relationships, agreements, and compromises.

The Seventh House belongs to Venus-ruled Libra in the natural Zodiac. Natives with this placement express great pride in their ability to have successful close relationships. They are motivated to become well liked. It is not uncommon for individuals with this placement to become good negotiators and public relations advocates. Depending on their Sun sign, especially Scorpio, Pisces, or Gemini, these natives can be excellent counselors. People are naturally drawn to them and want to share their personal life. Fairness is important to them, and they will pursue perceived injustices to themselves and others.

theatrical. Their pursuit of pleasure can become compulsive and interfere with productivity.

Sun in the Sixth House

The Sixth House governs daily routines, acts of service, the work-life balance, health, due diligence, pet care, coworkers, and employees.

The Sixth House is associated with Mercury-ruled Virgo. They derive a sense of fulfillment from producing work they can be proud of. The work that they do and the services that they offer are important to their sense of identity. They have the Virgoan tendency to seek perfection and distinction from their work. Day-to-day activities and habit patterns are important to natives with this placement. This position of the Sun can give these natives a sensitive constitution. They do best with life-supporting daily regimens and regularity in their routines.

Gift: Individuals with this placement can be charming and have a knack for establishing harmony in relationships. They love to share and give of themselves to those close to them. As a result, they attract strong, loyal partnerships into their lives, whether personal or business partnerships.

Shadow: The shadow side of this placement occurs when the individual puts their own objectives aside for the sake of creating harmony in a relationship. Continuingly putting their own needs on the back burner can weaken their sense of self and ultimately cause illness or heartache. They have a need for boundaries so that close relationships become a win-win situation for each of the parties. It is easy for these natives to fall into imbalanced relationships in order to be liked. They can overidentify with partnerships and take others' responses too personally.

Sun in the Eighth House

The Eighth House rules joint ventures, intimacy, sex, death, transformation, and psychic dimensions.

In the natural Zodiac, the Eighth House belongs to Pluto-ruled Scorpio. The native is drawn to exploring an interest in the deeper mysteries of life, including areas related to birth, death, and transformation. They have an interest in personal growth and self-development as well as personal and social evolution. Scorpio is the opposite sign to Taurus and the Second House, which rules the finances, values, talents, and resources of an individual. The Eighth House rules the same for partners, both at the personal level and in business. Therefore, at the mundane level, attention is placed on a partner's finances, values, and resources. The Eighth House also rules sex, death, legacies, insurances, and inheritances. An Eighth-House Sun can

be intense for the native based upon the fundamental nature of the change and transformation that the native undertakes. The Sun in the Eighth House can bring recognition after death.

Gift: These natives believe in transformation and change as a way of life. They are intent on growth since they instinctively know that constant change promotes their self-awareness and ultimately their spiritual growth. With this placement of the Sun, the individual is not fully satisfied operating at superficial levels. They have an urge to delve deeper into areas of life in which they are interested. Metaphysical and occult studies will often be of interest to them. These natives are magnetic and often sexually attractive.

> It is easy for these natives to get pulled off their centers due to their out-of-control desires.

Shadow: Difficulties or failed litigation can ensue over a partner's finances and joint resources. Pride and pomp can be overinflated, as related to the Eighth House are issues that include a partner's finances, inheritances, and legacies. Their desires are strong and powerful, and it is not easy for them to let go of what they want, even if they have to resort to unscrupulous means. It is easy for these natives to get pulled off their centers due to their out-of-control desires.

Sun in the Ninth House

The Ninth House rules higher education, long-term goals, foreign travel, publicity, adventures, religion, and philosophical and ethical pursuits.

These natives have a deep need to see the big picture and put the present day into a perspective that they can understand and

Natives with a Tenth House Sun want to shine. Naturally attuned to putting their best foot forward, they may also tend to be show-offs.

fillment from putting others at ease with their zany quips and sense of humor. Inspiration and flashes of insights are not uncommon for these natives. Many can have a prophetic side to their nature, whereby they receive information from dreams, visions, and hunches. These natives can abide by strong moral convictions that guide their lives.

Shadow: These natives can be snobbish about their spirituality, knowledge, and studies as a result of an excess of pride and an overly inflated ego. They can be condescending and overly moralistic toward others. Fanaticism and self-righteousness are possible. With Jupiter and its shadow tendency toward excess ruling of Sagittarius and the natural ruler of the Ninth House, these adventurous natives can get carried away and be reckless. Also, with their orientation toward the future, they can forget to live in the present.

Sun in the Tenth House

The Tenth House rules public achievements, reputation, authority, and prestige.

Natives with a Tenth-House Sun want to shine in every way possible. Typically, these natives are born within an hour or two of high noon. With their Sun at the top of the natal chart, they are not likely to keep their activities under wraps for very long. Reputation is important to them, and any missteps are in full view. Saturn-ruled Capricorn is the natural ruler of the Tenth House, and Saturn can be a taskmaster. These individuals are achievement oriented, and they will work hard to acquire the necessary knowledge and skills needed to move up the ladder of success.

be comfortable with. Jupiter-ruled Sagittarius is the natural ruler of the Ninth House. Natives with the Sun in this house have a deep need to understand the world around them. They do not tire of gathering knowledge. They are proud of the knowledge they have accrued, and they take great pride in transmitting their knowledge to others. These natives are adventurous and love to acquire firsthand knowledge through travel and other adventures. They have a strong interest in people of different cultures or those who live in foreign lands. Truth and higher law are important to those with this placement of the Sun. They often have an interest in religious and spiritual pursuits.

Gift: Individuals with this placement are natural philosophers and gain much ful-

Gift: These individuals excel in the professional world. They are naturally attuned to putting their best foot forward and making

the best presentation possible. They are well suited to be leaders since they are noticed in spite of themselves. Often, these individuals are born into families of high social standing, so they are aware of moral responsibility and personal dignity. They take pride in setting a good example for others.

Shadow: These natives can be show-offs. Their material ambition can take a toll on their personal development, family life, and significant relationships. The Tenth House makes a grand cross with the First, Fourth, and Seventh Houses. Ideally, each of these areas need attention for balance and fulfillment to occur. Their love of power and position can lead to their using unscrupulous means to achieve it. This can lead to reversals in their standings.

Sun in the Eleventh House

The Eleventh House rules friends, hopes, wishes, groups, and a sense of belonging in the world.

The Eleventh House is ruled by Aquarius in the natural Zodiac. Their Uranian influence inspires these natives to be unique and original. They embrace humanity and take pride in treating everyone as equals. They have great respect for human dignity. Friendships are important to an Eleventh-House Sun, and generally, natives with this Sun position will have many friends and partake in various group activities. Their nonjudgmental orientation and openness contribute to their popularity and the ease with which they interact with others. The Eleventh-House Sun has high hopes and wishes. The unbounded influence of Aquarius opens the door to thinking outside of the box. An attitude is present that anything is possible and that they can look at life in terms of opportunities.

Gift: These individuals are gifted in leading and overseeing group activities, whether these be small or large group undertakings. They intuitively know how to give each person their time in the Sun, and they promote an atmosphere where everyone feels special and accepted. Their drive to gain recognition for their achievements and original inventions and designs can be helped by friends with power and influence. Individuals with this placement are respected by their colleagues and friends for their high ideals and refusal to compromise their humanitarian goals and beliefs.

Shadow: The Aquarian influence can like everyone and still keep others at a distance with their personal detachment, where everyone is special and yet no one is really special. They can be too impersonal. The shadow side of this placement is someone who wants to dominate group dynamics or personal friendships for selfish purposes. An air of superiority can be present based on their unique and special talents and abilities.

Sun in the Twelfth House

The Twelfth House rules secrets, unconscious patterns, karma, closure, institutions, connections with higher sources, enlightenment, and undoing.

Neptune, the natural ruler of Pisces and the Twelfth House, softens the Sun's natural desire to radiate, with a more introspective orientation coupled with a subtle understanding of humankind. The will is directed toward exploring the resources of their unconscious. Typically, these individuals work best behind the scenes or in situations where they are the leader behind the scenes. They can find self-expression in positions of service or through work in large institutions geared toward service to others such as hospitals, human service and spiritual organizations, and places of confinement.

Gift: A highly compassionate orientation that does well being of service to the betterment of humanity characterizes this placement. An innate understanding of both mystical depths and levels of spiritual attainment is present. The desire for spiritual attainment can be a driving force for these natives to dive deeply into releasing past karma and old hurts. Similarly, they have an inner awareness to stay clear of generating new debts to individuals and to society.

Shadow: A sensitivity is present to the collective consciousness and all the worldly chaos and noise with this placement that can incline the native to not feeling at home in the outer world. Hence, this individual can choose to reside in their inner world and not take advantage of opportunities and challenges that can lead to growth and self-awareness. Resistance to letting go and to the process of change in general can be present. Unconscious egotism and desire for power and recognition does not work out so well for these individuals and can ultimately have the opposite effect.

> The desire for spiritual attainment can be a driving force for these natives to dive deeply into releasing past karma and old hurts.

SUN COMBINATIONS

Planetary bodies partner together to blend their uniquely characteristic energies. This blending can bring support and strength to the inherent energies of each planetary body whereby their gifts are bestowed upon the individual. When functioning at an unconscious level, the blending of the planetary bodies can weaken or compete with each other, thereby manifesting the shadow side of the planetary combinations.

Sun/Moon

The Sun indicates purpose, self-expression, creative life force, and conscious will.

The Moon symbolizes feelings, habit patterns, and the unconscious.

Moon/Sun combinations reflect the integration of the conscious and subconscious in the individual's psyche.

Gift: The Sun and Moon combined create a basic inner balance, whereby the native can stand fully behind who they are, what they want, and why they want it. They have a harmonious orientation toward life and seek harmony and peace in their outer experiences. These individuals are comfortable with male-, female-, and other-oriented individuals. Their self-expression has an easy flow. Generally, these natives are confident and seek to expand their conscious awareness.

Shadow: Natives can feel tension between their feelings and their conscious will that manifests as a hesitancy to be fully behind oneself. The conscious and the subconscious are at odds with each other, which can lead to tension in areas of self-expression and self-actualization. The native can have a tendency to be moody and off-balance, particularly when surrounded by mixed groups of masculine and feminine energies.

Sun/Mercury

The Sun indicates purpose, self-expression, creative life force, and conscious will.

Mercury rules communication, mental processes, and the logical mind.

Due to the proximity of Mercury to the Sun, relatively speaking, these two planetary

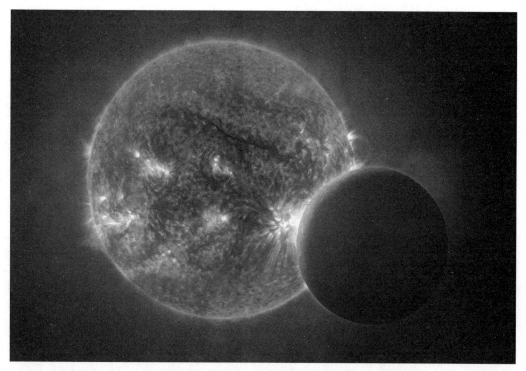

The connection between Mercury and the Sun bestows a sharp, witty mind. When Mercury combusts or comes too close to the Sun, the mind can become agitated and overheated, creating momentary blind spots in thinking.

bodies are never more than 28 degrees apart. The only significant connection they can make together is the Conjunction.

Mercury is considered to be "combust" to the Sun if it is between 0.5 and 4 degrees conjunct to the Sun. This can create a situation where Mercury gets overloaded and possibly overheated by the Sun's rays. It can create momentary blind spots in thinking.

Mercury is considered to be "casimi" or "cazimi," according to Medieval astrology, when Mercury is less than 0.5 degrees from the Sun. (Any planet is considered to be in the heart of the Sun—"casimi" or "cazimi"—when less than 0.5 degrees from the Sun. Late Medieval and Renaissance astrologers use the tighter value of 16 minutes from the Sun.) This connection means good luck and opportunity due to an alignment between the wave patterns of Mercury and the Sun. The Sun represents the will, and when combined so closely with Mercury, great will occurs, influencing mental expression. Mercury is considered to be at the heart of the Sun.

Gift: The gift of a close connection between Mercury and the Sun is the ability to shine with words. This connection bestows a sharp, witty mind that is energetic and thinks a lot about what they want.

Shadow: The mind can become agitated and overheated when Mercury combusts or comes too close to the Sun. A stronger need for relaxation and the use of meditation and other tools that calm the mind occurs.

Sun/Venus

The Sun indicates purpose, self-expression, creative life force, and conscious will.

Venus represents love, relationships, beauty, values, comfort, and material resources.

Venus is located between Earth and Mercury and is closer to the Sun than Earth. Venus can only be 48 degrees away from the Sun, so few combinations of these two energies are possible. According to traditional astrology, the only combinations that the Sun and Venus can make are the Semi-Sextile (30 degrees), Semi-Square (45 degrees), or Conjunction (0.5–10 degrees). As with Mercury, the beneficial "casimi" or "cazimi" situation would apply when the two planetary bodies are less than 0.5 degrees from each other. When the Sun is conjunct with Venus, a more stabilizing effect occurs than with the Sun/Mercury combination. Venus adds harmony and serenity to the Sun.

Venus becomes invisible under the rays of the Sun when it is closer than 8 degrees. Some ancient astrologers thought that when she is invisible, she should therefore be distrusted. A modern interpretation is that the Sun allows for the full expression of one's love of nature, beauty, and creativity.

Gift: The qualities of Venus are aligned with the individual's ego or drive for significance. They are able to project the traits of Venus easily and judiciously. They are cheerful, charming, optimistic, and magnetic. They are able to shine and excel at creating harmony and bringing people together. This combination offers the ability to be comfortable in one's own skin.

Shadow: Overindulgence is possible with the shadow side of a Sun/Venus connection. The native may need to be continuously reassured of admiration and love from others. These natives can have an edgy kind of charm, where they may be judgmental of others or not comfortable in social situations.

Sun/Mars

The Sun indicates purpose, self-expression, creative life force, and conscious will.

Mars rules assertiveness, energy, drive, and courage.

Combining Mars with the Sun is similar to having the Sun in Aries or the Sun in the First House, the natural home of Aries. This combination is courageous, energetic, impulsive, ambitious, and charming. Natives with a strong Sun/Mars combination can have a strong will with an abundance of energy at their disposal for getting things done in a hurry.

Gift: Expending energy or doing activities can be incredibly easy. I call this combination the "whistle while you work" combination. When the Sun and Mars work in harmony, great ease in moving about occurs, with little resistance in performing required actions. When asked to perform a task, these individuals are often up and at it before you know it. This combination knows how to energize their drive for significance or their purpose in life.

Shadow: The ego can get out of control, and too much self-aggrandizement and boasting can occur. The shadow side of this combination occurs when drives, desires, and impulses do not align with the individual's purpose and drive for significance; too much drive or not enough energy may be applied to an activity or life goal. Hence, the individual can be overly aggressive or not aggressive enough, cranky, and resistant to taking action. Resentments and grievances can be expressed unintentionally when the shadow side emerges. The native can use cantankerousness and irritability as a means to get attention.

Sun/Jupiter

The Sun indicates purpose, self-expression, creative life force, and conscious will.

Jupiter represents the higher mind, greater truths, expansiveness, hope, and optimism.

The expansive nature of Jupiter brings optimism and generosity to the individual's self-expression. Their life force is generally enhanced, and these natives typically exhibit a charitable disposition. Too much of anything ceases to be helpful, however, and natives with this combination will need to master balance in order to gain the most benefit from its influence. As a greater benefic, Jupiter is known to bestow luck unless contraindicated by other combinations in the chart.

> The expansive nature of Jupiter brings optimism and generosity to the individual's self-expression.

Gift: These natives are enthusiastic, generous, and see the glass as half full. They are likely to positively evaluate situations before them and have faith in their undertakings. Their upbeat nature contributes to their popularity. Others feel better after being around them. The connection between the Sun and Jupiter gives these individuals an edge in successfully manifesting their dreams. They have an aversion to pettiness and stinginess. They love to expand their horizons, which includes travel, interacting with different cultures, and expanding their knowledge base.

Shadow: The shadow side of this influence can make it difficult for these individuals to know where their boundaries

lie. Jupiter is expansive, and a tendency to overspend, overestimate, overindulge, and imbibe in other excessive behavior can occur. Similarly, the ego can get overblown, and their self-image can be unrealistic and exaggerated. These natives may brag, flaunt their talents and abilities, and aggrandize their accomplishments.

Sun/Saturn

The Sun indicates purpose, self-expression, creative life force, and conscious will.

Saturn rules responsibility, adjustments to limitations, sustainability, and structure.

Saturn in combination with the Sun brings discipline and responsibility to the conscious will. These natives are responsible and mature, and they will work hard for what they want. Saturn has a sobering effect on the luminous energy of the Sun. These natives can be serious and approach problems with deliberation and practicality. The Saturnian influence can also affect these natives' sense of humor. Every now and then, they will come out with very funny, sarcastic one-liners.

Gift: A strong sense of responsibility and trustworthiness is characteristic of the gift from this combination. This individual takes responsibility for themselves in any situation. They bring a practical orientation to problem solving. They have good follow-through. The organizational ability and disciplined nature of Saturn assists the Sun in achieving self-realization and manifesting their higher purpose.

Shadow: The dampening effect of Saturn on the Sun's ambition, although frustrat-

Natives with a Sun/Saturn combination have a strong sense of trustworthiness and take responsibility for themselves in any situation. They can be hard on themselves, feeling they never do enough, but can also experience ultimate fulfillment by accepting their limitations and being willing to work through them.

ing, can yield ultimate fulfillment once the native accepts limitations and is willing to work through them. Saturn will be the first to point out ego aggrandizement and shortcuts should the native choose to follow that path. Saturn is the master teacher and, once embraced, will lead to a much better result. Saturn looks to create resilient structures that can pass the test of time. Natives with a Sun/Saturn combination can be hard on themselves, as they feel that no matter how much they do, it is never enough. Excessive criticism and thwarted ego fulfillment from their upbringing can lead to self-consciousness that inhibits their self-expression and ambition. These natives can get caught up in a plethora of "should" and "should not," which may have initially come from their upbringing but has now been internalized, along with all of the guilt and self-abnegation that goes along with it.

Sun/Uranus

The Sun indicates purpose, self-expression, creative life force, and conscious will.

Uranus rules intuition, originality, individuality, and the sudden and unexpected.

Individuals with a Sun/Uranus combination are free-spirited, freedom-oriented, and individualists in that they follow the beat of their own drum and respect others who do so as well. The last thing they want to do is conform to a stereotype, especially one that isn't of their own making. Uranus is electrifying and activates planets that it touches in an individualistic and often re-bellious way. Uranus rules electricity, and these natives can often have highly sensitized nervous systems. They are often interested in or resonate to higher-frequency energies and planes of existence.

Gift: Sun/Uranus people are charismatic and magnetic. Their magnetism complements their uniqueness and enthusiasm, which inspires others, bringing them popularity. It is almost as if people aren't sure what to make of individuals with this combination, but they like it nonetheless. They are original, creative, and future oriented. They usually have a natural attunement to technology and other new ways of doing things. These individuals are not pretentious. They tend to be humanitarians who believe in the equality of all people, the universal brotherhood, where everyone is equal. Their open-mindedness and nonjudgmental stance contribute to the diverse opportunities and situations they are able to navigate. They are straightforward and expect the same from others. Truth and honesty are highly valued.

Shadow: Eccentric and erratic behavior may occur. This energy combination, although inventive and highly original, can lack the steadfastness and practicality necessary to carry.out their ideas. Personal freedom can come at a high cost when their ego becomes overly identified with doing things their own way. Rebelliousness for its own sake can become their mantra. People who do not understand their purpose can deem them unpredictable and eccentric.

> Uranus rules electricity, and these natives can often have highly sensitized nervous systems. They are often interested in or resonate to higher-frequency energies and planes of existence.

Sun/Neptune

The Sun indicates purpose, self-expression, creative life force, and conscious will.

Neptune rules ideals, creative imagination, transcendence, compassion, and vision.

The Neptunian influence brings added grace and sensitivity to the Sun's self-expression and conscious will. The higher dimensional orientation of Neptune brings a desire to exceed worldly ambition and constraints of the ego and help others who are less fortunate. They seek to enrich their lives through characteristic expressions that are ruled by Neptune that include art, music, photography, theater, spirituality, psychic phenomena, and healing.

Gift: They can have deep-rooted compassion and regard for mankind that is attributed to a Sun/Neptune combination. These natives feel Universal Oneness, which can extend to include all living things. They are highly sensitive to the suffering of others and are often regarded as empathic. The combination of the Sun and Neptune gives a highly refined nature that tunes in to the subtleties of the senses. A softness in their eyes can have a mesmerizing effect on others, perhaps due to their lack of brusqueness or the smoothness of their moves, as if they don't want to offend or hurt anyone. They excel in any talents and expressions that make use of their sensitivity and refinement, which includes those talents that are dependent on well-developed senses, all five of them, and includes sixth-sense expressions.

Sun/Neptune combination natives feel the universal oneness that can extend to include all living things. They are highly sensitive to the suffering of others and are often regarded as empathic.

Shadow: These natives love to embrace fantasy, which isn't to say that their perceptions don't have a kernel of truth in them. They need to figure out how much of this is real and how much of it is playing on their hopes and wishes and their unrealistic expectations or assessments. They can be easily led astray due to their innocent and trusting nature. It can seem at times that they are living in another dimension besides here on Earth. They can have memories of a more ideal existence, which can lead to disappointment and even depression when the realities of an ordinary existence with others who are less sensitive and aware hits home. The shadow side of a Sun/Neptune combination boils down to frustration and disappointment that can ensue from either setting unrealistic expectations or losing one's sense of self or one's self-identity in order to please

or help others. The tendency to sacrifice cannot be at one's own expense.

Sun/Pluto

The Sun indicates purpose, self-expression, creative life force, and conscious will.

Pluto represents regeneration; transformation; and a compelling, fundamental approach.

Investigative Pluto combines with the illuminating Sun, and you can be sure that an individual with this combination does not see anything at face value. They have a laser focus and persistence that gets to the bottom line sooner rather than later. This is a combination that will go all in, with no halfway. They do not stick their toe into the water.

These natives like to hold their cards close to their hearts. They don't like to expose their vulnerabilities for fear that it will lessen their power and reduce their ability to control a situation. They are as intense about controlling themselves as they are about controlling their environment. These natives often have a fascination with the dark side of life and all that is considered taboo, as if it unleashes a challenge for them to have power over the hidden and potentially uncontrollable.

Gift: This native believes in the ability to change, transform, and regenerate, which can give an innate healing ability and an all-around desire to grow and evolve. Keen perceptive abilities allow this native to see below the surface and get to the root of an issue. The person is a natural at taking adverse situations and using them for self-empowerment. These individuals go through many periods of self-transformation and self-renewal. They are capable of brilliant and profound insights, which gives them a great deal of power and strength.

Shadow: The shadow side of a Sun and Pluto combination can see the world through the lens of control and power. Sometimes in their life, they might have to make serious decisions as to whether they want to take the high road or give in to ego-driven impulses that go against their own well-being as well as those of others. Their desires are strong and often obsessive, overshadowing common sense and egging them on toward what can become self-destructive behavior. Their desire for intensity can lead them to seeking the challenge of going right to the edge. A lot can be going on below the surface with these individuals, which can include jealousies, deep-rooted vulnerabilities, paranoia, and a nagging suspicion of others' motives. Getting in touch with and facing these darker patterns can begin the transformation process, where the native can ultimately relieve their gnawing discomfort and release the creative energy held within.

The Sun's strength and courage coupled with Chiron's drive to heal promotes the full flourishing of the individual's growth and evolution. In this first-century fresco, Chiron's namesake centaur instructs young Achilles in the art of the lyre.

Sun/Chiron

The Sun indicates purpose, self-expression, creative life force, and conscious will.

Chiron represents core wounds and the desire to overcome them, and healing.

The combination of the Sun and Chiron yields a powerful combination that can influence the native in several ways. The purposeful rays of the Sun can combine with the healing nature of Chiron and deliver a soulful urge to bring healing to the planet. The individual's strong desire to heal may be the result of having had to wrestle with deep wounding to their self-esteem and confidence after a debilitated upbringing, wherein they had to struggle to assert themselves. They can then become a coach to help others develop confidence so that they can ultimately shine. Through helping others, these natives can develop the confidence that they needed all along. The wounded healer archetype is powerful and very real and tells the Chiron's story of crossing the bridge from the material to the spiritual realms.

The Sun conjunct with Chiron represents the instinct of the human spirit to manifest itself and leave something immaterial behind. Our spirit-seeking manifestation represents our "gift to the world." The Sun is our individuality, what makes us unique, our divine mission in this lifetime. The Sun conjunct with Chiron is the compelling drive to push beyond your existing boundaries to find your true zone of genius. The process of learning about your true self, the process of becoming who you are meant to be, cannot be an easy one, hence the wound.

Gift: The Sun brings hope and confidence to the native to delve into the deeper recesses of their psyche that are hampering their ability to shine. The Sun brings perpetual light to issues and to the psychological wounds that the native must overcome in order to express the creativity that wells up inside of them. The power of this combination is the strength and courage that is inherent in the Sun when coupled with Chiron's drive to heal the nagging discomforts and vulnerabilities that are preventing the full flourishing of the individual's growth and evolution.

Shadow: These natives may have a lifelong challenge to find out who they are at their core. A deep wounding to the ego has occurred. Who am I? Why am I here? They have difficulty in being themselves. Their lack of purpose can be daunting. With Chiron in combination with the Sun, they have the drive to find out. A perpetual glimmer from the Sun's rays gives them a chance to find the inner meaning to their struggle. They have the power to transform from seeing themselves as empty and lonely to wanting to express their inner light in spite of their acknowledged vulnerabilities.

Sun/Eris

The Sun indicates purpose, self-expression, creative life force, and conscious will.

Eris represents the determination to remove limitations that impede the soul's evolution.

Sun/Eris combinations foster the native's will to evolve and sustain integrity of purpose. These natives can use whatever means are at their disposal to reach their desired end goal.

Gift: When Eris combines with the Sun, the native is on a mission to express their authenticity in all aspects of their lives. They are aligned to the discovery of their true soul's calling and mission in life. They are likely to assist others in finding their true purpose as well.

Shadow: These individuals get caught up in ego identification with their mission to find authenticity in their own lives and in society. They may flaunt their beliefs with arrogance, which ultimately creates divisiveness. Their efforts may be unproductive and discordant.

Sun/North Node

The Sun indicates purpose, self-expression, creative life force, and conscious will.

The North Node represents future direction, soul guidance, and fulfillment.

The North Node emphasizes the importance for the native to develop the attributes represented by the Sun. This suggests that worldly success, recognition, and a life filled with purpose and creative self-expression are part of the destiny that the native will be drawn to fulfill.

Gift: The native is aligned and consciously aware of their purpose and what brings them happiness and fulfillment. A higher force has stirred them in a direction that may be different from the one they initially followed, as if circumstances showed up at the right time and place to influence important life choices. Once on the path that brings fulfillment, a sense of being on autopilot and going along for the ride occurs.

Shadow: The individual's ego or sense of identity isn't aligned with the direction that will most benefit them to pursue. A disconnect occurs between how the ego values the urges of the true self, perhaps as a result of imposed restrictions from their upbringing or from societal norms. The struggle that ensues is feeling out of place or never fully satisfied in spite of achievements, material comfort, and recognition. An underlying nagging feeling can occur for these natives that they need to take a chance, follow their heartfelt urges, and do what makes them happy.

Sun/South Node

The Sun indicates purpose, self-expression, creative life force, and conscious will.

The South Node represents familiarity, gratification, and the path of least resistance.

Those with a Sun and South Node connection have likely achieved a high level of success in the past, although they have the urge to find a new direction. They have an inherent self-confidence that can carry them into new realms of experience and fulfillment.

Gift: Individuals with this combination know how to be successful. They know what it feels like to know when they are on the right path. This inherent knowing can be applied to whichever new direction resonates with them to pursue. They are at a definite advantage having the wherewithal to put themselves out into the world. The key is for them to stay attuned to when it is time for them to move on to something new that aligns to the soul's growth and evolution.

Shadow: These natives can be so connected to the past due to accolades bestowed upon them for their achievements

in the early part of their lives that it is difficult for them to pursue other avenues of expression. Whatever had worked before is no longer satisfying or is not coming together as easily as before. It is not as easy to be in the limelight as it once was. Bragging and self-aggrandizement may not be received well by those they are looking to impress. They need to bring their old self up to the present day and find a new future self in order to feel good about themselves.

Sun/Ascendant

The Sun indicates purpose, self-expression, creative life force, and conscious will.

The Ascendant represents one's approach, orientation, and the window through which one sees the world.

The Sun's powerful life force combines with the Ascendant to energize and strengthen these individuals' physical constitution, creative self-expression, and conscious will. Just as the Sun is exalted in Aries, this combination can create a powerhouse that basically lives in the present moment as it approaches life with zeal and enthusiasm.

> The Sun's powerful life force combines with the Ascendant to energize and strengthen these individuals' physical constitution, creative self-expression, and conscious will.

Gift: The Sun and Ascendant combination is charismatic, self-confident, warm, and energetic. They possess leadership capabilities. Others are drawn to their light and energy. They are naturally noticed, which is a trait that they do not shy away from. These natives often have a strong constitution and possess courage and determination.

Shadow: The shadow side of this combination can create an impression that is overbearing and out of sync with the environment that they want to interact with. They are arrogant and conceited and distract others by their intense desire to be the center of attention. In spite of their warmth, they are not likely to be easygoing and cooperative. They have a self-centeredness that is intent on getting their own way.

Sun/Midheaven (MC)

The Sun indicates purpose, self-expression, creative life force, and conscious will.

The Midheaven (MC) represents image, outer aspirations, and career orientation.

When the Sun is positioned at the top of the chart (a position called the *medium coeli*, or MC), the native shines brightly for all to see. They are apt to have a strong impact on their careers and social circles. People will naturally look up to them just as one glances at the Sun and is aware of its intensity and power.

> When the Sun is positioned at the top of the chart, the native shines brightly for all to see. They are apt to have a strong impact on their careers and social circles.

Gift: Individuals with this combination are generally well received by others and do well in occupations where they are out front in the public view. They naturally exude an aura of importance and authority, and others are attracted by their warmth and friendliness.

Shadow: The shadow side of the Sun/Midheaven combination is an arrogant, bossy, and self-aggrandizing person that is blinded by ambition and power. Self-centeredness and a need to be the center of attention, even when not deserved, is characteristic of the shadow side of this combination. When the Sun is at

the Midheaven, their actions and foibles are noticed by others, and they can become victims of gossip and slander.

THE MOON

The Moon fluctuates within its monthly cycle and also is connected with the daily fluctuations of tidal waters throughout the world. Underlying this fluctuation, which may seem capricious if we don't pay attention to life's rhythms, are regular cycles and predictability. Compared to other planets, the Moon of Earth is the largest in size, proportionally speaking. As a result, the Moon stabilizes the rotation axis of Earth. This factor contributes to making the conditions on Earth more conducive to the evolution of life.

When the Moon is closest to Earth, known as its perigee, it is noticeably closer than when it is at its furthest distance from Earth, known as its apogee. The Moon's orbit has been the subject of intensive study by astrodynamicists because of the many factors affecting its orbit.

THE MOON IN THE SIGNS

The Moon symbolizes feelings, habit patterns, and the unconscious.

Moon in Aries

The emotionally oriented Moon in fiery Aries can be inspiring, enthusiastic, or prickly, as this placement heats the emotional tone of the moment with potent expressions. It is easy to read an individual with an Aries Moon since their mood is generally visible on their face. Whatever

Where your natal moon lies may seem to work at odds or in harmony with your sign's nature.

the emotion, it is embraced with presence and passion.

Gift: An individual with this Moon sign can warm the atmosphere with their enthusiasm and courageous spirit. They have an innocence combined with a confident, "I can do it" approach that is stimulating and inspiring to onlookers. They can overcome emotional crises more easily than other placements of the Moon.

Shadow: Caution is advised to ensure that decisions are not made from a place of impatience and restlessness. Headstrong and impulsive, this native can find themselves in some awkward situations. They can be overly reactive and may take things personally. Luckily, they are brave souls who don't mind the challenge!

Moon in Taurus

The Moon is well placed in Venus-ruled Taurus, where it is considered to be exalted.

The Moon loves the nurturing, sensually oriented energy of Taurus, which ensures all-around mental stability and peace of mind. In turn, their inner emotional stability comforts others. The Moon's placement in a Fixed Earth sign supports a stable, practical, and calm manner that can maintain an emotional mood that is grounded amid chaos and confusion.

Gift: With a naturally pleasant disposition, this native can woo any opponent with its soothing voice and charm. This Venus-ruled Moon sign can bestow its native with a well-proportioned face that is easy to look at. People with the Moon in Taurus exude a stable and warm presence. Enjoying the good things in life bring them great pleasure and joy.

Shadow: Natives with a Taurus Moon can be resistant to change. Subsequently, they can stay in relationships, residences, and jobs longer than is healthy. It is uncommon for a Taurus Moon to be aggressive, but when they get upset, it's hard to calm them down. They can be possessive of people and things. Natives with a Taurus Moon can stubbornly dig in their heels when they are confronted in a way that threatens their perceived emotional and material security.

Moon in Gemini

The Moon in Mercury-ruled Gemini produces natural communicators. They enjoy connecting and relating with people of different ages and from different walks of life. These are the individuals who will start a conversation with other people in line with them at the grocery store or the movie theater. They are young at heart and want to enjoy life. As a Mutable Air sign, individuals with a Gemini Moon are emotionally adaptable to life's changing tides and circumstances. They love to gather information and are able to converse on a variety of topics.

Gift: Individuals with the Moon in Gemini are adaptable and well versed in many topics. It is the combination of these talents that adds to their charm and popularity. They are natural spokespeople and writers. They have nimble fingers and can be talented with their hands since Gemini rules the hands. Natives with a Gemini Moon are able to handle and execute multiple tasks at one time, which makes them good multitaskers.

Shadow: Mercury-ruled Gemini Moon natives can be restless and lack focus. Overstimulation can cause stress and make them scattered and unproductive. Their logical orientation can sometimes lack empathy and compassion.

Moon in Cancer

The Moon is strongly placed in Cancer, the natural placement for the Moon. These natives are highly sensitive to the ebb and flow of life and have no problem picking up even the slightest of innuendos. People with the Moon in Cancer in their natal chart tend to be compassionate and nurturing. They can worry about the ones they love even though they may not always show their feelings. The symbol for Cancer is the Crab, and it is this protective shell that prevents them from being vulnerable. They may not always show when they are hurt; however, they have the potential to take everything very personally.

> People with the Moon in Cancer in their natal chart tend to be compassionate and nurturing.

Gift: These natives bring gifts of nurturing, protecting, and caring to those in their inner circle. They may only show their true caring side when they feel safe. These natives have active imaginations, which often manifest in their creative undertakings. The Cardinal Water orientation of the placement of the Moon activates their feelings, and it is not surprising for them to show up when help is needed. Any show of support and appreciation will be remembered and returned in kind. These natives have good memories.

Shadow: Cancer Moon people can retreat back into their shells, like a crab, when they are hurt or if they don't feel safe, which can make them difficult to reach. It may take some time before they are ready to come out and share their feelings. Security is important to them, and they can become overly protective to themselves and their family. They can sometimes go too far in taking others' actions and words personally.

Moon in Leo

People with the Moon in Leo need to be shown affection and love. They are happiest when they feel loved and are the center of attention. They especially love to be put on a pedestal. When they are happy, they will exude love, warmth, and magnanimity. The Fixed, Fiery nature of Leo lends itself well to being a loyal partner and companion.

Gift: Natives with a Leo Moon in their natal charts can be warm, loving, and generous. They can put others at ease with their magnanimous nature. They possess a dramatic flair, which can be handy when they want to make a pitch, whether in business or if they need to express something they believe in. They can be convincing, with an air of authority. They are usually creative in their presentation and approach, and they do well if they run their own business.

Shadow: These individuals thrive on compliments and encouragement and wither when they don't receive the attention they desire. A false sense of pride can get in their way, especially if their confidence is not being sufficiently boosted. It is not uncommon for them to have a "how dare you" attitude for a slight offense that was taken way too personally. These natives love to give advice but do not take advice well.

Moon in Virgo

People with the Moon in Virgo like to analyze things and find the most practical solution. They do not overreact unless their desire for perfection is triggered, interfered with, or hindered. This can cause their delicate nervous systems to become overwhelmed. Too much nervous tension can affect their digestive system, especially their intestines.

These natives can give good advice to anyone who asks. Mercury-ruled Virgo is a Mutable Air sign, which lends itself to a variety of practical and logical solutions. They are not as adept in giving emotional support unless they have other influences in their chart.

Virgo Moon individuals can be organized, but they may be the only ones who can find things in their organization. You can always count on their attention to detail, which gives them an edge if you buy into the expression "The devil is in the details."

Gift: These natives are highly discerning and can be called upon to find a needle in a haystack. They intuitively know when something is out of place or "off," and their input can be invaluable in making anything better. They are deeply fulfilled when they are productive, especially when they can be helpful to others. Their humble nature is their gift to those who know them as well as those who benefit from their desire to help.

Shadow: Individuals with a Virgo Moon strive for perfection, and they can forget that everyone, including themselves, are human beings, mere mortals. Humans on Earth are perfect in their imperfection. Their highly logical nature and the mental orientation of Mercury-ruled Virgo can make these natives highly critical of themselves and others. This can lead to low self-esteem and feelings of not being enough.

Moon in Libra

Individuals with their natal Moon in Venus-ruled Libra have a need for partnerships, friendships, and close relationships.

Those with the Moon in Libra have a knack for meaningful interactions and easy win-win negotiations. At times, their desire to create peace and harmony can make them seem unduly wishy-washy.

They are fulfilled by having meaningful contacts with people and by being surrounded by harmonious, aesthetically pleasing environments.

They have little tolerance for injustice and whatever they perceive to be unfair. Libra is a Cardinal Air sign, and individuals with the Moon in Libra will instinctively respond to any injustice to those in either their inner circle or to humanity as a whole.

These natives are romantic, socially aware, compromising, and appreciative of the finer things in life.

Gift: The Moon in Libra has a knack for creating a pleasing and aesthetic environment, which sets the stage for meaningful interactions and easy, win-win negotiations. They care about their physical appearance and are often physically attractive. They learned how to be pleasing at a young age,

and now, these qualities are deeply engrained in their being, often exemplified by their social ease and grace and their somewhat consistently gracious smile.

Shadow: Libra's Seventh-House orientation can give undue credence to others' opinions and feelings. As a result, they can be indecisive and appear wishy-washy even though they are not. Their emotions can lack intensity at times due to their desire to create peace and harmony, coupled with their high level of social refinement. As a result, other people don't always know where they really stand on any issue.

Moon in Scorpio

The Moon is in detriment in Scorpio, meaning that an easy blend does not occur between the Moon and the qualities of Scorpio. The Moon illuminates, reflects, and brings light into darkness. Scorpio is secretive, prefers dark corners, and doesn't open up easily. The Moon's placement in this Fixed Water sign can have very controlled emotional reactions. They do not like to be surprised.

Individuals with the Moon in Scorpio take their relationships very seriously. This is a very sensual and no-nonsense placement. They like to analyze and observe people and situations, not taking anything at face value. They have a strong desire by nature that can sometimes become overwhelming to them when their wants are not met. They have deep, intense feelings.

Gift: Loyal and caring to those in their inner circle, individuals with this placement can be very helpful and present in any emergency. They can give their full attention to the situation at hand. As a result, they make good therapists and healthcare workers. They are not squeamish when dealing with the nitty-gritty issues of life.

These individuals have an intense and deep emotional need to give themselves freely to those they care about. The Scorpio Moon aims to grow and evolve, which means that they will grow with a relationship or a situation should the need arise.

Shadow: Scorpio's number-one lesson is that of trust. Scorpios don't trust easily because they feel that the world can be a dangerous place to live in. They can be on high alert and suspicious, believing that people will let them down or that a disaster could strike at any time. Because of that, they are always on guard and don't like to share their innermost feelings. They can be prone to jealousy and possessiveness in their personal relationships. They can be overshadowed by their negative emotions and have difficulty letting them go.

Moon in Sagittarius

Natives with their natal Moon in Jupiter-ruled Sagittarius often have personalities that are straightforward, enthusiastic, happy-go-lucky, and easygoing. They have a need for excitement and a need for freedom. Sagittarius is a Mutable Fire sign, and those with this Moon placement need space to follow their inspirations. They don't do well when they feel confined or when a lot of demands and restrictions are put upon them. Truth is important to them, and it can be a deal-breaker if they are lied to. You can count on a Sagittarian to speak their truth, like it or not.

Travel, study, higher education, and communion with nature will generally uplift their spirit and provide these individuals with a fresh perspective.

Gift: Honest and straightforward, these natives are intent on bringing justice to the world. They are independent, forward-thinking, and can overcome issues pretty quickly.

They make great teachers and enthusiastically share what they are passionate about.

Shadow: These individuals can lack a realistic view of life due to their lofty and expansive nature. Disappointment can result. Too much attention can be given to the future, resulting in not enough attention being paid to the present moment. Innately philosophical, they can be influenced by religious or other belief systems from their environment or their early upbringing. This can lead to narrow-mindedness or a holier-than-thou attitude.

Moon in Capricorn

The emotionally expressive Moon is not well placed in Saturn-ruled Capricorn. These individuals prefer to grin and bear their burdens rather than show what they perceive to be their weakness. This Moon placement is diligent and serious, and they are not generally comfortable asking for help. They like to be seen as strong and powerful.

Capricorn Moon natives are ambitious, hard workers. They like climbing the ladder to success. Their active seeking of money, power, and status for themselves and their families can lead them to pursuing personal vested interests rather than those that would benefit global social interests.

Gift: These individuals have an innate business sensibility and often do well owning their own business or helping to build a business. Capricorn is a Cardinal Earth sign. Tangible results bring them personal fulfillment. They are responsible, reliable, faithful, and sometimes stoic. These are good people to have around when you have a tight deadline.

Shadow: Moon in Capricorn individuals can be insecure about their own worth.

Aquarian Moon natives prefer to stand back, observe, and remain a bit detached rather than have a knee-jerk emotional response, which can be misinterpreted by others as aloof and uncaring.

These natives are friendly and can embrace many different types of people. They have an inherent respect for authenticity, and they won't impose their will upon others. Similarly, they are not particularly tolerant of others imposing their will upon them.

Gift: Aquarian Moon natives have the capacity to sympathize with the needs of humanity. Their respect for individuality gives them the strength to stand up to their strongly held beliefs and create their own paths. They value friendships and are respected for their kindness by those who know them.

Shadow: Individuals with this placement can have an irrational need for freedom at all costs. They can be fearful that close emotional involvements pose a threat to their personal freedom. Their detached facade can be misinterpreted by others as aloof and uncaring, which is hardly the case. A risk is present of thinking so much that they neglect their feeling nature.

They may have lingering emotional wounds resulting from excessive criticism that they received in their formative years. As a result, some of these natives can have a lot of guilt, even in situations when guilt isn't warranted. These natives can become cynical when their ambitions aren't realized.

Moon in Aquarius

People with their natal Moon in Aquarius prefer to stand back, observe, and remain a bit detached rather than have a knee-jerk emotional response to situations. Aquarius is a Fixed Air sign, and these natives like to rationally analyze a situation first and then clearly and calmly communicate their response. They are kind, innovative, unconventional, and great at giving detached advice.

Moon in Pisces

Natives with their Moon in the Neptune-ruled Pisces are open, sympathetic, and easily connect with people. Emotionally sensitive and extremely impressionable on both conscious and unconscious levels, the Mutable Water nature of Pisces assesses and responds to the needs of others, sometimes to their own detriment. They will react as if they are experiencing the pain of another. Self-sacrifice is not foreign to their nature. As a result, they do well in caring professions. They like to protect the weak and will sometimes favor the underdog.

Piscean Moon natives are imaginative, spiritually oriented, and strongly intuitive.

Gift: People with this placement have a vivid imagination, which can result in poetic, musical, or artistic talent. Their attunement to layers of undercurrents and subtleties are apparent in both their artistic pursuits as well as in their décor. They make good chefs because of their knack for combining subtleties of taste. These natives are generally kind, considerate, and sympathetic because of their sensitivity to the feelings of others.

Shadow: These individuals absorb energies around them and can take on the issues of others if they don't learn how to protect themselves from negative vibrations. Their idealistic and self-sacrificing nature can result in disappointment when their generosity isn't returned in kind. They need to set boundaries in their relationships and set realistic expectations of others. They can become the victim or the savior in their relationships.

THE MOON IN THE HOUSES

The placement of the Moon in each of the 12 houses of the natal chart represents the department of life most strongly affected by the instinctive soul expression of the individual. Subconscious conditioning and automatic behavior patterns will be felt and seen in the areas ruled by that particular house. The native is likely to express more emotion and be more sensitive in these sectors of life.

Moon in the First House

The First House rules appearance, health, general temperament, and sense of self. The First House defines you and the image you project to others.

The First House is naturally ruled by Aries and the "I am" principle. The Moon in

the First House is highly expressive and acutely sensitive to their surroundings. Their determination to respond to their own course in life is strong and dominates their attention. Their focus is on activities that further self-discovery in order to strengthen their personal identity.

> The First-House placement of the Moon gives the native keenly felt, direct, and spontaneous access to their feelings and their desires....

Gift: The Moon in the First House can have an astute awareness of their environment that is instinctive and deeply felt. Their sixth sense is alert and aware. The First-House placement of the Moon gives the native keenly felt, direct, and spontaneous access to their feelings and their desires, so they know exactly what they want and, more importantly, what they don't want.

Shadow: Natives with a First-House Moon easily overreact to environmental situations that include people they come into contact with. They are likely to take feedback and reactions from others personally, even when they weren't directed toward the native. They can become overshadowed by their personal needs to the exclusion of others' needs. They can also be distracted by their feelings and miss out on support provided by partners and teammates. They have a tendency to be moody and have variable ups and downs.

Moon in the Second House

The Second House is connected with finances, values, material possessions, talents, and resources. The Second House represents the value we give to ourselves and, in turn, that which we possess.

The Moon in the Second House of talents, resources, values, self-worth, and earnings

As the natural house of Gemini, Third House natives are likely to rely on what feels right and be very convincing in their points of view but are prone to changing ideas and opinions due to a strong sensitivity to others' way of thinking.

gives the individual a strong need for security and stability. This Moon position has some of the qualities of the Moon's exaltation in Taurus. They can feel emotionally off-balance when they are uncomfortable or when their physical needs are not being met in the way to which they are accustomed. Personal belongings take on a special meaning, and these natives can be highly sentimental.

Gift: Individuals with their Moon in the Second House are highly resourceful, talented, and creative. They are likely to excel in endeavors associated with the arts, crafts, or music. They have a well-developed, instinctive business sensibility, especially in matters that strongly reflect their values or the quality of their life. A comfortable lifestyle is a major incentive for them, which they will value and preserve wholeheartedly.

Shadow: The shadow side of this placement is an individual who is possessive and holds on to people, places, and things long beyond their utilitarian value. Too much emphasis is placed on material possessions, which can skew their values and actions. The Moon is cyclical, and similarly, these natives can experience ups and downs regarding their earnings and spending habits. Their self-worth can be volatile and overly dependent on their possessions or lack of material resources.

Moon in the Third House

The Third House is connected with ideas, communication, siblings, neighbors, and short journeys.

As the natural house of Gemini, the Third House describes all forms of communication. A desire is present to receive self-validation through mental accomplishments. These natives are naturally curious and are at ease in meeting and communicating with those in their nearby environment. An emotional closeness to a particular sibling or relative may be present.

Gift: Combining the intuitive, feeling nature of the Moon with the Third House's Mercurial influence can give these individuals an edge when it comes to making decisions or engaging in communications. They are likely to rely on what feels right at each step of their discourse and ultimately be very convincing in their points of view. A high level of comfort is present in speaking about feelings and personal information. Their sensitivity easily draws confidential information from others. They like to feel comfortable in their work and home neighboring environments, and they take the time to congenially engage those whom they meet.

Shadow: Emotional factors, both conscious and unconscious, can have a strong influence on thoughts and interactions. Logic and reason can become distorted by emotional biases. Their strong imagination and even fantasy can influence their thinking. These natives are likely to change their mind often depending on their mood of the day. Similarly, they are prone to changing ideas and opinions due to a strong sensitivity to others' way of thinking.

Moon in the Fourth House

The Fourth House is about the home, family, genetic inheritance, foundational stability, innermost feelings, later life, and the end of matters.

The Fourth House is naturally ruled by Cancer and the Moon, and an individual with this lunar placement wants and needs a place they can call home. This home, which includes family life, has to nurture them and give them a feeling of comfort, safety, and security. It is their refuge, and they will keep moving until they find the right place. These natives have strong family ties, especially to the mother figure growing up.

Gift: With the double Moon influence, these individuals naturally tune in to the emotional needs of those around them. They are naturally nurturing and supportive and derive much personal fulfillment from their home life. Proud of their family heritage, they carry forward many subconscious influences and traditions from their upbringing. Their natural instincts often lead them to excel in matters pertaining to food, real estate, children, and the home.

Shadow: These natives can have difficulty stepping out of the roles and patterns that were reinforced by early parental conditioning. Many of these habit patterns are buried deep in the unconscious and require persistent attentiveness to unearth. Their emotional stability can be deeply affected when problems or disturbances occur at home. Similarly, when the native is disturbed emotionally, consciously or unconsciously, they will generate a lack of harmony in the home.

Moon in the Fifth House

The Fifth House rules creative self-expression, children, love, passion, romance, playfulness, and joy.

Natives with the Moon in the Fifth House have a natural inclination to express their emotions and feelings through creative arts, drama, romantic ventures, or simply through expressive play. They have a sensibility for knowing how to have fun, which they approach with enthusiasm and gusto. Love affairs can be emotionally intense, and these natives are prone to moodiness and fluctuations in their desires.

> The challenge with the Moon in the Fifth House is not to be emotionally immature or childish. Natives with this placement relish being the center of attention....

Gift: When the Moon is in the Fifth House, an instinctive *joie de vivre* orientation energizes the environment, uplifting those around them. They exude self-confidence and presence. These natives are comfortable expressing their feelings, often doing so with imagination and dramatic flair. Promoting themselves is easy and fun. A natural attunement occurs with children, pets, and babies.

Shadow: The challenge with the Moon in the Fifth House is not to be emotionally

Individuals with the Moon in the Sixth House value being organized, practical, and a good fit for the job they are doing. Insufficient appreciation can inadvertently affect their health and well-being.

satisfaction from tending to their daily affairs, although they may not do so in a strictly routine manner. Their moods may interfere with efficiency and a systematic approach to these matters.

Health concerns can be influenced by emotions. Further clues to health matters can be derived from the sign placement of the Moon as well as planetary connections to the Moon and the ruler of the sign on the cusp of the Sixth House.

Gift: Individuals with the Moon in the Sixth House value being organized and practical. They gain emotional satisfaction from successfully accomplishing their day-to-day work requirements. They are intuitively aware of the tasks that go into manifesting a desired outcome. Their emotional well-being is tied to their dedication to their service. When they feel that they belong or that they are a good fit for the job they are doing, they excel in their devotion and commitment to doing an outstanding job.

Shadow: Individuals with a Sixth-House Moon can have subjective, disproportionate emotional responses to their coworkers, employees, and employers as well as to anyone in their home, social group, or organization that these natives are assisting. Insufficient appreciation from any of the above can trigger emotional destabilization and, if prolonged, can inadvertently affect their health and well-being. These natives can change jobs frequently because they never feel that they are in the right job.

immature or childish. Natives with this placement relish being the center of attention, which can result in behavior that is overly demanding and egotistical. Their affections can be changeable because of emotional instability. They can also depend too much emotionally on their romantic partner. Impulsiveness can lead to unwise speculation and risk-taking through gambling or investments. Recreational activities can be an area where unconscious motives overwhelm their sensibilities and lead them to experiment in imprudent behaviors.

Moon in the Sixth House

The Sixth House governs daily routines, acts of service, the work-life balance, health, due diligence, pet care, coworkers, and employees.

The Sixth House is associated with Mercury-ruled Virgo. When the Moon is in this house, the natives have an emotional need to be useful and helpful to those they want to support. They derive emotional

Moon in the Seventh House

The Seventh House rules close personal relationships, agreements, and compromises.

The Seventh House belongs to Venus-ruled Libra in the natural Zodiac. Individuals with this placement of the Moon have a strong emotional need to be in a deeply fulfilling relationship. They have a heightened sensitivity to the wants and needs of others and are keenly motivated to be liked and accepted by them.

The Libran influence of the Seventh House gives these natives an extra dose of sensitivity to acts of unfairness or injustices to themselves and others. They can unconsciously strive for balance between opposing points of view.

Gift: Individuals with this placement have an instinctive ability to tune in to others' needs and vulnerabilities, and they make good counselors, negotiators, and public relations advocates. Their gentle and caring dispositions give them a knack for establishing harmony in relationships. They are successful mediators. They love to share and nurture those close to them. They seek emotional fulfillment through relationships, and they seek partners who are able to provide emotional support to them.

Shadow: These natives can be overly sensitive to others' responses. They are apt to be exceedingly subjective and take the slightest innuendo as a personal affront. Their strong need to please everybody can result in a pattern of trying to be all things to all people. They can put their own objectives aside for the sake of creating harmony in a relationship. Eventually, their unconscious and repressed emotional needs come to the fore, and they want to move on, developing a pattern of relationship dissatisfaction. Alternatively, they can be overly dependent on having partnerships and relinquish discernment as to whether these partners will be fulfilling to them.

Moon in the Eighth House

The Eighth House rules joint ventures, intimacy, sex, death, transformation, and psychic dimensions.

In the natural Zodiac, the Eighth House belongs to Pluto-ruled Scorpio. The Moon is considered to be in its fall in Scorpio. This placement can lead the native to be continually pushing their limits in the process of finding emotional fulfillment. They can be challenged to constantly reinvent themselves emotionally through the entanglements they participate in.

These natives are drawn to the deeper mysteries of life, including areas related to birth, death, and transformation. They have an interest in personal growth and self-development as well as personal and social evolution.

An Eighth-House Moon can be emotionally intense for the native based upon the essential nature of the transformation that the native undertakes. They are not emotionally satisfied operating at superficial levels of engagement. They will be instinctively drawn to metaphysical and occult studies.

Gift: The Eighth House governs sectors of life that include sex, death, transformation, crisis, reinvention, birth, personal growth, and revival. Natives with their Moon in this house gain emotional fulfillment through their participation in these areas. They are able to help others going through crises. They have an innate understanding of emotional intensity. They are not afraid of expressions of emotional depth, and they are not hesitant to participate and be helpful. They believe in transformation as a way of life. They demonstrate an incredible ability to reinvent themselves, regenerate, and recoup from sadness, loss, and pain.

Shadow: Natives with an Eighth-House Moon can lose track of their own vulnerabilities as they subject themselves to precarious situations. They can have underlying self-destructive motivations that move them to engage in situations, including sexual entanglements, that they cannot handle. Their desires are strong and powerful, and it is not easy for them to let go of what they want, even if they have to resort to unscrupulous means. It is easy for these natives to get pulled off their centers due to their out-of-control desires.

Moon in the Ninth House

The Ninth House rules higher education, long-term goals, foreign travel, publicity, adventures, religion, and philosophical and ethical pursuits.

Moon in the Ninth House natives have high ethics and morals. Jupiter-ruled Sagittarius is the natural ruler of this house, and the Jupiterian influence contributes to their optimistic, philosophic orientation. Emotional stability for them hinges on being able to put their daily concerns into a perspective that they can understand and be comfortable with. They have a need to see the big picture and understand the world around them. Travel provides these natives with a fresh, new perspective that they want and need.

Gift: Individuals with this placement have a high code of ethics and a strong moral creed. They are natural philosophers and gain emotional fulfillment from helping others formulate a higher perspective. They can have an active dream life from which they garner information. Hunches and inspirations can be a guidepost for them. They love to share their knowledge with others, whether it be their philosophic perspective or new information they think would be helpful. A highly intuitive visionary side is present to their nature.

Shadow: Moon in the Ninth House natives can overly identify with parental

moral and religious values so as to limit the scope and depth of their own spiritual understanding. Rather than develop their own ethical code, they project a strong emotional bias and affinity with parental attitudes and dogma. These natives can have escapist tendencies, where they are always looking for a place where the grass is greener. The visionary side of their nature can overshadow their need to be realistic and live in the present moment.

Moon in the Tenth House

The Tenth House rules public achievements, reputation, authority, and prestige.

Natives with a Tenth-House Moon have an instinctive memory of how to achieve prominence and recognition. The ability to work hard to acquire the knowledge and skills to succeed is in their bones. They understand at a deep level the importance of preserving their reputation. Their upbringing set an example for ambition and achieving a high standing in their field.

The Tenth House is ruled by Saturn, and Saturn can be a taskmaster. These natives are at peace emotionally when they are leading a responsible life and have attained a level of recognition or acknowledgment. It is important for them to live up to the expectations of their family.

Gift: These individuals have an innate sense of how to work well with the public. They know instinctively what the public wants, which gives them an edge for receiving the recognition that, in turn, nourishes them and brings the emotional fulfillment they need. It is natural for those with this placement to manage other people, and they are frequently found in positions of leadership. They are dependable and caring and will often go the extra mile to make sure that those who work for them, or those they are responsible for, are well taken care of.

Shadow: These natives are sensitive to criticism or lack of appreciation in the work that they do. When they aren't sufficiently recognized for their efforts, they can be moody and upset. Ambition and dedication to their career or public image can take a toll on their personal development, family life, and significant relationships. The Tenth House makes a grand cross with the First, Fourth, and Seventh Houses. Ideally, each of these areas need attention for balance and fulfillment to occur.

Moon in the Eleventh House

The Eleventh House rules friends, hopes, wishes, groups, and a sense of belonging in the world.

The Eleventh House is ruled by Aquarius in the natural Zodiac. Aquarius rules friends, groups of people, and communities, all of which serve a very important purpose in addressing our need for inclusion and belonging. Individuals with their Moon in the Eleventh House have a strong need to feel included. It is easy for them to take others' responses personally and feel left out even when they aren't.

The Uranian influence of this house placement activates an innate instinct to be unique and original. They embrace humanity and take pride in treating everyone as equals. They have great respect for human dignity.

Friendships are important to an Eleventh-House Moon. It is easy for them to make friends and participate in different types of group activities. Their nonjudgmental orientation and openness contribute to their popularity and the ease with which they interact with others.

The Eleventh-House Moon sets their sights high. They innately feel that they

Natives with a Tenth-House Moon have an instinctive memory for how to achieve prominence and recognition.

can attain goals they set for themselves. The unbounded influence of Aquarius opens the door to thinking outside the box. They have an attitude that anything is possible and that they can look at life in terms of opportunities.

Gift: Moon in the Eleventh House individuals are gifted in leading and overseeing small and large group activities. They intuitively know how to keep a sharing and congenial vibe in any group. They naturally promote an atmosphere where everyone feels special and accepted. They have a deep need to gain recognition for their achievements and will rise to the occasion to have that need met. Individuals with this placement are respected by their colleagues and friends for their honesty, high ideals, and refusal to compromise their integrity.

Shadow: These natives can feel like outsiders, as if they are excluded from society even when they are not. Their interactions with friends and group dynamics can be riddled with anxiety or with predisposed feelings of not belonging or of being inherently different. A need for safety and predictability can clash with their need to be true to themselves. The Aquarian influence can like everyone and still keep others at a distance with their personal detachment, where everyone is special and yet no one is really special. They can be too impersonal.

Moon in the Twelfth House

The Twelfth House rules secrets, unconscious patterns, karma, closure, institutions, connections with higher sources, enlightenment, and undoing.

Neptune, the natural ruler of Pisces and the Twelfth House, gives the native a naturally dreamy, compassionate, and introspective orientation. They can derive emotional fulfillment from positions of service or through work in large institutions geared toward service to others, such as hospitals, human service, and spiritual organizations and places of confinement.

Their emotional nature can be preoccupied with subtle feelings that barely rise to the level of conscious awareness. They often have delayed reactions to their own emotional experiences. Their naturally private nature coupled with their lack of identification with their own emotions and feelings can lead to feelings of isolation or of feeling misunderstood.

The suffering and sorrow these natives absorb subconsciously can have a significant impact on their psyche, requiring them to seek regular periods of silence and solitude to recharge their batteries.

Gift: These natives are compassionate and caring toward others, including those who are disadvantaged or infirmed. They derive emotional fulfillment when they can help

those in need or when they can participate in the betterment of society. They are naturally attuned to psychic impressions and nuances as well as to the trends and subtleties of society. This gives them an intuitive understanding of mankind and the sufferings they have had to endure. They have an instinctive urge to delve into their own subconscious in order to release past karma and old hurts that are holding them back from their soul's growth and evolution. They have an inner awareness to stay clear of creating any new karma or debts to individuals and society.

Shadow: A Twelfth-House Moon is extremely sensitive to worldly chaos and the woes of the world. They pick up on these outer energies and vibrations and lose track of their own feelings and emotions. These natives may need to withdraw into their inner worlds in order to regroup and discover their own emotional needs. Otherwise, they can feel vulnerable and moody and not exactly know why. These natives can have a subconscious desire to run away from the realities of life that prevent them from participating in their present-day experiences and relationships.

MOON COMBINATIONS

The Moon symbolizes instinctive awareness. When combined with planets, the energy of that planet will flow easily, and the native will own the qualities of that planetary energy, or else blockages will occur in how the energy is expressed.

Moon/Sun

The Moon rules the soul, core instincts, the personality, and subconscious conditioning.

The Sun indicates purpose, self-expression, creative life force, and conscious will.

The gift of a Moon/Sun combination is a harmonious orientation toward life. These natives seek harmony and peace in their outer experiences, with an easy flow of self-expression, and are comfortable with male-, female-, and other-oriented individuals. They are generally confident and seek to expand their conscious awareness.

Gift: The Sun and Moon combined create a basic inner balance, whereby the native can stand fully behind who they are, what they want, and why they want it. They have a harmonious orientation toward life and seek harmony and peace in their outer experiences. These individuals are comfortable with male-, female-, and other-oriented individuals. Their self-expression has an easy flow. Generally, these natives are confident and seek to expand their conscious awareness.

Shadow: Natives can feel tension between their feelings and their conscious will that manifests as a hesitancy to be fully behind oneself. The conscious and the subconscious are at odds with each other, which can lead to tension in areas of self-expres-sion and self-actualization. The native can have a tendency to be moody and off-bal-ance, particularly when surrounded by mixed groups of masculine and feminine energies.

Moon/Mercury

The Moon rules the soul, core instincts, the per-sonality, and subconscious conditioning.

Mercury rules communication, mental processes, and the logical mind.

When Mercury combines with the energy of the Moon, communication of one's feelings is highlighted. This combination will reflect the native's ability to have ac-cess to their emotions and genuinely ex-press how they feel.

Gift: This combination is sometimes known as the silver tongue. It represents an individual who can put their feelings into words and express them with confidence and ease. Even when speaking on subjects that are deeply passionate, they have an ability to choose words that reflect a balance between the head and the heart, so they are listened to. They have a natural rhythm to the tone and tempo of their voice and their communication style.

Shadow: Irrational thought processes often plague this individual, and it is difficult to communicate their deepest feelings. An overly logical approach can ensue that is devoid of emotion. Contrarily, communication can be overly emotional and lacking in logic. Basically, a disconnect occurs between emotions and logic.

Moon/Venus

The Moon rules the soul, core instincts, the personality, and subconscious conditioning.

Venus represents love, relationships, beauty, values, comfort, and material resources.

The gift of a Moon and Venus connection is emotional availability to close friends and intimate partners. Besides having a pleasing disposition and an open personality, they know how to put people at ease. They are not afraid to express their feelings, and they do so graciously. Both Moon and Venus are receptive energies, and when they work well together, they smooth out rough edges and bring affection and softness to situations.

Gift: These individuals are aesthetically sensitive to their own appearance as well as to their surroundings. Often personally attractive, they innately know how to add a pleasing touch to their surroundings.

Shadow: The shadow of this planetary combination can be expressed in a reluctance to express love and affection for fear of vulnerability. Their emotions can interfere with their love nature. Natives may subconsciously hold back their feelings, which can create an awkward social presence.

Moon/Mars

The Moon rules the soul, core instincts, the personality, and subconscious conditioning.

Mars rules assertiveness, energy, drive, and courage.

The combination of the Moon and Mars is similar to having an Aries Moon; a Moon in the First House; and, to some degree, Mars in Cancer. In all cases, the native will express their feelings with passion and will generate strong feelings and passionate responses.

Gift: Ample passion and enthusiasm occur when the energies of the Moon and Mars combine. Individuals with this combination can inspire others with their energy and charisma. These individuals can be inspirational, and they can easily motivate others with their energetic and instinctive responses. Activities are undertaken readily and with emotional ease. Anger is channeled into productive activities. When emotionally connected to a cause or particular item, they can be inspiring leaders or do well in fields that relate to sales and marketing.

> Ample passion and enthusiasm occur when the energies of the Moon and Mars combine. Individuals with this combination can inspire others with their energy and charisma.

Shadow: The shadow side of combining the Moon with Mars can result in an overly impulsive and arrogant nature that is prone to outbursts of anger. Emotional sensitivity is heightened, and these individuals can overreact and take an insignificant slight personally. They can jump to conclusions and overreact. Impatience, crankiness, and unwarranted aggressiveness can overshadow otherwise good deeds and negatively affect relationships. An imbalance of Mars can generate excess heat in the body, causing inflammation and infections.

Moon/Jupiter

The Moon rules the soul, core instincts, the personality, and subconscious conditioning.

Jupiter represents the higher mind, greater truths, expansiveness, hope, and optimism.

An optimistic, warm-hearted nature oozes from all levels of the conscious and subconscious when the Moon combines with expansive Jupiter. These natives are kind and authentic and bring their deeply caring nature to others. Just as Jupiter is exalted in Moon-ruled Cancer, these natives are often devoted to home and family, which can often include their extended family and friends.

Gift: A Moon/Jupiter combination brings forth the gift of good karma and generosity of spirit. They have a contagious optimism that makes it easy for others to be around. They are sought after for their uplifting sensibility and fresh perspective that they openheartedly extend to others. They are generally trusted for their honesty and sincerity and, in return, are likely to receive cooperation and help from others. It is not uncommon for them to have a pleasant disposition and a good sense of humor.

Shadow: The shadow side of this combination is a tendency toward overindulgence and a dislike of having limitations imposed upon them. Excessiveness coupled with a lack of prudence can work to their disadvantage. Overdoing can get carried too far, causing health problems and weight issues. They can exaggerate their emotional reactions to people and events and then feel let down when the desired response is not provided. It is not uncommon for them to promise more than they can deliver due to their generous nature, leading others to think of them as unreliable.

Moon/Saturn

The Moon rules the soul, core instincts, the personality, and subconscious conditioning.

Saturn rules responsibility, adjustments to limitations, sustainability, and structure.

Saturn can have a sobering effect on the Moon, which can, at times, inhibit one's emotional expression. These natives are very sensitive and feel very deeply, although they may have difficulty opening themselves to others. In turn, the native may be more apt to identify with material things and daily mundane activities. The Saturn influence bestows an inclination toward orderliness, discipline, and moderation.

Gift: These individuals are naturally responsible and responsive emotionally to others. They are realistic, persevering, and innately possess a good amount of common sense. Others appreciate that they follow through on their commitments and their mature attitude. They understand hardship and can offer empathy and realistic solutions. These natives are accomplished. They do not let their emotions get in the way when performing essential and critical activities and tasks. They are gifted with self-control and discipline.

Natives with a Moon and Saturn combination are naturally responsible—sometimes overly so—and do not let their emotions get in the way when performing essential tasks. They may feel emotionally unsupported and stuck as if a situation will never change.

Shadow: An undercurrent of guilt can plague these individuals. They may be overly responsible and thereby feel that they are never toeing the line. On the other hand, the shadow of this combination can manifest as an inherent pessimism, which can manifest as someone who is overly critical of situations they encounter and of others they engage with. It may be difficult for them to trust others. Saturn can feel depressing, stuck, as if any situation will never change. Emotions may not flow freely. These natives may feel emotionally unsupported. The heightened pessimism of the Saturnian influence on the Moon can magnify the potential for a negative outcome. These natives can become overshadowed by their fears and potential vulnerability.

Moon/Uranus

The Moon rules the soul, core instincts, the personality, and subconscious conditioning.

Uranus rules intuition, originality, individuality, and the sudden and unexpected.

The combination of the Moon with Uranus brings an aloofness or detachment to emotional expression. Uranus is electrical in nature, and natives with this combination move quickly, as if their synaptic responses are continually alert and ready to respond. They can be high-strung or totally present, with a rapid and apt response.

Gift: These natives are generally highly intuitive and think outside the box. Their personalities are lively and vibrant. Something about them is different, which intrigues others. They willingly express their individuality and respect others for their diversity and uniqueness. Others sense their openness, and they are comfortable expressing aspects of themselves that they may have previously kept private. This combination bestows an emotional honesty upon the individual. They do not appreciate pretense and deceptiveness of character. They value kindness and, at the same time, are able to tell it how it is.

Shadow: Natives displaying the shadow side of Moon/Uranus connections can be prone to mood swings, restlessness, and erratic behavior. Since the Moon rules habitual and instinctive behavior patterns and Uranus can rule aspects of the sensory nervous system, these individuals are prone to sensory overstimulation and anxiety that can be destabilizing. They have little tolerance for restriction and need to find a balance between emotional independence and intimacy.

Moon/Neptune

The Moon rules the soul, core instincts, the personality, and subconscious conditioning.

Neptune rules ideals, creative imagination, transcendence, compassion, and vision.

Neptune sensitizes an already sensitive Moon with heightened compassion and strong emotional empathy for all living things. They feel the discomfort of others as well as their joy. Neptune brings idealism and spirituality to the native's conscious awareness. These natives are naturally attuned to meditation and contacting higher realms of consciousness.

Gift: Fanciful Neptune enhances the imagination and responsiveness to sensory input, enriching musical, artistic, theatrical, and photographic talents for these natives. Their tastes are super refined, which contributes to their culinary gifts. They are particularly sensitive to subtleties of tone in both visual and musical realms. These natives are psychically attuned to the emotions of others as well as to environmental stimuli. The Moon/Neptune combination sees and relates to the best in others and can inspire them to be their best selves.

Shadow: Emotions can be subject to illusions and fantastical assumptions. A need to sacrifice can be attributed to unconscious feelings of not doing enough, as if an ideal exists that can never be reached. Neptune adds confusion to emotional issues. Self-pity and martyrdom can ensue as a result of their overly sensitive nature. Escapism is too often a viable option to experiencing the pain that they would otherwise feel. These natives can have a strong reaction to toxic substances due to the sensitivity of their constitution.

Moon/Pluto

The Moon rules the soul, core instincts, the personality, and subconscious conditioning.

Pluto represents regeneration; transformation; and a compelling, fundamental approach.

Pluto combining with the Moon brings emotional intensity. Their feelings are keenly felt, which is perhaps the trigger that leads them to want to take a deep dive into understanding their subconscious makeup. A desire is present to be in control of their feelings rather than having their emotions be a dominating influence over them.

Gift: These natives are willing to delve into their emotional discomfort and figure out its root cause. They believe in peeling back the layers to get to the crux of an issue. Self-empowerment is their goal, and they have an innate understanding of the right use of power. They are natural therapists and healers, helping others figure out what is motivating them. They have the courage and determination to overcome obstacles. They believe in transformation, and they are not limited to cultivating their inner lives. They do not hesitate to improve their outer environment with renovations and makeovers.

Shadow: Huge emotional fluctuations can occur due to the intensity of their emotions. As much as these natives want to have some control over their feelings, their strong desire by nature can lead them to self-destructive actions. Obsessive and compulsive behaviors can be daunting to these natives, making it difficult for them to find inner peace. The shadow side of a Moon/Pluto combination manifests as suspicion, jealousy, out-of-control anxiety, and trepidation.

> Uranus is electrical in nature, and natives with this combination move quickly, as if their synaptic responses are continually alert and ready to respond.

Natives with a Moon/Chiron combination can be very powerful healers, with acute sensitivity and heightened compassion for others.

Moon/Chiron

The Moon rules the soul, core instincts, the personality, and subconscious conditioning.

Chiron represents core wounds and the desire to overcome them, and healing.

The combination of the Moon and Chiron can indicate an individual who instinctively uses their healing abilities. These individuals are extremely sensitive, and their sensitivity senses emotional blocks that interfere with full self-empowerment and the development of consciousness.

Gift: Natives with a Moon/Chiron combination can be very powerful healers. Their attunement to their own soul urges and their awareness of the power of emotions when channeled positively as a tool for manifestation are gifts that they can share with others. They can be an example of someone who has been through a major emotional crisis and came out at the other end, i.e., the wounded healer archetype. Their acute sensitivity and heightened compassion for the suffering of others align them to practices that involve one of the many forms of healing.

Shadow: Deep-rooted problems can exist that are connected to issues around giving and receiving nurturance. The native may have been denied the encouragement and support that they needed to feel safe in their upbringing. In any case, they are coming from a position of lack. As a result, their strongly emotional nature is continually seeking compensation for the emptiness within from sources that are never going to give them the fulfillment they crave.

Moon/Eris

The Moon rules the soul, core instincts, the personality, and subconscious conditioning.

Eris represents the determination to remove limitations that impede the soul's evolution.

Gift: These natives have an innate gift for spotting phoniness and inauthenticity. They strive to uncover false belief systems and subconscious programming that resulted from society and parental conditioning. They desire to help others unveil their true selves.

Shadow: Subconscious competitiveness and a propensity to create strife and discord can characterize these natives in situations when they consciously want to improve their lives and the lives of those around them. They can be abrasive.

Moon/North Node

The Moon rules the soul, core instincts, the personality, and subconscious conditioning.

The North Node represents future direction, soul guidance, and fulfillment.

Individuals with a North Node/Moon connection have a deep, intuitive urge to embark upon the path indicated by the sign and placement of their North Node.

Gift: As karma would have it, these natives have an advantage in that they emotionally connect to the path of destiny that lies before them. They can feel comfortable that they are on the right path, and they instinctively know when they wobble away from it. They have the know-how needed to take advantage of trends and attain popularity. Sales, marketing, public relations, advertising, entertainment, and politics are areas that they can excel in, depending on the sign and placement of the Moon and the North Node.

Shadow: These individuals have a nagging feeling that something more is out there for them, that they don't fit in with what they are doing and the direction they are going in. They feel out of place, as if something is missing from their lives. They can be overly attached to parental or societal expectations that have led them to pursue avenues that they were never fully aligned to.

Gift: The gift of the South Node is using skills that have been developed in the past and bringing them forward to incorporate them into the destiny indicated by the sign and placement of the North Node. With the Moon associated with the South Node, gifts that can be gleaned include a warm, generous personality that is nurturing. They have a knack for connecting with the public and instinctively know how to sense and take advantage of whatever is trending.

Shadow: These natives can have strong emotional ties to the past. It may be very difficult for them to break away from expectations instilled upon them from early childhood. They may feel bound to enter into a field associated with family, like a family business or a field with deep roots to their ancestral lineage. In any case, they may embark in areas that bring them dubious satisfaction. They can have deep-rooted, subconscious habits and emotional patterns that no longer serve them. A lack of emotional fulfillment can plague them, and they can feel that they don't receive the nurturing and support they need. They can have feelings of isolation and aloneness.

> With the Moon associated with the South Node, gifts that can be gleaned include a warm, generous personality that is nurturing.

Moon/South Node

The Moon rules the soul, core instincts, the personality, and subconscious conditioning.

The South Node represents familiarity, gratification, and the path of least resistance.

Natives with a Moon/South Node connection may feel that they have to redo something they have done previously. They may, by happenstance, find themselves in a field that is very familiar to them.

Moon/Ascendant

The Moon rules the soul, core instincts, the personality, and subconscious conditioning.

The Ascendant represents one's approach, orientation, and the window through which one sees the world.

Moon/Ascendant combinations bring huge amounts of sensitivity to the native's approach to any situation. A major focus is on feelings and emotions, which can

The Moon at or near the Midheaven may mean that the emotional conditioning and imprints of early childhood have a strong influence on adult career choices.

manifest in a few ways. These natives can be overly shy and withdrawn or exceptionally sensitive and empathic to others' needs. Moon on the Ascendant individuals can have round, moonlike faces.

Gift: These natives are favorably received by others due to their sensitivity and soft, caring nature. They have a nurturing quality that can vary in strength depending on the sign the Moon is located in. They are easily moved by the plight of others and can bring comfort to those in need. They have lively imaginations and good memories, perhaps due to their strong connection to the past.

Shadow: These natives can be overly sensitive and find it hard to function. Their moodiness can make them difficult for others to be around. They can have a defensive stance due to their highly subjective nature, where they take every slight and innuendo personally. They can be overly impressionable, whereby they pick up and

retain dissonant energies that they come into contact with.

Moon/Midheaven (MC)

The Moon rules the soul, core instincts, the personality, and subconscious conditioning.

The Midheaven (MC) represents image, outer aspirations, and career orientation.

The Moon at or near the Midheaven is the Moon culminating, meaning that the emotional conditioning experienced in early childhood has a strong influence on career and social standing. Adult career choices may connect to imprints established in childhood, such as identification with a parent and their family business, or to strong environment influences, such as television and movie characters.

Gift: Individuals with a Moon/Midheaven connection can be highly charismatic and exude warmth and caring. They know how to intuitively connect with the public and bring forward issues that the public cares about. Their highly sensitive nature knows how to read their audience if they are in a leadership position, which is not unlikely since they can have an emotional need to be a public figure. The Moon rules habit patterns, giving these natives the subconscious memory of what it takes to be popular.

Shadow: The strong emotional makeup of these individuals can usurp their ability to be popular based upon emotional outbursts and other behavior patterns that are not condoned by society. The Midheaven is at the top of the chart, so it is difficult to keep secrets for very long. They can be victims of gossip and propaganda if in public roles, which requires a thick skin. It will be up to the native to not take every criticism too personally.

The Ascendant

The Ascendant, as well as the opposite point, the Descendant, of a chart are determined by the person's specific position on Earth at the exact moment in time that they take their first breath. The Ascendant is marked by the precise degree, minute, and second of the sign on the eastern horizon—more precisely, the point of intersection on the eastern horizon and ecliptic. It is that celebrated first impression that marks the dawning of a new life on planet Earth. The Ascendant is that awakening consciousness, in much the same way as the Sun's appearance in the east marks the dawn of a new day.

The Ascendant is one's automatic response to their environment. The Ascendant represents one's approach, orientation, and the window through which one sees the world.

The Ascendant reflects how one first appears to others, the first impression of the outer personality that is projected. It is that carryover from their first impression that they received upon arriving on Earth.

In order to calculate the chart's Ascendant, it is necessary to know the exact time and place of birth. The Ascendant or Rising sign changes approximately every two hours.

THE RULING PLANET

The ruler of the sign on the Ascendant designates the chart's ruling planet. Each sign has a ruling planet that governs it and imbues it with certain traits. Some signs, like Scorpio, Aquarius, and Pisces, have two ruling planets, the classical or original sign ruler, referred to as the coruler of the sign, as well as the modern house ruler.

Note the chart below. The planet in parentheses is the coruler of the sign.

Aries—Mars

Taurus—Venus

Gemini—Mercury

Cancer—Moon

Leo—Sun

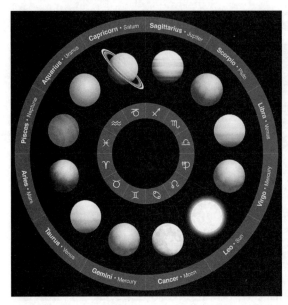

The ruler of the sign on the Ascendant designates the chart's ruling planet that governs it, imbuing the sign with certain traits.

Virgo—Mercury

Libra—Venus

Scorpio—Pluto (Mars)

Sagittarius—Jupiter

Capricorn—Saturn

Aquarius—Uranus (Saturn)

Pisces—Neptune (Jupiter)

The house position of the ruling planet, as well as how its gift and its shadow manifest for the individual, tell a story that offers additional information in chart interpretation. Some astrologers reference the ruler of the Sun sign as the ruling planet; however, I find that the ruler of the Ascendant or Rising sign is more significant, although both are important.

The ruling planet carries extra meaning when interpreting a chart. The ruler of the sign governing the First House is all about the Self. It describes physical appearance, general temperament, and the

person's sense of their relationship to being on Earth. It represents the surface of their personality, what they show to the world on a day-to-day basis. Think of it as the cover of a book, the first impression. It's enough to get an idea, but it is not the whole story.

The planet that rules the Ascendant or Rising sign is the ruling planet. For instance, for an Aries Ascendant, the ruling planet is Mars. For a Scorpio Ascendant, the ruling planet is Pluto, although Mars is the coruler of Scorpio.

The sign that rules each house cusp also has a ruling planet. Similarly, additional information is gleaned about the traits, ease of functioning, and gifts encountered in the areas of life governed by each of the 12 houses.

ARIES RISING

Aries Rising has Mars as the planetary ruler, propelling these individuals out into the world with their bold presence. They are the warriors of the Zodiac, ready to take on whatever is before them, and they come off as brave and independent. They are competitive and courageous, although a closer look at their ruling planet, Mars, in their chart will determine whether they will put their gloves where their initial impulse lies.

Gift: Their initial instincts are usually right on target. The gifts manifested by their ruling planet, Mars, will indicate the manner and the area of life where they are most apt to utilize their gifts. These action-oriented natives go after their objectives without wasting time.

Shadow: Aries Rising can be intimidating in situations where a more receptive approach is warranted. Too much bluster and not enough substance can occur, especially if the ego is out of whack. Not particularly receptive to the vibes around them, their initial approach can be gruff, with an undertone of anger, irritability, and insensitivity.

TAURUS RISING

Taurus Rising individuals present themselves with an aura of solidity and strength. They take in the situation at hand prior to responding. With Venus as their ruling planet, they are not likely to initially jump to conclusions without some prior assessment. They are likely to have a gentleness in their facial features with softness in their eyes as they take in the environment surrounding them.

Gift: These natives are unassuming and pleasant and are a welcome addition to most situations. They are naturally charming, with Venus as their planetary ruler. Their specific gifts will be based upon the sign and house position of their natal Venus.

Shadow: The shadow side of Taurus Rising is most obvious when adaptability is needed. They can dig their heels in and present quite an immovable force if either their environment or comfort level require flexibility.

GEMINI RISING

The Mercurial rulership of Gemini Rising gives these individuals a very adaptable persona, willing to approach new situations with curiosity and vigor. They are typically agile and quick-moving. As a Mutable Air Rising sign, these individuals will be garbed in appropriate yet easy-to-move-about attire. They have expressive hands, which they somehow make noticeable. They have an intellectual look about them.

Gift: Their adaptability and willingness to adjust to any situation is a welcome gift to those they encounter. They appear charming and well-spoken, and they are good conversationalists. They are a perfect addition to any social setting.

> Gemini Rising natives can get overwhelmed in their desire to do everything at once.

Shadow: Gemini Rising natives can get overwhelmed in their desire to do everything at once. When in doubt, they move about rather than delve into the situation at hand. They can resort to being too talkative when they forget to listen and assess their surroundings. They are not known for emotional sensitivity.

CANCER RISING

Moon-ruled Cancer is a sign that is often not comfortable in the spotlight. Shy, reserved, and sometimes retiring, Cancer prefers to spend time with either those whom they are very much at ease with or in a comfortable surrounding, such as their home, where they can focus on activities close to their heart. With the Moon as their planetary ruler, these natives will often be easily identified by their roundish-shaped face and soft eyes and features.

Gift: A sincere aura emanates from a Cancer Rising individual due to the depth of their emotions and the feeling that they want to put their arms around you to let you know that everything is okay. Their

Generating harmony is a goal for Venus-ruled Libra Rising natives. Gracious, polite, and diplomatic, they are genuinely cooperative and have the ability to see any matter from the viewpoint of others.

desire to nurture comes across especially to those in their inner circle.

Shadow: Cancer Rising can add just enough emotional dissonance and reticence that it limits one's effectiveness. An inherent moodiness is present that is apropos for the Moon-ruled Cancer Rising sign that can include swings in emotions and an inconsistency that is difficult for others to initially understand.

LEO RISING

Sun-ruled Leo Rising individuals will confidently present themselves with an aura of grandeur and flair. They emanate warmth and a sunny spirit. People tend to notice them when they walk into a room. They are stylish and generally have a noticeable feature, if not their attire, then their hair or makeup.

Gift: Leo Rising persons give off warmth, confidence, and strength. They project dignity and are generally fun-loving, should the occasion arise. After all, why not? The Sun can shine on regardless of whatever else is happening.

Shadow: Leos can have strong egos and overcompensate, especially when they are feeling insecure. This can show up as their demanding attention, even when it is not warranted. They can come off as bullies in their determination to dominate situations.

VIRGO RISING

This Mercury-ruled Earth sign is always looking at details and analyzing how they can make any situation they enter into better. Highly observant and self-aware, they take in as much as they put out. Confidence is not their trump card, and they can become reticent unless they are on a mission to improve a condition. They will often have a clean, simplified look with chiseled features.

Gift: The Virgoan nature is adaptable, and they will make themselves available to do whatever needs to be done. Their service-oriented nature makes them a useful addition to any situation. Their mental acuteness is expressed in practical matters. No details are too small for them to notice or expound upon. They often have a way with words.

Shadow: The perfectionist nature of Virgo Rising can inhibit these natives and prevent them from challenging themselves. They can stay within a small bubble of experience for fear of venturing forward into new realms of experiences. Their perfectionist air can be intimidating at times.

LIBRA RISING

Venus-ruled Libra Rising natives are gracious, polite, and diplomatic. They express beauty and grace in their actions and persona, and they have a knack for putting others at ease. They have a strong sense of justice, which will propel them to take action or, at least, speak up sharply, albeit diplomatically.

Gift: Generating harmony is a goal for Libra Rising individuals, and they want those around them to be happy. They are genuinely cooperative and have the ability to see any matter from the viewpoint of others. Aesthetics is an intrinsic aspect of their nature, and they have a sense of how to visually improve environments they are in.

Shadow: Libra Rising folks can be indecisive, which can end up being a nonstarter for them. Interference from their desire to please others can work against their realization of fulfilling their own hopes and desires. At times, their Venusian nature comes off as flirty and self-involved.

SCORPIO RISING

Scorpio Rising has Pluto as its ruling planet, with Mars as a coruler. Is it no wonder that they present themselves with intensity, energy, and willpower? Fixed in their intentions, they are highly focused and driven toward attaining their goals. Scorpio Rising intensity is generally obvious in their quiet, magnetic charisma, which captures the attention of others

while they move forward in their desired outcomes.

Gift: This no-nonsense Ascendant is unstoppable in attaining their desired outcomes. They have a knack for combining an alluring and magnetic charm with a focused intent to accomplish their objectives. They have the ability to draw on hidden sources of power to attain their ends.

Shadow: These natives can be manipulative when their intense desires become obsessive and overwhelm their better judgment. Much will depend on how they handle the hidden shadows inherent in the planetary combinations with their ruling planet, Pluto. The shadow side of Plutonian influence can be innately destructive to themselves and others.

SAGITTARIUS RISING

High-minded, Jupiter-ruled Sagittarius Rising people approach life with a glass-half-full orientation. They are straightforward and expect others to be so as well. Outspoken and opinionated, they can be counted on to say what no one else dares to speak of.

Gift: Jupiter-ruled Sagittarius Rising individuals have an enthusiasm for life that enlivens the atmosphere around them. Their optimism is infectious, inspiring those around them to subscribe to their way of thinking.

Shadow: Sagittarius Rising natives can take the outcome of situations for granted. Their Jupitarian approach to life can lack realism. A tendency to overlook important details may occur. These natives think big and sometimes overestimate their abilities with an overbearing amount of zest and gusto.

CAPRICORN RISING

Realistic and serious-minded, Capricorn Rising individuals are prepared for whatever situation they might encounter. Many of them aren't always serious, though. They are realistic and will live life to the fullest, to everyone's surprise, given their otherwise mature and sometimes somber persona. They will say it as it is, sometimes with caustic humor and sarcastic cynicism.

Gift: Capricorn Rising people can be counted on. They are serious-minded, responsible, and prepared. Everything they do has a purpose and is designed to achieve a practical end. Patience is a virtue that they understand to their core. Having learned some lessons of life the hard way, they have developed wisdom that they can share with others.

Shadow: Melancholy can overtake these serious-minded natives with their glass-half-empty approach to life. To their own chagrin, they can generate fear in others when they overdo the strict disciplinarian role.

AQUARIUS RISING

A Zen-like approach to situations characterize those individuals with Aquarius Rising. They remain cool, calm, and collected until they aren't. Uranus is their planetary ruler, and unexpected fluctuations in demeanor can apply, although as a Fixed Air sign, they can soon return to their detached and rational orientation to life. They are original, straightforward, creative, and independent.

Gift: Aquarius Rising individuals are people-oriented and friendly in an impersonal way. They do very well in group settings and have an innate knowledge of what brings the greatest good for the group. Individuality and originality are highly valued, and it is not uncommon for them to display these predispositions in their appearance.

Shadow: The overly rational orientation of an Aquarius Ascendant is likened to someone who has their head in the sand. Emotional interactions can be uncomfortable for them; they prefer a more logical approach, which can contribute to a lack of empathy and compassion. They like the idea of being compassionate more than they like the reality of it.

PISCES RISING

Neptune-ruled Pisces Rising individuals are dreamy, mysterious, and alluring. They have a refined sensibility and approach people with understanding, compassion, and empathy. Piscean eyes are deep and mesmerizing, reflecting the openness and vulnerability inherent in this Ascendant.

Gift: Compassion and empathy describe those with a Pisces Ascendant. They detect the subtle energies in their surroundings, responding openly and innocently to those who may need to be heard. Their subtle, ethereal approach gives them an edge when it comes to penetrating the human experience. They are idealistic and speak to the best in others.

Shadow: With Neptune as their ruling planet, these individuals can have their head in the clouds. Avoidance is their defense mechanism of choice and can have serious escapist tendencies. It is not unusual for these natives to carry worrying to the extreme. They can work themselves into a forsaken state of mind.

Mercury

Mercury, or Hermes, is the messenger of the gods. He rules over all forms of communication, including language, speech, online communication, and writing; short trips, transportation in general, and commuting; siblings and neighbors; and commerce and trade.

Mercury, as a divine messenger, can be the purveyor of wisdom. Mercury can also be a trickster. Mercury can represent thievery and cunning, yet on the other hand, Mercury can trick one into higher consciousness. Mercury is hard to put your finger on. Anyone who has ever attempted to try to capture a ball of mercury from a broken, old-fashioned thermometer knows that it is not easy to do.

Greek mythology portrays Hermes as a clever trickster who gets sent out on missions by Zeus and other Olympian gods to do their dirty work. Based upon this interpretation, Hermes denotes the Mercurial adaptability of the mind, which must survive through its abilities, dexterity, and ingenuity.

Mercurial thinking is restless and active. Mercury is about swift thinking and reasoning. Mercury rapidly assesses possibilities, formulates opinions, and has the ability to rationalize.

Mercury/Hermes carries a magic wand known as a "caduceus" that was gifted to him by Apollo, who is also referred to as the Sun God. The caduceus symbolizes the spinal column, the central channel for the nervous system, which, in turn, feeds into all of the organs and body parts. The caduceus is made up of two snakes, one representing the sympathetic nervous system and the other the parasympathetic nervous system. The places where the snakes cross represent the spinal energy centers, or chakra centers.

Mercury is the smallest of all the planets, and it is also the planet closest to the Sun

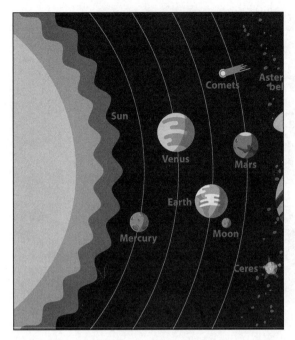

Mercury, the smallest of all the planets, is closest to the Sun and has the most eccentric orbit. From our vantage point on Earth, the "trickster planet" appears to change direction three times a year for a three-week period known as Mercury retrograde.

Mercury is related to the learning style and type of information the person is interested in and how they relate to the world, including the first impressions they formulate and receive.

Mercury in the heavens has a reputation for changing direction three times a year for about three weeks each time. This period is known as Mercury retrograde. During these periods, Mercury has been called the trickster planet. It is not uncommon that people who don't know much more about astrology than their Sun sign have heard that Mercury is retrograde. When Mercury changes direction, it shifts the focus from the logical, thinking right side of the brain to the more intuitive left side of the brain, supporting a period for reevaluation and review. Someone born with Mercury retrograde can be more right-brain oriented, have more spatial orientation, and recognize patterns and may or may not be primarily logical.

and with the most eccentric orbit, now that Pluto has been reclassified as a dwarf planet. Mercury is never more than 28 degrees from the Sun and takes about 88 days to complete its orbit around the Sun. Because the Sun and Mercury are so close, it will naturally fall in the same sign as the Sun or in the sign before or after the Sun sign.

Mercury is Mutable and readily takes on the qualities of the sign and house in which it is placed. Individuals with a Gemini Sun have Mercury as the depositor of their Sun. Subsequently, Gemini natives with Mercury in Taurus, Mercury in Gemini, or Mercury in Cancer will behave differently and have dissimilar characteristics because their Mercury has taken on the qualities of the sign it is placed in.

MERCURY IN THE SIGNS

Mercury in Aries

Mercury in Mars-ruled Aries can be sharp, with their witty one-liners and mental agility. The Martian influence doesn't make for a patient listener, but you can count on an enthusiastic and somewhat impatient response. These natives can come up with original and bold ideas.

Gift: The charm and quick wit of this placement can inspire the most somber audience and render them enthusiastic and engaged. Their reaction time is super quick, and coupled with their well-developed dexterity, these natives are adept at verbal sparring and not so bad at physical sparring, either.

Shadow: The attention span for an individual with this placement can be somewhat meandering and easily distracted. Impatience can be easily triggered, especially when the task at hand is drawn out or when the conversation gets boring. These natives have been known to put their foot in their mouth, especially when irritability and their quick reaction time are at play. Impulsiveness is not their friend, either. They can make decisions that they can later regret.

MERCURY IN TAURUS

Mercury combines with Venus-ruled Taurus to deliver a generally calm and patient individual who often prefers to listen rather than speak unless they have something worthwhile to contribute to the conversation. They lean toward being influenced by the usefulness, financial implications, or the extent to which an idea will add value to their life. They generally have good powers of concentration, and they are able to block out peripheral disturbances.

Gift: Patience coupled with a deliberate and organized approach is a characteristic held by an individual with this placement. They usually have a calm, multisensory, and pleasant communication style that entices their listeners. Taurus rules the throat, and the Venusian influence contributes to a melodious speaking voice. These natives excel in offering common-sense, practical solutions to everyday problems. They can do well in mathematics and physical sciences.

Shadow: The stubbornness that is characteristic of Fixed Earth Taurus can mean that this individual does not change their mind easily unless presented with a non-confrontational, logical reason why they should, and even then, don't count on it. Their slow response time can be a detriment in emergency situations, although they will likely have a good plan in place once they do execute it.

MERCURY IN GEMINI

As the natural ruler of Gemini, Mercury is well placed in this sign. These natives are worthy communicators, witty and agile in their style and choice of words. Innately curious, their interests are far-reaching, and their mental databases contain several folders packed with information. Multitasking and carrying on two conversations at the same time is easy for them, although they can easily end up with sensory overload due to the Mutable Air characteristics of Gemini and Mercury's adaptability.

> Mercury in Gemini folks are natural conversationalists who are witty, knowledgeable, and entertaining.

Gift: Mercury in Gemini folks are natural conversationalists who are witty, knowledgeable, and entertaining. They enjoy playing with words and generally make good writers, speakers, and communicators. Their versatility in knowledge as well as their ability to employ various communication milieus gives them great leeway in expression. They are friendly and congenial, with the ability to put others at ease.

Shadow: These natives bore easily. Coupled with their intense curiosity, they run the risk of spreading themselves too thin and dividing their attention too often. Their highly sensitive nervous systems are constantly subject to sensory input from

Natives with Mercury in Leo often speak with a distinctively self-confident flair, viewing conversations as a performance in which they are on center stage.

can be strong, especially when one's own emotions are not involved. The combination of the Moon with Mercury gives these natives a silver tongue, whereby they are able to express and communicate their feelings and deep-felt desires, leaving a distinct impression and convincing those who are listening. These individuals have excellent memories, and they are able to recount important aspects of their past with feeling, likely due to the multisensory fashion with which they initially absorbed the experience.

Shadow: Mercury in a sign ruled by the ever-changing Moon cycles can be moody and defensive, which prevents objective thinking. Self-reflection can be helpful prior to important conversations. Unconscious influences can affect clear and logical thinking and affect the native's ability to focus. These natives are defensive and quick to jump to conclusions.

external stimulation, which can affect their attention span and ability to focus. These natives need periodic time-out periods to regroup and refocus.

MERCURY IN CANCER

Logical Mercury meets up with the sensitive and emotionally oriented, Moon-ruled Cancer. This combination can open thought processes beyond logical standards as long as the emotions don't cloud clear thought. As with all the Cancer placements, a willingness to continually let go of the past needs to be present, which includes both positive and negative experiences.

Gift: Mercury in Cancer natives are sympathetic and protective, and someone with this placement has a knack for saying caring words in stressful situations. Intuition

MERCURY IN LEO

Natives with Mercury in Leo, a sign ruled by the luminous Sun, like to speak with authority, and they are often aided by a dramatic and distinctively self-confident flair. They can view conversations, speeches, and dialogue as performances where they are on center stage.

Gift: The energy and self-confidence behind their statements make them good organizers, bosses, and leaders. Their commands are given with conviction, and they bestow an air of positivity when tackling issues or directing behavior. They are persuasive and can animate their audience with their heartfelt words and gift of drama. Leo is the sign of creative self-expression, so theater and the arts are areas where their creative mind can flourish. These natives do well communicating with children and animals. Their expressive flair helps to get their point across.

Shadow: Excessive mental arrogance and pride can be by-products of this placement when their forceful manner is carried too far. Tall tales can ensue. They tend to see things more in generalities rather than focusing in on the details, especially when they don't have a passionate interest in the topic. Having Mercury in the Fixed sign of Leo can lead to fixed opinions that are slow to change.

MERCURY IN VIRGO

Mercury, as the natural ruler of Virgo, is exceptionally well placed since Mercury is also exalted in Virgo. This double dose of Mercurial influence gives this placement an edge for analyzing problems and finding solutions. Mercury in Virgo is highly discriminating, precise, and has the capacity for high levels of data crunching.

Gift: Mercury in Virgo natives streamline and simplify. They can get their points across with a list of bullet points rather than with long, flowery metaphors. They observe all the innuendos of their surroundings, and they are highly detail-oriented when they participate in conversations, listen to all types of media, and engage in social gatherings. As a result, they can recount their experiences with accuracy and detail. These natives are apt comedians, though not always consciously, resulting from the descriptive detail of their observations combined with the dose of cynicism they often possess due to their perfectionist nature.

Shadow: Their highly critical nature and perfectionist orientation can lead these natives into believing that no one can do a job better than them. In many cases, they are correct in their assumption; however, they don't give others the opportunity to gain their own experience and grow. They give off an air of superiority and can use their highly critical nature to make others feel inferior and aggrieved.

MERCURY IN LIBRA

Mercury in Venus-ruled Libra makes for excellent negotiators. The Venusian influence adds to their desire for peace and harmony unless they perceive a lack of fairness and justice. They rise to the occasion, consider all sides, and shine as the capable diplomats that they are. Weighing the pros and cons of any issue or situation characterizes this placement of Mercury. Their decision-making process is well thought out.

Gift: Those with Mercury in Libra are natural diplomats who are able to resolve conflicts, even in difficult situations. Good conversationalists, they enjoy interacting and pay attention to what others think. Maintaining open channels of communication is especially important to them in their relationships, and they are ill at ease when they feel out of touch from those closest to them.

Shadow: Mercury in Libra natives can lack conviction in their own beliefs and favor the views of others in order to be agreeable or accepted. They can be super polite and cater to others' opinions. Indecisiveness can come into play when these natives are off-center or out of balance with their own identity. They can become stymied or mentally frozen for fear of making a mistake or displeasing others.

MERCURY IN SCORPIO

Mercury in Scorpio natives probe deeply and have a knack for getting to the bottom of any issue they are engaged in. These natives are highly analytical and make excellent researchers, troubleshooters, and detectives. They excel at problem solving, as they peel back each layer systematically and with precision.

With dual rulers of Scorpio, Mars, and Pluto, these natives have a willingness to go where others may fear to tread. Don't count on them to reveal personal information or knowledge that they either want to or committed to keep secret. Small talk is not their thing, nor is engaging in superficiality. They won't mince words to spare the feelings of others.

Individuals with this placement of Mercury can be scheming and plotting and have ulterior motives that are not obvious to those around them.

Gift: Pluto-ruled Mercury in Scorpio natives have the mental focus and desire to ferret out the inherent truth in any situation. Penetrating beneath the surface of whichever issue is before them is normal for these natives, whether it be an impediment in their path, an interpersonal hurdle, or even what others might consider normal conversation. They are capable of profound insights and are highly capable of piercing to the crux of human behaviors and motivations.

Shadow: Unconscious or subconscious ruminations and emotional unrest can lead these natives to overreact to dialogue that is not meant to be personal. They can be overly suspicious and even paranoid when they are emotionally out of sorts. The strong desire naturally associated with Scorpio can lead to compulsive and obsessive thinking patterns. The same thoughts can have a hold on their minds, keeping these natives from finding peace and inner harmony.

MERCURY IN SAGITTARIUS

Mercury in Jupiter-ruled Sagittarius aims for the big-picture view and will then conceptualize how all the pieces subsequently fit in. They prefer to see a glass as half full and will usually find a construct that will support their thinking.

Mercury in Sagittarians enjoy conversations replete with philosophical insights and higher truths. They are forward thinkers who love to banter about all kinds of ideas and share what they know or recently learned.

> With dual rulers of Scorpio, Mars, and Pluto, these natives have a willingness to go where others may fear to tread.

Mercury in Sagittarius is in its detriment, according to traditional astrology, because it is opposite Gemini, the sign ruled by Mercury. Not only is Sagittarius opposite Gemini, a sign concerned with factual information, but it also squares Virgo, another Mercury-ruled sign that is highly detail-oriented.

Gift: These natives can be visionaries, and they can have prophetic insights. They often have a good grasp of what is trending and how these movements are affecting humanity at large. Truth is important to individuals with this placement, and they will often say exactly what they think.

Shadow: Mercury in Sagittarius natives can be more concerned with big-picture concepts and attitudes than with facts. They can lose track of what is actually true by not paying enough attention to details and objective information. The phrase "the devil is in the details" can apply to this placement of Mercury, where their optimism outweighs realistic outcomes. These natives can lack tactfulness. Truth can be hurtful when blurted out, especially if passion or emotion is behind it. Sensitivity is not employed at times when it could help these individuals make their point.

MERCURY IN CAPRICORN

Mercury in Saturn-ruled Capricorn natives are highly pragmatic, serious, cautious, and deliberate. They like to receive information in an orderly fashion, so they can process it carefully and clearly. "Clearly" to a Mercury in Capricorn may mean processing input in black-and-white terms.

Individuals with Mercury in Capricorn have an innate business sensibility. They can weed out information that will build and improve an existing business or assess whether the necessary components are sufficient to initiate a new deal or form a new business. Capricorn is a Cardinal Earth sign, so they like to initiate new deals and ventures; however, it is important to them that they can move forward on a firm footing.

Gift: People with Mercury in Capricorn are focused, capable of extended concentration, methodical, and highly organized. They move their initiatives and projects forward one step at a time. Although not necessarily original, their patience and discipline are a plus in areas such as science, business, architectural, and financial positions, which necessitate a tried-and-true approach. Mercury in Capricorn natives are natural teachers. They can break down and impart information in an organized and systematic manner that is easy to ingest.

Mercury in Jupiter-ruled Sagittarius aims for the big picture view, and prefers to see a glass as half full. They can be more concerned with big-picture concepts, not paying enough attention to details and objective information.

Shadow: The Saturnian influence of Capricorn can affect these individuals' interactions and communication skills. People with this placement can suppress emotions and override human values in favor of their material goals and ambitions. As a result, these natives have been characterized as narrow-minded, judgmental, cold, ruthless, and status-seeking.

MERCURY IN AQUARIUS

Mercury in Uranus-ruled Aquarius natives are intuitive, inventive, original, and progressive thinkers. They are not afraid to express their unique ideas or go against collective belief systems. They excel at separating their emotions from their thoughts, which can lead others to interpret their communication style as distant and aloof.

Mercury-in-Pisces natives have a well-developed sixth sense. They may not be able to explain why they know something; they just know, and it feels right. They excel in an array of creative pursuits.

Mercury is considered to be exalted in Aquarius, meaning that the planet of thinking and communication functions with ease. Uranus is called the higher octave of Mercury by esoteric thinkers. Aquarius is futuristic, and Mercury in Aquarius can be one step ahead of the collective thinking outside of the box. Astrologers have differing points of view as to whether Mercury is exalted in Virgo or Aquarius.

As a Fixed Air sign, the Aquarian influence lends a fixed focus and a constancy in their opinions. Determining the truth is their ultimate goal, and once they have settled upon that truth, they believe that they have reached their goal.

Gift: The highly intuitive nature of Mercury in Aquarius natives accounts for the originality of thought that they are capable of. They enrich humankind with fresh ideas and offer out-of-the-box solutions to the most mundane of tasks. Their willingness

to accept the unknown, combined with their openness to diverse opinions, pushes their boundaries of thought. Mercury in Aquarius has a neutrality that lends itself comfortably to involvement in groups and large organizations. This placement resonates well with humanitarian, scientific, and technology-oriented activities.

Shadow: Mercury in Aquarius natives can lack sensitivity to the emotions of others. They can be more dedicated to concepts and their version of the truth than to people. When their ego gets involved, their know-it-all persona comes to the fore, and they are not open to the opinions of others. They will judge views they don't agree with as subjective, believing that their own thinking is neutral and objective. Self-reflection is not a strong suit for a Mercury in Aquarius individual when their emotions are involved. They prefer to remain detached, and it can take them a while to realize that they are coming from a subjective perspective.

MERCURY IN PISCES

Mercury operates beneath the surface or from the subconscious realm rather than in the realm of the obvious or pure logical thought when it is in Pisces. These natives have a well-developed sixth sense that snuffs up impressions, tendencies, and motives that formulate their opinions and ideas. They may not be able to explain why they know something; they just know it, and it feels right. They are visionaries who excel in an array of artistic, musical, and other creative pursuits.

These natives are private and do not like to divulge information that is highly personal to them. You can count on them to keep a secret.

Gift: Mercury in Pisces natives have amazing compassion for humans and animals alike. They are good listeners, sympathetic and empathetic, and offer comfort and good insights. Their kindness and adaptability endear them to others. These natives can sense the tone of interactions, and they will adjust accordingly in order to maintain a positive energy exchange. They make others feel important and needed. Natives with this placement of Mercury are extremely sensitive to subtleties in color and light and make excellent photographers, painters, and interior designers. Extreme sensitivity combined with a well-developed imagination incline them toward poetry and story writing.

Shadow: Mercury rules Virgo, the sign opposite Pisces, and is therefore considered to be debilitated in Pisces. Here, logical and analytical thinking ability is not as readily employed as is creative imagination and intuition. It can be difficult for these natives to distinguish dreams and visions from reality. The Mutable Water modality of Pisces can be inconsistent, vague, and meander into other realms rather than stay focused. They can be described as spaced-out, forgetful, and disorganized when they are off their game. Due to their sensitivity, individuals with this placement can interpret the words of others as personal criticism even when it is not intended. Unconscious emotional patterns can trigger distortions in their perceptions.

MERCURY
IN THE HOUSES

Mercury is linked to the mind, and its sign and house position give a view into the areas and activities of life that dominate one's mental activity. The house placement influences Mercury's expression based upon the natural ruler of each house. For example, Aries is the natural ruler of the First House, Taurus is the natural ruler of the Second House, etc.

MERCURY IN THE FIRST HOUSE

The First House rules appearance, health, general temperament, and sense of self. The First House defines you and the image you project to others.

Ideas are expressed directly and spontaneously when Mercury is in the First House. The First House carries the influence of Mars-ruled Aries. The native energetically expresses their ideas and opinions, and they don't hesitate to speak out of turn. They can be preoccupied with their self-image and how others are seeing them since the First House rules self-identity. It is likely that they want to be perceived as clever and alert.

Gift: Mercury in the First House individuals can be inspiring, and they bring enthusiasm and energy to any situation. Depending upon Mercury's sign placement, they can be witty, innovative, and resourceful thinkers who adapt to fast-moving situations and settings. They are comfortable communicating, and ideas come easily to them.

Shadow: The Martian influence of this placement inclines these natives to impatience, nervous excitability, and a quick temper. Words are expressed spontaneously and often without being well thought out, leading to a foot-in-mouth situation. They can skip from one topic to another without finishing a train of thought. Focusing on a particular task or goal for any length of time is not easy for them. Their sensory input gets overwhelmed easily and needs frequent time-outs.

MERCURY IN THE SECOND HOUSE

The Second House is connected with finances, values, material possessions, talents, and resources. The Second House represents the value we give to ourselves and, in turn, that which we possess.

Mercury in the Second House is concerned with money, both how to earn it and how to spend it. The sign that Mercury is placed in can determine whether they are likely to gather and save or spend and enjoy the comforts of life. Mercury in Cancer natives may be more security-minded, whereas Mercury in Leo natives may be more inclined to find value in having fun and enjoying life.

Gift: A Second-House Mercury native gives the ability to gather and manage financial and material resources. They are naturally disposed to intuitively understand the inherent value of all kinds of material assets. They can easily prioritize what is important to them and how and where they should expend their time and energy. They are practical and like to focus on what can produce concrete and lasting results.

Shadow: Mercury in the Second House natives can get carried away with shopping and acquiring possessions. They can overrate material values at the expense of more humanitarian ones. As a result, they can cling to their personal belongings rather than enjoy them or share with them with others. They are likely to store more than they will ever use.

MERCURY IN THE THIRD HOUSE

The Third House is connected with ideas, communication, siblings, neighbors, and short journeys.

Mercury is well placed in the Third House, which is naturally ruled by Mercury-ruled Gemini.

Gift: These natives know how to get their point across. They are natural communicators, witty, and adept at wordsmithing. They make good writers, speakers, and conversationalists and are often dexterous in their movements. They are versatile in their interests and can communicate on a variety of topics to a wide range of people. It is not uncommon that individuals with this placement of Mercury are good imitators. They pick up on the subtleties of speech and notice innuendos in others and communication patterns.

Shadow: Mercury in the Third House natives can tell tall tales, either consciously or unconsciously. They can generate a lot of talk and no action and ultimately create difficulties for themselves where promises, contracts, and agreements are concerned. These individuals can get caught up in gossip and superficial conversations.

MERCURY IN THE FOURTH HOUSE

The Fourth House is about the home, family, genetic inheritance, foundational stability, innermost feelings, later life, and the end of matters.

Mercury in the domain of Cancer focuses on issues of security, family, and the home. Early home life likely helped to formulate their mental orientation. Family discussions and their favorite books and movies are likely to be imprinted in their memory. They are likely to frequently recall aspects regarding their background and how they were raised.

Gift: Mercury in the Fourth House natives are sensitive and perceptive by nature, and they enjoy heart-to-heart communication with friends and family, preferably in their comfortable home environment. Even with a busy schedule, they are likely to make space for family members and those they

Natives with a Fifth-House Mercury placement are highly expressive and creative. They make great teachers, gifted when communicating with children and younger people. They place a value on fun and play, which can appeal to all ages.

consider to be like family. They often surround themselves with reading material, communication devices, and other articles of interest. Working from home is up their alley, including working remotely and working on their own projects. Ancestry and family lineage may be of particular importance to these natives. They can devote time to learning about their genetic inheritance in order to understand themselves more clearly.

Shadow: Parental imprinting may overshadow these natives' opinions, viewpoints, and ideas. Unconscious habits may have been formed based upon communication styles in the home, especially if a parent was overcritical or highly opinionated. The shadow side of Mercury in the Fourth House can manifest as the individual being very private and secretive about their childhood.

MERCURY IN THE FIFTH HOUSE

The Fifth House rules creative self-expression, children, love, passion, romance, playfulness, and joy.

Mercury with a Leo influence natives love to reflect on romantic escapades and their artistic expressions. Creative self-expression that can include a variety of modalities and media formats indicates how these individuals like to fill their leisure time. These natives have a knack for communicating with little ones and pets.

A Fifth-House Mercury native is often inclined to take chances and risks. The Fifth House rules speculation and gambling as well as romantic adventures.

Gift: Natives with a Fifth-House Mercury placement are highly expressive, creative, and engage others with their energetic communication style and confidence. They have an ability to express themselves forcefully and dramatically in their speech as well as in writing and other forms of expression. They may be particularly dexterous in movement and sports activities. With their Fifth-House affinity for children, these individuals make great teachers. They are gifted when it comes to communicating with children and younger people. They place a value on fun and play, which can appeal to all ages.

Shadow: Mercury in Leo's house may devote too much time to figuring out how to get attention. Natives can be compelled to constantly project their self-image in order to get validation. Excessive boasting and constantly talking about their interests and children can result from insecurity and a low self-esteem. Gambling and speculation can get out of control. These natives can get addicted to the mental stimulation they receive from the games they play and the intricacies of financial and other types of speculations.

> The mental agility of Mercury gives these natives an edge on multitasking. They are detail-oriented and hardworking.

MERCURY IN THE SIXTH HOUSE

The Sixth House governs daily routines, acts of service, the work-life balance, health, due diligence, pet care, coworkers, and employees.

Mercury is well placed in the Sixth House, the natural home of Virgo. Individuals with this placement will think of all the details that others miss. They are generally hardworking and focused and like to work alongside others who share their work ethic.

Gift: Sixth-House Mercury individuals are great at sorting things out, organizing, and keeping day-to-day activities and chores on track. The mental agility of Mercury gives these natives an edge on multitasking. They are detail-oriented and hardworking. They tend to have good communication skills given the placement of Mercury in Virgo's domain. They are particularly good at presenting a logical and organized case for whatever it is they want to communicate. Their skill with details can also play out in the craftsmanship realm.

Shadow: Mental rest may not be easy to come by with this placement of Mercury. These individuals feel as though they could always be doing more, as if their daily chores are never done. They can be prone to health issues due to anxiety and stress. Their daily chores can take precedent over rest and relaxation as well as over human interactions. They can become obsessed with getting everything done perfectly. These individuals can get too caught up in their routines and lose track of the big picture. These natives can be hard on their employees or coworkers, expecting the same high standards from them that they place on themselves. Compassion and empathy can remain on the back burner when it is needed to be more up front.

MERCURY IN THE SEVENTH HOUSE

The Seventh House rules close personal relationships, agreements, and compromises.

Mercury in the Seventh House is influenced by Venus, bestowing upon these natives a good amount of charm, a pleasing disposition, and a genuine interest in others. They like to exchange ideas and have engaging conversations. The Libran influence of this placement gives these individuals a natural attunement as to what is fair and just. They make good mediators and arbitrators as a result.

Gift: Individuals with this placement excel at persuading and influencing people. They tune in to others' ways of thinking and are able to speak their language in order to get their point across. People will often come to those with this placement for advice. They can have an aptitude for counseling due to their orientation toward one-on-one communication. They are generally good listeners and have a genuine interest in understanding and evaluating different types of people.

Shadow: The Seventh-House placement of Mercury can put too much emphasis on what others think. It is easy for them to lose track of their own thoughts and ideas for the sake of being accepted by others. As a result, misunderstandings can develop, and broken agreements can occur. They can get caught up in searching for romance or someone who deeply understands them. The indecisiveness associated with Libra can make it difficult for these natives to make decisions concerning others. They may continually weigh the pros and cons of people and important relationships without the satisfaction of closure.

MERCURY IN THE EIGHTH HOUSE

The Eighth House rules joint ventures, intimacy, sex, death, transformation, and psychic dimensions.

Mercury in the Eighth House natives have a keen interest in the deeper, mysterious aspects of life, including the occult. They tend to have good analytical ability and do well in areas that involve research and probing into the inner workings of people and things.

The Scorpio influence on an Eighth-House Mercury inclines these natives to be particularly adept at perceiving what is going on beneath the surface.

The Eighth House belongs to Pluto, giving these natives an interest in understanding and then transforming and changing that which they come into contact with.

Gift: The Scorpio influence on an Eighth-House Mercury inclines these natives to heightened sensitivity and a well-developed sixth sense. They are particularly adept at perceiving what is going on beneath the surface. The ulterior motives of others are very obvious to them. As a result, they make excellent healers, therapists, detectives, and sleuths. It is not often that anyone can pull the wool over their eyes. They have the patience to continue searching until they find answers to their quests.

Shadow: These natives can be so focused on trying to read between the lines that they end up prone to undue suspicion and paranoia. They can become isolated as a result. This tendency is supported by their secretive and private natures. They do not easily forget the actions and slights of others and can hold grudges until they seek payback. Since the Eighth House rules partners' resources, these natives can be strategic and manipulative when they are highly motivated materially. The Eighth House also rules sex, and they can become mentally obsessed with sex and pornography.

MERCURY IN THE NINTH HOUSE

The Ninth House rules higher education, long-term goals, foreign travel, publicity, adventures, religion, and philosophical and ethical pursuits.

The expansive nature of Mercury in the Ninth House is influenced by Jupiter-ruled Sagittarius, the ruler of the Ninth House in the natural Zodiac. They are continually seeking ways to broaden their horizon. Philosophically inclined, these natives have a highly curious nature that loves to learn about cultures and traditions both near and far.

These natives love bantering about philosophical concepts and exchanging ideas. This placement usually suggests an individual who is highly educated either formally or through a sampling of learning modalities, including self-education, certification programs, and the exploration of cultures and experiences through travel and social interaction.

Gift: Mercury in the Ninth House offers the gift of reframing mundane mental deliberations and negative views into a larger perspective that offers hope. They are able to attain a broader perspective for themselves as a result of acquiring knowledge and additional relevant information, and they are able to help others by reframing their problems into a more easily digestible

context. This placement has a visionary component. These individuals often receive information through their dreams and revelations. They are able to reformulate these insights into a wide-ranging plan. Faith and hope are important to these individuals. It gives them the fuel to execute their ideas and stick to their plans and goals. An attunement to higher law and justice is generally likely, and they value ethics and integrity.

Shadow: A native with a Ninth-House Mercury placement can get caught up in the future attainment of their goals and lose track of being in the current moment. They can have their head in the clouds and not keep their feet on the ground in order to actually manifest their dreams and visions. These natives can be prone to intellectual pride and snobbery. They can also get carried away by dogmatic thinking and belief systems.

MERCURY IN THE TENTH HOUSE

The Tenth House rules public achievements, reputation, authority, and prestige.

Mercury in the Tenth House is influenced by Saturn due to its location in Capricorn's house in the natural Zodiac. The Saturnian influence provides these individuals with a practical, disciplined, and organized way of thinking, which they can then apply to self-betterment and professional aspirations. It is not unlikely for them to assume leadership roles in their professions since they are naturally attuned to making a good impression with decision makers. They strive for recognition and fame.

Gift: This placement of Mercury gives the ability to communicate with people in leadership positions and positions of power. They are able to break down the information that they want to impart clearly and concisely so that they can get their point across. This same ability to clearly organize information into smaller, easily digestible tidbits of information inclines them toward being excellent teachers and lecturers. Individuals with a Tenth-House Mercury will accept mental challenges, especially if they think that it will enhance their image in society. They are usually focused and self-directed, which helps them to manifest the aspirations they set out for themselves.

Shadow: The downside of this placement is that these natives can get caught up in social climbing and ambitious undertakings at the expense of relationships, family, and their own self-care. It is easy for them to get stressed out because they feel driven to achieve. They can also get caught up in society's impression of their mental acumen. The Tenth House cares about their reputation and will strive for approval, sometimes losing track of their own sense of who they are and what they really want. Respect is important to these individuals. They do not like to be contradicted or ridiculed. Their bruised egos can incline them toward shrewd and calculating competitive behaviors.

> This placement of Mercury gives the ability to communicate with people in leadership positions and positions of power.

MERCURY IN THE ELEVENTH HOUSE

The Eleventh House rules friends, hopes, wishes, groups, and a sense of belonging in the world.

The Eleventh House is ruled by Aquarius in the natural Zodiac. Mercury is well placed in this position due to its exaltation in Aquarius. Those with this placement have a humanitarian orientation, and they are often drawn to groups that support the betterment of mankind. Friendships are important to them, and they enjoy exchanging ideas and communicating with those who share their goals and objectives.

The Eleventh House supports the Tenth House, and Mercury in the Eleventh House helps to support the individual's public image.

Gift: These individuals are extroverted and easily make acquaintances and form alliances with friends. Their nonjudgmental orientation, openness to humanity, and appreciation of those from diverse backgrounds make it easy for them to attain a welcome position in several types of social groups and settings. Honesty is a virtue that is important to Mercury in the Eleventh House, as is an appreciation of impartiality, diversity, and originality. These individuals evaluate situations' objectivity and are able to maintain detachment and equanimity. All of these attributes contribute to maintaining group cohesion and sustaining important business alliances. These natives can be counted on to offer an innovative perspective and bring fresh ideas to most situations. They are generally highly intuitive and are able to tune in to futurist trends.

Shadow: Mercury in the Eleventh House natives run the risk of being too objective in situations that require more finesse. They are apt to blurt out what they perceive to be the truth without taking the pulse of the situation first. Their eccentricity can be carried to the point of being impractical. They have a rebellious streak,

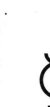

Mercury in the Twelfth House has a Neptune influence, giving these natives a dreamy, sensitive, and visionary mind attuned to art, music, and photography. But they can get caught up in a fantasy world and lose track of their objectivity.

Gift: Individuals with this placement are very observant and pick up impressions that others are apt to miss. They are comfortable sensing what is going on beneath the surface. Their insightfulness, compassion, and sympathetic nature give them an advantage in positions relating to healing and working with the disadvantaged. Their dreamy, sensitive, and visionary minds are attuned to art, music, and photography. Many have a good sense of color and tone. The Neptunian influence of the Twelfth House gives these natives a refined sensibility that tunes in to the subtleties of each of the senses. Their ability to pick up impressions and identify with others is a plus in performing in film and theater.

Shadow: Twelfth-House Mercury natives can get caught up in a fantasy world and lose track of their objectivity. Their fertile imaginations can assume slights and personal affronts that don't exist or that weren't meant to be personal. Their introverted tendency, combined with a powerful illusory bent, can lead to isolation and disorientation. Their heightened compassion and inherent defense for the underdog can make them too gullible in personal relationships, which leads to disappointment and disillusionment. These individuals can have trouble focusing on important details.

which can lead them to be contrary when not warranted.

MERCURY IN THE TWELFTH HOUSE

The Twelfth House rules secrets, unconscious patterns, karma, closure, institutions, connections with higher sources, enlightenment, and undoing.

Mercury in the Twelfth House has a Neptune influence, giving these natives a dreamy, impressionable orientation. They can be introverted and prefer to watch rather than join in. Planets in the Twelfth House can be blocked from expressing themselves, thereby causing frustration.

MERCURY COMBINATIONS

Mercury/Sun

Mercury rules communication, mental processes, and the logical mind.

The Sun indicates purpose, self-expression, creative life force, and conscious will.

Due to the proximity of Mercury to the Sun, relatively speaking, these two planetary bodies are never more than 28 degrees apart. The only significant connection they can make together is the Conjunction.

Mercury is considered to be "combust" to the Sun if it is between 0.5 and 4 degrees conjunct to the Sun. This can create a situation where Mercury gets overloaded and possibly overheated by the Sun's rays. It can create momentary blind spots in thinking.

Mercury is considered to be "casimi" or "cazimi," according to Medieval astrology, when Mercury is less than 0.5 degrees from the Sun. This connection means good luck and opportunity due to an alignment between the wave patterns of Mercury and the Sun. The Sun represents the will, and when combined so closely with Mercury, great will occurs, influencing mental expression. Mercury is considered to be at the heart of the Sun.

Any planet is considered to be in the heart of the Sun—"casimi" or "cazimi"—when less than 0.5 degrees, or 30 minutes, from the Sun. Late Medieval and Renaissance astrologers use the tighter value of 16 minutes from the Sun.

Gift: The gift of a close connection between Mercury and the Sun is the ability to shine with words. This connection bestows a sharp, witty mind that is energetic and thinks a lot about what they want.

Shadow: The mind can become agitated and overheated when Mercury combusts or comes too close to the Sun. A stronger need for relaxation and the use of meditation and other tools that calm the mind occurs.

MERCURY/MOON

Mercury rules communication, mental processes, and the logical mind.

The Moon rules the soul, core instincts, the personality, and subconscious conditioning.

When Mercury combines with the energy of the Moon, communication of one's feelings is highlighted. This combination will reflect the native's ability to have access to their emotions and genuinely express how they feel.

Gift: This combination is sometimes known as the silver tongue. It represents an individual who can put their feelings into words and express them with confidence and ease. Even when speaking on subjects that are deeply passionate, they have an ability to choose words that reflect a balance between the head and the heart, so they are listened to. They have a natural rhythm to the tone and tempo of their voice and their communication style.

Shadow: Irrational thought processes often plague this individual, and it is difficult to communicate their deepest feelings. An overly logical approach can ensue that is devoid of emotion. Contrarily, communication can be overly emotional and lacking in logic. Basically, a disconnect occurs between emotions and logic.

MERCURY/VENUS

Mercury rules communication, mental processes, and the logical mind.

Venus represents love, relationships, beauty, values, comfort, and material resources.

Mercury and Venus have a special relationship in that their orbits are both between Earth and the Sun. The other planets, dwarf planets, and asteroids have an orbit further out, beyond Earth. Mercury and Venus are therefore called personal planets due to their special connection to Earth.

Mars combining with Mercury bestows the native with an alert mind that speaks with energy and enthusiasm, good at getting their point across. But sometimes they don't think before they speak, leading to consequences.

combination of Mercury and Venus. These natives blend information in a pleasing manner, one that is easy for their listeners to hear. They are acutely aware of how their communication affects others. They often have pleasing voices, and many are good singers. Their harmonizing talents give these natives commendable negotiating skills, inclining them to be successful mediators and diplomats. They naturally know how to convince people to cooperate and get along. They speak and move with grace, harmony, and balance.

Shadow: Too much schmoozing and sweet talk can be distasteful, especially without any significant action to back it up. When Venus is out of proportion, a tendency to overindulge occurs. This can manifest as vanity, conceit, and irresolute behavior patterns. They can take on the persona of a social butterfly, one who leans toward being fickle and superficial.

MERCURY/MARS

Mercury rules communication, mental processes, and the logical mind.

Mars rules assertiveness, energy, drive, and courage.

The combination of Mars and Mercury is similar to having Mercury in Aries, Mercury in the First House, or Mars in Gemini. These natives have sharp, decisive minds, and they are able to think on their feet.

Gift: Mars combining with Mercury bestows the native with an alert mind that speaks with energy and enthusiasm. They can be direct, decisive, and emphatic. They say what they mean without hesitation. Their ability to speak with enthusiasm makes them good public speakers and interesting lecturers. They are good at getting their point across.

Mercury can only be within 28 degrees of the Sun, and Venus can only be within 48 degrees of the Sun. These planets can combine their energies in only a few ways since they cannot reside further than 47 degrees apart. These include a Conjunction, a Sextile, and a Semi-Square. A Sextile can only form when Mercury and Venus are on different sides of the Sun in the Zodiac, with one of them rising ahead of the Sun as a morning star and the other setting behind the Sun as an evening star.

The combination of Mercury and Venus offers a blend of artistic and mental qualities. They often have a talent for design and have a love of books and the written word.

Gift: An abundance of charm and grace are two of the gifts to be gained from the

Shadow: Mercury combined with Mars can be impatient and restless, and natives are likely to fidget when they are bored. They have an abundance of mental energy, and these individuals can overanalyze and get stressed out if they don't have tools to help calm their minds. They can be sharp-tongued and combative. Responses may not be well thought out, leading to misunderstandings and disagreements. Their minds can work so quickly that they don't think before they speak, leading to consequences for them down the road.

MERCURY/JUPITER

Mercury rules communication, mental processes, and the logical mind.

Jupiter represents the higher mind, greater truths, expansiveness, hope, and optimism.

Jupiter is an expansive energy that leans toward optimism and an idealistic point of view. When combined with Mercury, Jupiter will incline the native to think big. They can engage in planning on a grand scale, bringing enthusiasm and positive energy into their conversation.

Gift: These natives have a broad outlook. They can take mundane issues and problems and come up with long-range solutions that put the original problems into a grander perspective. Their orientation is philosophical, and they enjoy bantering about a wide array of topics, including those relating to spiritual, cultural, and political issues. They are enthusiastic and bring excitement to any con-

versation or negotiation, thereby having the ability to hold their audience's attention. These natives have a positive attitude, and it is likely that they have a good sense of humor. They can be fun to be around.

Shadow: The shadow side of a Mercury/Jupiter combination is a lack of realism. The idealistic nature of these natives may not evaluate their ideas and the situations before them realistically. They can have an aversion to imposing limitations and restrictions on the issues at hand even though they may be required. Their judgment can be impaired as a result. These natives can do more talking than listening, whereby they can miss out on important information.

MERCURY/SATURN

Mercury rules communication, mental processes, and the logical mind.

Saturn rules responsibility, adjustments to limitations, sustainability, and structure.

Combining Mercury and Saturn brings logic and structure to the thinking process. These natives are generally focused and well-disciplined in their thinking processes. They like to know what they are talking about and will usually go the extra mile to be sure they have all the facts.

Gift: These individuals have the discipline and focus to apply themselves to mentally challenging tasks. They are systematic in their approach and are excellent presenters, especially in situations that require a logical

> Mercury and Venus have a special relationship in that their orbits are both between Earth and the Sun.... Mercury and Venus are therefore called personal planets due to their special connection to Earth.

and well-thought-out approach. The pairing of Mercury and Saturn is favorable for sticking to verbal agreements and commitments as well as for dealing with any project that requires stamina and follow-through. Those with this combination are realistic and practical. They are good listeners and value learning from experience. Many natives with this combination are scientifically and mathematically oriented, and some natives are musically inclined, especially where a fixed rhythm and a lot of skill is required.

Shadow: The pessimistic side of Saturn can incline these natives to worry and depression. They can feel that they never know all that they should and have an inferiority complex that relates to the learning capabilities. A tendency to be rigid, narrow-minded, and unyielding can occur in situations that require more buoyancy and enthusiasm. The monotony of their tone can make it difficult for others to listen to them. They can be overly inhibited and fearful in social situations.

> The pessimistic side of Saturn can incline these natives to worry and depression.

MERCURY/URANUS

Mercury rules communication, mental processes, and the logical mind.

Uranus rules intuition, originality, individuality, and the sudden and unexpected.

Mercury rules ideas and communication, and Uranus rules breakthroughs and discoveries. This combination looks at things with an open mind and can think outside of the box. Sometimes called a combination of genius, inventive breakthroughs are possible, especially when a healthy nervous system is maintained.

Gift: Mercury combined with Uranus is highly intuitive and future-oriented, so they excel at innovative and original thinking and the ability to think outside of the box. These abilities can connote a particular type of genius, which can sometimes be erratic. They are prone to creative bursts of thinking and unexpected revelations. These natives are independent thinkers who prefer to be self-directed and autonomous. They are attracted to what's new and unusual. These natives are generally straightforward and direct. At least a few of the senses are well developed and extraordinary in their perception. Sometimes, these natives have very acute hearing or can be very sensitive to lighting and smell.

Shadow: An overactive mind with a highly sensitive nervous system can trigger anxiety and restlessness. This person can be easily overstimulated. Thinking can be so ahead of its time that ideas are rejected as eccentric. These natives can have a scattered mind and lack focus. Outside stimulation can be highly distracting to them.

MERCURY/NEPTUNE

Mercury rules communication, mental processes, and the logical mind.

Neptune rules ideals, creative imagination, transcendence, compassion, and vision.

Mercury in combination with Neptune can endow the native with a highly creative and vivid imagination. They have a highly developed sixth sense that can pick up information from the ether, both consciously and subconsciously.

Gift: This combination can contribute to inspirational thinking that can motivate others through their ability to logically communicate high-minded ideals and concepts. The combination lends itself to a mind prone to magical thinking with an affinity for the arts, music, and poetry. They are visionaries and often receive information through visions and imagery. These natives are not limited to logical thinking and can get impressions that others may miss. They can often see into motives and behavior patterns due to the subtleties that they pick up. As a result, they often excel in theater due to their ability to pick up on innuendos.

Shadow: This sensitive thinker can get easily confused when picking up impressions from others and from the environment. Difficulty focusing can occur. The truth can be mutable and unclear. Others can have an undue influence on their thinking due to a tendency to pick up on their thoughts and beliefs. These natives can be elusive and deceptive. They can live in their own fantasy world, where they lose track of reality.

MERCURY/PLUTO

Mercury rules communication, mental processes, and the logical mind.

Pluto represents regeneration; transformation; and a compelling, fundamental approach.

The combination of Mercury and Pluto results in a laser-focused mind that is capable of high levels of concentration and deep analysis.

Mercury in combination with Neptune can endow the native with a highly creative and vivid imagination. They often receive information through visions and imagery.

Gift: Natives with a Mercury/Pluto combination have remarkable investigative abilities and can gain insights that uncover information that others miss. Their skill set includes the ability to probe and comprehend hidden material and evidence, making them good detectives, medical practioners, and therapists. These individuals are strategic and persuasive thinkers who can get to the bottom of an issue and convince others with their persuasive communication skills. They make good strategists due to their ability to evaluate all angles of an issue. They are well equipped to do jobs that others may lack the focus, patience, and analytical skills to attempt.

Shadow: Natives with a Mercury/Pluto combination can have an obsessive mind that can't let go and move on. Their thought process can get caught up in looping, whereby the same thoughts keep returning over and over, spiraling into circular thinking patterns that stem from unconscious fears and self-limiting beliefs. Their strategic reasoning ability can embrace underhanded schemes, especially when they are overwhelmed by out-of-control desires. They can use force or pressure to get others to conform to their way of thinking. They can have a tendency to manipulate the truth.

MERCURY/CHIRON

Mercury rules communication, mental processes, and the logical mind.

Chiron represents core wounds and the desire to overcome them, and healing.

These individuals may be unconscious of how they project themselves mentally when speaking and otherwise communicating, learning, or teaching until a situation arises that triggers them. They then can become aware of their deficiencies or social skills. Analyzing the root cause of what is behind why they were triggered in the first place is a sign of healing that can be under the influence of Chiron.

Gift: Unexplained bouts of anxiety, stress, or depression can cause the native to delve deeper into their unconscious patterns and ultimately release memories from childhood or delve into inherited family patterns. The gift that ensues is expanded awareness of the initial problem or a medical solution that ultimately diminishes the discomfort they initially experienced. This individual can help others who may be experiencing similar issues if they so choose. These natives can choose to rewire their thinking patterns through positive affirmations, various forms of therapies, and

fastidious conscious awareness of their disempowering thoughts. These individuals can use voice, sounds, thoughts, and language for healing purposes.

Shadow: The shadow side of this combination of Mercury and Chiron can indicate that the cognitive functioning of the native has been diminished or overpowered by one's subconscious wounding or sensitivity. Similarly, discomfort can occur in social situations or when speaking in public, which can be explored. A well of mental creativity may not yet be unleashed due to the resistance to explore the psyche. Pain can occur from not having their voice heard.

MERCURY/ERIS

Mercury rules communication, mental processes, and the logical mind.

Eris represents the determination to remove limitations that impede the soul's evolution.

Gift: These natives make great spokespeople for enlightening others on the disparaging influences of the collective unconscious. They can express their own stories in an effective manner that helps others.

Shadow: The communication style of these natives serves to alienate others, so they don't hear or receive what the native wants to convey. They can be on a mission that is ineffective.

MERCURY/NORTH NODE

Mercury rules communication, mental processes, and the logical mind.

The North Node represents future direction, soul guidance, and fulfillment.

When Mercury connects with the North Node, the native's mental capacity has added potential in the areas represented by the North Node sign and house placement. A strong emphasis can be placed on the intellect and further developing the intellect, communication modalities, and other Mercurial talents.

Gift: The native may possess a versatile mind that is quick, witty, and adaptable with their destiny linked to fulfilling aspects of their Mercurial skills: speaking, comedy, writing, research, teaching, or public relations. They may feel that they have a gift for languages. An ease in communicating is present that can lead to career and personal fulfillment.

Shadow: These natives can fall into a trap of dispersing an inadvertent amount of energy gabbing and pursuing social media at the expense of a more constructive use of the talents and abilities they may have.

Individuals with a Mercury/South Node connection have a well-developed communication style that is easy for others to understand and can be super dexterous in their movement or with their hands.

MERCURY/SOUTH NODE

Mercury rules communication, mental processes, and the logical mind.

The South Node represents familiarity, gratification, and the path of least resistance.

The native has well-developed mental faculties that are intuitive and skilled in various forms of communication. In Vedic astrology, this combination is indicative of a spiritual thinker.

Gift: Individuals with a Mercury/South Node connection may have been precocious as children and young adults. They have a well-developed communication style that is easy for others to understand. They can be super dexterous in their movement or with their hands, contrib-

uting to skillfulness in dance, gymnastics, or areas involving craftmanship. Languages are easy for them to learn.

Shadow: These natives can have communication barriers that can be overcome such as learning disabilities or dyslexia. They can also be restless and prone to stress and anxiety due to a highly sensitive nervous system.

MERCURY/ASCENDANT

Mercury rules communication, mental processes, and the logical mind.

The Ascendant represents one's approach, orientation, and the window through which one sees the world.

A Mercury/Ascendant combination produces a quick-witted, mentally gifted individual with a somewhat agile body that moves easily and quickly.

Gift: These natives think before they act and before they speak, and they express themselves clearly and easily. They are quick to sense and evaluate their physical environment. They are witty and communicative and gain much fulfillment through interfacing with the outside world. They are friendly, sociable, and agreeable, or at least willing, to negotiate. These natives have a youthful appearance or express themselves with a youthful air throughout their lives.

Shadow: Natives with Mercury on the Ascendant have the gift of gab, although they may not actually say much. They can be prone to verbosity and may come across as anxious and stressed. They can have a brusque and abrasive tonality to their presentation and be overly focused on themselves.

MERCURY/MIDHEAVEN (MC)

Mercury rules communication, mental processes, and the logical mind.

The Midheaven (MC) represents image, outer aspirations, and career orientation.

The sign on the Midheaven (also called *medium coeli*, or MC) will give more information on how Mercury will express itself and also which career choices the native will more likely be drawn to.

Gift: Mercury/Midheaven combinations often engage in professions that are involved in communication in some form. They are noticed by their superiors for their intelligence and well-developed communication skills. They do well as teachers, writers, researchers, and in public relations and social media fields.

Shadow: People in authority and the public at large will take notice of the substance as well as the manner in which these individuals express themselves. Others may get by with their foibles unnoticed; however, when Mercury is on the Midheaven, they are in the limelight, and little will get past their superiors and the public unnoticed.

Named after the Roman goddess of love and beauty, we inevitably associate Venus with love and relationships. She was worshipped historically in many civilizations: as Aphrodite in Greece, Ishtar in the Middle East, Freya in Scandinavia, and Cybele in Asia Minor. Venus has always been connected with love, beauty, creative artistry, sexual pleasure, and relatedness.

More basically, though, Venus is associated with what we like and what we dislike, with what we value and what we don't value. Love and relationships are a direct result of how we feel about other people. Similarly, Venus rules money, possessions, and personal values because money, possessions, and personal values are a direct result of how we feel about ourselves. What do we really want out of life, and what are we willing to give up to get it?

Venus is unique in several ways, including its orbit around the Sun. According to *Scientific American*, "Our neighboring planet

Venus is an oddball in many ways. For starters, it spins in the opposite direction from most other planets, including Earth, so that on Venus, the sun rises in the west."

In our solar system, Venus and Neptune have nearly circular orbits. Neptune is considered the higher octave of Venus in esoteric astrology. Most planets have slightly elliptical orbits. Also, Venus rotates very slowly; it takes 243 Earth days to complete one rotation.

When plotted from an Earth-centered perspective, a noticeable rhythm occurs in the motion of Venus. Every eight years, Venus returns to the same place in our sky on about the same date, known as the eight-year cycle of Venus. This cycle was of great interest to the ancient people, such as the Maya.

In a January 7, 2022, post in *Earth Sky* by Guy Ottewell, "The word pentagram—or five-sided figure—is used because, over

As if scribed by a celestial Spirograph, Venus's apparent orbit as seen from Earth creates a surprisingly elegant design that some call the Rose of Venus.

the eight years, each phenomenon—each relative position of Earth, Venus, and the sun—occurs five times. Then, over the next eight years, they repeat five times almost identically."

Every eight years, Venus dances with Earth, forming a nearly perfect geometric pattern that looks like a rose. It is called the Rose of Venus or the Pentagram of Venus. Incidentally, Venus rules roses.

The Rose of Venus as seen from Earth is a reminder of the sacred geometry and mystical patterns that always exist in life. Venus is also known as the planet of love and relationships through its skill at reconciling opposites and the creation of harmony and beauty.

In the natal chart, Venus can only be in a sign up to 48 degrees from the location of the Sun. This means that at most, Venus will be in a sign only two signs away from the Sun sign.

VENUS IN THE SIGNS

Venus is the planet of love, relationships, beauty, values, comfort, money, and material resources.

Venus moves through the signs of the Zodiac, providing information how a person expresses themselves in relationships, the types of things they value, how they use their material resources, and their social and aesthetic values. Venus also relates to our own value and self-worth and the ease and manner in which our value is expressed in society.

Venus in each of the signs and houses and in combination with the other planetary energies can indicate how we reach out to others as well as how we respond to others when they reach out to us.

VENUS IN ARIES

Venus in Mars-ruled Aries can be assertive in pursuing objects of their interest. They do not tend to be shy and reticent. Rather, they can be charming and romantic and will make a good first impression. They are comfortable with the chase and perhaps less comfortable being pursued. They fall in love quickly and can have an instinctive knowledge of whether they have a chemistry with those they pursue.

In traditional astrology, Venus is considered to be in detriment in Mars-ruled Aries since it opposes Venus-ruled Libra. Venus in Aries doesn't inherently strive for balance and peace. Their job is to keep the spark going in relationships and social gatherings.

They are attracted to free-spirited and independent partners who are not overly dependent. Nonetheless, they want their partner's attention when they are ready for it. They value bravery and directness in themselves and in others.

Gift: These natives lend enthusiasm and sparkle to social gatherings as they mingle about with great ease. In personal relationships, natives with this placement are ardent, passionate, and romantic lovers. They generate an air of excitement in mutual activities and are generally not at a loss for keeping those around them stimulated and engaged. They can be gallant and charming and are the equivalent archetypes to the knight in shining armor or Wonder Woman.

Shadow: Flirtatious and aggressive in their approach, individuals with this placement can get too hung up in the chase and not end up with the personal fulfillment that they want and need. They can demand a lot of personal attention and place their own needs in front of those of their close personal relationships. Their mannerisms can be coarse, unrefined, and off-putting when they are on a quest.

VENUS IN TAURUS

Venus is at home and has a natural affinity with the earthy, sensual qualities of Venus in the Fixed Earth sign of Taurus. The characteristics of Venus are especially strong and expressed easily and naturally. Their sense of touch is highly developed, and they enjoy surrounding themselves with sensual fabrics and comfortable surroundings.

They have an innate sense of the value of material resources. They are practical and can weigh the value of long-lasting quality with the immediate need of the moment.

Gift: Venus in Taurus natives are easygoing, pleasing to look at, and tend to have a sex appeal that is inviting and nonthreatening. They seek to attract rather than pursue those they desire to be in their orbit. They emanate a vibratory frequency that is magnetic and can attract to themselves what they need. Emotional security and stability are important to these individuals. They can be counted on for lasting affection and a consistent attitude toward love, although they may approach relationships at a slow pace. Venus in Taurus natives like to show their appreciation for kind gestures. They enjoy giving and receiving considerate gifts. Since Taurus rules the throat and larynx, these natives often have rich, melodious voices.

Shadow: Although loyal and steadfast in their affection, Venus in Taurus natives can be possessive and jealous if their emotional security is threatened. They can dig in their heels and be uncompromising and stubborn in situations where material resources are at stake. Excessive hedonism that can interfere with their health and ultimate well-being is possible with this placement due to the heightened sensuality and the tendency to overindulge.

VENUS IN GEMINI

Venus in Gemini brings a Mercurial quality to all things Venusian, which includes what the native values, social and personal relationships, and personal aesthetics. Communication becomes a top priority in all important relationships. Mental and intellectual connections are valued, as these natives love to banter about ideas, feelings, and plans.

People with this Venus position need a good amount of freedom in their close personal relationships. They generally

Venus in Cancer natives put those around them at ease, coming across as caring, emotionally perceptive and good listeners.

people they attract into their orbit. This gift, when carried to the extreme, can make them fickle, where they don't take the time and energy to garner full appreciation for these things. Their curiosity and ability to adapt and communicate can lead them to become social chameleons. These individuals can be overly chatty, where they want to fill any and all silent moments with often meaningless and irrelevant conversation.

VENUS IN CANCER

Venus in the nurturing sign of Cancer feels comfortable when combined with the energy of the Moon. Venusian qualities flow easily, bringing a natural gentleness and sweetness. This native enjoys making a beautiful, comfy, and nurturing environment for those nearest and dearest.

Individuals with this placement are sensual and affectionate when they are in a safe and trusting environment. The symbol for Cancer is the Crab, and those with Venus in this sign can retreat into their shell with the slightest provocation that threatens their emotional security. Their homes are places where they feel safest, and they will often prefer to entertain rather than be in an unfamiliar environment.

maintain good relations with siblings and neighbors.

These natives can come off as being light-hearted and noncommittal.

Gift: Venus in Gemini natives are willing to bring a refreshing opening to tense social situations. They excel at creatively opening up new channels of communication, even when it involves expressing themselves from new and different sides. In close personal relationships, they are willing to talk it out and bring new life into areas where stagnation may have occurred. Natives with this placement attract love by being witty, charming, and adaptable.

> People with this Venus position need a good amount of freedom in their close personal relationships.

These natives will remember good deeds and kind gestures directed toward them, and they will hold deep gratitude in their hearts and look to return in kind in the distant future.

They prefer their close relationships to be committed and predictable.

Shadow: Venus in Gemini natives love to seek variety in things that they own and

Gift: Venus in Cancer natives value the emotional bond that they have in close relationships. They put those around them at ease, coming across as caring, emotionally perceptive, and good listeners. These natives are instinctively nurturing and know how to make their friends, partners, and children feel cared for and nurtured. They are very impressionable and empathic and can pick up on the moods of those close to them, responding appropriately to comfort them.

Shadow: Venus in Cancer natives take a deep dive when it comes to falling in love until they've been hurt. Their heightened sensitivity makes them vulnerable, and they can be easily hurt and are often pouty and withdrawn. They are super self-protective, and they become wary of opening their hearts and trusting again. These natives can become overly sentimental and hold on to a lost love for several years, limiting opportunities for finding new happiness and fulfillment in their love life. They can be very fearful around showing their vulnerabilities and feelings. They may appear to be casual about their deepest feelings, but they are very careful about how much they reveal emotionally. As a result, partners and close relationships may get a wrong impression and feel that these natives don't care as much about them as they really do.

VENUS IN LEO

Venus in Fiery Leo natives are energetic, passionate, proud, and creative. Venus in Leo natives can amplify emotions and passion. These natives want to feel special. They thrive on romantic attention. They court their lovers with flair and zeal, and they love to be ardently wooed in return.

They typically support the arts and businesses connected with artistic development. They have a keen love of vibrancy, opulence, and color in art, décor, and other artistic forms.

They are fond of children, and their warm disposition and playful nature are engaging to children and adults of all ages.

Gift: Those with Venus in Leo are lovers of life. These natives are warm-hearted and fun-loving. As hosts and hostesses, they are great entertainers. They will always go the extra mile to make sure that their guests have a memorable time. Somewhat theatrical by nature, individuals with Venus in Leo make good actors and actresses. They have an innate ability to dramatize emotion and can be the life of a party. Their warmth is engaging, and they inspire people to open up and have fun. They are very loyal to those they deem worthy of their attention.

Shadow: The dark side of the Venus in Leo ego shows itself when the need for excessive amounts of attention leads to disappointment. They revert to childish behavior and, oftentimes, tall tales in order to gain back the focus of attention. Their pride can get in their way, and small slights and jealousies can trigger a dramatic response. The shadow side also manifests as snobbishness, selfishness, and overconcern with sex. These natives can be in love with love and not tune in to the needs of their partner.

VENUS IN VIRGO

Venus in Mercury-ruled Virgo natives are highly observant and aim to please. They express their love through practical gestures. These gestures can go unnoticed since these natives are not ostentatious about doing them. Nonetheless, they are very appreciative when their gestures and tokens of love are acknowledged.

Venus in Virgo natives often have a reserved quality, which is part of their appeal. They are not apt to make grandiose gestures in relationships until they have established a level of confidence in the connection.

Their analytical nature prevents them becoming overly dependent in relationships. With Venus in a Mutable Earth sign, these natives are generally adaptable and practical. They use common sense when determining the extent that they will engage in social and personal relationships. Similarly, these natives have practical spending habits.

Gift: These natives are good listeners, and through their observations, they instinctively sense what to do in order to be helpful. They can appear understated; however, they will be available to lend a helping hand. They want to have successful close relationships, and they will work toward that end. Individuals with Venus in Virgo are fastidious about their appearance and personal hygiene. They select their personal possessions with care and have a keen eye for their quality and utility. They appreciate the inherent beauty that exists in an ordered, working environment.

Shadow: In traditional astrology, Venus is in its fall in Virgo since Venus is exalted in its opposite sign of Pisces. The somewhat critical nature of Venus in Virgo can be off-putting to those closest to them even though the intention of these natives is not necessarily to hurt or offend. Their thinking is that they are trying to help you because they care. This overly analytical approach to love can cut off the flow in personal interactions and ultimately support the insecurity that a Venus in Virgo may have in personal interactions.

VENUS IN LIBRA

Venus is well placed in Libra since Venus is the natural ruler of Libra. Personal relationships are very important to these natives. Naturally tuned in to others, these individuals easily understand the feelings of those they are close to. They are able to put themselves in their place.

Naturally diplomatic, individuals with Venus in Libra look to create harmony in social situations as well as in their personal relationships. They can maintain a diplomatic stance even when confronted by unfair circumstances and situations that manage to engage their ire.

> With Venus in a Mutable Earth sign, these natives are generally adaptable and practical.

Venus in Libra natives are true romantics at heart and thrive when they are in a committed and loving partnership. They look to surround themselves with socially refined people who treat them with fairness and kindness.

Gift: Natives with Venus in Libra have a natural refinement. They have a highly developed aesthetic sensibility, which is generally observable in their personal surroundings and attire. Venus usually bestows well-proportioned features and general physical attractiveness to these natives. Their willingness to be present and attentive is a gift to those around them. This translates to mean that these natives are a pleasure to be with. Good manners, a refined disposition, grace, and charm are qualities that endear them to others. They make sure that a balanced give-and-take occurs in their personal and social interactions. They can create an easy and open rapport that endears them to potential partners. They are also gifted at creating a romantic mood, with all of the environmental accoutrements.

Shadow: Too much people-pleasing can leave them feeling empty and unfulfilled. Their desire to merge with another can offset common sense, and they may find, down the road, that they got together with another too soon. In their tendency to acquiesce to others and avoid unpleasant situations, they can inadvertently gloss over potential issues at play in their personal and social relationships. When they find themselves in over their heads, they can resort to avoidance behavior.

Venus in Libra usually bestows well-proportioned features and general physical attractiveness. Their willingness to be present and attentive is a gift to those around them.

VENUS IN SCORPIO

Natives with Venus in Scorpio demand intensity, passion, and total intimacy in their close personal relationships. Intimacy need not necessarily be limited to just the physical, as mental, emotional, and spiritual intimacy are also vital. They want to feel that they have an airtight connection with that individual. Venus in Scorpio natives strive to merge with another and thereby become a unique third entity that functions as one.

Venus in Scorpio is an "all or nothing" love nature. They do well with partners who are strong mentally, emotionally, and physically. Even though they can be controlling at times, they find it difficult to respect a partner who is passive or weak-willed.

In traditional astrology, Venus is in the sign of its detriment when it is in Scorpio since Scorpio is opposite Venus-ruled Taurus, where the Venusian energy naturally flows. Emotions and passions are strong and intense in Scorpio, so natives with this

position of Venus are not generally adept at creating harmony and peace. Their reactions to interactions can be overly personalized due to their underlying conscious and unconscious desires. This tendency can lead to misunderstandings and ruptures in relationships.

Gift: Venus in Scorpio individuals will work at improving their relationships. They believe in transformation and redemption, so they will go ahead and put substantial effort toward that end. Their dedication, intensity, and sensitivity, coupled with an innate charisma, create a highly seductive auric field around them that is attractive to those they want to bring into their sphere. They have a knack for boosting others' self-esteem and making them feel important.

Shadow: Jealousy and possessiveness can overwhelm individuals with Venus in Scorpio to the point that they become controlling in their close personal relationships. They can be overly suspicious of their mates and resort to spying and other devious behaviors. Even though these natives have a strong need for privacy, they have a tendency to probe into other people's personal lives. They have a knack for getting information out of others. Their intensity can be a turn-off to those they want to attract. They're not afraid of creating a crisis in order to test someone's devotion to them. This "all or nothing" approach to relationships can leave them out in the cold with nothing when a little moderation and self-confidence would have secured for them what they want.

VENUS IN SAGITTARIUS

Venus in idealist and high-minded Jupiter-ruled Sagittarius natives are friendly, sociable, outgoing, and adventurous. They can be outspoken about how they feel about you and not very good at keeping secrets, although they would never deliberately betray a trust.

Freedom is highly valued to these individuals. They are carefree and spontaneous and may not commit in their relationships as easily as other positions of Venus. They love excitement and spontaneity in their relationships, which is connected to their need to be free spirits. Controlling or overly possessive relationships don't work with these natives.

They love to travel and explore different cultures. Philosophical discussions, exchanging ideas, and sharing new experiences can be a turn-on for them.

> Jealousy and possessiveness can overwhelm individuals with Venus in Scorpio to the point that they become controlling in their close personal relationships.

Gift: Venus in Sagittarius individuals seek to be open and honest when expressing their feelings in relationships. They are not likely to be manipulative and calculating when addressing tough issues. They prefer to lay their cards out on the table and expect the same level of honesty from others. These natives are not always serious. They can be highly entertaining with their sense of humor, witty quips, and friendly, flirtatious behavior. These natives are attracted to relationships where they feel they can grow and expand their knowledge and awareness.

Shadow: Overly idealistic in their romantic relationships, these natives can be disappointed when practical considerations bring them down to Earth and reveal another side of their partners. They can dogmatically impose their viewpoints on others in their personal and social relationships. This position of Venus may try to convert their mates to their spiritual, religious, and moral beliefs. Their love of freedom can make these natives restless, noncommittal, and inconsistent in their display of feelings. They can temporarily disappear when they are feeling boxed in.

VENUS IN CAPRICORN

Venus is more traditional in the sign of Capricorn, which is ruled by Saturn. With this placement, one is more aware of stability and endurance. Saturn is exalted in Libra, indicating that the combination of Venus with Saturn can be beneficial for long-term commitments and relationships that endure the test of time. These individ-

The combination of Venus with Saturn can be beneficial for long-term commitments. These mature natives project an aura of competency and consistency that makes those who come in contact with them feel secure. They instinctively value effort and conscientiousness, and they don't shirk their responsibilities.

uals are serious about love, money, and their position in society. They like some measure of predictability in their relationships.

These natives can be material- and status-oriented. They care about what others think about them. Reserved in their public behavior, they dislike overt demonstrations of affection and emotion.

Individuals with this position of Venus will tend to seek older, more mature partners, especially when they are younger, and they tend to seek younger mates as they grow older.

Gift: These mature natives project an aura of competency and consistency that makes those who come into contact with them

feel secure. They instinctively value effort and conscientiousness and don't shirk their responsibilities. Individuals with Venus in Capricorn are realistic and practical and have an innate sense of how to build a sustainable relationship, with long-term ambitions for the lifestyle they desire. They are not dissuaded by the trials and tribulations that relationships encounter. When it comes to intimacy, they are sensual and earthy.

Shadow: Their serious nature can be off-putting, as these individuals can come across as lacking in warmth and spontaneity. Material possessions, social status, and impressing others can be disproportionately important to Venus in Capricorn natives. As a result, their close personal relationships can be emotionally unfulfilled and feel undervalued. These individuals can have fears centered around living up to others' expectations in love and romance as well as in social relationships. They fear being rejected or not being socially accepted, all of which pulls them away from appreciating what is happening in the moment.

VENUS IN AQUARIUS

Venus in Uranus-ruled Aquarius natives are open-minded and future-oriented. They are proud of their unique ways and their individualistic approach to life. Friendship is important to these individuals, and they want to feel that their romantic relationships are based upon a solid and congenial friendship. These friendships will often continue long after the romantic relationship disappears.

> As a Fixed Air sign, Aquarius takes a cool-headed mental approach to social, romantic, and aesthetic interactions.

Aquarian Venus placements are attracted to unusual and unconventional relationships. Their social mores can depart from so-called standard rules that are adhered to by much of society. Independence and freedom are high on their agenda. These natives dislike jealousy and possessiveness, and they will shy away from any relationship that aims to curtail their social freedom.

Venus in Aquarius natives are drawn to diverse types of romantic partners and friendships. The common thread is likely that each person is very much of an individual, and they love being themselves. Romantic attractions are often sudden and casual.

As a Fixed Air sign, Aquarius takes a cool-headed mental approach to social, romantic, and aesthetic interactions. In addition, it is likely that something is uncommon about their mindset. Their eclecticism inclines them toward unusual tastes. When it comes to their creative expression, they are likely to conjure up something with an original, and sometimes all-out eccentric, flair.

Gift: Venus in Aquarius individuals are kind, laid-back, open-minded, and generally straightforward. Honesty is highly valued and an integral part of the friendship that is the basis of their close relationships. They easily create a comfort level in their relationships based upon their easygoing nature that doesn't easily get ruffled. People around them can be themselves, and their individuality is appreciated and encouraged. Individuals with this placement of Venus are admired for treating everyone with the same honesty and respect.

Shadow: Venus in Aquarius adds an impersonal, aloof, and emotionally detached touch to the way that they relate to close personal and social relationships. They are not particularly sensitive to the emotional needs of others, which can limit the depth and sustainability of their romantic and social ventures. These natives do well to cultivate an open heart. Aquarius is the opposite sign to Leo, which rules the heart, and establishing a heart–mind balance can ultimately bring these natives more fulfillment and satisfaction in their lives. With Venus in a Fixed sign, they seldom compromise but rather believe that you should do whatever you want. It is as if any concession could mean the loss of their unique individuality.

VENUS IN PISCES

Natives with Venus in Pisces are fortunate to have their Venus positioned in the sign of its exaltation, which is characterized by a deeply sensitive, creative, and romantic heart. They are able to express their feelings freely and unconditionally, although they may not fully commit before allowing ample time to feel their way through the relationship.

Their highly compassionate nature turns their hearts toward sympathizing with those in need of help. They will give the underdog a chance and lend a helping hand.

These individuals prefer to be nonconfrontational, and they will let issues slide for fear that they might hurt someone close to them. They are forgiving and understanding.

Venus in Pisces natives have the innate ability for inspired musical and artistic creativity.

Gift: Venus in Pisces natives bring healing and comfort to anyone in distress, with their highly empathetic and extremely compassionate nature. Their soft-hearted presence is soothing to anyone who is in the midst of physical, mental, or emotional pain and suffering. They do not shy away from those who are in need of a little help. These natives understand unconditional love. They do not keep a scorecard, nor do they let their egos get in the way of expressing their love and sympathetic nature. Venus in Pisces natives take love to its highest spiritual level. Neptune is the higher octave of Venus, and this placement produces an emotional connection with all living creatures. They have an extraordinary capacity to see the best in those they interact with.

Shadow: Idealistic Venus in Pisces natives can easily ignore red flags and danger signals in their existing or potential romantic partners. Disappointment and forsakenness can result when reality doesn't match the fantasy built up by these natives. Martyrdom can ensue. The heightened sensitivity of Venus in Pisces gives these natives the ability to pick up on every want and need of those they care about. As much as their empathic nature benefits persons in their inner circle, these natives can neglect taking care of their own needs. Unless they learn to establish discrimination and set boundaries, their own health and well-being can suffer. Hypersensitivity, lack of discernment, and overdependence on others can stand in the way of them finding mutually beneficial and supportive relationships. They allow themselves to be victimized by others.

VENUS IN THE HOUSES

Venus is the planet of love, relationships, beauty, values, comfort, money, and material resources.

As Venus moves through each house of the Zodiac, she expresses herself through the areas governed by that house. The house position provides information about how the person expresses themselves romantically, artistically, and socially.

VENUS IN THE FIRST HOUSE

The First House rules appearance, health, general temperament, and sense of self. The First House defines you and the image you project to others.

The First House is ruled by Mars in the natural Zodiac since it is the house of Aries. In traditional astrology, Venus is con-

Venus in the First House bestows a magnetic charm and attractiveness with personal grace and an easy-to-approach demeanor. Some can place disproportionate importance on seeking approval and adoration.

cupation with appearance can occur, and they can place disproportionate importance on seeking approval and adoration.

VENUS IN THE SECOND HOUSE

The Second House is connected with finances, values, material possessions, talents, and resources. The Second House represents the value we give to ourselves and, in turn, that which we possess.

Venus is well placed in the Second House, which is the natural ruler of Taurus in the natural Zodiac.

Gift: Venus in the Second House loves to possess beautiful things. They have good taste and appreciate the indulgences in life. A comfortable, easy lifestyle that includes their favorite luxuries brings them great joy and comfort. They can be musically or artistically talented. It is likely that they have a melodious voice; good, solid values; and a charming personality.

Shadow: These natives can flaunt their personal possessions in order to gain social status and attract love. They can be extravagant and enticed by outer, superficial appearances, missing out on the authentic goods.

VENUS IN THE THIRD HOUSE

The Third House is connected with ideas, communication, siblings, neighbors, and short journeys.

The Third House belongs to Gemini in the natural Zodiac. Venus in the Third House combines the adaptability of Mercury with Venus.

Gift: Venus in the Third House natives are polite, tactful, articulate, and creative communicators. Their artistic talent may

sidered to be in its fall since Venus naturally rules Libra, the sign opposite Aries.

Gift: Venus in the First House bestows a magnetic charm and attractiveness. These individuals have a personal grace; pleasing, gentle mannerisms; and an easy-to-approach demeanor. They show a natural ease when working with others and are generally well received. They are likely to have artistic talent and a well-developed aesthetic. They have an eye for style and design and like to incorporate an artistic flair in their personal appearance or environment.

Shadow: Charm, beauty, and physical attractiveness can be used negatively to influence others for selfish ends. A preoc-

be expressed through their hands. They are expressive writers and communicators. They can be flirtatious and witty. They tend to have good relationships with their neighbors and siblings.

Shadow: Their silver tongue can serve these natives in manipulative ways, using flattery and sweet talk for selfish ends. Mind games have an inordinate appeal to them. They are the neighborhood gossipers and busybodies.

VENUS IN THE FOURTH HOUSE

The Fourth House is about the home, family, genetic inheritance, foundational stability, innermost feelings, later life, and the end of matters.

The Fourth House is ruled by Cancer in the natural Zodiac. Venus in the Fourth House combines the instinctive qualities of the Moon with the desire to create harmony that is inherent in Venus.

> Venus in the Fourth House creates a comfortable, loving, and nurturing home for themselves and their family.

Gift: Venus in the Fourth House creates a comfortable, loving, and nurturing home for themselves and their family. These natives desire harmony, beauty, and calm in their household. They are sentimental, which is expressed through their nurturing and caring nature. Parental influence plays a strong role in their life. Emotional closeness to their parents is indicated, which brings happiness to the native.

Shadow: Venus in the Fourth House natives can be smothering, melodramatic, manipulative, and commanding. A parent may have been overprotective and indulgent, which influences the native through-out their life. They tend to have inherited illnesses related to the sign that Venus is placed in. Disruptions on the home front can throw these natives into a tailspin.

VENUS IN THE FIFTH HOUSE

The Fifth House rules creative self-expression, children, love, passion, romance, playfulness, and joy.

The Fifth House is naturally ruled by the Sun since the Fifth House is the area of the chart that correlates with Leo.

Gift: Love and romance are important themes to individuals with this Venus placement, especially in their younger years. Their innate flair for drama and creativity comes across as self-confidence. They are fun-loving and understand the value of play and pleasure. They bring joy to others by reminding them to let loose and have fun. In social situations, these individuals are well liked and welcomed into social circles. Young at heart, these natives are creative, and their creativity will express itself based on the sign that Venus is placed in. They have a natural affinity for children and pets.

Shadow: Hedonism and decadence can easily evolve into debauchery when Venus is in the Fifth House. Moderation is not in this native's vocabulary. Gambling, excessive sexual exploits, and living high on the hog are all tendencies when the shadow side of this placement is expressing itself. They can be in love with love and not see their mates clearly but rather as love objects.

THE ASTROLOGY GUIDE

Those with a Seventh-House Venus placement will go to great lengths to create balanced and harmonious relationships. They are considerate of others and have an edge in fields involving public relations and diplomacy, with a knack for putting others at ease with their agreeable and magnetic charm.

VENUS IN THE SIXTH HOUSE

The Sixth House governs daily routines, acts of service, the work-life balance, health, due diligence, pet care, coworkers, and employees.

The Sixth House is the natural home of Virgo, which is ruled by Mercury. The body you are born with is governed by the First House, whereby choices made over time that create the current body are governed by the Sixth House.

Gift: Natives with Venus in the service-oriented Sixth House are thoughtful and seek to be helpful, especially to those they care about. They are kind and humble and gain satisfaction working for the welfare of others. They will have harmonious relationships with coworkers and people who work for them. These natives are generally health-conscious and will work toward maintaining a healthy, attractive body.

Shadow: This placement can incline the native to feel like they are never doing enough. Their focus on how to be helpful can lead to selling themselves short. Preoccupation with daily chores and activities can cause them to miss out on opportunities. They can be weak in the areas of the physical body connected to the sign that Venus is in. These natives can have a sweet tooth that can affect their health and well-being.

VENUS IN THE SEVENTH HOUSE

The Seventh House rules close personal relationships, agreements, and compromises.

The Seventh House is the home of Libra in the natural Zodiac. Venus is comfortable and at home here.

Gift: Those with a Seventh-House Venus placement will go to great lengths to create balanced and harmonious relationships. They are pleasing and considerate of others and have successful social interactions with the general public, giving them an edge in fields involving public relations and diplomacy. They have a knack for putting others at ease with their agreeable and magnetic charm.

Shadow: Venus in the Seventh House natives can pay too much homage to everyone but themselves. Without a strong sense of self, they can relinquish their personal identity in their close partnerships. They can feel lost when they are not in a partnership.

VENUS IN THE EIGHTH HOUSE

The Eighth House rules joint ventures, intimacy, sex, death, transformation, and psychic dimensions.

Venus is in the house of Scorpio, the sign of Venus's detriment. Identifying the shadow aspects in one's psyche and bringing these patterns to the forefront of consciousness is highly important in manifesting the gifts that the placement offers.

Gift: Venus in the Eighth House can bring financial gain through partnerships, which can include inheritances, shared investments, and insurances. These natives seek an intense connection in their love re-

lationships. They love passionately and expect total devotion and commitment in return. Their relationships can have a transformative effect on them since they give wholeheartedly.

Shadow: Venus in Scorpio's house can manifest as an excessive or compulsive emphasis on sex. Overly intense emotions, jealousy, and possessiveness are possible with this placement of Venus. An Eighth-House Venus native can keep secrets and be drawn to secretive relationships or relationships based on power themes and taboos. A partner's resources can be the motivating factor in engaging in a relationship.

VENUS IN THE NINTH HOUSE

The Ninth House rules higher education, long-term goals, foreign travel, publicity, adventures, religion, and philosophical and ethical pursuits.

Venus in Jupiter-ruled Sagittarius combines the energies of Venus and Jupiter. Both planets are described in traditional astrology as benefics, meaning that they are fortunate and will generally provide favorable results in a chart.

Gift: Venus in the Ninth House is adventurous, flirtatious, idealistic, and culturally oriented. The Jupiter influence of the Ninth House provides these natives an expansive purview for socializing. It is not uncommon for them to meet significant relationships when traveling or engaging in cultural events. They enjoy philosophical and spiritual discussions, sharing dreams and visions, and expanding their

> The Ninth-House placement of Venus can be fixated on beliefs that they then impose on those close to them. They can be obsessed with the exotic to the exclusion of relationships....

horizons either through adventures or through educational, spiritual, and philanthropic groups.

Shadow: The Ninth-House placement of Venus can be fixated on beliefs that they then impose on those close to them. They can be obsessed with the exotic to the exclusion of relationships that could bring them a higher level of satisfaction and joy. The idea of love can be romanticized. Planets in the Ninth House can incline the individual to want to live in the future rather than the present. As a result, they can find themselves in a difficult relationship, with the belief that it will get better in the future rather than realistically work on current issues.

VENUS IN THE TENTH HOUSE

The Tenth House rules public achievements, reputation, authority, and prestige.

With Venus in a house ruled by Saturn, these natives will be mindful of putting their best foot forward. They know how to make a good impression.

Gift: These natives will have many admirers for a good reason. They have a charming disposition, a pleasing manner, and are generally stylish based upon whatever image or impression they want to create. The upshot is that they can enjoy good relationships with their employers and those in positions of power. It is likely that these individuals will be noticed and appreciated. Organizing successful social events is natural for them.

Shadow: A Tenth-House Venus native has to guard themselves against being too wrapped up in the image they want to project out in society. They could be

viewed as pretentious or superficial. They can also be perceived as a social climber who forgets their close friends or people who helped them along the way.

VENUS IN THE ELEVENTH HOUSE

The Eleventh House rules friends, hopes, wishes, groups, and a sense of belonging in the world.

The Eleventh House is ruled by Uranus with a coruler of Saturn in traditional astrology. These natives can feel a level of social responsibility or align with humanitarian ideals. Groups and group activities can prove to be beneficial for attaining their hopes and wishes.

Gift: Venus in the Eleventh House values friendship. Close personal relationships, lovers, and business partnerships need to withstand the criteria for friendship before these individuals would consider them to be genuine and worthwhile. They are apt to retain the friendship long after the romance or business venture has faded away. Their friends are generally artistically talented, visually attractive, or well put together or have a humanitarian orientation.

Shadow: These natives can have so many friends and social connections that they don't develop depth in any of their close relationships. They are preoccupied with social engagements and don't establish bonds that are nurturing or involve personal responsibility to each other.

VENUS IN THE TWELFTH HOUSE

The Twelfth House rules secrets, unconscious patterns, karma, closure, institutions, connections with higher sources, enlightenment, and undoing.

Venus in the Eleventh House values friendship. These individuals can feel a level of social responsibility or align with humanitarian ideals. They are apt to retain friendships long after a romance or business venture has faded away.

The Twelfth House is ruled by Pisces in the natural Zodiac, and Venus is exalted in Pisces, affording this placement with a general ease of functioning.

Gift: Venus in the Twelfth House is romantic, kind, and charitable. They exhibit great compassion to those who may need their help. They can be attracted to people from all walks of life, although they favor those who work toward the benefit of others as well as those who are disadvantaged in some way. These natives are highly sensitive and intuitive, which gives them the ability to easily attune to unconscious and subtle trends. This ability can be expressed in musical and artistic pursuits.

Shadow: The merging qualities ascribed to Pisces and the Twelfth House can leave these natives without clearly defined boundaries. They can lose track of their own needs while indulging in the needs of others. They can easily get hurt or feel used and underappreciated by unconsciously correlating love with sacrifice or martyrdom. Their romantic needs can be kept

hidden, and they can feel like they are being selfish or don't deserve to express them.

VENUS COMBINATIONS

Venus/Sun

Venus represents love, relationships, beauty, values, comfort, and material resources.

The Sun indicates purpose, self-expression, creative life force, and conscious will.

Venus is located between Earth and Mercury and is closer to the Sun than Earth. Venus can only be 48 degrees away from the Sun, so few combinations of these two energies are possible. According to traditional astrology, the only combinations that the Sun and Venus can make are the Semi-Sextile (30 degrees), Semi-Square (45 degrees), and the Conjunction (0.5–10 degrees). As with Mercury, the beneficial "casimi" and "cazimi" situation would apply when the two planetary bodies are less than 0.5 degrees from each other. When the Sun is conjunct with Ve-

The gift of a Moon and Venus connection is emotional availability to close friends and intimate partners. They are not afraid to express their feelings, and they do so graciously.

nus, a more stabilizing effect occurs than with the Sun/Mercury combination. Venus adds harmony and serenity to the Sun.

Venus becomes invisible under the rays of the Sun when it is closer than 8 degrees. Some ancient astrologers thought that when she is invisible, she should therefore be distrusted. A modern interpretation is that the Sun allows for the full expression of one's love of nature, beauty, and creativity.

Gift: The qualities of Venus are aligned with the individual's ego or drive for significance. They are able to project the traits of Venus easily and judiciously. They are cheerful, charming, optimistic, and magnetic. They are able to shine and excel at creating harmony and bringing people together. This combination offers the ability to be comfortable in one's own skin.

Shadow: Overindulgence is possible with the shadow side of a Sun/Venus connec-

tion. The native may need to be continuously reassured of admiration and love from others. These natives can have an edgy kind of charm, where they may be judgmental of others or not comfortable in social situations.

VENUS/MOON

Venus represents love, relationships, beauty, values, comfort, and material resources.

The Moon rules the soul, core instincts, the personality, and subconscious conditioning.

The gift of a Moon and Venus connection is emotional availability to close friends and intimate partners. Besides having a pleasing disposition and an open personality, they know how to put people at ease. They are not afraid to express their feelings, and they do so graciously. Both Moon and Venus are receptive energies, and when they work well together, they smooth out rough edges and bring affection and softness to situations.

Gift: These individuals are aesthetically sensitive to their own appearance as well as to their surroundings. Often personally attractive, they innately know how to add a pleasing touch to their surroundings.

Shadow: The shadow of this planetary combination can be expressed in a reluctance to express love and affection for fear of vulnerability. Their emotions can interfere with their love nature. Natives may subconsciously hold back their feelings, which can create an awkward social presence.

VENUS/MERCURY

Venus represents love, relationships, beauty, values, comfort, and material resources.

Mercury rules communication, mental processes, and the logical mind.

Mercury and Venus have a special relationship in that their orbits are both between Earth and the Sun. The other planets, dwarf planets, and asteroids have an orbit further out, beyond Earth. Mercury and Venus are therefore called personal planets due to their special connection to Earth.

Mercury can only be within 28 degrees of the Sun, and Venus can only be within 48 degrees of the Sun. These planets can combine their energies in only a few ways since they cannot reside further than 47 degrees apart. These include a Conjunction, a Sextile, and a Semi-Square. A Sextile can only form when Mercury and Venus are on different sides of the Sun in the Zodiac, with one of them rising ahead of the Sun as a morning star and the other setting behind the Sun as an evening star.

The combination of Mercury and Venus offers a blend of artistic and mental qualities. They often have a talent for design and have a love of books and the written word.

Gift: An abundance of charm and grace are two of the gifts to be gained from the combination of Mercury and Venus. These natives blend information in a pleasing manner, one that is easy for their listeners to hear. They are acutely aware of how their communication affects others. They often have pleasing voices, and many are good singers. Their harmonizing talents give these natives commendable negotiating skills, inclining them to be successful mediators and diplomats. They naturally know how to convince people to cooperate and get along. They speak and move with grace, harmony, and balance.

Shadow: Too much schmoozing and sweet talk can be distasteful, especially

without any significant action to back it up. When Venus is out of proportion, a tendency to overindulge occurs. This can manifest as vanity, conceit, and irresolute behavior patterns. They can take on the persona of a social butterfly, one who leans toward being fickle and superficial.

VENUS/MARS

Venus represents love, relationships, beauty, values, comfort, and material resources.

Mars rules assertiveness, energy, drive, and courage.

When the inner feminine and the inner masculine energies are balanced, conscious inspired action occurs that is guided by heart wisdom without overexerting and becoming energetically depleted.

Gift: The gift of balance between the Yin and Yang principles occurs when Mars and Venus harmoniously combine. The Venusian principle of attraction can be energized by Mars, and similarly, the assertive principle of Mars can be refined by the influence of Venus. These natives can be artistically inclined and often find it easy to relate to others. They instinctively know how to balance the energies they interact with when relating one-on-one or as part of a group. They can be productive without dominating and diplomatic and personable leaders.

Shadow: Too much Yang can occur when more Yin is required and vice versa. The Yin–Yang balance is off, causing confusion and issues, especially in close personal relationships. A lack of refinement can occur in social interactions or too much passivity when a more active role is more appropriate. Sensual desires can be strong and can overshadow emotional sensitivity.

VENUS/JUPITER

Venus represents love, relationships, beauty, values, comfort, and material resources.

Jupiter represents the higher mind, greater truths, expansiveness, hope, and optimism.

Venus and Jupiter are both known as benefics in astrology, meaning that this combination can bring good luck, positive outcomes, and ease. The expansive nature of Jupiter enhances everything that is ruled by Venus and can bring radiance and opportunities to social and personal relationships, finances, artistic endeavors, and all that is valued by the native.

Gift: A generosity of spirit occurs that, when coupled with a supportive attitude, fosters love and trust. This is an open-hearted, joyous combination that attracts positivity, prosperity, and popularity. The native exudes an uplifting aura that adds positivity and sparkle to an environment. Their happy spirit and general liking of people brings friends and many social contacts to them. They possess social grace and a refinement that makes them welcome guests. This combination can incline the individual toward artistic pursuits, which they likely will, in turn, be successful at.

Shadow: Too much of a good thing can bring overindulgence and an overinflated ego, which can outweigh the generosity of spirit that could otherwise be present with this combination. Overreach can occur in relationships due to overconfidence and a sense of entitlement. A cocky attitude can result when this otherwise delightful combination is displaying its shadow side. An increased appetite for spending and sensual and sexual indulgence can manifest with this combination.

VENUS/SATURN

Venus represents love, relationships, beauty, values, comfort, and material resources.

Saturn rules responsibility, adjustments to limitations, sustainability, and structure.

Venus and Saturn energies work well together, as exemplified by the exaltation of Saturn in the Venus-ruled sign of Libra. Saturn gives concrete expression to the artistic tendencies of Venus. Saturn also produces committed and sustainable personal relationships.

Gift: Venus can tone down the harsher, more serious, and judgmental side of Saturn by adding a down-to-earth approach to awkward situations. Saturn brings added responsibility and commitment to partnerships and social relationships. These natives are not easily dissuaded by minor squabbles and disagreements. They understand the more serious side of relationships, which can have its ups and downs. They have a practical orientation as to what is entailed in order to have successful relationships. They add a sense of fair play and presence to social situations. The Venus/Saturn combination can be helpful to artists and those engaged in creative undertakings. Saturn can bring concrete expression to their Venusian tendencies. These natives can be skilled in business and financial affairs, whereby Saturn adds practicality and good judgment to their endeavors.

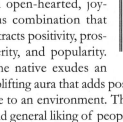

The Yin–Yang balance is off, causing confusion and issues, especially in close personal relationships.

Shadow: The shadow side of a Venus/Saturn combination can manifest as a fear of abandonment. These natives can hold on to difficult experiences in life where they were disappointed by love. The memory of past situations that did not work out for them can overshadow their present-day personal and social relationships. They can become reticent and avoid social situations in general. Saturn can dampen the freer-flowing, pleasure-oriented side of Venus. A melancholic disposition can follow that causes them to be shy, stiffly formal, or totally withdrawn for social contact.

VENUS/URANUS

Venus represents love, relationships, beauty, values, comfort, and material resources.

Uranus rules intuition, originality, individuality, and the sudden and unexpected.

Natives with connections between Venus and Uranus bring a unique and inventive flavor to social encounters that adds brilliance to any stagnant situation. They delight in surprising others with their unexpected and creative responses to everyday occurrences.

Anyone with a Venus/Uranus combination in their birth chart needs more of a sense of freedom in those Venus-ruled areas of life, including relationships, financial affairs, the arts, and entertainment. Uranus loves to think outside of the box and needs the freedom to be able to do so. Natives with connections between Venus and Uranus are inclined to sudden attractions. They have vibrant personalities that make them popular and sometimes not well understood.

Gift: Uranus adds a unique kind of genius to Venus that can manifest in a host of different ways. These individuals bring a unique and inventive flavor to social encounters, which adds brilliance to any stagnant situation. They delight in surprising others with their unexpected and creative responses to everyday occurrences. A person with this combination is a breath of fresh air when it comes to surprises, and

it is unlikely that a relationship with them will become stale or predictable. They have a distinctive artistic flair that extends to all of the creative arts. Their effervescence and spontaneity especially add to the performing arts. These natives have a magnetic charm that engages others into their sphere of influence. Undoubtedly, they will be noticed and remembered.

Shadow: A Venus/Uranus combination can manifest as an individual who cannot stand to be tied down to any kind of commitment. They can be unpredictable as a mate or even as a friend unless a mutual understanding occurs going into the relationship. These natives have little tolerance for any kind of pressure to be a certain way or to behave as far as the status quo is concerned. They dance to the tune of their own drummer in both appearance and in the realm of social and relationship mores. Traditions hold little merit unless they add their own interpretation to it. Their overwhelming desire for freedom can come off as irresponsible.

VENUS/NEPTUNE

Venus represents love, relationships, beauty, values, comfort, and material resources.

Neptune rules ideals, creative imagination, transcendence, compassion, and vision.

Neptune is the higher octave of Venus. Venus is the planet of love, relationships, beauty, values, comfort, money, and material resources. Neptune rules our dreams and visions. Venus is exalted in the sign of Neptune-ruled Pisces, which lends itself to the highest and purest form of spiritual love.

Gift: Unconditional, pure love is a beautiful gift that natives with this combination can experience in their life. People are often elevated in the company of this individual due to their unique ability to relate to the highest and best in them. A romantic at heart, they have a knack for helping others feel special. These natives are aesthetically sensitive and perceptive. Their vivid imagination and refined sensitivity incline these natives toward music, photography, and mystically inspired art. They excel at perceiving the subtleties of artistic expression. Their heightened sensory awareness gives them an edge in any creative expression, whether it entails the visual arts, cooking, music, or the performing arts.

Shadow: Yearning for something or someone that doesn't exist is typical of the shadow side of this combination. This individual can be always looking for the perfect life, the perfect relationship, the perfect love, only to be disappointed once reality sets in. When expectations run hay-wire, they become set up for frustration and disappointment since their expectations are often not met. These natives can lose themselves in others, where they give up any semblance of personal boundary and dedicate themselves to another's expectations and happiness. The result is an emptiness when their sacrificial gestures are not returned in kind.

VENUS/PLUTO

Venus represents love, relationships, beauty, values, comfort, and material resources.

Pluto represents regeneration; transformation; and a compelling, fundamental approach.

When Venus and Pluto connect, a desire occurs to transform and be transformed through love. Emotional intensity and passion in their connections occur, whether they be romantic, personal, or social. Transformation can occur either through conscious effort based upon not having their needs met or through outer events that the native feels that they don't have control over.

Individuals with this combination will likely experience intense emotional deaths and rebirths at some point, which will mark a major turning point in their life.

Gift: These natives are passionate and ardent partners and lovers. This planetary connection can indicate the capacity for regenerating a relationship to a highly spiritual level. They can feel that the relationship was destined and part of a cosmic plan. A strong desire occurs to connect and merge at all levels—physically, emotionally, mentally, and spiritually—yielding an airtight relationship and union. These natives can be artistically talented, which is passionately expressed through their artistic milieu. In each case, the artwork will be captivating and absorb onlookers.

Shadow: The shadow side of a Venus/Pluto combination occurs when emotions and passions get out of control and trigger compulsive behavior patterns. Usual triggers include jealousy, possessiveness, sexual desire, and control of financial and material resources. Sometimes, the shadow side will manifest as the need to find passion at any cost. These natives can create experiences for the sole sake of creating a stir. These natives are not beyond playing games to get a rise out their significant other or people close to them. These natives can be fascinated and ultimately obsessed by the unknown and the forbidden. They can be inordinately stimulated and involved in sexual passion and indulgence. Clandestine encounters appeal to them.

Individuals with this combination will likely experience intense emotional deaths and rebirths at some point, which will mark a major turning point in their life.

VENUS/CHIRON

Venus represents love, relationships, beauty, values, comfort, and material resources.

Chiron represents core wounds and the desire to overcome them, and healing.

Combinations between Venus and Chiron involve getting in touch with how the individual expresses love and healing obstacles that prevent the full expression of love. The individual can have old relationship traumas that require healing. This combination can lead to healing and to questioning values and self-worth.

Gift: Long-term subconscious blocks that have prevented fulfilling love relationships are released. Inherited genetic patterns are sought and revealed, giving way to a conscious awareness of those patterns that have caused disappointment or lack of relationships. Awareness is brought to views and attitudes surrounding money, finances, and material resources. Values are redefined, where those imparted to the native from their upbringing are replaced by ones more suitable to their beliefs and ideals. This individual can use what they gleaned from their own healing to help others, particularly women, with relationship issues and self-worth.

Shadow: The native keeps encountering the same relationship issues over and over again. Issues occur involving the principle of attraction in both relationships and financial matters. Areas of the physical body connected with Venus may be more vulnerable and be in need of healing. Issues can occur with gender identity that need attention.

VENUS/ERIS

Venus represents love, relationships, beauty, values, comfort, and material resources.

Eris represents the determination to remove limitations that impede the soul's evolution.

Gift: These natives attract to themselves like-minded souls that accompany them on their journey to their next level of evolution. They seek to find purity and authenticity in their relationships.

Venus in combination with Eris natives attract to themselves like-minded souls that accompany them on their journey to their next level of evolution, seeking purity and authenticity in their relationships.

Shadow: Their exceedingly strong competitive nature can cause these individuals to seek love for the sake of love. Their lack of discernment can send them barking up the wrong tree. They are inclined to create strife and discord in social situations, whereby they become an outcast, without the comraderie they desire.

VENUS/NORTH NODE

Venus represents love, relationships, beauty, values, comfort, and material resources.

The North Node represents future direction, soul guidance, and fulfillment.

These individuals may be attractive and sensitive but are not able to sustain a suitable relationship until they consciously learn how to be in a relationship and make it work. They may find little value in money and material resources.

Gift: A Venus/North Node connection indicates that relationships are or will be important to these individuals. Love and significant relationships of all types may be a central theme that will impact them. They may feel intuitively destined to one day meet their soulmate. Their charm and charisma increase as they age. Others may be instinctively drawn to them, and it may turn out that these are destined connections.

Shadow: These natives can use their magnetism and charm to deceive and manipulate others. They can continually engage in frivolous relationships without any intent to develop a deeper connection or commitment. They can be spendthrifts.

VENUS/SOUTH NODE

Venus represents love, relationships, beauty, values, comfort, and material resources.

The South Node represents familiarity, gratification, and the path of least resistance.

Relationships are familiar territory for these individuals. Situations will deter these natives from forming superficial relations that don't further their growth and development.

Gift: Natives are naturally magnetic, graceful, and charming and have a knack for putting others at ease. They are experienced in interacting in social situations. Connecting with others comes naturally to them. These natives may have to learn the true meaning of love. They may have taken for granted people who loved them in the past. These individuals likely have artistic or musical talents that were previously developed. These abilities may show up at a young age.

Shadow: The shadow side of the Venus/South Node connection is that these individuals may need to become more independent. A pattern of codependence can occur that feeds into their relationship patterns. Unconscious motivations affect the individual.

VENUS/ASCENDANT

Venus represents love, relationships, beauty, values, comfort, and material resources.

The Ascendant represents one's approach, orientation, and the window through which one sees the world.

Venus in combination with the Ascendant brings an aesthetically attractive quality to the native.

Gift: These individuals are generally charming and attractive. They approach situations with grace and ease. Their personal mannerisms are pleasing, and they like to create aesthetically pleasing and harmonious environments. They have a warm and friendly disposition that attracts others to them.

Shadow: These natives can place a disproportionate amount of importance on appearance and less importance on sub-

stance. A tendency toward narcissism and a strong need to be appreciated and complimented can occur.

VENUS/MIDHEAVEN (MC)

Venus represents love, relationships, beauty, values, comfort, and material resources.

The Midheaven (MC) represents image, outer aspirations, and career orientation.

Gift: The connection between Venus and the Midheaven (also called the *medium coeli*, or MC) connotes a person who is favorably noticed for their talents and abilities. It favors those in artistic, diplomatic, and social relation professions. They also have the ability to attract financial benefits through their social and business connections. They are likely to be stylish and make a good impression on people in prominent positions.

Shadow: These natives may be prone to social ambition. They can use their charm and attractiveness to promote their careers even if they do not have the talent and ability to sustain the position that they attain.

Mars

Mars is an expressive and initiating creative force. Mars is brave, adventurous, and instinctual.

Mars is the planet of desires, passion, and action. Mars's placement in the birth chart tells a story of how one asserts themself and pursues their goals. It tells a story of how one chooses to use courage and what motivates one to be competitive. Mars also indicates how to express a raw, primal nature and creative urges. Mars is connected to sexuality, vitality, verve, life force, and the ability to get up and go.

Mars shapes our destiny since hard work, dynamism, physical power, sports, and various forms of aggression are connected with Mars. All areas of life connected with Mars come up as heated, energetic, and result-oriented, as it is Mars's nature to test limits, fire up energy, and use assertiveness to get desired results and be a trailblazer in that area of the chart. As a planet of action, Mars is driven and straightforward in its approach and likes to draw clear boundaries. "Do this, not that" and "this is mine and that is yours" are the mantras of Mars.

Mars rules Aries, the first sign of the Zodiac, the pioneer and the initiator. Mars and Pluto are corulers of Scorpio, a sign connected with passions, instincts, and desires.

A strong, well-placed Mars makes a person confident, successful, courageous, passionate, and energetic.

The shadow side of Mars is characterized by expressions such as rage, volatility, reactivity, and more aggressiveness, forcefulness, or competitiveness than is required. Mars is argumentative and ready to fight. Mars's shadow is connected with resentments, health concerns, and financial losses. Acknowledging how, when, and where Mars is working in the chart brings conscious awareness to this strong and sometimes overwhelming force. After

Mars rules Aries and is the co-ruler of Scorpio. Both of these signs share the gifts associated with the planet's namesake, the ancient Roman god of war.

trapped and repressed anger, resentments, and frustrations are recognized, Mars's gifts can be fully be recognized and utilized for achieving goals in life.

At the physical level, Mars is connected with heat and can trigger inflammation and sensitivity in areas of the body governed by the sign that Mars is placed in. For example, Mars in Cancer can indicate a sensitive stomach, and individuals with Mars in Aries may be prone to headaches.

Mars is about half the size of Earth, with a highly tenuous atmosphere and no magnetic field, unlike Earth. The surface temperature of Mars can be as high as 70 degrees Fahrenheit and as low as −220 degrees. The tilt of Mars's rotation axis is similar to that of Earth; Mars is 25 and Earth is 23. One day on Mars is 24 hours and 37 minutes, almost the same as Earth.

Mars takes about 2–2.5 years to transit each sign. Mars is retrograde approximately every 2 years.

MARS IN THE SIGNS

Mars rules assertiveness, energy, drive, and courage.

MARS IN ARIES

As the natural ruler of Aries, Mars is at home in this sign and is assertive, energetic, and directed at attaining desired outcomes. Mars in Aries can be likened to driving a very fast car, which is great on a highway, but not so much so on a windy, mountainous road.

Gift: Assertive, confident, and brave are keywords that describe Mars in Aries. Mars in Aries can be the spark that gets new endeavors off the ground. When actions are coupled with forethought, the daring, adventuresome spirit of this energy can be very gallant and charming. They can choose to be all in when on a mission or pursuing a cause. You can count on Mars in Aries to get the ball rolling when energy is stuck.

Shadow: The confidence inherent in Mars in Aries can turn to arrogance when taken for granted. Similarly, a headstrong approach can be a turn-off in situations where more finesse and thoughtfulness are required. The shadow side of Mars in Aries can be a native who easily becomes argumentative and aggressive. They have to be mindful of looking before they leap, lest their impulsive actions cause them regret.

MARS IN TAURUS

Mars in Taurus has a slow and steady determination and can plod along with surprisingly good results as long as they are not confronted in their process, at which point they will dig in their heels until circumstances are more amenable to their way of functioning. They are slow to anger, but don't let that fool you; their inner bull can unleash when they are pushed beyond their comfort zone or prodded before they are ready to move.

Mars in Taurus is the combination of Martian and Venusian energies, so their passions run high for earthy and sensual pleasures. They don't tire easily when motivated by their desire for comfort, material or personal security, or their fondness for acquiring possessions.

Gift: Mars in Taurus emanates steadfastness and maintains an even keel when they have a deadline, even if anxieties surround them. They emit a quiet, yet tireless air of calmness while staying on track. They possess an inner sensibility that leads them to spend the least amount of energy in order to accomplish a goal. This placement does well in areas that require quiet determination, and you will find them in the cuisines, the arts, and musical professions where staying power is needed. They are deliberate and not easily swayed.

> Mars in Taurus is the combination of Martian and Venusian energies, so their passions run high for earthy and sensual pleasures.

Shadow: Mars in Taurus is not known for being adaptable, and they can dig in their heels and refuse to budge when pushed. Highly competitive situations may not be their forte unless they feel very well prepared and comfortable. Their penchant for stubbornness can be most visible when they are asked to do something they really don't like doing. Mars in Taurus can garner a reputation for being lazy and indulgent

when they are distracted by sensual pleasures. Mars in Taurus can be stubborn and bullheaded when pushed or confronted, and they don't like doing anything that they don't want to do, although you may be able to lure them with the right payoff. Don't count on a Mars in Taurus native to make a spectacle of themselves when competition is required, although they could end up on top in their own quiet way.

MARS IN GEMINI

Mars in Gemini combines the feistiness of Mars with the mental acuity of Mercury. Here, you have a quick-witted mental energy that would rather negotiate or find an efficient strategy than use elbow grease. Spirited conversation is favorite pastime, as the energy of Mars can influence their communication skills.

Gift: Mars in Gemini has the ability to outwit their competition while sweet-talking them during the process. With their agile bodies and nimble fingers, they excel in activities that require fast action and a quick response. When angered, these natives will prefer having a conversation to hash things out, and once they do, their irritation will quickly dissipate.

Shadow: Easily distracted, Mars in Gemini can and often will start on a new track before completing what they originally started. Don't be surprised if every now and then, the original task gets completed since the mental orientation of Gemini never stopped thinking about what they had left undone. Boredom is not their favorite state, and you can find these natives tapping their

Mars in Cancer is motivated to protect others and especially those about whom they care, and they make good caretakers in every sense. Their gentle, calm energy can be soothing and supportive.

hands or feet, frequently changing position, or doodling when they are restless. These natives possess ingenuity but not necessarily perseverance.

MARS IN CANCER

Mars in Cancer is in its fall since Cancer is the opposite sign to Capricorn where Mars is exalted. The combination of Mars with the Moon can make for an emotional and sensitive individual who directs their energy toward taking care of others' needs and tending to their own home and hearth.

Mars in Cancer can be moody, and these natives like to feel comfortable and secure before putting themselves in a challenging situation. By the same token, since Cancer, like Capricorn, is a Cardinal sign, a desire is present to take some action to move

the energy forward, creating an inner conflict. It is often an emotional impulse that finally moves them ahead.

Gift: Although cautious, Mars in Cancer can be very tenacious, especially when emotional and security needs are at stake. Mars in Cancer is motivated to protect others, especially those they care about, and they make good caretakers in every sense. They exude a gentle, calm, and sensual energy that can be soothing and supportive, especially when they feel comfortable and secure.

Shadow: Moodiness and emotional frustrations combine to make this placement less deliberate and steadfast than some other Mars placements. It is important for these natives to find outlets for their anger and resentments so that they avoid brooding, which can lead to long-term issues with their stomach and digestion. Mars in Cancer natives can be uncomfortable with confrontation or with displays of anger since it makes them feel vulnerable. Nonetheless, they can benefit from being mindful that passive-aggressive behaviors don't ensue. Holding on to past slights can easily turn into excessive dwelling that affects their digestive system.

MARS IN LEO

Mars in Leo people are a strong, confident, charismatic, fun-loving lot who cares a lot about their image. Sun-ruled Leo likes to shine, and with Mars in Leo, they are more than willing to glean the spotlight unless they have other planetary influences in Cancer or Virgo, which will subdue their desire. When Mars in Leo is angry, they might as well be onstage because they can make a performance out of it. Leos are natural-born leaders, so expect them to direct their energy toward achieving their goals.

Gift: Mars in Leo is passionate, which, more often than not, comes with dramatic flair. A person with this placement is not apt to back down when presented with a challenge that only strengthens their resolve. The Lion—and who would want to tangle with a lion?—symbolizes Leo. They know how to be the life of a party, and people are drawn to their natural charisma. They thrive on having a sense of purpose, which is par for Sun-ruled Leo and incredibly important to them. They must have meaning in their lives. They are fiercely loyal to their loved ones and expect the same kind of devotion in return. This is someone who likes to work hard and play hard. They can be a fun partner or friend to have around.

Shadow: Pride and ego can get in their way, triggering a "how dare you" attitude if they are confronted or criticized. They are jealous; they can be self-centered, boastful, strong-willed, or obstinate; and they love to be appreciated and admired. A little flattery will go a long way.

MARS IN VIRGO

Mars in Virgo knows what has to be done, and they do it with a certain amount of ease and without unnecessary fuss or flair. When they don't have something to do, the Virgoan Mercurial influence can make them feel restless and useless.

They are likely to approach each task logically and with great rationality, and you can be sure that they can be a stickler when implementing their self-imposed schedule and their rules are threatened. Giving them reassurance for a job well done can go a long way.

Gift: Mars in Virgo is productive, detail-oriented, skilled, and orderly. Mars in an-

alytical Virgo strategizes and approaches problems with surgical precision. They love helping people and are motivated when they are of service to others.

Shadow: Mars combining with Mercury-ruled Virgo can trigger nervous energy, especially when their high standard of perfection is not maintained. Expect a few critical jabs if you are working alongside them and don't live up to their high standard.

MARS IN LIBRA

Mars in Venus-ruled Libra is motivated by romance, one-on-one relationships, and any affront to their high standard of fairness and justice. They excel at prioritizing personal connections and are often successful at bridging the gaps that divide us.

Mars can be frustrated in Libra, which is why it's classified as being in detriment here. Mars is the planet of war and action, but Libra is ruled by Venus, the planet that prefers harmony. The symbol for Libra is the Scales, and these natives can be indecisive when the situation calls for an immediate response. They can procrastinate because they feel the need to weigh all of the alternatives before taking action.

Gift: Diplomacy, compromise, and the art of persuasion are innate talents associated with Mars in Libra. They prefer a softer approach to head-on confrontation and can usually find the most palatable way to present an argument or disagreement before rushing into disagreements with others. They have a gift for seeing both sides of a situation whenever they are in a mediating role. Mars in Libra would prefer to charm and win you over with niceties and compliments rather than with direct confrontation. Nonetheless, they are very good at compromise and intuitively prefer to play fair and use the power of persuasion to get their point across.

Shadow: As a by-product of their concern for fairness and justice coupled with their Libran orientation toward the other, a Mars in Libra native can be guilty of passive-aggressiveness when their anger and frustration don't have an outlet. As an avoidance mechanism, this can take the form of sneaky and indirect behaviors that undermine their relationships—the very thing they want to preserve. Too much weighing in of options can lead to indecision at moments when an immediate or timely response is called for. Don't think that Mars in Libra won't notice when their actions are not reciprocated. Fairness is high on their agenda, and although they won't make a fuss about it, they will nonetheless be disappointed.

MARS IN SCORPIO

As the coruler of Scorpio, Mars is well placed in the passionate and intensely focused sign of Scorpio. These people love a challenge and won't back down from a good fight, although their intent may not be obvious on the surface.

They are strategists and know how to veil their strong desires and keep their competitors off guard and at a distance. These individuals can show a poker face when the stakes are high. With their undying passion for things that interest them, their attention is not easily diverted.

Gift: Survival instincts are strong when Mars is in Scorpio, and this gives these individuals very good recuperative and regenerative abilities. They may appear as if their chips are down but suddenly leap back on their feet like a cat with nine lives. Natives with this placement have a myste-

rious, albeit magnetic, sexy air. They know how to engage you in a way that captures your attention; they lure you in and then stir your imagination so that you want more. Trust is very important to these natives, and if you make it into their inner circle, they will protect you with the same vigor that they guard themselves. Natural sleuths, Mars in Scorpio have a sixth sense for unraveling a puzzle or solving a mystery. They make excellent detectives.

Shadow: Mars in Scorpio natives love to win, and they won't hesitate to manipulate the outcome in secretive and unobtrusive ways. Psychological warfare is not beneath them, and they are not known for moderation or superficial charm. Obsessive-compulsive or paranoid behavior patterns are possible manifestations of the shadow side of Mars in Scorpio when Mars is heavily afflicted. When threatened, these natives are formidable opponents. They can, at times, be ruthless. A Mars in Scorpio native won't hesitate to use secrets or perceived insecurities to sting others.

MARS IN SAGITTARIUS

"Shoot for the stars" is the motto for a Mars in Sagittarius individual with optimistic Jupiter propelling their Martian instincts. These natives are independent, goal-oriented, courageous, and playful. They love to motivate others, and their playful, energetic demeanor does just that.

These natives do well in sports, and their athletic disposition serves them well when it comes to burning off excess energy. They can be philosophic about their anger, which may not serve them in the long run unless they have set up appropriate ways to blow off steam. They love to banter ideas and are good at coming up with one-line perspectives that seem to capture the situation.

Mars is well placed in the passionate and intensely focused sign of Scorpio. These people love a challenge, and they won't back down from a good fight. They are strategists and know how to keep their competitors off guard. With a sixth sense for unraveling a puzzle or solving a mystery, they make excellent detectives.

Gift: Their enthusiasm and goal-oriented instincts are a winning combination for inspiring others both in business and sports. They do well in any situation that needs a jump-start. They are straightforward, sometimes blunt, and are not apt to hold a grudge because philosophically, it doesn't make sense for them to do so; they have so many other things to do. Their natural athletic skill is a by-product of the ease and enthusiasm that propels them to take action. They can sometimes spend too much time in their mind philosophizing and planning, which makes sports and other high-energy activities a good outlet for burning off excess energy.

Shadow: The combination of Mars and Jupiter bodes well for an impulsive self-starter but not so well for curtailing how much energy to expend in any given activity. They are enthusiastic but not necessarily efficient or strategic. Optimistic Jupiter can lead these natives astray when it comes to taking a gamble. Their innate good nature isn't easily daunted, even when they lose. Mars in Sagittarius does not do well when confined. They are very independent and need a lot of freedom. Their mantra is "don't fence me in." They can shoot their arrows indiscriminately in all directions and be the proverbial "loose cannon," lacking clear direction and being a danger to themselves and others.

MARS IN CAPRICORN

Mars in Saturn-ruled Capricorn is industrious and has incredible staying power

Mars in Aquarius natives value friendship and are generally kind, but a rebellious side shows itself whenever the need for personal freedom and individuality is squashed. Fiercely independent, they want to do their own thing in their own way without anyone telling them what to do.

when they deem the task worthwhile. These natives are ambitious and set their sights high. It is important for them to rise to the top and be the best. Via an abundance of patience and discipline, they are likely to get there, just as the Mountain Goat, the symbol for Capricorn, easily makes its way to the top of the mountain.

Gift: Mars is exalted in Capricorn, and individuals with this placement are highly efficient planners and hard workers. They have a knack for completing a task efficiently while expending the least amount of personal energy. Mars in Capricorn will approach a task like a nimble mountain goat does when it heads up the side of a mountain. They like to get the hard

part over with, so they put themselves in overdrive, and off they go with their head tilted downward, just like a goat tilts its horns down when moving quickly up a hill.

Shadow: Mars in Capricorn can be serious and border on becoming melancholic when frustrated. This is not a match with the flow placement. Instead, these individuals are coolly realistic and will pick themselves up by their bootstraps and keep on going. The Saturn influence keeps them grounded in a no-frills way, and they don't expect all their needs to be magically met. Their shadow side can be ruthless, cold, and calculating when their ambitions are threatened or if their material needs are threatened.

MARS IN AQUARIUS

Mars in humanitarian Aquarius is less personal and more focused on outside interests and the general good. Ruled by Uranus, Aquarius wants the freedom to be themselves, and Mars will fight for it here. The combination of Mars with Uranus is fiercely independent, especially if what is at stake is for them to do their own thing in their own way without anyone telling them what to do.

Gift: Mars in Aquarius can be highly philosophical, socially active, and humanitarian in its nature. It supports the breakdown boundaries of race, age, status, nationality, and religion, with the intent of ushering in a feeling of oneness with all of humanity. Natives with this placement value friendship, and they are generally kind.

Shadow: Mars in Aquarius has a rebellious side, which shows itself whenever the need for personal freedom and individuality is squashed. The transition from friendliness and general well-being to impatience, arrogance, and irritability can occur without warning. As quickly as this sudden state of being occurs, it can dissipate without grudge or resentment, as if nothing had happened. It is part of the unpredictability of the placement of Mars in Aquarius.

MARS IN PISCES

Mars and Pisces don't appear to have much in common. Mars acts, and Neptune-ruled Pisces feels and merges vibrationally with its surroundings. Mars is focused on its own wants and desires, whereas Pisces is focused on the needs and wants of others. Mars in Pisces can be idealistic and inspirational, with a sixth sense that is tuned in to other realms simultaneously, as they are present in this realm.

Gift: Mars in Pisces can be highly creative and prolific and can channel higher-dimensional artistic, musical, and spiritual pursuits with ease and grace. A "go with the flow" approach to life is present that can generate ease, especially when the individual with this placement is aware and purpose-oriented. Their inspired and spiritually attuned orientation can be stimulating and uplifting to others. Mars in Pisces will fight on behalf of the defenseless. Sensitive Pisces is aware of others' needs, and they are on top of stepping into the role of protecting those needs.

Shadow: The desire to avoid direct confrontation can lead to unclear or clandestine actions that could lead to further consequences down the road. Mars in boundary-challenged Pisces can be so loose and scattered that it is difficult to manifest one's desires.

MARS IN THE HOUSES

Each house indicates a department of life, and Mars in a particular house shows which aspect or department of life the individual most often expresses their actions, passions, and desires. It shows where the individual exerts energy and initiative and which areas of life their gifts are more likely to emanate from. Similarly, the house where Mars resides can show specific areas of life where the shadow side of Mars is most obvious and where healing needs to occur in order to bring forward the inherent gifts of Mars in that particular sign. Any planetary combinations affecting Mars need to be considered as well. Therefore, we have three variables in total that we are looking at that will ultimately give a picture of Mars in your natal chart: the sign that Mars is in, the house that Mars inhabits, and the influences that Mars receives from other planetary bodies casting their energy on Mars.

MARS IN THE FIRST HOUSE

The First House rules appearance, health, general temperament, and sense of self. The First House defines you and the image you project to others.

Mars in the First House can influence physical features since the First House rules the body and can also affect how the individual approaches life. Mars is strong in the First House since the First House corresponds to Aries, and Mars rules Aries, giving these natives heaps of vitality and energy. They like to feel strong and often will innately have well-developed musculature. The sign that Mars is in will influence the kind of energy that is projected outward. Usually, these natives like to be where the action is, projecting their own particular gifts as well as the shadow side of their Mars placement outwardly. In any case, some impulsiveness is likely to be in their disposition coupled with some amount of pleasure in engaging in competition. The First House is where we try to figure out who we are as well as how we project it to the outer world.

> Usually, these natives like to be where the action is, projecting their own particular gifts as well as the shadow side of their Mars placement outwardly.

Gift: These natives are energetic and enthusiastic, with a strong body that can develop muscles more easily than other placements of Mars. The First House position of Mars will direct a lot of passion and energy toward self-development and self-improvement. Mars in the First House blesses the native with great confidence, courage, and high energy.

Shadow: These individuals can display an overaggressive, impulsive, and rash disposition, with a tendency to act without thinking through the ramifications of their actions. Their pushiness can work against them and come off as contentious even if their motivation is to help. Sometimes, these natives will have a scar on their head or face or striking features that catch the attention of others.

MARS IN THE SECOND HOUSE

The Second House is connected with finances, values, material possessions, talents, and resources. The Second House represents the value we give to ourselves and, in turn, that which we possess.

An individual with Mars in the Second House will actively pursue financial gain and material security. This gives them good earning ability as well as good spending ability, depending on the sign that Mars is in. For example, Mars in Cancer will be more apt to save material possessions in case anyone needs them.

Mars in the Second House will also fight to protect their personal property as well as their deeply held values, which are likely to include physical prowess and assertiveness.

Gift: These individuals easily find ways to earn money and accumulate possessions, and, as a result, they can do well in business. This is someone who will fight for his or her values and convictions.

Shadow: Material possessions can take on too much importance, and the ends may not always justify the means.

MARS IN THE THIRD HOUSE

The Third House is connected with ideas, communication, siblings, neighbors, and short journeys.

Mars in the Third House individuals have an active intellect and like to put their energy into communication and storytelling, such as speaking, writing, marketing, film, and photography. These individuals are usually quick thinkers and can be good to have around in an emergency.

Mars in the Third House individuals have an active intellect and like to put their energy into some form of communication that can include speaking or writing as well as other forms of visual communication, including marketing, film, and photography. Since the Third House rules neighbors and the immediate community, these natives are generally friendly; however, depending on the sign Mars is in and planets that are influencing their Mars placement, they can be in competition with siblings and neighbors.

Gift: A passion is present for communication and storytelling. These individuals are usually quick thinkers and can be good to have around in an emergency.

Shadow: A tendency can occur to jump to conclusions or be sharp-tongued when they are not getting their point across. Bu-

ried aggression can show itself indirectly when driving. This placement can be indicative of annoyances with neighbors when the shadow side of Mars is dominating.

MARS IN THE FOURTH HOUSE

The Fourth House is about the home, family, genetic inheritance, foundational stability, innermost feelings, later life, and the end of matters.

The Fourth House is naturally ruled by Cancer, so it is appropriate that an individual with Mars in the Fourth House will be apt to focus their attention and energy on both the home and family. Home improvement is high on their list along with tending to the needs of family.

Gift: This placement gives a strong constitution with sustainable energy. The Fourth

House rules the end of matters, so their energy is strong into old age if other planetary combinations to Mars are favorable.

Shadow: Depending on the assertiveness of the Mars placement by sign and the influence of planetary combinations, a desire can occur to dominate the home front. Domestic disputes could be the outlet that is most often used to let off steam if home-improvement projects are not high on their list.

MARS IN THE FIFTH HOUSE

The Fifth House rules creative self-expression, children, love, passion, romance, playfulness, and joy.

The Fifth House is the natural home of Leo, and sunny, passionate Leo rules love, romance, and all forms of creative self-expression. Leo rules children, and an individual with this placement will engage energetically with their offspring and all children. These natives actively pursue love, romantic connections, and having fun. This is a good placement for deriving pleasure and excelling in competitive sports.

Gift: This individual knows how to have fun and has a talent for bringing enthusiasm and dynamism to any situation. In a social setting, it is not unlikely for them to be the life of the party. Their natural athletic ability combined with an affinity for children often leads them into coaching scenarios. They are very dramatic, creative, self-confident, and assertive.

Shadow: Not shy romantically, their passion can turn to jealousy depending on their Mars placement and the planetary combinations of Mars in their natal chart. Some individuals with this placement love risk and gambling. Common sense is a good balance to the passion inherent in this placement. These natives can be arrogant, egotistical, and fixed in their opinions.

MARS IN THE SIXTH HOUSE

The Sixth House governs daily routines, acts of service, the work-life balance, health, due diligence, pet care, coworkers, and employees.

When Mars is in the Sixth House, the native focuses their energy on their work and day-to-day tasks and routines. They are usually very productive and organized and are not comfortable until their to-do list is wiped clean.

> Not shy romantically, their passion can turn to jealousy depending on their Mars placement and the planetary combinations of Mars in their natal chart.

Gift: These individuals are hard workers, and they are generally well organized. They do well in service-oriented positions based on their work ethic and desire to be helpful.

Shadow: Individuals with this placement can become obsessive and need to stop and smell the roses. Stress can affect the health of those with this placement, and the sign on the cusp of the Sixth House may indicate the area of the body that is most likely to bear the brunt of too much stress and the subsequent inflammation that stress can trigger. It is important that they incorporate rest, relaxation, and good nutrition into their daily routines. This placement can be demanding on those around them, including their coworkers and people working under them.

MARS IN THE SEVENTH HOUSE

The Seventh House rules close personal relationships, agreements, and compromises.

Individuals with Mars in the Seventh House prefer to work in conjunction with others, either in business partnerships or marriage. They are generally aggressively involved in personal or business partnerships or in working with the public. The Seventh House is naturally aligned to Libra, so these natives can be passionate about fighting for fairness and the rights of the people.

Gift: Close personal relationships can be passionate, and these individuals can be exciting partners who love adventure and shared activity.

Shadow: With Mars in the Seventh House, the individual may be drawn to others who are more assertive and aggressive than the native. Often, the partner takes the brunt of repressed or unexpressed anger, especially if Mars is in a sign that tends toward passive-aggressive behavior patterns. This placement can be overly competitive and lack compassion and empathy.

MARS IN THE EIGHTH HOUSE

The Eighth House rules joint ventures, intimacy, sex, death, transformation, and psychic dimensions.

In the natural Zodiac, the Eighth House belongs to Scorpio, so Mars is powerfully placed here. Their nature is strong, passionate, and determined, and their sexual desire can be strong.

Gift: Energy can focus on self-transformation and healing with this placement, especially when a strong natal Mars is present or when Mars is combined with Jupiter, Neptune, or Pluto.

Shadow: Sexual desire can become overly important and overwhelming to these individuals. A strong desire to bond and merge with other Mars in the Eighth House individuals is present, and it can be difficult to let go of jealousy and possessiveness. These tendencies may need to be reined in with conscious awareness.

MARS IN THE NINTH HOUSE

The Ninth House rules higher education, long-term goals, foreign travel, publicity, adventures, religion, and philosophical and ethical pursuits.

With Mars in the Ninth House, a strong focus on education, learning, and travel is present. The orientation is toward finding a perspective in life due to the Sagittarius influence of the Ninth House. Spiritual pursuits as well as philosophy and religion are areas that can offer a bigger picture. Changing location, especially traveling to visit different cultures, not only offers a fresh perspective but has the added advantage of being educational. Meditation and other spiritual practices offer an opportunity to travel to other dimensions, which can also provide an alternate perspective on life.

Gift: Individuals with Mars in the Ninth House can be inspiring with their personal philosophies since they enjoy a wide range of interests and partake in a variety of experiences.

Shadow: A tendency can be present to place too much emphasis on the future and not spend enough time being present

With Mars in the Ninth House, there is a strong focus on learning, traveling to visit different cultures, meditation, and other spiritual practices that can provide an alternate perspective on life.

Gift: Having Mars in this section of the chart can bring the impetus to rise up and be productive. The Tenth House is concerned with doing their part for the planet and, if possible, getting noticed for it. Reputation is important to the area of the chart governed by Capricorn, and these natives have a knack for being visible with positive acts and contributions.

Shadow: A desire for fame and power at any cost can be present, especially if Mars is in a strong sign and if Mars combines with the nodes of the Moon, Uranus, or Pluto. The shadow side of Mars in the Tenth House can yield a bad reputation or reversals in fortune. Planets in the Tenth House are out there for everyone to see, for better or for worse.

to what is happening in their own backyard. The grass is always greener somewhere else, which can lead to never being fully satisfied in the current moment.

MARS IN THE TENTH HOUSE

The Tenth House rules public achievements, reputation, authority, and prestige.

A strong focus is placed on attaining status and fame with Mars in the natural home of Capricorn. These natives desire meaningful work, and they can energetically pursue a career that will give them fulfillment and notoriety if supported by other planetary positions in the chart. The Tenth House, and the Midheaven specifically, is what we reach for. Picture standing with both feet flat on the ground with your arms stretched high above your head.

MARS IN THE ELEVENTH HOUSE

The Eleventh House rules friends, hopes, wishes, groups, and a sense of belonging in the world.

Someone with Mars in the Eleventh House is apt to expend energy on developing or maintaining friendships. They are likely to participate or take the initiative in organizing group functions and activities. The Eleventh House is the natural area of the chart ruled by the humanitarian sign Aquarius, also indicating that social reform and social justice are important to them and that they can be successful in leading groups in these areas.

Gift: An individual with this placement is goal-oriented and can generally be successful in attaining their goals, especially if Mars is in a strong sign. The Eleventh House is also known as the house of hopes and wishes, and they are usually able to go after what they want. Mars in the Eleventh House can bring enthusiasm to group activities and social endeavors, and they are a natural at event planning.

Shadow: Conflicts with friends can occur when the shadow side of Mars is overly competitive or when Mars is placed in a sign that exhibits a passive-aggressive expression of the Mars energy. Impulsive actions can hinder otherwise good intentions for social reform and in group activities, creating a situation where the individual is rejected by the group.

MARS IN THE TWELFTH HOUSE

The Twelfth House rules secrets, unconscious patterns, karma, closure, institutions, connections with higher sources, enlightenment, and undoing.

Mars in the Twelfth House can be overly impulsive and too quick with intimacy since the effect that planets in the Twelfth House have is not often seen clearly by the individual. The Twelfth House is the area of the chart that is ruled by Pisces and Neptune, so often a veil exists that prevents, exaggerates, or inhibits the full expression of any planet that is in the Twelfth House.

The individual with a Twelfth-House Mars placement may think that they are being assertive when they are not. They are simply more aware of the Mars energy in their subconscious field. They can also misinterpret another person as being aggressive to them when they are not.

Similarly, they may not see their own aggressive nature and may overcompensate or undercompensate for it.

Gift: Someone with Mars in the Twelfth House may direct their energy toward helping others. These natives will often work behind the scenes and not look for recognition for their efforts.

Shadow: Actions and desires are strongly influenced by the unconscious. These individuals can benefit from exploring their unconscious and looking at where they may have tucked away self-loathing or where anger toward others has been repressed. This can be a nonconfrontational placement unless Mars is in a confrontational or aggressive sign. With the Piscean and Neptunian influence, a desire can be present to work or conduct activities in secret or in seclusion.

MARS COMBINATIONS

Mars/Sun

Mars rules assertiveness, energy, drive, and courage.

The Sun indicates purpose, self-expression, creative life force, and conscious will.

Combining Mars with the Sun is similar to having the Sun in Aries or the Sun in the First House, the natural home of Aries. This combination is courageous, energetic, impulsive, ambitious, and charming. Natives with a strong Sun/Mars combination can have a strong will with an abundance of energy at their disposal for getting things done in a hurry.

Gift: Expending energy or doing activities can be incredibly easy. I call this combination the "whistle while you work" combination. When the Sun and Mars work in harmony, great ease in moving about occurs, with little resistance in performing required actions. When asked to perform a task, these individuals are often up and at it before you know it. This combination knows how to energize their drive for significance or their purpose in life.

Natives with a strong Sun/Mars combination can have an abundance of energy for getting things done in a hurry, often up and at it before you know it.

The combination of the Moon and Mars is similar to having an Aries Moon; a Moon in the First House; and, to some degree, Mars in Cancer. In all cases, the native will express their feelings with passion and will generate strong feelings and passionate responses.

Gift: Ample passion and enthusiasm occur when the energies of the Moon and Mars combine. Individuals with this combination can inspire others with their energy and charisma. These individuals can be inspirational, and they can easily motivate others with their energetic and instinctive responses. Activities are undertaken readily and with emotional ease. Anger is channeled into productive activities. When emotionally connected to a cause or particular item, they can be inspiring leaders or do well in fields that relate to sales and marketing.

Shadow: The ego can get out of control, and too much self-aggrandizement and boasting can occur. The shadow side of this combination occurs when drive, desires, and impulses do not align with the individual's purpose and drive for significance; too much drive or not enough energy may be applied to an activity or life goal. Hence, the individual can be overly aggressive or not aggressive enough, cranky, and resistant to taking action. Resentments and grievances can be expressed unintentionally when the shadow side emerges. The native can use cantankerousness and irritability as a means to get attention.

Shadow: The shadow side of combining the Moon with Mars can result in an overly impulsive and arrogant nature that is prone to outbursts of anger. Emotional sensitivity is heightened, and these individuals can overreact and take an insignificant slight personally. They can jump to conclusions and overreact. Impatience, crankiness, and unwarranted aggressiveness can overshadow otherwise good deeds and negatively affect relationships. An imbalance of Mars can generate excess heat in the body, causing inflammation and infections.

MARS/MERCURY

Mars rules assertiveness, energy, drive, and courage.

Mercury rules communication, mental processes, and the logical mind.

MARS/MOON

Mars rules assertiveness, energy, drive, and courage.

The Moon rules the soul, core instincts, the personality, and subconscious conditioning.

The combination of Mars and Mercury is similar to having Mercury in Aries, Mercury in the First House, or Mars in Gemini. These natives have sharp, decisive minds, and they are able to think on their feet.

Gift: Mars combining with Mercury bestows the native with an alert mind that speaks with energy and enthusiasm. They can be direct, decisive, and emphatic. They say what they mean without hesitation. Their ability to speak with enthusiasm makes them good public speakers and interesting lecturers. They are good at getting their point across.

Shadow: Mercury combined with Mars can be impatient and restless, and natives are likely to fidget when they are bored. They have an abundance of mental energy, and these individuals can overanalyze and get stressed out if they don't have tools to help calm their minds. They can be sharp-tongued and combative. Responses may not be well thought out, leading to misunderstandings and disagreements. Their minds can work so quickly that they don't think before they speak, leading to consequences for them down the road.

> The Venusian principle of attraction can be energized by Mars, and similarly, the assertive principle of Mars can be refined by the influence of Venus.

MARS/VENUS

Mars rules assertiveness, energy, drive, and courage.

Venus represents love, relationships, beauty, values, comfort, and material resources.

When the inner feminine and the inner masculine energies are balanced, conscious inspired action occurs that is guided by heart wisdom without overexerting and becoming energetically depleted.

Gift: The gift of balance between the Yin and Yang principles occurs when Mars and Venus harmoniously combine. The Venusian principle of attraction can be energized by Mars, and similarly, the assertive principle of Mars can be refined by the influence of Venus. These natives can be artistically inclined and often find it easy to relate to others. They instinctively know how to balance the energies they interact with when relating one-on-one or as part of a group. They can be productive without dominating and diplomatic and personable leaders.

Shadow: Too much Yang can occur when more Yin is required and vice versa. The Yin–Yang balance can go off, causing confusion and issues, especially in close personal relationships. A lack of refinement can occur in social interactions or too much passivity when a more active role is more appropriate. Sensual desires can be strong and can overshadow emotional sensitivity.

MARS/JUPITER

Mars rules assertiveness, energy, drive, and courage.

Jupiter represents the higher mind, greater truths, expansiveness, hope, and optimism.

This power combination can bring immense inspiration and goal-centered action. This individual is always looking to expand their territory and enrich their life. They are the ones who are not afraid to take a calculated risk, an adventurer at heart.

Gift: Individuals with a prominent and well-aspected Mars and Jupiter combina-

With discipline and a positive attitude, the bright side of a Mars/Saturn combination can manifest, resulting in noteworthy accomplishments.

tion are not afraid to go after their desires with gusto and enthusiasm. They possess a courage and boldness that can be smooth and easy to an onlooker. With Jupiter's help, endeavors are likely to succeed.

Shadow: An excess of this energy can lead to an individual who casts away any semblance of efficiency and overestimates much of what they do. A grandiosity can overcompensate for a lack of information or a basic insecurity. As a result, the foot can stay on the gas pedal to the point where they become careless and hasty, and they need modulating.

MARS/SATURN

Mars rules assertiveness, energy, drive, and courage.

Saturn rules responsibility, adjustments to limitations, sustainability, and structure.

Saturn can stymie the "go for it" side of Mars. This combination is compared to hav-

ing one foot on the gas pedal and the other on the brake. Saturn is the taskmaster. Saturn wants to bring order and discipline to the impulsive Mars energy. With discipline and a positive attitude, the bright side of a Mars/Saturn combination can manifest, resulting in noteworthy accomplishments.

Mars is exalted in Saturn-ruled Capricorn. This combination is steadfast and consistent, and the conscious balance between these two energies can hold the key to successful manifestation.

Gift: Just enough restraint, just enough push is the best outcome for this combination, which can be highly productive when directed and combined with a step-by-step approach. The discipline of Saturn can be used to direct anger, frustration, impatience, and the passion of Mars to yield positive outcomes.

Shadow: Some degree of defiant unwillingness can be expected when the shadow side of the Mars and Saturn combination is dominating. A feeling occurs of being stuck, comparable to applying the gas and the brake at the same time. Frustration, impatience, and outbursts of anger can ensue when these energies are not being managed and used consciously. The shadow side of this combination can include anger and frustration resulting from situations and instances when self-control is tested. Staying flexible physically is helpful to anyone with a Mars/Saturn combination in their chart. Mars rules the muscles, and Saturn rules the joints and bones. Exercise modalities that are supportive to musculature and skeletal systems will be beneficial.

MARS/URANUS

Mars rules assertiveness, energy, drive, and courage.

Uranus rules intuition, originality, individuality, and the sudden and unexpected.

The combination of Mars and Uranus yields sudden, unpredictable actions that can be serendipitous or shocking, depending on the circumstance. Similar to Mars in Aquarius, the combination of Mars and Uranus is highly innovative and freedom-oriented.

Gift: When Mars and Uranus are working well together, the body has its own natural intuitive flow. The body knows what to do without thinking about it and will spontaneously take the best action for the given situation. This combination can contribute to the native being innovative, inventive, and an asset in any crisis situation.

Shadow: Simmering tensions can suddenly boil over out of the blue. Harnessing this daring and erratic energy can be a worthwhile challenge. When out of control, this combination can be accident-prone at worst or at least highly inconsistent. Revolutionary actions can be appealing as a way to clear stuck energy, and a large amount of energy can be released all at once. Similarly, an overwhelming urge to seek freedom from constricting circumstances can occur.

MARS/NEPTUNE

Mars rules assertiveness, energy, drive, and courage.

Neptune rules ideals, creative imagination, transcendence, compassion, and vision.

The combination of Mars and Neptune is comparable to having Mars in Pisces. These

> Neptune can dilute the forcefulness of Mars, which can be a detriment in competitive situations or situations that require focus.

individuals are inspiring, generally helpful, and artistically or musically inclined.

Gift: Individuals with Mars and Neptune in combination are helpful and can often be found in healing and service professions. These natives are intuitive and very good at inspiring others. It is natural for them to want to find a higher meaning in their action. They have a talent for creative visualization that is an asset in creative endeavors.

Shadow: Neptune can dilute the forcefulness of Mars, which can be a detriment in competitive situations or situations that require focus. The natures of these two planetary energies are very different from each other: Mars is highly directed, and Neptune is not. Confusion over desires and actions that lead to accomplishments are likely. Goals may be more fanciful than realistic. Setbacks can lead to disillusionment, whereby the native loses intention or abandons any inspiration to keep on going.

MARS/PLUTO

Mars rules assertiveness, energy, drive, and courage.

Pluto represents regeneration; transformation; and a compelling, fundamental approach.

Mars and Pluto are a power-packed duo, where Pluto is the higher octave of Mars. These planetary energies can be explosive together or, when used consciously, can be highly energetic and productive. Similar to Mars in Scorpio, the native can be driven, compulsive, and sometimes feel as though they are superhuman, which energetically can be true at times. "Don't stop until you drop" is a motto for these folks.

Gift: The gift that the persistence of this combination bestows is the ability to rise to the task or mission, whatever that mission happens to be at the time. This is a "don't stop until you drop" energy combination, where desire combines with directed actions. This combination has a regenerative quality and can bestow an ability to self-heal when directed accordingly.

Shadow: Passions and desires can be overwhelming, and regret, shame, and serious consequences can occur as a result. An unconscious acting out of inner wounds and held resentments can also occur. Personal affronts can be difficult to release and can fester, thereby triggering misdirected anger and rage. Obsessive behavior patterns or a power-hungry drive for power, control, and domination can occur.

MARS/CHIRON

Mars rules assertiveness, energy, drive, and courage.

Chiron represents core wounds and the desire to overcome them, and healing.

The combination of Mars and Chiron can indicate that deep wounding is likely regarding any of the following: aggression, anger, sexuality, courage, or the ability to fulfill desires.

Gift: Discomfort in any of the areas ruled by Mars, which include lack of assertiveness, uncontrolled anger, sexual disfunction, the inability to fulfill desires, and abusive behavior, can lead the native to probe into their subconscious motivations. Releasing primal wounds in any of the above areas can bring newfound comfort and

conscious awareness to the native. Post-healing, the native can help others heal their wounds.

Shadow: Perpetuating negative behavior patterns associated with Mars without engaging in soul-searching and the subsequent healing keeps the native in their wounds.

MARS/ERIS

Mars rules assertiveness, energy, drive, and courage.

Eris represents the determination to remove limitations that impede the soul's evolution.

Gift: Combining the energies of Mars and Eris, mythically known as brother and sister, warrior and warrioress, is a force to be reckoned with when the goal is generating change. This combination can focus in on what is inauthentic and unfair where the betterment of society is at stake.

Shadow: These natives can lose track of what they are fighting for. Personal issues can overshadow the purity of their quest.

MARS/NORTH NODE

Mars rules assertiveness, energy, drive, and courage.

The North Node represents future direction, soul guidance, and fulfillment.

Gift: Strength and courage are assets for these individuals. They have the drive and stamina to get fully involved in life and take on situations that can at first glance appear daunting and require a stick-to-it, energetic approach. They can surprise themselves and others with the ease with which they can accomplish these types of activities and gain further cooperation and support. They can pursue various types of adventures from which they can gain notice.

Shadow: For the sake of getting notice and attention, these individuals can overdo bravery and courage and take on self-destructive activities. Their ambition can be overly ego-driven and come off as excessive to those they are wanting to impress. They can lack sensitivity to others as well as to situations around them.

MARS/SOUTH NODE

Mars rules assertiveness, energy, drive, and courage.

The South Node represents familiarity, gratification, and the path of least resistance.

These natives can be too familiar with an aggressive and competitive approach to situations that others find overwhelming. They are naturally courageous and will fight for what they want. Once they learn to integrate these traits into a more harmonious and diplomatic approach, they will find that their success yields appreciation from others.

Gift: Natives with this combination of Mars with the South Node are not afraid to lend a hand in situations and activities that require courage, strength, and fortitude. They can be naturally energetic and enthusiastic, although they can have a tendency to be overly impulsive if not kept in check. They are willing to fight for their beliefs and pursue causes that are at the forefront of innovation. These are the original pioneers. Tactics and strategy come naturally to them.

Shadow: Anger and sexual energy can be mired in the past or old habits. These natives may need to learn to walk away

Strength and courage are assets for individuals with Mars in the North Node. However, with ambition that can be overly ego driven, they may overdo the bravery and courage and take on self-destructive activities.

from a fight or take time out before initiating any kind of hasty action that won't ultimately benefit them. This combination can also imply a lack of assertiveness based upon unsuccessful endeavors from the past. Overcompensation can ensue, and the native can become fearful and phobic about ever taking the initiative. Repressed Mars energy can show up as negative, aggressive patterns or behavioral issues.

MARS/ASCENDANT

Mars rules assertiveness, energy, drive, and courage.

The Ascendant represents one's approach, orientation, and the window through which one sees the world.

Mars connected to the Ascendant will approach situations with passion and gusto. They can take on more responsibilities than they can realistically handle thanks to their energetic approach. It is not uncommon for those with this combination to look younger than their biological age due to their high energy level.

Gift: Natives with this combination approach life with courage and strength. They are able to take on situations that others may not attempt. Their enthusiasm is infectious, and they can make good leaders in positions that require courage, passion, and strength. They are generally not afraid to stand up for themselves. These individuals are usually dynamic, confident, and straightforward. They are driven to accomplish their goals and do well in fast-paced environments.

Shadow: The shadow side of a Mars/Ascendant combination is a native who jumps into the deep end without paying attention to obstacles in the pool. They can lack sensitivity and rely on brute strength rather than any amount of finesse in their dealings with other individuals as well as with situations. They can have a tendency to overdo activities, which can lead to unhealthy burnout and exhaustion. They can be dominating and obnoxious.

> Anger and sexual energy can be mired in the past or old habits.… This combination can also imply a lack of assertiveness based upon unsuccessful endeavors from the past.

MARS/MIDHEAVEN (MC)

Mars rules assertiveness, energy, drive, and courage.

The Midheaven (MC) represents image, outer aspirations, and career orientation.

Drive and ambition are characteristic of an individual with the combination of Mars and the Midheaven. Their energy is directed toward achieving prominence and standing in their professional life.

These natives can be found in highly competitive professions and those professions that are involved in Martian activities, such as the military, politics, sports, or branches of law enforcement, where courage and strength are valued.

Gift: Natives with the combination of Mars and the Midheaven can work tirelessly toward activities and actions that help them achieve their long-term goals. They are highly ambitious and don't hesitate to take the initiative in areas that reap rewards or elevate their status. They can be called upon to take quick and decisive action in a timely manner. This combination can be highly inspirational to others due to the confidence and lack of hesitancy with which they handle situations.

Shadow: The shadow side of this combination is that the native can display frustration and irritability that is noticed by others. They don't go unnoticed in any displays of anger and aggression. Missteps involving their highly competitive nature will be visible since Mars is connected to the top of the chart for all to see. These natives may prefer doing things their own way and may not excel in cooperative ventures. They can challenge their superiors or those in positions of authority in an untimely manner or with inappropriate motivations.

The Social Planets: Jupiter and Saturn

The outer planets—Jupiter, Saturn, Uranus, and Neptune—are located far from the Sun, past the asteroid belt that separates Mars and Jupiter. The asteroid belt is occupied by rocks, debris, and numerous irregularly shaped bodies, including many thousands of asteroids and the dwarf planet Ceres.

The outer planets are also considered the collective planets. They set the tone for what is going on not just on a personal level but on a collective level. They tell the story about the evolution of humanity and what is happening in the realm of the collective unconscious.

Jupiter and Saturn, the social planets, represent distinct trends in our society that include culture, religion, and the economy.

JUPITER

Jupiter is a sky god whose position in the heavens gave him the ability to be omnis-cient, omnipotent, and omnipresent. He was in charge of laws and higher order. As the largest planet in the solar system (10 times larger than Earth), Jupiter bestows the gifts of expansiveness, generosity, a higher wisdom and philosophical orientation, and the potential for prosperity, luck, and good fortune when well positioned in the chart.

As a correlation with Jupiter's magnanimous presence, Jupiter's massive gravity has caused the orbits of many solar system bodies to become altered such that it helped to create a stable environment for life to begin on Earth.

Jupiter is inclusive and embracing and expresses a warming, optimistic, and expansive energy. Jupiter can lift one out of a limited mindset, offer a fresh perspective, and impel one to reach for a higher vision. A well-placed Jupiter can inspire others without being pushy or self-righteous. Jupiter is the outgoing expression of posi-

Named for the king of the Roman gods, our solar system's largest planet, Jupiter, has an expansive influence on the traits of whichever sign it's found in.

tivity and goodness, which magnetically attracts to the individual what they need to further their growth and development.

Jupiter signifies expansion, abundance, knowledge, wisdom, children, pets, luck, and good karma.

The shadow side of Jupiter can overdo and overreach, thus magnifying the negative effects of the planets that it is in a relationship with. Jupiter can be extravagant, overzealous, boisterous, and suffer from false optimism and poor judgment.

JUPITER IN THE SIGNS

Jupiter's sign position indicates how an individual uplifts themselves, how they express their spirited nature, their highest ideals, and what they do to grow and develop. The sign position can also indicate the traits they have been endowed with and how they share those gifts as their contribution to society.

Jupiter in Aries

Jupiter in the sign of enthusiasm and leadership, Aries, is motivated, clear, and energized; these natives have an abundance of initiative and assertiveness.

Gift: These natives emanate the gift of maintaining a positive attitude, even when the odds are against them. Their charm can be endearing. With Jupiter in Mars-ruled Aries, they love competition and definitely don't shy away from a challenge. They have the courage and enthusiasm to make what they want to have happen in life. Inspiration and motivation are gifts that they bring forth to others. They attract positive energy to themselves when taking the lead and initiate, motivate, and inspire others.

Shadow: Their impulsiveness and impatience can work against them, especially when they overreact or move too quickly. Carelessness can ensue. They can be overzealous and find themselves in situations where they are in over their heads. Keeping it real works to their advantage.

Jupiter in Taurus

Jupiter in Venus-ruled Taurus can be a lucky combination for attracting material resources. These individuals enjoy the "good things in life" and place a high value on the quality of their life.

Gift: These natives can infuse higher ideals and spiritual values into the exchange of material resources and goods. Taurus rules values, and Jupiter can enhance and uplift what the native values and how they use their resources. Quality can be more important than quantity, and environmental concerns can enter their decisions regarding the use and disposal of items. Self-worth is important to these natives and something that they value. They have good instincts for financial endeavors and can be appropriately generous.

Shadow: Too much sensory indulgence can cause these natives problems with health, particularly with weight gain and sugar metabolism. They may be particularly sensitive to sugar imbalances, with the abundance of Venusian energy. This can activate the indolence and laziness so often attributed to Taurus. Jupiter in Tau-

rus natives can place too much emphasis on their possessions and material resources at the expense of their personal relationships. Hoarding can be a tendency with this combination.

Jupiter in Gemini

Jupiter in Mercury-ruled Gemini natives love information and facts, and they are often quite knowledgeable about an array of subjects. Gemini rules the hands, and these individuals can have skillful hands and dexterous movements.

Gift: These natives are inquisitive and have an intellectual curiosity that has an expansive influence on their mental development throughout the course of their lives. Their repertoire of information is vast. They are particularly good at spotting trends due to the broad array of data that they have gathered. Jupiter in Gemini minds are spry and energetic, filled with ideas that they enjoy conversing about. Social venues with neighbors and friends are frequently a platform for the exchange of ideas. They put others at ease with their openness, versatility, and friendly disposition. They like to become familiar with their immediate environment. They are often recognized and welcomed in local shops and venues for their warm and friendly nature.

> Jupiter in Gemini minds are spry and energetic, filled with ideas that they enjoy conversing about.

Shadow: Jupiter rules Sagittarius and is considered to be in its detriment in Gemini, the opposite sign that it rules. Nonetheless, Jupiter is a beneficial influence in any sign. The shadow side of Gemini can be a tendency for them to become intellectual snobs. Gossip and nosiness are also possible. It is easy for their curious

Jupiter in Leo is noble, proud, confident, and ambitious. They inspire confidence and positivity in others, command authority, and make good leaders.

nature to get so caught up in this and that and minding others' business that they neglect more important matters.

Jupiter in Cancer

Jupiter in Cancer, its sign of exaltation, means that Jupiter can exhibit its maximum potential. Jupiter provides good fortune, prosperity, optimism, and protection.

Gift: Natives with this placement understand the concepts of kindness, gentleness, and morality at a deep level. They realize the importance of taking care of things and of being kind to others. Jupiter's expansive nature enhances all that Cancer rules, which includes all that is related to the home, food, and children. They love their food, beverages, and comfortable home environments. Family, and oftentimes strangers, are warmly welcomed and fed. Jupiter in Cancer individuals are charitable and generous.

Shadow: Jupiter in Cancer natives are likely to have grand and expressive emotions, which can incline them toward mood swings and oversentimentality. Their generous and caring nature can lack discernment, and they can put their trust into undeserving people who take advantage of them. Too much food and drink can also fall under the expansive and indulgent nature of Jupiter in Cancer. They can be overly extravagant or be prone to overestimating or underestimating the value of things.

Jupiter in Leo

Jupiter in the sign ruled by the Sun is noble, proud, confident, and ambitious. They are the archetype of the warm and jolly ruler or person in charge whom people like to be around.

Gift: Jupiter in Leo is warm, magnanimous, confident, and expressive, and natives inspire confidence and positivity in others. These natives can turn on their dramatic flair in a flash and easily grab the attention of those around them. They command authority and therefore make good leaders. The Leo nature is organized even though it may not always seem obvious, with their warm and congenial mannerisms. Jupiter expands their leadership ability as well as their heartfelt and benevolent capacities.

Shadow: Jupiter in Leo is proud; however, they can have a false sense of pride or a bloated sense of themselves that turns into a "how dare you" attitude at the smallest slight. Their egos can overinflate, and they can come across as self-important and superior. Jupiter expands Leo's leadership abilities, which can turn into bossiness and a controlling nature. The overindulgent side of Jupiter can go haywire in Leo, where eating, drinking, and being merry is concerned, and they can take unnecessary risks.

Jupiter in Virgo

Jupiter enhances the "let me help you" side of Virgo. They love to be of service and prefer to be helpful and provide a service rather than give a nonessential gift.

Gift: Natives with Jupiter in Mercury-ruled Virgo are capable, reliable, and responsible. Virgo's analytical skills are enhanced by Jupiter's expansive nature. They can logically drill down to find solutions, even when they are confronted with large amounts of information. They notice details that others miss, making these natives highly suited for jobs that require precision and accuracy.

Shadow: The shadow side of Jupiter in Virgo can be excessively critical and exhibit pettiness, which is due to an exaggerated attention to detail. They are prone to anxiety and stress due to their high standards for perfection, a standard that is not always realistic or attainable. Natives with this placement can be workaholics. Again, relating back to their standard of perfection, they can put so much pressure on themselves that they lose track of human limitations. Jupiter in Virgo natives can lose track of the big picture that is so much a part of Jupiter's influence. Jupiter is considered to be in its detriment in Virgo since Jupiter rules Pisces, the sign opposite Virgo.

Jupiter in Libra

Jupiter in Venus-ruled Libra natives have a well-developed aesthetic and social sensibility. They have a keen eye for beauty and style. Relationships are often prioritized. Fairness and equality are valued in all their interactions. Their highly mannered nature can be disrupted when they come into contact with injustice, although they will tend to maintain their sense of dignity.

Gift: Jupiter in the sign of the Scales natives are good mediators and have a gift for negotiating and being highly attuned to all that is fair and balanced. Their use of charm and grace assists them in navigating through difficult situations with uncooperative participants. They are fair-minded and treat others with respect and dignity, which draws others to them. The Venus influence in this placement can imply artistic talent, especially in areas that require a refined aesthetic.

Shadow: The shadow side of Jupiter in Libra is the expansion of the indecisiveness that is so characteristic of Libra. Weighing pros and cons can be difficult when one is so highly invested in fairness and equality. Similarly, they can put the needs of others ahead of their own. Cooperation is great, but not at the expense of getting one's own needs met. A tendency to be snobbish occurs when things aren't so pretty or refined. They can be overly concerned with their impression on others.

Jupiter in Scorpio

Jupiter in Pluto-ruled Scorpio natives are driven by a deep desire to put into perspective the deeper meanings of life and death. They have a longing to constantly unveil the mysteries of life, including all that is taboo and deeply psychological. They have a knack for uncovering that which is buried in the untapped resources of the subconscious.

Gift: Jupiter in Scorpio natives love to solve a good mystery. They have well-developed probing skills that gain tremendous satisfaction getting down to the bottom of an issue. Highly determined, these individuals know what they want and have

With Jupiter in Sagittarius, expansion, travel, knowledge, and abundance are all front and center. Their fiery enthusiasm and adventurous nature inspire others while fostering ethical behavior and goodwill.

the resolve to dedicate themselves to getting it. They are highly resourceful. Jupiter enhances Pluto's urge to transform, and change gives these individuals an edge on changing whatever is not working. They are not only capable of finding solutions, but they can easily let go of whatever wasn't working to begin with.

Shadow: Jupiter in Scorpio natives can get so caught up in their desires and obsessive behaviors that they forget to look at the bright side of life. The Scorpio influence of looking beneath the surface and not trusting veneers can become overdone, whereby these natives become overly suspicious of everything and everyone. Their lack of trust can plague them, and they can fall into antisocial behavior patterns. Excessive secrecy and a desire for power and control can grow out of proportion.

Jupiter in Sagittarius

Jupiter rules Sagittarius, giving the bountiful nature of this placement a distinctive advantage. Sagittarius loves freedom. With this placement, expansion, travel, knowledge, and abundance are all front and center. They appreciate the broader fabric of humanity and seek understanding of cultures and philosophies. They have high ideals and an expansive vision.

Gift: Jupiter in Sagittarius has a fiery enthusiasm and an adventurous nature that inspires others while fostering ethical behavior and goodwill. They love to learn and seek to expand their level of knowledge, especially in the cultural, philosophical, and spiritual arenas. They have an optimistic outlook that seeks the big-picture interpretation of problems large and small. Faith is important to them, and they can inspire others with their expansive perspective and conviction that things will work out. Their positivity attracts positive outcomes to these natives.

Shadow: An individual with this placement can be overzealous and inclined to force their beliefs on others or try to convert them to their way of thinking. Their optimistic nature can be blindsided and lead to extravagance, gambling, risk-taking, and poor judgment. Responsibilities and routines are often interpreted as interfering with their freedom to be.

Jupiter in Capricorn

Jupiter in Capricorn natives are diligent and efficient. Capricorn is the sign of debilitation for Jupiter, meaning that the attribute of seeing the big picture requires a more fastidious approach in order to maintain faith and trust through difficult times. The more practical, constructive, and Saturn-oriented aspects of Capricorn are expanded with this placement.

Gift: Natives with Jupiter in Capricorn are resourceful. The expansive energy of this placement manifests in the native's ability to make plans, produce structures, and implement goals and credible solutions. Their logical and technical orientation are geared to handle complex situations. They are honest and sincere, and they keep their promises. Jupiter in Capricorn is highly disciplined. They bring themselves honor and recognition through their high moral and ethical code. Their efforts rarely go unnoticed, and they are rewarded for their honesty and integrity.

Shadow: Jupiter in Capricorn natives can get caught up in material success, social status, greed, and power or become unduly pessimistic when a more optimistic attitude would help them achieve their goals. Contrarily, they can be overly optimistic when they really need a reality check. This placement can buy into, and further expand, the Saturnian belief that less is more and that they endorse the school of hard knocks. This results in these natives being too proud to ask for help.

Jupiter in Aquarius

Expansive Jupiter in Uranus-ruled Aquarius is humanitarian, original, and highly idealistic. Personal freedom is valued for themselves as well as for others. These natives are inventive and highly individualistic, which is often displayed in their unusual presentation and avant-garde style, which, in the extreme, borders on eccentric.

Gift: The Aquarian value of friendship is enhanced when Jupiter is in this sign. Aside from being a friend to all, these in-

dividuals hold the ideal of accepting all in a nonjudgmental way. They appreciate diversity and help others feel comfortable for being who they are. Their open and progressive outlook is socially conscious, and they are likely to participate in and support humanitarian causes. Kind and generous, they value honesty and integrity. They especially respect others being true to themselves and will be supportive and generous to that end.

Shadow: Jupiter in Aquarius, in their acceptance of equality for all, can underestimate their own value and self-worth. Their strong need for personal freedom can keep others at arm's length. Love interests may not take these natives seriously due to their objectively friendly nature. The keywords for Aquarius are "I know," and Jupiter can expand their know-it-all attitude to incline them to be dogmatic about their personal beliefs where they are not open to listening to others' good ideas and beliefs. Their original, quirky ideas, although initially impressive, may not actually work because they are not realistically possible.

> Expansive Jupiter in Uranus-ruled Aquarius is humanitarian, original, and highly idealistic. Personal freedom is valued for themselves as well as for others.

Jupiter in Pisces

Spirituality and inspiration are abundant for anyone born with Jupiter in Pisces. Jupiter is the coruler of Pisces, and expansive and idealistic Jupiter is very much at home in this sign. They are motivated by a universal vision of peace and harmony and faith in the goodness of life.

Gift: A belief in magic, a belief that anything is possible, occurs with Jupiter in Pisces. Their vivid imagination and ability

$2\!\!\!\downarrow\!\!\hbar$

to contact transcendent realms open these natives to otherworldly inspiration, where anything can take shape and become a reality. Their faith is strong, and it guides them through darker times. They help others move through difficult circumstances via their extreme compassion and empathic nature. In many instances, they have been there themselves and can provide the understanding and inspiration necessary for healing. These natives watch out for the underdogs and those who cannot help themselves.

Shadow: Jupiter magnifies the Piscean need to establish boundaries. Their heightened compassion and empathy permeate their being, making them vulnerable to absorbing negativity and despair from others. This, along with an overly idealistic nature, can trigger depression and despair. These natives may engage in avoidance behaviors so that they can cope with the harsh realities of life. They may indulge in substance abuse and various forms of fantasy and escapist behaviors, which can ultimately lead to addictions and delusional activities.

JUPITER IN THE HOUSES

Jupiter's sign position indicates how a person shares what has been given to them, how they reach out in generosity to the larger social order, and the benefits they receive in return. Jupiter in the houses shows where you can find your luck.

Jupiter in the First House

The First House rules appearance, health, general temperament, and sense of self. The First House defines you and the image you project to others.

Jupiter is strong in the First House and lends itself to having a glass-half-full approach to life. When combined with either a Sagittarius or Pisces Ascendant, the individual can be well suited to scholarly or philanthropic endeavors, where they bring a high-minded perspective to the table.

Gift: An individual with this house placement brings wisdom and a fresh perspective to situations that are associated with the sign that Jupiter occupies. They have a generosity of spirit and openness that puts others at ease.

Shadow: Overindulgence and an excessive nature can lead to health problems if not balanced with good health habits. Poor judgment can result from too much optimism that lacks a reality check when dealing with shady individuals or potentially dangerous situations.

Jupiter in the Second House

The Second House is connected with finances, values, material possessions, talents, and resources. The Second House represents the value we give to ourselves and, in turn, that which we possess.

Jupiter in Taurus's natural home enhances the ability to acquire and ultimately possess material resources. Values and a solid philosophy of life are important to these natives.

Gift: Generally, these natives obtain abundant financial resources from various sources, including good fortune, successful investments, and family inheritances. They have the ability to make long-term plans for achieving financial success. As luck would have it, and depending on the sign Jupiter is placed in, these natives can have a definite advantage in their choice of options for acquiring monetary gain. Their glass-half-full approach helps those with this placement have the confidence to fully develop their talents and further expand their potential.

Jupiter in the Second House enhances the ability to acquire material resources. Their glass-half-full approach gives them confidence to fully develop their talents and further expand their potential, but they need to be watchful lest that Jupiterian optimism preclude realistic risk assessment.

Shadow: These natives need to be watchful that they do not accumulate so many material possessions that they become a burden for them. They can have a tendency to hoard. Gambling and speculation can exceed their luck for acquiring gain, and they can end up short. Excessive Jupiterian optimism can preclude a realistic risk assessment prior to investing. Impulsive spending can be an issue, as can placing too much importance on material possessions.

Jupiter in the Third House

The Third House is connected with ideas, communication, siblings, neighbors, and short journeys.

Jupiter in a house governed by Mercury can incline these natives to the accumulation and dissemination of facts and information and can bring the native benefits from siblings, acquaintances, neighbors, and close relatives.

Gift: Natives have wide-ranging interests, intellectual curiosity, and a lively communication style, all contributing to the ease with which they interact with others. All modes of communication are included in their repertoire. They love to share information. People tend to enjoy their company and conversation. They are mentally optimistic and embrace philosophical and spiritual concepts. The Third House rules short journeys, so it is likely that these natives are fond of travel. Their cars are frequently considered to be a valued second abode. The Third House is also the house of running errands and getting things done. This placement enjoys exploring their immediate environment. They like to know what is going on around

♃♄

them. They are often recognized and welcomed in local shops and venues for their warm and friendly nature.

Shadow: These natives are frequently mentally restless and not fond of constrictive routines. Multitasking at the wrong time can work to their detriment. Overconfidence and recklessness can overtake them when driving or traveling. These natives can indulge in gossip and small talk and cast discernment aside, which can come back and bite them.

Jupiter in the Fourth House

The Fourth House is about the home, family, genetic inheritance, foundational stability, innermost feelings, later life, and the end of matters.

Jupiter in the Cancer-ruled Fourth House is dignified since Jupiter is exalted in Cancer. This placement brings great benefits to an individual with this placement. They are generally confident and have a nurturing and helpful disposition.

Gift: These natives have strong instincts. They trust their gut responses, which help guide them and bring them luck. Integrity along with a strong moral code was likely reinforced during their upbringing. They generally have congenial family relationships and enjoy the comforts of home. The Fourth House rules the latter part of life, and these natives generally have good fortune in general during the second part of life.

Shadow: One or both parents may have been indulgent during the native's upbringing. They subsequently developed indulgent habits as their go-tos when they feel insecure, which can lead to immaturity and moodiness.

Jupiter in the Fifth House

The Fifth House rules creative self-expression, children, love, passion, romance, playfulness, and joy.

Natives with Jupiter in Leo's Fifth House are gallant, charming, warm, and confident. They can excel in the arts as well as in sports.

Gift: Natives of expansive Jupiter in the Fifth House of creative self-expression are generally artistically talented and good performers if they are so inclined. They are warm and generous and have a special relationship with children and pets. They understand the value of play, which they also derive great benefit from. It gives them joy, which is important for an individual with Jupiter in the Fifth House.

> Natives with Jupiter in Leo's Fifth House are gallant, charming, warm, and confident. They can excel in the arts as well as in sports.

Shadow: Gambling and unwise speculation can cause large financial losses. These natives tend to overextend themselves not only financially but also in other areas ruled by Leo, which include an out-of-proportion penchant for romantic affairs, daring adventures, and wild forms of entertainment and play. They can lack foresight and get themselves into a heap of trouble as a result.

Jupiter in the Sixth House

The Sixth House governs daily routines, acts of service, the work-life balance, health, due diligence, pet care, coworkers, and employees.

The Sixth House belongs to Mercury-ruled Virgo, which inclines these natives to find fulfilling work in service-oriented areas. They are conscientious and take great pride in being helpful.

Gift: Jupiter gives these individuals a strong moral code in their business dealings with others. They have beneficial relationships with coworkers and employees. As a result, they are favored by those they interact with and generally have an easy time finding employment. Conscientiousness generally applies to handling daily routines and matters pertaining to health and healing. Nutrition and exercise are areas that attract them, at least in principle.

Shadow: These natives can get overwhelmed in their attempt to perfectly tend to their day-to-day routines. They can get overly concerned with minute details. At the same time, they tend to overindulge in rich foods and drinks that do not benefit them from a health perspective. Jupiter rules the liver and the Sixth House is a health house, so the native benefits from carefully watching their diet and alcohol consumption.

Jupiter in Venus-ruled Libra's house is fortunate for close, committed partnerships, plentiful in charm and grace. Honesty and fairness characterize their exchanges, and relating as equals is important to them.

Jupiter in the Seventh House

The Seventh House rules close personal relationships, agreements, and compromises.

Jupiter in Venus-ruled Libra's house is fortunate for close, committed partnerships, including those that are business related. Charm and grace are plentiful in their exchanges with others.

Gift: Jupiter in the Seventh House natives have a strong sense of justice, which is exhibited in their dealings with others. Honesty and fairness characterize their exchanges, and they expect the same in return. Relating as equals is important to them. They are talented mediators and be-lieve in negotiating when conflicts are at play. They tend to do well in legal transactions brought on by another. Jupiter stimulates a desire to be kind, generous, and supportive as a partner. Their strong moral code and spiritual values regarding relationships usually result in close, rewarding partnerships.

Shadow: The shadow side of this placement occurs when these individuals become overly idealistic and then expect too much from others. They can easily engage with many different types of people and have difficulty settling on what and who they want from a relationship. Their high-minded approach to partnering can neglect embracing some of the darker aspects of relationships that often have to get worked out first. Others can take advantage of their generous and benign disposition in business dealings.

Jupiter in the Eighth House

The Eighth House rules joint ventures, intimacy, sex, death, transformation, and psychic dimensions.

Jupiter in Pluto's house of transformation contributes a broad and expansive perspective for handling major life passages, crisis situations, and other upsets. Belief in the power of transformation and change is a huge asset for these individuals.

Gift: The Eighth House pertains to shared resources, inheritance, debt, alimony, and divorce. Jupiter brings benefits to the handling and potential outcome of all of these areas. Jupiter's sign and planetary combinations will determine the extent to which these individuals will benefit in each of these areas. These natives believe in their ability to heal and transform themselves. They see change as an integral part of life. It is not uncommon for them to appreciate the value of various avenues of psychology and other therapies for probing into areas of the unconscious in order to release blocks that interfere with change and achieving full potential. They can have a strong interest in birth and death as well as in life after death. Some have experiences communicating with energies in other dimensions.

> The shadow side emerges when they become obsessed with the process to the exclusion of other life-supporting activities.

Shadow: This placement has an attraction to the forbidden. This can include information that they think is being withheld from them. The shadow side emerges when they become obsessed with the process to the exclusion of other life-supporting activities. They can also become paranoid, thinking that partners or others are hiding resources and information from them. Whenever Pluto is in the equation, a risk exists of overdoing, even when no valid reason is present.

Jupiter in the Ninth House

The Ninth House rules higher education, long-term goals, foreign travel, publicity, adventures, religion, and philosophical and ethical pursuits.

Jupiter is very much at home in the Ninth House, which belongs to Jupiter as the ruler of Sagittarius. Faith and a high-minded approach to life comes easily to them and helps them navigate through difficult circumstances they may encounter.

Gift: Individuals with a Ninth-House Jupiter placement are optimistic and open to new possibilities and situations that attract beneficial prospects to themselves. They easily connect to the big picture and can inspire others by offering a fresh perspective and a new way of looking at the same issues. These natives are adventurous and generally love to travel and explore new venues and different cultures. They are enthusiastic teachers, lecturers, and party guests, as they relate their experiences to others. Learning is always on their agenda, and they benefit from their appetite for knowledge and explorations of philosophies and spiritual practices. The inspiration they glean from formulating their own philosophies on life and the truths of existence elevate their faith and keep them at peace.

Shadow: These natives need a lot of stimulation and adventure, and they can get restless and seek excitement in places that may not benefit them. Their belief systems can carry a lot of weight for these natives, and they can want to impose their beliefs on others. A rigidity can develop where they are not open to other thinking.

Jupiter in the Tenth House

The Tenth House rules public achievements, reputation, authority, and prestige.

Jupiter in Capricorn's Tenth House, a placement primarily associated with career and reputation, brings professional opportunities to the native. Jupiter in this position is all about growth and expansion in the professional arena.

Gift: A Tenth-House Jupiter native shines down upon the chart, bringing with it confidence and a strong likelihood of success. Others will notice them, as a prominent Tenth House native puts these individuals in the public eye. Here, they are noticed for their positivity, knowledge, benevolent disposition, and high-mindedness. Ambition is strengthened in this position, and their confident and open temperament attracts opportunities and favor. Typically, these individuals display professionalism and sophistication, providing them with an image that is welcome in professional circles. Ethical principles and a high moral code are applied to their business dealings and social responsibilities.

Shadow: The shadow side of Jupiter is generally associated with excess and indulgence, and with this placement, the native can overdo opportunist tendencies and turn off those they want to impress. Their hunger for growth and expansion can imply a lack of satisfaction and fulfillment with their current position. They may be constantly plagued by the impulse to seek greener pastures. Another possible pitfall is that these natives can acquire a cocky and overconfident attitude due to the ease and good luck they may have experienced in the past. They can be remiss

in doing the work and preparation required for the notoriety they are seeking.

Jupiter in the Eleventh House

The Eleventh House rules friends, hopes, wishes, groups, and a sense of belonging in the world.

Jupiter in the Eleventh House, traditionally ruled by Aquarius with the dual rulership of Uranus and Saturn, indicates natives who receive benefits via friends and group activities. They are usually well liked and attract friends who are influential and helpful. Teamwork is their strength, and they are generally successful at networking.

Gift: These natives are humane and generally progressive by nature. They are open to new approaches for meeting their goals and objectives, which bring them fresh and innovative opportunities. Friends and influential social associations see these natives in a favorable light and can be helpful and supportive. This placement of Jupiter brings a spirit of cooperation and a high moral standard to friendships, group endeavors, and organizational structures. They are welcomed and respected, which adds to the success of group undertakings. Successful ventures can include those from foreign cultures, philanthropic organizations, institutions of higher learning, and prominent members of society.

Shadow: These natives can take friendships for granted and not give back the required attention and respect they would like. They can be social climbers, where friendships are built on ulterior motives and the desire for social prominence.

Jupiter in the Twelfth House

The Twelfth House rules secrets, unconscious patterns, karma, closure, institutions, connections with higher sources, enlightenment, and undoing.

Jupiter in the Eleventh House indicates natives that are usually well liked, attracting influential and helpful friends. Humane and generally progressive by nature, they are welcomed and respected, with teamwork being their strength.

Jupiter in the Twelfth House is well placed and inclines the native toward spiritual growth and personal evolution. The native can display profound insights on the inner workings of the collective consciousness. They can be imaginative with lofty ideals and receive divine inspirations from transcendent realms.

Gift: This position of Jupiter bestows good karma upon the individual. My teacher, Isabel Hickey, considered this placement as a guardian angel position. Deep in their subconscious is the knowledge that they are protected and that all is good. An instinctive trust in the universe brings them peace of mind. They often favor meditation practices and other modalities that encourage contact with transcendental realms. Jupiter in the Twelfth House has great compassion for those in need. They can derive emotional satisfaction from helping others. It is not uncom-

mon for them to be involved in acts of service to the disadvantaged or connected to institutions such as hospitals, prisons, or monasteries.

Shadow: These natives can be overly trusting and optimistic, where they lack discernment with those they choose to help. Their enthusiasm and positive outlook can blindside them to the shadowy motives of others. The Twelfth House is also known as the house of self-undoing. These natives have the potential to work against their better interests through overindulgence, extravagance, laziness, and negligence.

JUPITER COMBINATIONS

Jupiter/Sun

Jupiter represents the higher mind, greater truths, expansiveness, hope, and optimism.

The Sun indicates purpose, self-expression, creative life force, and conscious will.

The expansive nature of Jupiter brings optimism and generosity to the individual's self-expression. Their life force is generally enhanced, and these natives typically exhibit a charitable disposition. Too much of anything ceases to be helpful, however, and natives with this combination will need to master balance in order to gain the most benefit from its influence. As a greater benefic, Jupiter is known to bestow luck unless contraindicated by other combinations in the chart.

Gift: These natives are enthusiastic, generous, and see the glass as half full. They are likely to positively evaluate situations before them and have faith in their undertakings. Their upbeat nature contributes to their popularity. Others feel better after being around them. The connection between the Sun and Jupiter gives these individuals an edge in successfully manifesting their dreams. They have an aversion to pettiness and stinginess. They love to expand their horizons, which includes travel, interacting with different cultures, and expanding their knowledge base.

> Too much of anything ceases to be helpful, however, and natives with this combination will need to master balance in order to gain the most benefit from its influence.

Shadow: The shadow side of this influence can make it difficult for these individuals to know where their boundaries lie. Jupiter is expansive, and a tendency to overspend, overestimate, overindulge, and imbibe in other excessive behavior can occur. Similarly, the ego can get overblown, and their self-image can be unrealistic and exaggerated. These natives may brag, flaunt their talents and abilities, and aggrandize their accomplishments.

Jupiter/Moon

Jupiter represents the higher mind, greater truths, expansiveness, hope, and optimism.

The Moon symbolizes feelings, habit patterns, and the unconscious.

An optimistic, warm-hearted nature oozes from all levels of the conscious and subconscious when the Moon combines with expansive Jupiter. These natives are kind and authentic and bring their deeply caring nature to others. Just as Jupiter is exalted in Moon-ruled Cancer, these natives are often devoted to home and family, which can often include their extended family and friends.

Gift: A Moon/Jupiter combination brings forth the gift of good karma and generosity of spirit. They have a contagious optimism that makes it easy for others to be around them. They are sought after for their uplifting sensibility and fresh perspective that they openheartedly extend to others. They are generally trusted for their honesty and sincerity and, in return, are likely to receive cooperation and help from others. It is not uncommon for them to have a pleasant disposition and a good sense of humor.

Shadow: The shadow side of this combination is a tendency toward overindulgence and a dislike of having limitations imposed upon them. Excessiveness coupled with a lack of prudence can work to their disadvantage. Overdoing can get carried too

When combined with Mercury, Jupiter will incline the native to think big. They can engage in planning on a grand scale, bringing enthusiasm and positive energy into their conversation. They have a positive attitude and can be fun to be around.

Gift: These natives have a broad outlook. They can take mundane issues and problems and come up with long-range solutions that put the original problems into a grander perspective. Their orientation is philosophical, and they enjoy bantering about a wide array of topics, including those relating to spiritual, cultural, and political issues. They are enthusiastic and bring excitement to any conversation or negotiation, thereby having the ability to hold their audience's attention. These natives have a positive attitude, and it is likely that they have a good sense of humor. They can be fun to be around.

Shadow: The shadow side of a Mercury/Jupiter combination is a lack of realism. The idealistic nature of these natives may not evaluate their ideas and the situations before them realistically. They can have an aversion to imposing limitations and restrictions on the issues at hand even though they may be required. Their judgment can be impaired as a result. These natives can do more talking than listening, whereby they can miss out on important information.

far, causing health problems and weight issues. They can exaggerate their emotional reactions to people and events and then feel let down when the desired response is not provided. It is not uncommon for them to promise more than they can deliver due to their generous nature, leading others to think of them as unreliable.

Jupiter/Mercury

Jupiter represents the higher mind, greater truths, expansiveness, hope, and optimism.

Mercury rules communication, mental processes, and the logical mind.

Jupiter is an expansive energy that leans toward optimism and an idealistic point of view. When combined with Mercury, Jupiter will incline the native to think big. They can engage in planning on a grand scale, bringing enthusiasm and positive energy into their conversation.

Jupiter/Venus

Jupiter represents the higher mind, greater truths, expansiveness, hope, and optimism.

Venus represents love, relationships, beauty, values, comfort, and material resources.

Venus and Jupiter are both known as benefics in astrology, meaning that this combination can bring good luck, positive outcomes, and ease. The expansive nature of Jupiter enhances everything that is ruled by Venus and can bring radiance and opportunities to social and personal relationships, finances, artistic endeavors, and all that is valued by the native.

Gift: A generosity of spirit occurs that, when coupled with a supportive attitude, fosters love and trust. This is an open-hearted, joyous combination that attracts positivity, prosperity, and popularity. The native exudes an uplifting aura that adds positivity and sparkle to an environment. Their happy spirit and general liking of people brings friends and many social contacts to them. They possess social grace and a refinement that makes them welcome guests. This combination can incline the individual toward artistic pursuits, which they likely will, in turn, be successful at.

Shadow: Too much of a good thing can bring overindulgence and an overinflated ego, which can outweigh the generosity of spirit that could otherwise be present with this combination. Overreach can occur in relationships due to overconfidence and a sense of entitlement. A cocky attitude can result when this otherwise delightful combination is displaying its shadow side. An increased appetite for spending and sensual and sexual indulgence can manifest with this combination.

Jupiter/Mars

Jupiter represents the higher mind, greater truths, expansiveness, hope, and optimism.

Mars rules assertiveness, energy, drive, and courage.

This power combination can bring immense inspiration and goal-centered action. This individual is always looking to expand their territory and enrich their life. They are the ones who are not afraid to take a calculated risk, an adventurer at heart.

Mastery occurs when striking a balance between Jupiter, "The Great Benefic," and Saturn, "The Great Malefic," in traditional astrology.

Gift: Individuals with a prominent and well-aspected Mars and Jupiter combination are not afraid to go after their desires with gusto and enthusiasm. They possess a courage and boldness that can be smooth and easy to an onlooker. With Jupiter's help, endeavors are likely to succeed.

Shadow: An excess of this energy can lead to an individual who casts away any semblance of efficiency and overestimates much of what they do. A grandiosity can overcompensate for a lack of information or a basic insecurity. As a result, the foot can stay on the gas pedal to the point where they become careless and hasty, and they need modulating.

Jupiter/Saturn

Jupiter represents the higher mind, greater truths, expansiveness, hope, and optimism.

Saturn rules responsibility, adjustments to limitations, sustainability, and structure.

Jupiter and Saturn, although seemingly contradictory energies representing expansion and contraction, work in combination to bring structure and practical steps to the manifestation of ideals and aspirations.

The late astrologer Nick Anthony Fiorenza aptly described the energies of Jupiter and Saturn on his website Lunarplanner.com: "Jupiter is inclusive and embracing while Saturn is exclusive and segregating. Saturn imposes boundaries, walls, rules and regulations. Saturn forces us to confront our fears and Jupiter impels us to claim our wisdom. Saturn demonstrates and validates by con-

♃♄

The combination of Jupiter and Uranus can bring good luck exactly when it is needed. Unexpected situations can awaken consciousness for these natives, who can open the door to "aha!" experiences.

cretizing in form that which Jupiter expands to embrace."

Gift: Mastery occurs when striking a balance between Jupiter, "The Great Benefic," and Saturn, "The Great Malefic," in traditional astrology. Gifts derived from this blending include realistic optimism, a mature moral code and set of ethics, and sustainable expansion that is based upon the establishment of solid structures and jurisprudence. The individual is able to strike a balance between freedom and responsibility, blend logic with philosophy, and combine patience and good judgment in all types of business and bold undertakings. These natives are able to bring faith, trust, and patience to situations when obstacles are encountered and when snags arise. They benefit from employing discipline and commitment to their visions and goals, and they can bring perspective to life's hardships and difficulties.

Shadow: The shadow side of a Jupiter/Saturn combination is periods of disproportionate gain, extravagance, and over-indulgence followed by periods of little gain or even loss, frugality, and tremendous discipline. Rather than integrating the above attitudes and behaviors, the native sticks with one type of extreme behavior pattern and then, when obstacles arise or when goals are not met, their behavior patterns switch to opposing behaviors. These natives have difficulty keeping the faith and may go from periods of confidence and optimism to periods of being depressed and pessimistic. They have difficulty integrating the opposing energies of expansion and contraction, faith and discipline, and cautiousness and foolhardiness.

Jupiter/Uranus

Jupiter represents the higher mind, greater truths, expansiveness, hope, and optimism.

Uranus rules intuition, originality, individuality, and the sudden and unexpected.

At the personal level, the combination of Jupiter and Uranus in the chart can bring unexpected good luck exactly when it is needed. The occurrence of unexpected situations and sudden events happen that awaken one's consciousness and redirect them into more purposeful activities.

A new Jupiter/Uranus synodic cycle occurs every 13.81 years, which infuses society with innovation and cultural shifts. Culturally, the Jupiter/Uranus energy combination can lead to following one's own belief systems rather than conform to any traditional teachings.

Gift: Natives with a Jupiter/Uranus combination can be ahead of their time. They have a futuristic vision that can bring forth cultural shifts and inventions. They are able to recognize and open the door to innovations, personal and societal insights, and "a-ha" experiences. Uranus can awaken trust in the divine or in a higher power due to having had experiences where things end up working out somehow in the end. These individuals can be true humanitarians and advocates for personal freedom.

Shadow: Jupiter expands whatever energies it touches and can thereby enhance rebellious tendencies when combining with Uranus. These natives can become overzealous reformers in areas relating to cultural, religious and spiritual issues. They can have brilliant ideas that lack follow-through in terms of their execution. An abundance of optimism and goodwill can be present, but their actions and ideas don't materialize into desired outcomes due to the scattering of energy and difficulty with maintaining focus. The Uranian energy is highly charged and makes the native overly receptive to sensory stimulation, which, in turn, affects focus and concentration.

Jupiter/Neptune

Jupiter represents the higher mind, greater truths, expansiveness, hope, and optimism.

Neptune rules ideals, creative imagination, transcendence, compassion, and vision.

A Jupiter/Neptune combination can open pathways to the celestial realms, expanding access to the individual's highest visions and dreams. On the other hand, the Neptunian influence can also dissolve boundaries, and when Jupiter combines with Neptune, the result can expand collective illusions, delusions, and deception. Neptune is visionary but is also potentially delusional.

Gift: The combination of Jupiter and Neptune opens the native to the possibility of

miracles. They are inclined to transcend and connect with the spirit and the field of all possibilities and creativity. These individuals seek internal peace regardless of external conditions. This combination can bring an outpouring of compassion and an increase in spiritual and metaphysical interests. They are charitable, sympathetic, humanitarian, highly visionary, and imaginative. This planetary combination can indicate a transcendent breakthrough with access to divine realms or a spectacular blunder prompted by deception and fantasy.

Shadow: Jupiter tends to "think big," and it is not unlikely for Jupiter to expand the amorphous borders of reality and think too big at times. Individuals with this combination can lack discernment and be charitable and too trusting to the undeserving. They need frequent reality checks whenever speculating or investing their time and money. Jupiter expands Neptune's ability to absorb and hold toxins. Natives with this combination need to be mindful of toxic fumes and other environmental factors. It is likely that they are super sensitive to certain medications, drugs, and alcohol, which all come under the influence of Neptune.

Jupiter/Pluto

Jupiter represents the higher mind, greater truths, expansiveness, hope, and optimism.

Pluto represents regeneration; transformation; and a compelling, fundamental approach.

Jupiter expands and Pluto transforms, making this a power combination that can bring immense inspiration, strong desires, and resourcefulness that can implement change and transformation.

Gift: The combination of Jupiter and Pluto can generate the desire for the attainment of personal empowerment. Natives need to get to the bottom of anything that interferes with growth so that the next phase of change and rebuilding can occur. This desire applies to both identifying and removing internal subconscious blocks as well as to external problem-solving so that progress can continue. These natives demonstrate good judgment that can be applied to any kind of issues before them. They can be persuasive, as they key into underlying motivations and speak to others' subconscious needs and desires. They can harness enthusiasm for growth, change, and evolution, even making this process into an adventure.

Shadow: The shadow side of the Jupiter/Pluto combination is that it can increase the desire for power and control beyond appropriate limits. Jupiter can expand whatever energies it touches, and Pluto, also known as the god of the Underworld, can lead the native down a rabbit hole in search of the taboo, the forbidden, control, and power. Pluto can be extreme, and Jupiter can enhance Pluto's intense, polarized nature. The result can be a tendency to go overboard, compulsive behavior patterns, power struggles, and manipulation. These natives can be inclined to overreach and have an all-or-nothing approach when they would be better served by a more gentle and moderate approach.

Jupiter/Chiron

Jupiter represents the higher mind, greater truths, expansiveness, hope, and optimism.

Chiron represents core wounds and the desire to overcome them, and healing.

Jupiter in combination with Chiron can relate to a need to overcome a wounding related to faith and trust in a positive outcome. Fear is present that the rug can get pulled out at any time, causing deep-rooted, subconscious distrust of the divine.

Gift: These natives hold a strong belief in the power of healing. They can have a personal philosophy where they have gained mystical wisdom connected to their own wounding and subsequent healing. They have found a perspective with which they can integrate their negative experiences and reestablish stasis. These natives can profess ethical and ideological convictions around helping others. Themes that might interest them from a societal point of view include the involvement with solutions for those connected to banishment, ridicule, and unfortunate life circumstances, especially in early childhood. Judgment of others is kept in check through a realization that everyone has positive and negative traits and that with the proper training and opportunity, negative behaviors can be healed. They believe in redemption of the soul through faith and knowledge. As luck would have it, Jupiter can bring to awareness, through situations and personal interactions, places where hurt and pain is ready to be released and healed.

Shadow: The shadow side of a Jupiter/Chiron combination can manifest as a quest to find meaning in life. These individuals can get lost in the discomfort of the pointless turmoil of life, placing their faith and trust in one school of thought after another. As seekers, they may chase after various gurus and teachers,

> Jupiter in combination with Chiron can relate to a need to overcome a wounding related to faith and trust in a positive outcome.

never finding peace or a sense of well-being, only reinforcing their distrust of some promise for healing and reinforcing a belief in suffering and pain. Their early worldview may have been built upon the concept of terminal suffering and pain, and the native has struggled to put their early life experiences into perspective. These natives may not be open to seeking help, preferring to indulge their pain.

Jupiter/Eris

Jupiter represents the higher mind, greater truths, expansiveness, hope, and optimism.

Eris represents the determination to remove limitations that impede the soul's evolution.

Gift: Expansive Jupiter can lend perspective to Eris's quests and assist the native in ascertaining beneficial outcomes in their personal and societal ventures.

Shadow: Jupiter has been known to overdo, and when these two energies combine, the process for attaining their desired result can be fraught with too much fight and determination.

Jupiter/North Node

Jupiter represents the higher mind, greater truths, expansiveness, hope, and optimism.

The North Node represents future direction, soul guidance, and fulfillment.

The North Node emphasizes the importance for the native to develop the attributes represented by Jupiter. This suggests that a philosophy of life that assists the native in fostering faith and trust will be beneficial.

Gift: Jupiter in combination with the North Node can bring a life theme chock full of opportunities and good fortune.

They may be known for their positive attitude and easygoing nature. Their generosity, high moral standard, and benevolence to all peoples open doors for them, leading to circumstances and people that support their causes. These people are frequently in the right place at the right time. They feel the support of nature, which becomes a guidepost for them and affirms that they are on the right path.

Shadow: The individual's social views and values may not support their path of destiny. They can be overly judgmental of others and limit themselves from interactions and opportunities that they could benefit from. Wanderlust can keep these individuals from staying in one place, where their fate would like them to be. They can take too much for granted and miss out on opportunities that require follow-through. Blind optimism can lead them down a less advantageous path. Overindulgence and greed can be tendencies that prevent these natives from taking advantage of opportune breaks and prospects.

Jupiter/South Node

Jupiter represents the higher mind, greater truths, expansiveness, hope, and optimism.

The South Node represents familiarity, gratification, and the path of least resistance.

The combination of Jupiter and the South Node bestows a deep-rooted sensibility that luck is on their side. They likely come from deeply spiritual roots and have earned good karma that they can bring forward in this life.

Gift: These natives are innately easygoing and generous. They have a life philosophy that carries them forward through difficult circumstances. It is easy for them to put their experiences in perspective, and they

Jupiter in combination with the Ascendent describes a good-natured, adventurous individual who approaches life with a positive attitude, confidence, and optimism. This can open doors for them but may also put them in dangerous situations.

are able to help others by providing an alternate and more expansive point of view. They are naturally attuned to people of other cultures and able to integrate cultural experiences into their current life path.

Shadow: The shadow side of the Jupiter/South Node combination is a lack of determination and stick-to-itiveness. They are used to receiving life's bounties on a silver platter and do not have the wherewithal to forge their path when circumstances are tough. They can have an inflated view of themselves that is not in alignment with their capabilities.

Jupiter/Ascendant

Jupiter represents the higher mind, greater truths, expansiveness, hope, and optimism.

The Ascendant represents one's approach, orientation, and the window through which one sees the world.

Gift: Jupiter in combination with the Ascendant describes a good-natured, adventurous individual who approaches life with a positive attitude, confidence, and much optimism. Doors open before them, and they can feel generally supported.

Shadow: The shadow side of a Jupiter/Ascendant combination can be an over-inflation of one's capabilities. These natives can have delusions of grandeur, and as a result, they take on more than they can handle. Their optimism and adventurous nature can put them in dangerous situations. These natives have a tendency to overindulge, and they can put on weight in their later years.

Jupiter/Midheaven (MC)

Jupiter represents the higher mind, greater truths, expansiveness, hope, and optimism.

The Midheaven (MC) represents image, outer aspirations, and career orientation.

With Jupiter at the top of the chart, good deeds and benevolent acts are readily noticed, bringing fame and accolades to the individual.

Gift: This individual has an easy time reaching their career aspirations. Opportunities appear for these natives exactly when they are ready for them. They are well liked by their superiors for their good nature, honesty, and confidence, and they easily attain prominence.

Shadow: The shadow side of this combination can manifest as a lack of humility, practicality, and common sense. Others will take note of blunders resulting from these behavior patterns. They can exaggerate their competencies when applying for professional positions and overestimate their capabilities in general.

SATURN

Saturn can pose an enigma that many do not understand. Saturn rewards, and Saturn challenges. Saturn's gifts are long-lasting and enduring. Saturn points out areas of vulnerability. Saturn's purpose is to strengthen, stabilize, and make resilient.

No better teacher exists than Saturn. Saturn brings lasting rewards for righteousness and good karma. Saturn can present obstacles, delays, and retribution as well so that a course correction can be embarked upon. This process brings forth major transformations.

Saturn is a teacher, guide, and ally, even when it feels exactly the opposite. It isn't always easy to view Saturn as an ally. Certainly, sometimes Saturn limitations can feel unfair, depressing, and downright difficult. Saturn is also about growth and maturation and creating or building the structures that sustain and support all aspects of the true self. Saturn can be a taskmaster that points out behavior patterns that are not sustainable or resilient.

Although Saturn is correlated with "Old Father Time," Saturn also has a feminine association. Saturn has to do with structures, form, and matter. Matter has its roots in the word "mother," hence the feminine association with Saturn. Also, Saturn rules Capricorn, which is a feminine Earth sign that has to do with the Circle of Grand-

mothers. An evolved perspective of Saturn integrates its feminine side. Saturn is not a punishing, judgmental, masculine god, as described by the patriarchy, though it certainly can feel that way at times.

Saturn represents physical and material realities, responsibilities, structures, delays, obstacles, and limitations. Saturn also rules time, patience, discipline, adversity, lessons, losses, and setbacks. Saturn can reinforce an individual's ability to persevere through life's many difficulties. Saturn shows where and how the individual is being tested and what they need to do to be more disciplined and patient so that they can realize and fulfill their purpose. Saturn wants everyone to grow up and take responsibility.

Alice A. Bailey says in *Esoteric Astrology*, "Saturn is the planet of discipleship and of opportunity; it is exceedingly active today, presenting to the world disciple those difficult situations and crises which will involve free choice, discriminative pioneering, wise response and correct decision, thus bringing about the destruction of that which hinders—without the relinquishing of any true values of which humanity may be aware."

Stephen Arroyo, in his book *Astrology, Karma & Transformation: The Inner Dimensions of the Birth Chart*, has this to add:

> According to Dane Rudhyar, Saturn refers to a person's "fundamental nature," the purity of one's true self. It seems that Saturn has come to have negative meanings in the minds of many astrologers and students of astrology because most people do not live in terms of their fundamental nature, but rather in terms of fashions, social patterns and traditions, and ego games. Hence, Saturn

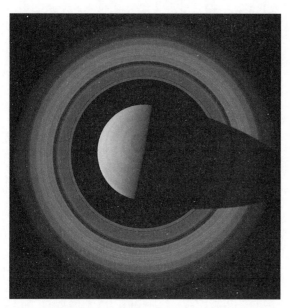

Saturn's sign has a lot to do with things such as work and responsibilities in ones life, and it indicates what is working and not working for a person, too.

pening. With a one-step-at-a-time approach, situations are handled with little to be overwhelmed by and with less stress. Saturn bestows wisdom. That wisdom is gained by responding to obstacles and challenges with a patient and grounded approach. When it is understood that success may not be easy but will be rewarding, the native develops the discipline and perseverance to be successful. It is helpful to understand that Saturn is the planet of strength, discipline, effort, sustainability, and responsibility and how and where to apply these principles. Saturn makes you uncomfortable, and that discomfort provides the impetus to make changes. Saturn is down-to-earth, and it's also the planet that denotes common sense.

Shadow: The shadow side of Saturn is an amplification of fear coupled with a tendency to live in the past rather than to put one foot in front of the other and move forward in a practical and grounded manner. Saturn projects the feeling that no matter what anyone does, they get the same outcome that life is unfair and everything is hard. The task is to learn how to play the hand you have and do the best you can with it; the rewards will come.

SATURN IN THE SIGNS

Saturn's sign position in the birth chart indicates the manner in which the person needs to shoulder responsibility so they can develop discipline and attain maturity. Saturn exposes the limitations of the sign it is in and points out what is working for the individual and what is not working. The energetics and characteristics of the sign in which Saturn is placed are generally taken seriously by the individual. They are likely to want to accomplish something of lasting value based upon the nature of the sign placement.

is often experienced as a "stern reproach" or a challenging act of "fate" in order that we begin to heed the needs of our fundamental nature within. Saturn is indeed a rough taskmaster, as many of the old books say, but is particularly rough when we have deviated from manifesting our true nature.

An expression in the astrological community says, "Do your Saturn and the rest of your chart will be happy."

Gift: Saturn can be a huge ally when an individual is willing to take responsibility. The word "responsibility" breaks down to response-ability, the ability to respond. When one is present to the current moment, they are able to respond to any situation by placing one foot in front of the other. It is amazing how much can be accomplished by simply staying grounded and being present to exactly what is hap-

Saturn in Aries

Saturn is in its fall in the sign ruled by Mars; it is not considered to be well placed since Saturn is exalted in the sign opposite Aries, which is Libra. Aries is a sign of enthusiasm and leadership that is generally motivated and energized with an abundance of initiative and assertiveness. These are exactly the characteristics that Saturn will pressure the native to develop and maintain in spite of obstacles and limitations. Aries rules the beginning, the initial spark, whereas Saturn develops strength and wisdom over time, so these natives are always working at what they feel is a disadvantage. They don't feel that time is on their side.

Gift: Saturn in Aries individuals value self-control, practicality, and determination, all qualities that the native knows are important for them to develop with Saturn in Aries. They are ambitious and exemplify the best qualities of a Mars/ Saturn combination when they take seriously that developing these qualities will accelerate their growth and well-being. They are rewarded for self-sufficiency and for taking the initiative.

Shadow: These natives can be headstrong, arrogant, somewhat inflexible, and highly self-oriented. The shadow side of this sign placement can show up as an underlying fear of failure and a lack of confidence. Insecurities can result and, when combined with the subliminal pressure of Saturn, can result in headaches since Aries rules the head.

Saturn in Taurus

Saturn in Venus-ruled Taurus places an emphasis on developing practical solutions that stand the test of time. Sustainability is a highly valued objective and will manifest in several areas, especially in the area governed by the house that Saturn is in. These natives can have an interest in preserving Earth's resources and the right use of her precious reserves.

Gift: These individuals seek financial and material security. They will be highly motivated to find stable career positions that will provide them with the lifestyle they desire. As a result, they are stable and reliable workers and business owners. They have a salt-of-the-earth persona that others find comforting and welcoming. Their dependable, common-sense type of wisdom increases as they age. Taurus rules values, and with Saturn in Taurus, the native is highly aware of the importance of strong moral values. They will stand up for what they believe is important.

Shadow: The shadow side of this placement is excessive materialism. They can overly identify with their material possessions at the exclusion of more human-oriented qualities. Stubbornness and obstinacy can result from this placement. These natives can have a narrow vision and a restricted perspective, which can evolve from putting too much attention on material resources. They can be frugal and lack a generosity of spirit.

Saturn in Gemini

Saturn in Mercury-ruled Gemini slows down the chitter-chatter side of Gemini and seeks thought-out communication over random gossip and extraneous words.

> Sustainability is a highly valued objective and will manifest in several areas, especially in the area governed by the house that Saturn is in.

Saturn in Cancer natives take family responsibilities seriously, watching over the other members of the tribe. They will protect those who are important to them more through their actions than through their display of emotions.

Gift: Individuals with Saturn in Gemini are mentally organized and focused. They may have learned early on that if they want to get their point across, they are more effective when they know what they are talking about and when they present their information in a logical and organized manner. These natives learn how to master the art of using bullet points in their presentations and communication modalities. Saturn in Gemini natives enjoy learning, and they will tend to focus on a couple of streams of knowledge that they can delve into more thoroughly rather than knowing random facts about a host of topics. Their ideas are evaluated on the basis of their practical utility.

Shadow: Saturn in Gemini natives can impart doubt and hesitation when communi-

cating. They can have an incredibly high standard for themselves and don't ever feel that know enough about what they want to say. They may fear being viewed as unintelligent. As a result, these natives can find ways to avoid situations where they will have to present information or engage in consequential communications.

Saturn in Cancer

Saturn is in its detriment in the sign of Cancer because Cancer is the opposite sign to Capricorn, which is ruled by Saturn. Saturn can inhibit the expression of emotion that is characteristic of Moon-ruled Cancer. They are likely to prefer logical explanations over emotional displays.

Gift: Saturn in Cancer natives take family responsibilities seriously. They can be the

♃♄

resilient and exemplary member of a family unit who watches over the other members of the tribe. They will protect those who are important to them more through their actions than through their display of emotions. They understand the importance of showing respect for family members and, likewise, the value of honoring family and ancestral traditions.

Shadow: Just as crabs are known to retreat to their shells, Saturn in the sign of the Crab can lead these individuals to have the same impulse when emotions are running high. They can be emotionally inhibited and not know how to handle their own feelings, nor those of others, with any amount of ease and grace. Self-isolation or emotional defensiveness can appear to be viable options for them. They don't know how to be vulnerable and will go all out to hide their feelings so that others don't see their sensitive nature.

Saturn in Leo

Saturn in the sign ruled by the Sun learns over time how to develop solid foundations upon which to support their confidence and self-esteem. They are highly aware of authenticity and work hard to establish an identity that supports their view of themselves.

Gift: The gift of having Saturn in Leo is that the native is willing to put forth the effort necessary to gain recognition in an area of their choosing. They realize at some point that it won't be handed to them on a silver platter. Through willpower and determination, they stay on the right path and continually fortify themselves with the training

and accomplishments that they need in order to feel that they are on a firm footing. As a result, their confidence and self-esteem continue to grow, and they shine as the Leo energy should.

Shadow: Individuals with Saturn in Leo can get entrenched in their egos and forget how to be humble. They are apt to run into situations that bring up subconscious murmurings of "how dare you?" They are prone to taking innocent comments and gestures from others as personal affronts rather than realizing that they were objective comments not meant for them. These natives don't quite know why they are not the center of everyone's universe. They have an unconscious need for recognition and for feeling that they are important. They may want to be in charge; however, they don't have the required skills to achieve the status they desire.

Saturn in Virgo

Saturn in Mercury-ruled Virgo has an eye for detail and precision, which, through hard work and perseverance, moves them toward the perfection and efficiency they seek.

Gift: Saturn in Virgo has an innate sensibility about how to streamline their tasks and routines in order to achieve the best results. They developed this discernment over time and know that anxiety and frustration can occur if they don't. They cultivate their everyday wisdom, which keeps them and those around them on track with workable routines that are sustainable. They do well in positions that others would tire of. Those around them, whether on a project, at work,

> They cultivate their everyday wisdom, which keeps them and those around them on track with workable routines that are sustainable.

or in the home, admire and respect their dedication and work ethic.

Shadow: The shadow side of Saturn in Virgo is a pettiness that loses track of the big-picture perspective of what it is they are wanting to achieve. They can get hung up on rules and regulations to the extent that they fail to achieve the overriding goal. It can be difficult for others to get along with them due to them being detail-orientated and having a perfectionist nature. They need to cultivate an awareness of human limitations, their own as well as those of others. Worry and overwhelm can take a toll on their health and well-being. They are challenged to take a step back and see the big picture every now and then. Perfectionism can hold these natives back from possible fulfillment and ultimate success.

Saturn in Libra

Saturn in Venus-ruled Libra is well placed. Libra is the sign of exaltation for Saturn, a placement that recognizes the value of mutual honor and respect. An exalted Saturn in Libra is an attestation that diligence and grit are necessary to create relationships that sustain the test of time.

Gift: Libra is the sign of balance, fairness, diplomacy, and cooperation. Saturn is upping the ante on these important components, which are needed in order to have successful relationships. Natives with Saturn in Libra are likely to master these principles over time through diligence and hard work. Balance comes into play because Libra is the natural ruler of the Seventh House and Saturn rules Capricorn, the natural ruler of the Tenth House. Balancing a relationship with career demands is challenging if one wants to do justice to both. Compromise is integral to successful relationships, where neither party is dom-

inant and both parties function as equals. Saturn in Libra can assist the native in realistically assessing relationships.

Shadow: Natives with Saturn in Libra fear loneliness. Saturn in Libra can delay a serious relationship at various times during the individual's life. These delays are usually to assist the native in further self-development and help them set realistic relationship expectations. Responsibility and give and take in partnerships may be learned via trial and error. This applies to both personal and business relationships.

Saturn in Scorpio

Saturn in Scorpio, the sign of transformation, challenges the native to let go of whatever doesn't work. Scorpio is deeply penetrating and can get to the crux of any situation. This placement of Saturn is serious and persistent.

Gift: The gift that Saturn in Scorpio bestows upon the native is an unrelenting commitment to their personal growth. These natives can be fastidious about self-help routines, consciousness development techniques, and therapies that further awareness and personal development. Saturn can put the brakes on out-of-control passions and help the native learn how to be in control of their passions and desires rather than have their passions and desires be in control of them.

Shadow: The shadow side of Saturn in Scorpio is an emotional intensity that, if suppressed or sublimated, can manifest in indirect ways. This placement can lead to compulsive, obsessive, and manipulative behavior patterns. Subconscious motivations will keep presenting themselves until patterns are cleared. The nature of this placement is that it will create pressure until the native is ready to dig in and get to the bottom of their issues, clearing emotional blocks that are causing these painful behaviors.

Saturn in Sagittarius

Saturn in Jupiter-ruled Sagittarius combines the energies of Jupiter and Saturn, thereby assisting the native in balancing their expansive, visionary instincts with a reality check. They take a serious approach to education and spirituality and a down-to-earth approach to their philosophy of life.

Gift: Individuals with Saturn in Sagittarius can tell the truth even when circumstances make it difficult to do so. They learned over time the value of honesty and a straightforward approach to tackling issues. They seek honesty and integrity in all of their daily dealings and interactions. They have a great deal of respect for cultural and spiritual traditions. Personal freedom is important to these natives; however, they have learned how to mitigate their need for freedom and adventure with their business and personal responsibilities. Intellectual achievement is important, and they will endure difficulties so that they can reach their educational goals. Many have aspirations to be an authority in an area of knowledge. They desire to have their opinions taken seriously. An endearing aspect of a Saturn in Sagittarius placement is that these natives retain the ability to laugh at themselves.

Shadow: The shadow side of this placement occurs when the native chooses to disregard honesty in their dealings. They have a karmic need to tell the truth, and when they don't, they are likely to experience complications. Unwise speculations run the risk of not working out well. Self-righteousness can get carried too far, and these natives can impose their philosophic and religious beliefs on others.

Individuals with Saturn in Sagittarius seek honesty and integrity in all of their daily dealings and interactions, and they have a great deal of respect for cultural and spiritual traditions.

Saturn in Capricorn

Saturn is at home in Capricorn. This double Saturn influence bestows these natives with great responsibility, high ambition, and self-discipline. They are diligent and efficient in their quest to make their mark on worldly affairs. These natives are good organizers, tend to be serious, and carry an aura of dignity.

Gift: Individuals with Saturn in Capricorn will rise to the occasion in spite of their own emotional state. They are mature and show their maturity by being able to balance their emotions while carrying out their responsibilities. This placement gives individuals an edge on dealing with the harsh circumstances of life. They are able to put one foot in front of the other and stay in the present moment as they walk toward their cherished goals and objectives. They don't look for shortcuts. This is something they learned at an early age after possible missteps.

Shadow: The shadow side of this placement is a stoic pragmatism that disregards human values. At the extreme, they can be incapable of facing their feelings, and their behavior can border on being hardhearted and cold. Many come up through the ranks as a result of hard work, overcoming obstacles each step of the way. Compassion and empathy are not usually attributes that are highly valued. These natives risk becoming rigid in their attitudes and opinions. Unscrupulous means can be used to achieve social standing and be recognized for their ambitions.

Saturn in Aquarius

In traditional astrology, as the coruler of Aquarius, Saturn is considered to be well placed in this sign. When combined with its modern ruler, Uranus, this placement knows how to prioritize their goals so that they can get their desired results. The Uranian influence acknowledges the value of their own individuality, their friendships, and the importance of paying homage to all of humanity. These natives are able to truly understand the human condition, with all of its ups and downs.

Gift: The Fixity of Aquarius combined with the discipline of Saturn gives these natives the ability to have an unwavering focus on their goals and objectives. Saturn compels the native to learn how to manage their time and prioritize which goals are based upon realistic ideas. Saturn will also help to formulate concrete steps in order to reach those goals. These natives have an impetus to break through restrictions of the past and create new, original, and innovative structures. Saturn in Aquarius will help these individuals express their in-

dividuality in a mature way rather than expressing themselves as rebellious adolescents. They are instead strong and accomplished individuals who stand up for an ideal that they believe in. Social relationships are important to them, and they will abide by a high code of ethics in their interpersonal and social relationships.

Shadow: The shadow side of this combination shows up as immature rebelliousness that can go as far as being belligerent and ostentatious about being different. They will flaunt their differences as a means of gaining attention. Natives with this combination can be domineering and self-centered in their relationships with friends, where they expect others to play by their rules. Saturn in Aquarius natives can be aloof in their relationships.

Saturn in Pisces

Saturn in Pisces can be difficult, as Pisces is the sign of completion as well as the sign of self-sacrifice. Natives can become trapped in their memories of the past or their fears that an area of their life will end before they are ready for it to be completed. This placement can ultimately help them overcome their irrational fears. Life can force these individuals to become more understanding and compassionate. Those with this placement may need more quiet time so that they can process past memories and fears of the future. Meditative time and some amount of peaceful solitude can also help them get in touch with their own needs when they have been too caught up in helping others at their own expense.

Gift: Saturn in sensitive Pisces will serve to develop a more spiritual approach to life as the native experiences the value of faith. The life circumstances they have faced, along with an awakened compassion and empathy for the pain and suffering of

Saturn in Pisces natives may need more meditative time and some amount of peaceful solitude so that they can process past memories and fears of the future. Their life's circumstances may have awakened compassion and empathy for others, strengthening their faith, while they must learn to set boundaries to respect their own well-being.

others, further strengthen their faith along with a desire to care for those who are less fortunate. At the same time, these individuals are learning how to set boundaries and discernment so that they develop a healthy respect for their own well-being while they sustain their compassion for others.

Shadow: The shadow side of Saturn in Pisces is an innocence that does not realistically assess who needs help and who may be taking advantage of their good nature. Eventually, after a boatload of negative experiences, these individuals learn to apply their sensitivity as a tool for discernment and let Saturn do its job of setting limits. Romanticizing others and self-sacrificing at their own expense are shadow sides of this placement that Saturn is more than willing to point out.

SATURN IN THE HOUSES

Saturn in each of the houses indicates the area of life where learning based upon sign placement will take place. These are areas where the native will develop the discipline and responsibility that will contribute to their maturation process. Saturn points out wherever weaknesses exist and gives the individual a choice to make changes and grow up or experience a less than fulfilling life.

Saturn in the First House

The First House rules appearance, health, general temperament, and sense of self. The First House defines you and the image you project to others.

Saturn in the First House brings self-imposed limitations. The native will likely be prone to restricting themselves or their behavior for one reason or another. The placement also helps the native to develop a realistic approach to life's circumstances and experiences. As time goes on, a strengthening of character and fine maturation of their persona occurs that bestows wisdom and good judgment.

Gift: Natives with Saturn in the First House are realistic about who they are and what they can offer. They are mature, disciplined, responsible, and hardworking. They are not easily dissuaded by challenges and obstacles. Saturn is in the house ruled by Aries in the natural Zodiac, and the Martian nature of this placement gives the native fortitude and courage. These natives are generally self-sufficient and take responsibility for their own destiny and actions.

Shadow: An ultraconservative approach to taking on life's challenges and adventures can occur. Aries is the sign of new beginnings, and Saturn in Aries's house may create self-imposed limitations in order to avoid venturing forth into unknown territory. They may prefer to go along with the tried and true at the expense of their own growth and development. These natives may have to deal with overriding fears and anxieties until they gain the courage to move forward. Once they do, they will develop added confidence and self-worth. The challenge of this placement is to be able to face fears, grow beyond limitations, and take well-calculated risks. The shadow side can manifest as a cold and calculating approach to life. The native can be overly materialistic and self-oriented. Much will depend upon the sign that Saturn is placed in and the other planetary energies that are affecting Saturn in the birth chart.

Saturn in the Second House

The Second House is connected with finances, values, material possessions, talents, and resources.

The Second House represents the value we give to ourselves and, in turn, that which we possess.

Saturn in Taurus's natural home will work hard to establish financial security and long-term investment stability. In the Second House, Saturn can exert discipline in regard to spending. They can successfully limit excess spending and curtail overindulgences so that they are able to stay within their budget. Since the Second House also rules self-worth, these individuals learn over time how to value themselves and not be underpaid or unappreciated for their value and worth. They seek realistic compensation for their value and experience.

Gift: Natives with Saturn in the Second House are persistent and hardworking. Building a solid financial structure is key on their agenda, and these natives are realistic about their investment strategies and will seek those opportunities that pay off in the long term. They are shrewd in business and understand value, so they are able to realistically assess how to get a good deal. The Second House is also connected to self-worth, and these natives will work to develop their talents and abilities throughout their lives. Since the Second House belongs to Venus-ruled Taurus, many have artistic gifts. As they acknowledge their various talents and abilities, they strengthen their self-image.

Shadow: The shadow side of this placement shows up as a poor self-image. The native may experience deprivation before they can get in touch with their real value. Saturn will sometimes work through placing obstacles and limitations before the native until they are forced to reassess their situation. These natives can also place too much emphasis on the acquisition of material resources. Hoarding and possessiveness can result from fear of not having enough.

Saturn in the Third House

The Third House is connected with ideas, communication, siblings, neighbors, and short journeys.

Saturn in a house governed by Mercury can incline these natives toward analytical and logical thinking.

Gift: The gift of Saturn in the Third House is that the native carefully chooses their words so that they can communicate clearly and effectively. These natives are logical and to the point. They are likely to possess good critical thinking skills along with good analytical abilities. Individuals with this placement possess mental discipline and don't share information unless they know what they are speaking of. They prefer to have a depth of knowledge on a few subjects rather than a little knowledge on a broad number of topics. They are willing to put in the necessary time and energy to be fully trained in any particular field.

Shadow: The shadow side of this placement is that these individuals find connecting with others challenging. Some may be limited by social inhibition or extreme shyness. The Third House is the area of the chart connected with communication, and Saturn here can represent blocks and limitations in this area. They can have a fear of speaking in public for fear of being judged and criticized. These natives can fear that they are intellectually inferior. Their childhood may have been marked by loneliness and feelings of isolation. The Third House rules siblings, and Saturn in this position can indicate sibling rivalry or difficulties with siblings or the lack of siblings. Natives with this placement can be prone to worry and negative thinking. They can also be overly critical of others.

Saturn in the Fourth House can indicate an individual who has strong attachments to the home and family. Ancestral legacies and family traditions are important.

Saturn in the Fourth House

The Fourth House is about the home, family, genetic inheritance, foundational stability, innermost feelings, later life, and the end of matters.

Saturn in the Cancer-ruled Fourth House can indicate an individual who has strong attachments to the home and family. Ancestral legacies and family traditions are important. These natives may be drawn to architecture and construction since Saturn is connected to structures.

Gift: Natives with a Fourth-House Saturn are dependable and will often take on added responsibilities for family members and people they care about. Family honor and respect for their ancestral heritage are important to them.

Shadow: Difficulties during early childhood or a strict upbringing can cause these individuals to become emotionally unavailable in their adult life. Parental approval may have been hard to come by, leading to deep-rooted insecurities. The shadow side of a Fourth-House Saturn can be blockages or difficulty in expressing one's feelings. They can feel isolated from their family, especially later in life. These natives may struggle with being able to provide for the family materially; added burdens may occur regarding the care of family members whom they are not able to meet.

Saturn in the Fifth House

The Fifth House rules creative self-expression, children, love, passion, romance, playfulness, and joy.

Natives with Saturn in Leo's Fifth House are likely to take a conservative and organized approach to creative self-expression and speculation. They are careful investors and do their research prior to any type of speculative venture. These natives are likely to take a more conservative approach to dating and romantic involvement.

Gift: Saturn in the Fifth House natives are organized and apply structure to their creative endeavors. This placement assists them in marketing and in combining their artistic expressions with business management. They can excel in fields that take a creative approach to business dealings or fields that deal directly with artistic expressions. They like to be well prepared and organized in any form of creative expression, marketing venture, or event planning. They can apply the same propensity for organization and structure to the education or management of children. These individuals have the patience and determination to master any creative art form that they are drawn to and enjoy.

Shadow: These natives can experience financial loss through their speculative ventures due to an unrealistic assessment prior to investing. They can overestimate the investment potential or not do their homework evaluating the people they are dealing with. Heavy responsibilities may occur around the care of children. These natives may find it difficult to interact with children and pets. A tendency to be overly strict can occur. They need to learn how to make time for fun and games. Their romantic expression may be blocked.

Saturn in the Sixth House

The Sixth House governs daily routines, acts of service, the work-life balance, health, due diligence, pet care, coworkers, and employees.

The Sixth House belongs to Mercury-ruled Virgo, which inclines these natives to take a highly organized approach to their schedules and day-to-day activities. Adaptation to healthy routines may occur following challenges in areas related to physical health, mental stressors, or health or workplace challenges.

> Saturn in the Sixth House can bring the native great pride and accomplishments in their jobs.

Gift: Saturn in the Sixth House can bring the native great pride and accomplishments in their jobs. They take their job responsibilities seriously and are organized in their methodologies and preparedness. They can be counted on for their high moral code and workmanship. They will often take on tasks that others may find arduous and unappealing. Once these individuals embrace healthy, life-supporting routines, they are able to stick to them and organize themselves, and others, accordingly. An important gift that individuals glean from this placement of Saturn is self-empowerment. They learn that they can take responsibility for their mental and physical well-being through adapting and embracing good habits and healthy routines. They understand the value of the upkeep and periodic maintenance that can be applied to several departments of life in order to further preservation and enhance sustainability.

Shadow: This native can be somewhat of a taskmaster. Relationships with coworkers and employees can be strained due to the heavy demands placed upon them. The workplace environment may be challenging or unsuitable, or these individuals may have difficulty in finding suitable work. Low self-esteem issues may have to be addressed in order to improve their presentation skills and preparedness. Failing health can result from poor daily health routines, a lack of proper nutrition, or negative habits in general. High stress and anxiety levels may require a reevaluation of daily routines and incorporating routines that serve to alleviate stress such as consistent exercise practices and nutritional counseling.

Saturn in the Seventh House

The Seventh House rules close personal relationships, agreements, and compromises.

Saturn in Venus-ruled Libra's house is fortunate for business and personal partnerships as well as dealings with the public. Saturn is exalted in Libra, and the Seventh House belongs to Libra, with its rulership over these areas. These natives understand that no man or woman is an island and that we all need each other. Through vigilance, fairness, and responsibility, they strive to bring harmony and fairness to all of their relationships, both business and personal.

Gift: Saturn in the Seventh House individuals seek to strengthen and deepen their personal and business relationships. They are conscientious regarding their participation in partnerships and seek the development of mutual respect and fair and honest interactions. They are loyal, dependable, and willing to work on issues as they develop. They dislike superficiality and relationships that lack substance. These natives are good strategic negotiators. They are able to logically organize key points that are up for discussion, they are fair-minded, and they operate within a code of integrity and honor.

Shadow: Individuals with this placement can have difficulty in forming close attachments due to their rigidity and air of detachment. Commitment can be scary for these natives, especially if previous commitments did not go well. It is likely that they have high standards for partnerships, possibly standards that are very hard to meet. The shadow side of this placement can be that they need to learn how to cooperate with others. Soul searching may be necessary in order to determine subconscious obstacles that are preventing the achievement of successful connections with others.

Saturn in the Eighth House

The Eighth House rules joint ventures, intimacy, sex, death, transformation, and psychic dimensions.

Saturn in Pluto's house of transformation provides the discipline and structure that is needed to make evolutionary changes in one's life. The Eighth House pertains to shared resources, and these natives can be organized and reliable in the management of other people's money and material resources. These individuals can be very private and secretive, although with Saturn in the Eighth House, they may have learned the hard way that honesty, honor, and integrity are the way to go.

Individuals with Saturn in the Eighth House are able to handle crises with the discipline and structure that is needed to make evolutionary changes in their life.

Gift: Individuals with Saturn in the Eighth House are competent in their ability to handle crises and cope with changes in their lives. They are able to take a step-by-step approach to get back on their feet. They are well aware of the value of transformation and will work hard to identify issues that are causing them mental, emotional, or physical pain and suffering. They believe in change and their ability to change, and Saturn in this position gives these natives the fortitude to stick with a path that will support that change. Their gift is that they are able to reinvent themselves as a means of coping with difficult situations.

Shadow: The shadow side of Saturn in the Eighth House can be a tendency to carry grudges and criticize others. Issues with shared resources can occur, and these natives may learn over time that a straightforward approach works better in the long run. The Eighth House also rules debt,

alimony, and inheritances, and these individuals can run into obstacles in these areas. They can wield power and control over others in order to benefit from shared possessions and monetary resources. Similarly, these natives can use manipulation and control tactics in their intimate relationships. Some repression or restraint can occur in the area of intimacy.

Saturn in the Ninth House

The Ninth House rules higher education, long-term goals, foreign travel, publicity, adventures, religion, and philosophical and ethical pursuits.

Saturn in Sagittarius's Ninth House works hand in hand with Jupitarian energy to manifest dreams and visions. Saturn adds a reality check to Jupiter's expansive, idealistic, and sometimes indulgent nature. It is important for them to subscribe to a philosophy that is practical and that makes sense out in the world. They can formulate their own philosophy or subscribe to existing spiritual, religious, scientific, or other ideological structures.

Gift: Individuals with Saturn in the Ninth House are generally seekers of knowledge, and they will often embark upon traditional educational paths for their education. They are studious and generally disciplined in their learning styles. They see the attainment of knowledge as a doorway to obtaining status and professional advancement. These natives can translate their knowledge into organized and logical curriculums that they can share with others. They can become effective educators. These natives are able to help others by offering them a fresh perspective that is replete with practical, common-sense solutions. They are well versed in the importance of maintaining perspective and will seek practices and ideologies that will redirect their attention from the mundane stressors in their daily lives. Travel can also provide much-needed perspective, which they are likely to pursue with much seriousness and a great deal of preparation.

Shadow: The shadow side of a Ninth-House Saturn placement is that these natives can be narrow-minded and have rigid viewpoints associated with their beliefs and closely held ideologies. Black-and-white thinking can alienate them from others. They may have difficulties in formulating a viable perspective that helps them cope with day-to-day stresses. As a result, they may suffer from depression. Insignificant occurrences and minor limitations can be overwhelming to them due to their inability to resort to faith in a higher power.

> The shadow side of a Ninth-House Saturn placement is that these natives can be narrow-minded and have rigid viewpoints associated with their beliefs and closely held ideologies.

Saturn in the Tenth House

The Tenth House rules public achievements, reputation, authority, and prestige.

Saturn is at home in Capricorn's Tenth House, a placement primarily associated with career, social status, and reputation. These natives are able to pursue a path that ensures that they are well prepared for any position that they set their sights on. They have an inherent understanding of what it takes to get to where they want to be.

Gift: A Tenth-House placement of Saturn promotes a healthy respect for authority and for those in positions of power. These natives possess moral integrity, honesty, and professionalism that gains notice and recognition from those in positions of authority and power. These natives are able

to sustain a strong focus and a disciplined approach to attaining success. They don't take shortcuts when it comes to achieving their professional goals.

Shadow: These natives can be drawn into power struggles with others. Their stubbornness and rigidity can be hindrances to the actual attainment of success that they so dearly strive for. These natives have a profound disregard for others. They are highly competitive and overly ambitious. Their desperation to be successful is palpable and works against them since planets in the Tenth House are at the top of the chart, so negative manifestations of the planetary energies are visible to all. Saturn in the Tenth House can also manifest as a lack of ambition due to poor self-esteem or other issues that have not been successfully resolved.

Saturn in the Eleventh House

The Eleventh House rules friends, hopes, wishes, groups, and a sense of belonging in the world.

Saturn in the Eleventh House is well placed since this house is traditionally ruled by Aquarius, with the dual rulership of Uranus and Saturn. The Eleventh House rules hopes and wishes, and with this Saturn placement, the native approaches manifesting their intentions in a practical and logical manner. These natives may enjoy a certain popularity; however, they take their friendships very seriously and prefer to limit those closest to them to a few.

Gift: Individuals with Saturn in the Eleventh House have a basic appreciation of

Saturn in the Eleventh House natives may enjoy a certain popularity, but they prefer friendships with a trusted few and will generally cultivate these friendships over a long period of time.

approach to society in general. As a result, they can worry over whom they should trust and who their real friends are. They can sometimes end relationships because they don't feel that these people are useful or helpful to their aspirations. The challenge for anyone with Saturn in the Eleventh House is to foster a deeper understanding of others and to relate to individuals they want to keep in their lives with loyalty and responsibility. Their focus on society in general and being part of something bigger can compete with their desire to have satisfying and fulfilling friendships.

Saturn in the Twelfth House

The Twelfth House rules secrets, unconscious patterns, karma, closure, institutions, connections with higher sources, enlightenment, and undoing.

Saturn in Pisces's domain, the Twelfth House, indicates a native who is intent on delving into and releasing unconscious fears and blockages so that they can merge with the divine. This is a meditative position of Saturn. Often, these natives need time alone so that they can turn their attention inward. The Twelfth House is known as a house of solitude, which is really about being alone with oneself. Saturn will create situations so that the native has to connect with themselves, whether they do it voluntarily or subconsciously create situations that force them to be solitary so that they can connect with themselves.

social networking from a practical point of view. Social interactions along with community collaborations and connections are supportive to both personal and group ambitions. These individuals can take advantage of technological solutions in order to reach larger numbers of people since Aquarius, the Zodiac's natural owner of the Eleventh House, rules technology and other innovative and futuristic approaches for reaching multitudes. The Eleventh House rules friendships. Natives with this placement prefer friendships with a trusted few, and they will generally cultivate these friendships over a long period of time. Honesty and integrity are important to them, and their authenticity is often admired by those who interact with them.

Shadow: These natives can come off as detached and aloof, and their motives can be easily misinterpreted by others due to their apparent lack of warmth and utilitarian

Gift: The gift of this placement is that these natives have a dedicated interest in connecting to the transcendent realms. They are focused on and will work hard to develop the spiritual side of their nature. Saturn's challenge in this position is to develop faith and trust. The Piscean energy is one of completion. These natives want to be complete with any issues on the material plane so that they can be at peace and connect with higher realms. Saturn gives them the discipline and focus to succeed. Saturn in this position has a sense of responsibility to those who are less fortunate. They are compassionate and sympathetic to the problems of others. It is not uncommon for them to find work in hospitals and other institutions of healing and rehabilitation, government agencies, and even large corporations.

Shadow: The shadow side of this position can manifest as a fear of being alone. The Twelfth House is also known as the house of karma, meaning that painful memories can be associated with this placement and yield a fear of solitude that may lead to the native having to delve into their deepest fears. Saturn, also known as the Lord of Karma, can facilitate subconscious fears and memories rising to the surface. This can include feelings of guilt and fears of being out of control. Subconscious fears may be overwhelming at times.

SATURN COMBINATIONS

Saturn/Sun

Saturn rules responsibility, adjustments to limitations, sustainability, and structure.

The Sun indicates purpose, self-expression, creative life force, and conscious will.

Saturn in combination with the Sun brings discipline and responsibility to the conscious will. These natives are responsible and mature, and they will work hard for what they want. Saturn has a sobering effect on the luminous energy of the Sun.

These natives can be serious and approach problems with deliberation and practicality. The Saturnian influence can also affect these natives' sense of humor. Every now and then, they will come out with very funny, sarcastic one-liners.

Gift: A strong sense of responsibility and trustworthiness is characteristic of the gift from this combination. This individual takes responsibility for themselves in any situation. They bring a practical orientation to problem solving. They have good follow-through. The organizational ability and disciplined nature of Saturn assists the Sun in achieving self-realization and manifesting their higher purpose.

> The Saturnian influence can also affect these natives' sense of humor. Every now and then, they will come out with very funny, sarcastic one-liners.

Shadow: The dampening effect of Saturn on the Sun's ambition, although frustrating, can yield ultimate fulfillment once the native accepts limitations and is willing to work through them. Saturn will be the first to point out ego aggrandizement and shortcuts should the native choose to follow that path. Saturn is the master teacher and, once embraced, will lead to a much better result. Saturn looks to create resilient structures that can pass the test of time. Natives with a Sun/Saturn combination can be hard on themselves, as they feel that no matter how much they do, it is never enough. Excessive criticism and thwarted ego fulfillment from their upbringing can lead to self-consciousness that inhibits their self-expression and ambition. These natives can get caught up in a plethora of "should" and "should not," which may have initially come from their upbringing but has now been internalized,

Saturn's sobering effect on the Moon generates orderliness, discipline, and moderation. These individuals are naturally responsible and responsive emotionally to others but can experience inherent pessimism, which may make them overly critical.

others. They are realistic, persevering, and innately possess a good amount of common sense. Others appreciate that they follow through on their commitments and their mature attitude. They understand hardship and can offer empathy and realistic solutions. These natives are accomplished. They do not let their emotions get in the way when performing essential and critical activities and tasks. They are gifted with self-control and discipline.

Shadow: An undercurrent of guilt can plague these individuals. They may be overly responsible and thereby feel that they are never toeing the line. On the other hand, the shadow of this combination can manifest as an inherent pessimism, which can manifest as someone who is overly critical of situations they encounter and of others they engage with. It may be difficult for them to trust others. Saturn can feel depressing, stuck, as if any situation will never change. Emotions may not flow freely. These natives may feel emotionally unsupported. The heightened pessimism of the Saturnian influence on the Moon can magnify the potential for a negative outcome. These natives can become overshadowed by their fears and potential vulnerability.

along with all of the guilt and self-abnegation that goes along with it.

Saturn/Moon

Saturn rules responsibility, adjustments to limitations, sustainability, and structure.

The Moon rules the soul, core instincts, the personality, and subconscious conditioning.

Saturn can have a sobering effect on the Moon, which can, at times, inhibit one's emotional expression. These natives are very sensitive and feel very deeply, although they may have difficulty opening themselves to others. In turn, the native may be more apt to identify with material things and daily mundane activities. The Saturn influence bestows an inclination toward orderliness, discipline, and moderation.

Gift: These individuals are naturally responsible and responsive emotionally to

Saturn/Mercury

Saturn rules responsibility, adjustments to limitations, sustainability, and structure.

Mercury rules communication, mental processes, and the logical mind.

Combining Mercury and Saturn brings logic and structure to the thinking process. These natives are generally focused and well-disciplined in their thinking processes. They like to know what they are talking about and will usually go the extra mile to be sure they have all the facts.

Gift: These individuals have the discipline and focus to apply themselves to mentally challenging tasks. They are systematic in their approach and are excellent presenters, especially in situations that require a logical and well-thought-out approach. The pairing of Mercury and Saturn is favorable for sticking to verbal agreements and commitments as well as for dealing with any project that requires stamina and follow-through. Those with this combination are realistic and practical. They are good listeners and value learning from experience. Many natives with this combination are scientifically and mathematically oriented, and some natives are musically inclined, especially where a fixed rhythm and a lot of skill is required.

Shadow: The pessimistic side of Saturn can incline these natives to worry and depression. They can feel that they never know all that they should and have an inferiority complex that relates to the learning capabilities. A tendency to be rigid, narrow-minded, and unyielding can occur in situations that require more buoyancy and enthusiasm. The monotony of their tone can make it difficult for others to listen to them. They can be overly inhibited and fearful in social situations.

Saturn/Venus

Saturn rules responsibility, adjustments to limitations, sustainability, and structure.

Venus represents love, relationships, beauty, values, comfort, and material resources.

Venus and Saturn energies work well together, as exemplified by the exaltation of Saturn in the Venus-ruled sign of Libra. Saturn gives concrete expression to the artistic tendencies of Venus. Saturn also produces committed and sustainable personal relationships.

Gift: Venus can tone down the harsher, more serious, and judgmental side of Saturn by adding a down-to-earth approach to awkward situations. Saturn brings added responsibility and commitment to partnerships and social relationships. These natives are not easily dissuaded by minor squabbles and disagreements. They understand the more serious side of relationships, which can have its ups and downs. They have a practical orientation as to what it takes to have successful relationships. They add a sense of fair play and presence to social situations. The Venus/Saturn combination can be helpful to artists and those engaged in creative undertakings. Saturn can bring concrete expression to their Venusian tendencies. These natives can be skilled in business and financial affairs, whereby Saturn adds practicality and good judgment to their endeavors.

Shadow: The shadow side of a Venus/Saturn combination can manifest as a fear of abandonment. These natives can hold on to difficult experiences in life where they were disappointed by love. The memory of past situations that did not work out for them can overshadow their present-day personal and social relationships. They can become reticent and avoid social situations in general. Saturn can dampen the freer-flowing, pleasure-oriented side of Venus. A melancholic disposition can follow that causes them to be shy, stiffly formal, or totally withdrawn for social contact.

Saturn/Mars

Saturn rules responsibility, adjustments to limitations, sustainability, and structure.

Mars rules assertiveness, energy, drive, and courage.

Saturn can stymie the "go for it" side of Mars. This combination is compared to having one foot on the gas pedal and the other on the brake. Saturn is the taskmaster. Saturn wants to bring order and discipline to the impulsive Mars energy. With discipline and a positive attitude, the bright side of a Mars/Saturn combination can manifest, resulting in noteworthy accomplishments.

Mars is exalted in Saturn-ruled Capricorn. This combination is steadfast and consistent, and the conscious balance between these two energies can hold the key to successful manifestation.

Gift: Just enough restraint, just enough push is the best outcome for this combination, which can be highly productive when directed and combined with a step-by-step approach. The discipline of Saturn can be used to direct anger, frustration, impatience, and the passion of Mars to yield positive outcomes.

Shadow: Some degree of defiant unwillingness can be expected when the shadow side of the Mars and Saturn combination is dominating. A feeling occurs of being stuck, comparable to applying the gas and the brake at the same time. Frustration, impatience, and outbursts of anger can ensue when these energies are not being managed and used consciously. The shadow side of this combination can include anger and frustration resulting from situations and instances when self-control is tested. Staying flexible physically is helpful to anyone with a Mars/Saturn combination in their chart. Mars rules the muscles, and Saturn rules the joints and bones. Exercise modalities that are supportive to musculature and skeletal systems will be beneficial.

Saturn/Jupiter

Saturn rules responsibility, adjustments to limitations, sustainability, and structure.

Jupiter represents the higher mind, greater truths, expansiveness, hope, and optimism.

Jupiter and Saturn, although seemingly contradictory energies representing expansion and contraction, work in combination to bring structure and practical steps to the manifestation of ideals and aspirations.

The late astrologer Nick Anthony Fiorenza aptly describes the energies of Jupiter and Saturn on his website Lunarplanner.com: "Jupiter is inclusive and embracing while Saturn is exclusive and segregating. Saturn imposes boundaries, walls, rules and regulations. Saturn forces us to confront our fears and Jupiter impels us to claim our wisdom. Saturn demonstrates and validates by concretizing in form that which Jupiter expands to embrace."

Gift: Mastery occurs when striking a balance between Jupiter, "The Great Benefic," and Saturn, "The Great Malefic," in traditional astrology. Gifts derived from this blending include realistic optimism, a mature moral code and set of ethics, and sustainable expansion that is based upon the establishment of solid structures and jurisprudence. The individual is able to strike a balance between freedom and responsibility, blend logic with philosophy, and combine patience and good judgment in all types of business and bold undertakings. These natives are able to bring faith, trust, and patience to situations when obstacles are encountered and when snags arise. They benefit from employing discipline and commitment to their visions and goals, and they can bring perspective to life's hardships and difficulties.

Shadow: The shadow side of a Jupiter/Saturn combination involves periods of disproportionate gain, extravagance, and overindulgence followed by periods of little gain or even loss, frugality, and tremendous disciplining. Rather than integrating the above attitudes and behaviors, the native sticks with one type of extreme behavior pattern and then, when obstacles arise or goals are not met, their behavior patterns switch to opposing behaviors. These natives have difficulty keeping the faith and may go from periods of confidence and optimism to periods of being depressed and pessimistic. They have difficulty integrating the opposing energies of expansion and contraction, faith and discipline, and cautiousness and foolhardiness.

Saturn/Uranus

Saturn rules responsibility, adjustments to limitations, sustainability, and structure.

Uranus rules intuition, originality, individuality, and the sudden and unexpected.

Saturn is interested in fortifying and preserving existing structures, whereas Uranus's job is to bring forward new and original structures that are more appropriate for the times. Saturn represents responsibility, and Uranus represents freedom. Individuals with these two planets in combination are bridge builders between old ways and new. They are dissatisfied with the status quo and see how circumstances can be improved.

Gift: These natives can be thrust into challenging situations, where they are called upon to reconcile the contradictory manifestations of Saturn and Uranus. They can facilitate a logical and well-thought-out execution of large-scale innovative plans and projects. They can successfully decode innovative technology solutions to those who are less technologically savvy. These natives work well at finding compromise between opposing factions in society. Astrologer Donna Cunningham, in

Jupiter and Saturn, although seemingly contradictory energies representing expansion and contraction, work in combination to bring structure and practical steps for the manifestation of ideals and aspirations.

an article published in the July 6, 2015, issue of *The Mountain Astrologer*, aptly coined individuals with Saturn/Uranus combinations as "grounded eccentrics and sane weirdos." She describes the blending of these energies as someone who is "self-directed and self-motivated" and "wise elders of their tribes."

Shadow: The shadow side of this combination is that these individuals can be prone to anxiety and indecision from continually being pulled into situations where they have strongly different urges. On the one hand, they want to be known as being responsible; on the other, they have the overwhelming urge to break free from expectations and obligations. It can be difficult for these natives to find inner peace because they feel that new frontiers are out there for them, yet they want to fulfill their responsibilities. They can be fearful and lack confidence to move forward, yet they resent having restrictions. These individuals may not trust that anything in their lives will stay constant.

Saturn/Neptune

Saturn rules responsibility, adjustments to limitations, sustainability, and structure.

Neptune rules ideals, creative imagination, transcendence, compassion, and vision.

Saturn is tasked with creating resilient and sustainable formats and structures, whereas Neptune dissolves boundaries and borders so that merging occurs with the unbounded. Saturn rules the material world, and Neptune rules the transcendent. Saturn rules fears, and Neptune rules trust.

Gift: Saturn can bring focus, structure, and organization to one's dreams and visions. These natives are able to successfully balance realistic expectations with faith and trust that their dreams can manifest. They have a belief that anything is possible. They are practical dreamers and visionaries who can achieve their dreams with grit, discipline, focus, vision, creativity, and a lot of trust. These natives are often seekers on a path to higher consciousness. They understand the basic laws of nature, including the law of cause and effect.

Shadow: The shadow side of a Saturn/Neptune combination is a fear that the rug will be pulled out from underneath them. These natives can feel ungrounded, that they cannot fully depend or trust anything or anyone in this world. It can be very difficult for these individuals to fully let go and trust. Instead, they can overperform for fear that they are not doing enough or underperform with an attitude of "why

bother?" They are prone to frequent episodes of depression and bouts of forsakenness. They have an underlying feeling of dissatisfaction with everyday life but lack the focus or will to do anything about it.

Saturn/Pluto

Saturn rules responsibility, adjustments to limitations, sustainability, and structure.

Pluto represents regeneration; transformation; and a compelling, fundamental approach.

The combination of Saturn and Pluto can produce tremendous discipline toward the process of self-regeneration and transformation, or this combination can bring forward the darker side of both energies. Deeply subconscious fears and paranoia may be stimulated. At the social level, when these two planetary bodies meet, events are triggered, including influenza and viral outbreaks, as well as other apocalyptic events that cause mass hysteria.

It is likely that circumstances will contribute to these natives having to reinvent themselves several times over the course of their lives.

Gift: The combination of Saturn and Pluto offers the individual the gift of a focused and disciplined approach to undertaking life's challenges and subsequent changes. They have tremendous discipline and display amazing fortitude and perseverance. These natives are strong in their convictions, and they believe in self-empowerment through transformation and regeneration. They are supportive of helping others take charge of their lives and make changes for their betterment. These individuals can effect subtle yet powerful changes in their own lives and in society.

♃♄

Shadow: The shadow side of the combination of Saturn and Pluto can bring great fear of the unknown. Subconscious fears that rise up and cause anxiety and panic are possible, making it necessary for the native to ideally pause and take stock of the core issues that can be buried. Paranoia can overshadow social interactions and personal relationships. These natives can be manipulative and self-serving and strategically attempt to control others for fear that others will exert control over them. Obsessive-compulsive behavior patterns are likely. Material goals and ambition can be sought at the expense of anyone or anything that gets in their path.

Saturn/Chiron

Saturn rules responsibility, adjustments to limitations, sustainability, and structure.

Chiron represents core wounds and the desire to overcome them, and healing.

The combination of Saturn and Chiron can indicate core wounds connected with authority figures. These natives can take a disciplined approach to their own healing and the healing of others.

Gift: Natives with a Saturn/Chiron combination can be influential in creating structures and programs for healing and the development of higher consciousness. They can apply discipline and focus for their own healing. These natives are likely to prefer following organized, established programs for healing and expanding their consciousness. They can be advocates for humanitarian causes and will often assist in contributing to their successful outcome.

Shadow: These natives may have a domineering, critical parent who undermined their confidence and self-worth. They can be prone to feelings of guilt and, in ex-

The combination of Saturn and Pluto offers the individual the gift of a focused and disciplined approach to undertaking life's challenges and subsequent changes, displaying amazing fortitude and perseverance.

treme cases, feel guilty for their own existence. They can be hard on themselves, never feeling that they are doing enough.

Saturn/Eris

Saturn rules responsibility, adjustments to limitations, sustainability, and structure.

Eris represents the determination to remove limitations that impede the soul's evolution.

Gift: Saturn can add structure to Eris's intentions so that social change can follow a step-by-step approach to reach their desired outcome. Saturn also adds patience and perseverance, which can tone down the impetuous nature of Eris.

Shadow: Limitations and setbacks can throw a monkey wrench into plans and

♃♄

actions undertaken by the native. The native may have to do more soul searching before ascertaining a successful outcome.

Saturn/North Node

Saturn rules responsibility, adjustments to limitations, sustainability, and structure.

The North Node represents future direction, soul guidance, and fulfillment.

The North Node emphasizes the importance for the native to develop the attributes represented by Saturn, which include discipline, focus, and responsibilities to accomplish their heartfelt desires.

> The North Node emphasizes the importance for the native to develop the attributes represented by Saturn....

Gift: These natives have an opportunity to develop mastery in this lifetime. Through discipline and responsibility, they are able to attain their destined path. These individuals are focused on overcoming challenges and obstacles in their path. They benefit from staying on a straight and narrow track and embracing a resolute moral code. They benefit from adhering to protocols regarding timing and formalities.

Shadow: Natives with a Saturn/North Node combination can have a pessimistic attitude and may resist challenges before them. They can tend to hold on to the past and resist moving forward when letting go of the past is precisely what is needed and required.

Saturn/South Node

Saturn rules responsibility, adjustments to limitations, sustainability, and structure.

The South Node represents familiarity, gratification, and the path of least resistance.

The combination of Saturn and the South Node can indicate that the native is familiar with limitations and able to handle responsibilities. They are likely to prefer solitude and a humble lifestyle.

Gift: Discipline and self-mastery are a given for these individuals. They are capable of working in isolation and may have had to learn to be self-reliant. These are traits that they can carry forward in achieving their current ambitions.

Shadow: These individuals can have rigid personalities that are not comfortable relating to others. They can be cold and calculating and may have issues trusting others. These natives may want to embrace attributes that contribute to a flourishing society and include cooperation and interdependence.

Saturn/Ascendant

Saturn rules responsibility, adjustments to limitations, sustainability, and structure.

The Ascendant represents one's approach, orientation, and the window through which one sees the world.

Gift: These natives are disciplined and responsible. They can be counted on in situations where serious work needs to be done. They take a serious, no-nonsense approach and do well in circumstances that require consistency and a focused presence.

Shadow: The shadow side of a Saturn/Ascendant combination is that the natives approach life with a glass-half-empty orientation. They carry the burdens of the world on their shoulders and are frequently depressed and lonely. They may have incurred difficulties in early childhood that set the tone of their adult life unless they strive to bring in more joy.

Saturn/Midheaven (MC)

Saturn rules responsibility, adjustments to limitations, sustainability, and structure.

The Midheaven (MC) represents image, outer aspirations, and career orientation.

With Saturn at the top of the chart, a strong drive to succeed and achieve recognition is present.

Gift: Natives with a Saturn/Midheaven combination possess the focus and discipline needed in order to achieve their career ambitions. They are likely to be successful and gain recognition from those in positions of authority. They make good executives and administrators, where they seek sound policies that can lead to the stability of the organizations they lead.

Shadow: The shadow side of this placement is ambition at all costs. They can ride roughshod over others and be at risk of a fall from grace. Planets at the Midheaven (also called the *medium coeli*, or MC), are visible to society, so any deviation in their moral code can cause them disgrace and dishonor.

The Outer Planets, Including Pluto

The earliest identified planets, visible to the naked eye, were seen as gods and goddesses. The ancient astrologers' knowledge of the cosmic world ended once Saturn was reached. When Uranus, Neptune, and Pluto were discovered, a new realm opened up. This new realm increased awareness into the more subtle spiritual realms.

The discovery of each of the outer planetary bodies—Uranus; Neptune; and the later reclassified dwarf planet, Pluto—each correlated with distinct outer events that are synchronistic with the planetary meaning. Uranus's discovery in 1781 correlated with revolutionary events: the French Revolution, the American Revolution, and the Industrial Revolution. The discovery of Neptune in 1846 correlated with initial murmurings of the subconscious and deeper psychological insights, and Pluto's discovery in 1930 with Nazi Germany, the Great Depression, and, 15 years later, the atomic bomb.

URANUS

Although initially discovered on March 13, 1781, it was another century or so before Uranus was really understood and used in astrology. Uranus is twice as far from Earth as Saturn.

Uranus, also known as the Awakener, moves slowly and stays in each sign for approximately seven years. Individuals born with Uranus in the same sign will have an effect on the collective and will want to enlighten others on the values associated with the sign it is placed in. Uranus is electrifying and will activate planets and houses that it touches in an individualistic and often rebellious way. Uranus's position in the birth chart indicates how the individual responds to authority and cultural norms. Uranus is unpredictable in nature, with its erratic magnetosphere. A magnetosphere is essentially the magnetism surrounding a planet, similar to the

Wildcard planet Uranus is symbolized by the brave and rebellious nature of Prometheus, who was punished eternally for stealing fire from the gods. Uranus is a great awakener that can be a powerful channel of awareness for new ideas.

is symbolic of the fire of knowledge, which, in turn, represents freedom since it is truth that can set you free from whatever you are bound to, karmically or otherwise.

Historically, the discovery of Uranus coincided with revolutionary times, including the French and American Revolutions as well as the Industrial Revolution. Uranus is associated with freedom, and these revolutions were involved in the fight for independence and freedom. The Industrial Revolution brought innovation, which is also ruled by Uranus.

Uranus is referred to as a quantum planet, meaning that it crosses the boundary between fate and free will. You can predict lightning, but you cannot predict where it will land. Astrologer Rick Levine aptly describes Uranus as the instantaneous resolution of irresolvable opposites, whereby Uranus releases tension from the expression that was not expressed. Uranus awakens us.

atmosphere. Unlike other planetary atmospheres, the magnetic field on Uranus turns off and on.

Uranus is called the sideways planet because its rotation axis is tilted by about 98 degrees. Most astronomers indicate that because it's tilted more than 90 degrees, the planet rotates in the direction opposite most of the planets. The fact that it is "lying on its side" may have been caused by a collision with another celestial body.

Uranus, the natural ruler of Aquarius, is connected with personal freedom, innovation, individuality, and the unexpected. Uranus is a wild card that cannot be controlled.

Mythically, Prometheus is symbolic for the planet Uranus. As the myth goes, Prometheus was chained to a rock as a punishment for stealing fire from the gods and bringing it to the people. The fire he stole

Dane Rudhyar describes Uranus as the planet of individual transfiguration, where we can personally become a focal point for the release of an aspect of the Universal Mind. As you experiment, a point of return exists when things fall into place because they make sense to you, then you have silence. You have arrived at your own knowing.

Uranus is connected with intuitive insights, spiritual awakenings, extreme fluctuations, unexpected events, individuality, and originality. Uranus is unstable, spontaneous, impulsive, and undisciplined. Uranus is further associated with invention, discovery, technology, genius, eccentricity, and electricity. Uranus seeks freedom and independence.

Uranus can be magical. Uranus activates in unpredictable ways.

Uranus is at home in the sign of Aquarius and in its detriment in the sign of Leo. Uranus is exalted in the sign of Scorpio and in its fall in the sign of Taurus.

Gift: Uranus is a great awakener that can be a powerful channel of awareness for new ideas. A strong, well-placed Uranus can bring forth a genius of sorts, through which new forms are innovated and new ways of thinking are illuminated.

Shadow: The shadow side of Uranus can leave you feeling wired, on edge, over-excited, or very restless. Uranus has an unexpected quality to it. Its sudden onset of events, symptoms, and revelations can lead to anxiety and frayed nerves when one is not grounded and balanced.

URANUS IN THE SIGNS

Uranus in each of the signs indicates how an individual manifests their individuality and their urge for freedom. The sign placement can also suggest the type of motivations that are behind a person's hopes and wishes.

It takes seven years for Uranus to move through each sign of the Zodiac and 84 years to move through all of the constellations. Everyone born during a given seven-year period has Uranus in the same sign except for those born at the very beginning or very end of a sign. Uranus can retrograde backward and then move forward again when moving between signs.

Sign placements are primarily generational for the outer planets. Uranus's house placement and the blending of Uranus with the other planetary bodies are more relevant factors when describing the soul's purpose and the individual's unique gifts.

Uranus in Aries
(1927–1935; 2010–2019)

Uranus in the sign of enthusiasm and leadership brings a clear and energized spark to whichever house placement and planetary body it touches. Uranus in Aries individuals are truly original, and the Aries placement gives them an edge in asserting their individuality.

Gift: These are the trailblazers who are daring and courageous. The Martian influence brings bravery, enthusiasm, innovation, inspiration, and wildness to whatever it touches. Personal freedom is important to these natives.

Shadow: The shadow side of Uranus in Mars-ruled Aries is a quick temper and an impetuous nature. This can be someone who seeks adventure for its own sake without forethought and without care for consequences to themselves or anyone else. Little follow-through results from the initial implementation.

Uranus in Taurus
(1934–1942; 2018–2026)

Uranus in Venus-ruled Taurus is a generation who is interested in original ways of using money and resources, updating outmoded values and traditions, and questioning the meaning of security as these principles relate to modern life. This placement can bring forth artistic and musical innovations as well as innovations that lead to the preservation of Earth's natural resources.

Gift: Uranus in Taurus brings a focus to the intrinsic value of material resources and the natural world. Innovations that relate to improving the quality of life are highlighted. Individuals born under this influence have a keen intuition for practical matters and are likely to have talents that can manifest in new and unusual ways.

The Uranus in Taurus generation is interested in original ways of using money and resources, updating outmoded values and traditions and questioning the meaning of security.

Shadow: The shadow side of Uranus in Taurus is a stubborn refusal to engage in innovations, an ardent adherence to convention and tradition, unstable finances, a disregard for Earth and its resources, and a possessiveness for material things.

Uranus in Gemini
(1941–1949; 2025–2033)

Uranus in Mercury-ruled Gemini produces a generation of people who bring forth new ideas and innovative ways of thinking. The combination of Mercury-ruled Gemini with Uranian originality can introduce technological advances and breakthroughs.

Gift: The sign placement of Uranus in Gemini produces innovation and original thinking in areas related to communica-

tion, the media, literature, education, transportation, and science. Natives born under this sign are intuitive thinkers who are here to seed new ways of thinking and communicating.

Shadow: The shadow side of this placement is extreme restlessness, a lack of follow-through on ideas, and eccentric thinking that is difficult to apply to life. Fickleness and possible dishonesty in relationships may come under the guise of personal freedom. This placement can yield social butterflies who don't seek substance in their interactions.

Uranus in Cancer (1948–1956)

The Uranus in Cancer generation is motivated to bring innovations to the family structure. This can include updating gender-based roles and domestic routines, modernizing family traditions, and expanding the boundaries of who we consider family.

Gift: Freedom of emotional expression is a gift that evolves out of the placement of Uranus in Cancer. Inhibitions that previously existed around the display of feelings, feelings centered around emotional support, and issues related to attachment and dependence are all brought out into the open so that innovative solutions can benefit society in general. These natives have an awakened appreciation for flashes of intuition and psychic impressions.

Shadow: The shadow side of Uranus in Cancer is a disregard for family values and a rebelliousness against parents and the family structure. These natives can lack respect for family members and want to disregard aspects of their upbringing rather than work through issues that may have developed. Sudden changes in mood and erratic emotional outbursts are likely.

Uranus in Leo (1955–1962)

Uranus in Sun-ruled Leo brings an awakened consciousness to love and romance; creative self-expression, including the arts and theater; and the upbringing of children. Technological advances are likely in art and entertainment fields.

Gift: Natives with Uranus in Leo seek freedom from traditions around courtship, dating, romance, and love. Technology solutions are implemented that change how people approach dating and romance. These individuals can be valiant, charming, and very expressive, and they are not afraid to be themselves.

Shadow: The shadow side of this placement is inflexibility and self-centeredness. These natives can be egomaniacal and uncooperative. They are overly dramatic and flaunt their eccentricities. Traditional views on loyalty and courtesy may not apply.

Uranus in Virgo (1961–1969)

The Uranus in the Mercury-ruled Virgo generation has brought innovative solutions to areas related to the health and service industries. This includes technical advancements in medicine, information processing, diagnostic services, and computer applications. These individuals went on to further revolutionize numerous technological and analytical tools that are helpful to the management of daily tasks.

Gift: Individuals with Uranus in Virgo excel at analyzing and distilling information in order to provide more efficient ways of doing everyday tasks. They like to get the most out of every situation, and as a result, they will employ groundbreaking tools that make their life easier.

> Natives with Uranus in Leo seek freedom from traditions around courtship, dating, romance, and love.

Shadow: Uranus in Virgo can exaggerate traits like perfectionism, black-and-white thinking, and critical propensities. They can be high-strung, prone to stress, and self-critical. These natives can lose track of the big picture. Technical tools support their tendency to drill down on details.

Uranus in Libra (1968–1975)

The generation with Uranus in Venus-ruled Libra is interested in bringing to light new ways of thinking regarding fairness, justice, and equality. Traditional views regarding marriage and partnerships are re-evaluated in regard to personal freedoms and shared responsibilities.

Gift: Those born with Uranus in Libra are likely to be gifted in artistic expression and the literary arts. Besides having an original way of expressing their talents, their appreciation includes new artistic, musical, and literary formats. These individuals have an awakened interest in law and the judicial system. "Equal rights for all" is a theme close to their hearts. Some may find themselves connected to societal structures that implement these changes.

Shadow: The shadow side of Uranus in Libra is that personal freedom becomes so important to the individual that they are commitment phobic and highly indecisive. Simple acts of cooperation can be difficult for them. As a result, they are highly unreliable and not able to get along with most people.

Uranus in Scorpio (1974–1981)

Uranus is well placed in Scorpio, the sign of its exaltation. This generation is inter-

The Uranus in Sagittarius generation is interested in updating the meaning of freedom as it relates to speech, beliefs, religion, and education. These individuals can talk about very difficult situations and are also able to laugh at themselves.

ested in making changes wherever it can, more specifically in areas connected to intimacy, health care, psychology, the management of resources, and the financial system as it relates to debt and working with other people's money.

Gift: Individuals with this placement are decisive, resourceful, and determined. They view change as necessary for society as well as in their personal lives. They are gifted in areas of research and analysis and have a knack for solving problems. They will find innovative solutions to release blockages in their unconscious and change troubling behavior patterns. They like to delve into life's mysteries.

Shadow: The Uranus in Scorpio influence can awaken obsessive and compulsive im-

pulses related to sex, anger, mortality, and jealousy. Their passions can get them into trouble. These natives can have control issues and resort to ruthless and manipulative behaviors. A propensity toward black-and-white thinking is present.

Uranus in Sagittarius (1981–1988)

The Uranus in Sagittarius generation is interested in updating the meaning of freedom as it relates to speech, beliefs, religion, and education. Innovations in progressive education and cultural interactions are likely. This generation values freedom and independence.

Gift: These natives think in terms of the big picture, and as a result, they excel in fields that relate to predicting trends. They tune in to futuristic waves of thought and are adept at getting ahead of the curve. These individuals are straightforward and can talk about very difficult situations. They are also able to laugh at themselves when they make a blunder.

Shadow: The shadow side of Uranus in Sagittarius is that these natives can have a rigid allegiance to eccentric religious and philosophical beliefs. Sagittarius is an energy of freedom, and with Uranus in this sign, the manifestation of freedom can be unorthodox and revolutionary. They can be brutally honest and lack sensitivity to others.

Uranus in Capricorn (1988–1996)

Innovations in business are front and center with the Uranus in Capricorn generation. They are likely to follow a more conservative approach to initiating these changes; however, the end result will bring innovative methods and new technologies that advance ways of doing business.

Gift: These are progressive innovators in government and business who can see where existing processes and structures are not fulfilling the needs of society. Their genius is bringing original yet practical and efficient solutions to all kinds of companies, institutions, and organizations, including the government and law enforcement. They are likely to consider every angle before initiating progressive innovations.

> Natives with Uranus in Pisces are highly idealistic, and they look for original ways to improve everyone's lives.

Shadow: The rebellious nature of Uranus can look to destroy societal structures and traditions for the sake of it. Individuals may challenge the government, laws, and authority figures, including law enforcement, without offering new and viable solutions. Individuals with this placement can be rigid and inflexible.

Uranus in Aquarius (1995–2003)

Uranus is well placed in Aquarius, and this placement brings forward individuals who are decidedly open-minded and those who will fight for moral principles. This generation acknowledges the value of humanity and the contributions of all people to the greater whole. Innovations in genetics, science, and technology will greatly excel at the hands of this group.

Gift: Individuals with this placement are highly original, independent thinkers. They are willing to accept people for their differences. Personal freedom is very important to them, and they understand that it is important to everyone else as well. They are open to new ideas and new ways of doing things, including the elimination of barriers between individuals and cultures and bringing scientific inventions and advances in technology to everyone.

Shadow: The shadow side of this placement manifests as extremes of unpractical eccentricity and an unwillingness to answer to anyone or anything. Extreme stubbornness and an "I don't care" attitude is possible.

Uranus in Pisces (2003–2011)

The Uranus in Pisces generation awakens universal compassion and brings attention to the less fortunate. Innovative implementations in humanitarian relief efforts and healing modalities are likely. A trend toward spirituality outside of dominant religious practices is present. Innovations are likely that will assist with substance abuse.

Gift: Natives with Uranus in Pisces are highly idealistic, and they look for original ways to improve everyone's lives. They are capable of understanding more abstract and transcendent concepts of human existence.

Shadow: The shadow side of this placement is impractical idealism that doesn't manifest into viable solutions. Deceptive practices and false narratives lead to perpetuating false truths and shadowy practices in all areas, especially those affecting the less fortunate. Drug and alcohol abuse can occur as a backlash to unrealistic expectations and ideals.

URANUS IN THE HOUSES

Uranus's house position indicates how a person will express their individuality and which area of life personal freedom will be highlighted for them. The house position can also indicate where the individual can expect sudden events and circumstances to influence their life. Uranus is a

Individuals with Uranus in the Second House are likely to find practical applications for new technologies and innovations, with a particular interest in preserving natural resources and humanitarian causes. They can appreciate others' individuality, and they value original ideas.

liberator, and the individual will want to break free from traditions and bring in new innovations.

Uranus in the First House

The First House rules appearance, health, general temperament, and sense of self. The First House defines you and the image you project to others.

Personal freedom is very important to individuals with Uranus in the First House. The First House is ruled by Aries in the natural Zodiac, so individuals with this placement are not shy about fully expressing their individuality in all of their actions. Uranus in the First House can bring a disruptive energy to situations and environments.

Gift: Uranus in the First House individuals take responsibility for their destiny and their actions. They are authentic in how they present themselves. They are generally honest and straightforward. Their intuition is well developed, and these natives have a sixth sense in their approach to people and situations. They have an altruistic desire to make changes in the world.

Shadow: The shadow side of this placement is someone who is strong-willed and not open to negotiating or compromise. It is their way or the highway. They can be restless, with a short concentration span. Their nervous systems are likely to be highly sensitive to noise and light, which can indirectly trigger anxiety. Their behavior is likely to be unpredictable and erratic.

Uranus in the Second House

The Second House is connected with finances, values, material possessions, talents, and resources.

The Second House represents the value we give to ourselves and, in turn, that which we possess.

These individuals are likely to find practical applications for new technologies and innovations. They have a particular interest in technologies related to natural resources and the preservation thereof.

Gift: Individuals with Uranus in the Second House have good intuition and can find innovative ways to earn money. Some do very well when self-employed or when they can find financial solutions that don't impede on their personal freedom. They can appreciate others' individuality and value original ideas. They often invest in or support humanitarian causes and original projects. Although they can find unusual ways to earn money, they are not materialistic in the traditional sense in that they care about human values and take into account the whole picture.

Shadow: These natives can have unsettled finances, with unexpected gains and losses. Gambling and speculation may appeal to these individuals; however, they may not take the time to fully investigate where they are putting their money. They prefer to go by hunches, which may not always guide them well. Financial and material losses can result.

Uranus in the Third House

The Third House is connected with ideas, communication, siblings, neighbors, and short journeys.

Uranus in a house governed by Mercury is well placed for innovative and even brilliant ideas. Open-mindedness and freedom of speech are important to them.

Gift: Individuals with Mercury in the Third House are intuitive thinkers who take a novel approach to solving problems, often

with out-of-the-box solutions. Their communication style can be offbeat and witty, and they present information in original and refreshing ways. These individuals are often involved in media and communication fields and have an unusual writing style, often choosing unconventional topics. They are open-minded and straightforward.

Shadow: The shadow side of this placement is a short attention span and varying opinions on the same topic. Mental instability is possible along with bouts of anxiety due to their overactive mental processes. Their restlessness makes them unable to follow through on their original and sometimes brilliant ideas. They can have up-and-down relationships with siblings.

Uranus in the Fourth House

The Fourth House is about the home, family, genetic inheritance, foundational stability, innermost feelings, later life, and the end of matters.

Uranus in the Fourth House can contribute to a home life or family structure that is different from the norm. They can have exceptional or unusual parents, or their homes may be a place frequented by community and family gatherings. Friends can be included as part of their extended family. Sudden changes of residence can occur.

Gift: These natives are open about discussing personal events that arise from their family background and upbringing. They prefer to bring issues out into the open so that they can be handled. These individuals will seek to bring innovative solutions to any festering difficulties. They are free spirits and are not likely to get attached to particular residences or places once they cease to support their current needs. They seek common values and ideas from those they call family, which may not always include their biological family.

Shadow: The shadow side of a Fourth-House Uranus placement is a restlessness that is hard to satisfy. Boredom occurs easily, and these natives may find it hard to completely relax in their environments. These individuals can become increasingly more eccentric as they age, thereby limiting their life experiences and potential fulfillment. They may be too independent to ever ask for help, even when they need it.

Uranus in the Fifth House

The Fifth House rules creative self-expression, children, love, passion, romance, playfulness, and joy.

Uranus in the Fifth House individuals take great pleasure in expressing themselves in their own unique way. Freedom of expression is a high priority, which can yield innovative and highly creative results.

Gift: Natives with Uranus in Leo's Fifth House are unusually creative, and they have innovative ways of expressing themselves. They are likely to have exceptional talent in some area of self-expression, which can include art, music, dance, or entertainment. Their children can have special and unusual gifts as well. Romantically, their flirtatious and zany behavior can be charming and magnetic. These individuals are masters of creative living and artists of life itself.

Shadow: Romantic life for these natives can be erratic due to their great need for personal freedom and dislike of conventional bonding patterns. These natives are often misunderstood since their passions can run hot and cold. Gambling and speculation can bring erratic results. They can experience losses due to quirky speculations that are not sound investments.

Uranus in the Sixth House

The Sixth House governs daily routines, acts of service, the work-life balance, health, due diligence, pet care, coworkers, and employees.

The Sixth House belongs to Mercury-ruled Virgo, which inclines these natives to seek daily routines. When Uranus is placed in this house, disruptions occur every time harmony is achieved.

Gift: Natives with Uranus in the Sixth House employ innovative solutions in their daily life both at home and at their jobs. Personal freedom is important to them, so they are willing to do what they can in order to make their lives more efficient since they are not fans of mundane tasks and humdrum routines. They prefer work that is unconventional and independent. They easily adapt to advanced technology solutions. Sixth-House Uranus individuals often adhere to alternate views on health care. They have strong intuitive insights and are likely to connect well with their bodily needs. Health, exercise, and nutrition guidance will likely come from their own insights and may differ from traditional views and even those of experts.

Shadow: The shadow side of this placement is that they can partake in unorthodox treatments that don't work and ultimately do them harm. They don't do well with most bosses and authority figures,

> Natives with Uranus in Leo's Fifth House are unusually creative, and they have innovative ways of expressing themselves.

who perceive them as incapable or irresponsible. Their defiant nature and poor listening skills can get them into trouble. Sudden and unexpected changes can occur in their employment if the native does not work for themselves.

Uranus in the Seventh House

The Seventh House rules close personal relationships, agreements, and compromises.

Uranus in Venus's Seventh House of partnerships enhances the native's need for independence in relationships. They do best in unconventional partnerships with mates who are unique and mentally stimulating.

Gift: Individuals with this placement are highly creative, and they have a knack for keeping relationships interesting. Honesty is highly regarded, and they are straightforward in their dealings in both personal and business relationships. Fairness and integrity are also valued as long as each person can be true to themselves. Codependency and undue clinginess are not on their agenda.

Shadow: The shadow side of this placement manifests as a cool, self-serving individual who cares more about their own justified ends. They can be commitment-phobic and irresponsible. Their rebellious side may show up in hurtful ways. Anxiety and restlessness can interfere with emotional and physical intimacy.

Uranus in the Eighth House

The Eighth House rules joint ventures, intimacy, sex, death, transformation, and psychic dimensions.

Uranus is in Pluto's house of transformation when it is placed in the Eighth House. Uranus is exalted in Scorpio, meaning that Uranus is well placed here. They are likely to facilitate change in new and unusual ways.

Gift: Individuals with an Eighth-House Uranus placement are highly intuitive and prone to frequent premonitions and insights. They are good detectives and have a sixth sense for intuiting dishonest and clandestine behaviors. They are not afraid of taboo topics and succeed in areas where others fear to tread. They do well in times of crisis and emergencies and can help others who are going through major life challenges and transitions. Their insights are usually spot-on in these situations. Many have a knack for procuring funding or finding alternative ways of working with funding modalities. The Eighth House rules inheritances and partners' finances, and unexpected circumstances can occur in these areas.

Shadow: The shadow side of Uranus in the Eighth House is a potential for drastic and destabilizing changes, as the rebellious aspect of this placement initiates change at any cost. Revolutions with little regard for humanity are possible. Defiance can be generalized, losing any purposeful intent.

Uranus in the Ninth House

The Ninth House rules higher education, long-term goals, foreign travel, publicity, adventures, religion, and philosophical and ethical pursuits.

Uranus in Jupiter-ruled Sagittarius is a visionary par excellence. Their intuitive insights mingled with innovative and futuristic thinking can tune in to and initiate trends that are not yet recognized. These individuals are adventurers and are likely to enjoy travel to lesser-known locations.

Gift: These natives are gifted with an open mind that is receptive to new concepts and independent views. They bring a refreshing atmosphere to stagnated belief systems and outworn philosophies. They can help others with their expansive perspective and

Uranus in Sagittarius is a visionary par excellence. Their intuitive insights mingled with innovative and futuristic thinking can tune into and initiate trends not yet recognized.

nonjudgmental approach to situations. The Ninth House rules journalism and publishing, which serve as venues for bringing forth their original ideas. Uranus rules technological advances, so they are likely to employ new methods as their platforms.

Shadow: The shadow side of this placement is an individual who can go overboard with fanatical ideas and conspiracy theories. They are stimulated by the pursuit of higher learning, and yet they may not ever use their knowledge in any way that benefits them. These individuals can focus on the future to the exclusion of living in the present moment.

Uranus in the Tenth House

The Tenth House rules public achievements, reputation, authority, and prestige.

Uranus placed in Saturn's Tenth House combines the energies of Saturn and Ura-

nus, the traditional with the innovative, the old and the new, conservative views with progressive thinking.

Gift: Natives with Uranus in the Tenth House are bridge builders. They can bring forth new ideas and new technologies and link them to conventional thinking and existing modalities. They are innovative yet steadfast in their approach. Their intuitive grasp of new ways of doing things makes them excellent teachers and organizers. They are brilliant leaders but prefer to maintain their own identity rather than conform to the status quo. They do best with their own unique career path.

Shadow: The shadow side of this placement is an individual who cannot adhere to any kind of routine or follow rules and regulations. It may take them a few negative experiences before they realize that they are most comfortable working for themselves. They can have unexpected ups and downs in their career path. As with other planets in the Tenth House, this energy is on display, so rebellious, unlawful, or insubordinate behavior will be on display for the public.

Uranus in the Eleventh House

The Eleventh House rules friends, hopes, wishes, groups, and a sense of belonging in the world.

Uranus is at home in the Eleventh House, the area of the chart that is naturally ruled by Aquarius.

Gift: Natives with Uranus in the Eleventh House are champions of diverse groups of people. They are able to lead or participate in groups that are composed of diverse members and bring the group together without judgment or partisanship. They are talented in working with group dynamics. Their sharp intuition and clear insights give them an edge in social situations. They are generally admired for their uniqueness and strong sense of their own identity. They are likely to have diverse types of friends, many of whom may not particularly choose to be friends with each other.

Shadow: These natives can feel that they are outsiders. It may be difficult for them to reconcile that they are different from many others and that their uniqueness is their gift. They will develop a higher level of ease as they develop their confidence and talents. Eventually, they will find groups that they resonate with. In the meantime, they can act out and overdo rebellious behavior or isolate themselves and become lone wolves.

Uranus in the Twelfth House

The Twelfth House rules secrets, unconscious patterns, karma, closure, institutions, connections with higher sources, enlightenment, and undoing.

Uranus in the Twelfth House can work behind the scenes. The Twelfth House rules unconscious patterns, and this can trigger unconventional and rebellious behaviors that the native is not fully aware of. They can act out at the wrong time and at the wrong place. On the other hand, these natives may come up with new ways to help the underprivileged and the oppressed.

Gift: An individual with Uranus in the Twelfth House can be highly intuitive and have an uncanny awareness of trends and patterns going on beneath the surface. They are ahead of their time and can foreshadow events and unfortunate indicators for the benefit of society. They can also bring forth cutting-edge solutions that can assist the underserved and less fortunate. They are advocates for change as it relates to oppressive institutions and dogmas that imprison the collective.

An individual with Uranus in the Twelfth House can be highly intuitive and have an uncanny awareness of trends beneath the surface. They can foreshadow events and bring forth cutting-edge solutions that can assist the underserved.

Shadow: With this Twelfth-House placement, unexpected events can occur that the native doesn't see coming. They can isolate themselves due to feelings of not being accepted by society. These are the true eccentrics and outcasts, and they may not always even know that they are. Their psychic impressions can be overwhelming and trigger anxieties until they learn how to protect themselves psychically and integrate and channel their abilities.

URANUS COMBINATIONS

Uranus/Sun

Uranus rules intuition, originality, individuality, and the sudden and unexpected.

The Sun indicates purpose, self-expression, creative life force, and conscious will.

Individuals with a Sun/Uranus combination are free-spirited, freedom-oriented, and individualists in that they follow the beat of their own drum and respect others who do so as well. The last thing they want to do is conform to a stereotype, especially one that isn't of their making. Uranus is electrifying and activates planets that it touches in an individualistic and often rebellious way. Uranus rules electricity, and these natives can often have highly sensitized nervous systems. They are often interested in or resonate to higher frequency energies and planes of existence.

Gift: Sun/Uranus people are charismatic and magnetic. Their magnetism complements their uniqueness and enthusiasm, which inspires others, bringing them popularity. It is almost as if people aren't sure what to make of individuals with this combination, but they like it, nonetheless. They are original, creative, and future oriented. They usually have a natural attunement to technology and other new ways of doing things. These individuals are not pretentious. They tend to be humanitarians who believe in the equality of all people, the universal brotherhood, where everyone is equal. Their open-mindedness and nonjudgmental stance contribute to the diverse opportunities and situations they are able to navigate. They are straightforward and expect the same from others. Truth and honesty are highly valued.

Shadow: Eccentric and erratic behavior may occur. This energy combination, although inventive and highly original, can lack the steadfastness and practicality necessary to carry out their ideas. Personal freedom can come at a high cost when their ego becomes overly identified with doing things their own way. Rebelliousness for its own sake can become their mantra. People who do not understand their purpose can deem them unpredictable and eccentric.

Uranus/Moon

Uranus rules intuition, originality, individuality, and the sudden and unexpected.

The Moon rules the soul, core instincts, the personality, and subconscious conditioning.

The combination of the Moon with Uranus brings an aloofness or detachment to emotional expression. Uranus is electrical in nature, and natives with this combination move quickly, as if their synaptic responses are continually alert and ready to respond. They can be high-strung or totally present, with a rapid and apt response.

Gift: These natives are generally highly intuitive and think outside the box. Their personalities are lively and vibrant. Something about them is different, which intrigues others. They willingly express their individuality and respect others for their diversity and uniqueness. Others sense their openness, and they are comfortable expressing aspects of themselves that they may have previously kept private. This combination bestows an emotional honesty upon the individual. They do not appreciate pretense or deceptiveness of character. They value kindness and, at the same time, are able to tell it how it is.

Shadow: Natives displaying the shadow side of Moon/Uranus connections can be prone to mood swings, restlessness, and erratic behavior. Since the Moon rules habitual and instinctive behavior patterns and Uranus can rule aspects of the sensory nervous system, these individuals are prone to sensory overstimulation and anxiety that can be destabilizing. They have little tolerance for restriction and need to find a balance between emotional independence and intimacy.

Uranus/Mercury

Uranus rules intuition, originality, individuality, and the sudden and unexpected.

Mercury rules communication, mental processes, and the logical mind.

Mercury rules ideas and communication, and Uranus rules breakthroughs and discoveries. This combination looks at things with an open mind and can think outside of the box. Sometimes called a combination of genius, inventive breakthroughs are possible, especially when a healthy nervous system is maintained.

Gift: Mercury combined with Uranus is highly intuitive and future-oriented, so they excel at innovative and original thinking and the ability to think outside of the box. These abilities can connote a particular type of genius, which can sometimes be erratic. They are prone to creative bursts of thinking and unexpected revelations. These natives are independent thinkers who prefer to be self-directed and autonomous. They are attracted to what's new and unusual. These natives are generally straightforward and direct. At least a few of the senses are well developed and extraordinary in their perception. Sometimes, these natives have very acute hearing or can be very sensitive to lighting and smell.

Shadow: An overactive mind with a highly sensitive nervous system can trigger anxiety and restlessness. This person can be easily overstimulated. Thinking can be so ahead of its time that ideas are rejected as eccentric. These natives can have a scattered mind and lack focus. Outside stimulation can be highly distracting to them.

Uranus/Venus

Uranus rules intuition, originality, individuality, and the sudden and unexpected.

When Mars and Uranus are working well together, the body has its own natural intuitive flow and will spontaneously take the best action for the given situation. Innovative and inventive, this native can be an asset in any crisis situation.

Venus represents love, relationships, beauty, values, comfort, and material resources.

Anyone with a Venus/Uranus combination in their birth chart needs more of a sense of freedom in those Venus-ruled areas of life, including relationships, financial affairs, the arts, and entertainment. Uranus loves to think outside of the box and needs the freedom to be able to do so. Natives with connections between Venus and Uranus are inclined to sudden attractions. They have vibrant personalities that make them popular and sometimes not well understood.

Gift: Uranus adds a unique kind of genius to Venus that can manifest in a host of different ways. These individuals bring a unique and inventive flavor to social encounters, which adds brilliance to any stagnant situation. They delight in surprising others with their unexpected and creative responses to everyday occurrences. A person with this combination is a breath of fresh air when it comes to surprises, and it is unlikely that a relationship with them will become stale or predictable. They have a distinctive artistic flair that extends to all of the creative arts. Their effervescence and spontaneity especially add to the performing arts. These natives have a magnetic charm that entices others into their sphere of influence. Undoubtedly, they will be noticed and remembered.

Shadow: A Venus/Uranus combination can manifest as an individual who cannot stand to be tied down to any kind of commitment. They can be unpredictable as a mate or as a friend unless a mutual understanding occurs going into the relationship. These natives have little tolerance for any kind of pressure to be a certain way or to behave as far as the status quo is concerned. They dance to the beat of their own drummer in both appearance and in the realm of social and relationship mores. Traditions hold little merit unless they add their own interpretation to it. Their overwhelming desire for freedom can come off as irresponsible.

Uranus/Mars

Uranus rules intuition, originality, individuality, and the sudden and unexpected.

Mars rules assertiveness, energy, drive, and courage.

The combination of Mars and Uranus yields sudden, unpredictable actions that can be serendipitous or shocking, depending on the circumstance. Similar to Mars in Aquar-ius, the combination of Mars and Uranus is highly innovative and freedom-oriented.

Gift: When Mars and Uranus are working well together, the body has its own natural intuitive flow. The body knows what to do without thinking about it and will spontaneously take the best action for the given situation. This combination can contribute to the native being innovative, inventive, and an asset in any crisis situation.

Shadow: Simmering tensions can suddenly boil over out of the blue. Harnessing this daring and erratic energy can be a worthwhile challenge. When out of control, this combination can be accident-prone at worst or at least highly inconsistent. Revolutionary actions can be appealing as a way to clear stuck energy, and a large amount of energy can be released all at once. Similarly, an overwhelming urge to seek freedom from constricting circumstances can occur.

> When Mars and Uranus are working well together, the body has its own natural intuitive flow.

Uranus/Jupiter

Uranus rules intuition, originality, individuality, and the sudden and unexpected.

Jupiter represents the higher mind, greater truths, expansiveness, hope, and optimism.

At the personal level, the combination of Jupiter and Uranus in the chart can bring unexpected good luck exactly when it is needed. The occurrence of unexpected situations and sudden events happen that awaken one's consciousness and redirect them into more purposeful activities.

A new Jupiter/Uranus synodic cycle occurs every 13.81 years, which infuses society with innovation and cultural shifts. Culturally, the Jupiter/Uranus energy combination can lead to following one's own belief systems rather than conform to any traditional teachings.

Gift: Natives with a Jupiter/Uranus combination can be ahead of their time. They have a futuristic vision that can bring forth cultural shifts and inventions. They are able to recognize and open the door to innovations, personal and societal insights, and "a-ha" experiences. Uranus can awaken trust in the divine or in a higher power due to having had experiences where things end up working out somehow in the end. These individuals can be true humanitarians and advocates for personal freedom.

Shadow: Jupiter expands whatever energies it touches and can thereby enhance rebellious tendencies when combining with Uranus. These natives can become overzealous reformers in areas relating to cultural, religious, and spiritual issues. They can have brilliant ideas that lack follow-through in terms of their execution. An abundance of optimism and goodwill can be present, but their actions and ideas don't materialize into desired outcomes due to the scattering of energy and difficulty with maintaining focus. The Uranian energy is highly charged and makes the native overly receptive to sensory stimulation, which, in turn, affects focus and concentration.

Uranus/Saturn

Uranus rules intuition, originality, individuality, and the sudden and unexpected.

Saturn rules responsibility, adjustments to limitations, sustainability, and structure.

Saturn is interested in fortifying and preserving existing structures, whereas Uranus's job is to bring forward new and original structures that are more appropriate for the times. Saturn represents responsibility, and Uranus represents freedom. Individuals with these two planets in combination are bridge builders between old ways and new. They are dissatisfied with the status quo and see how circumstances can be improved.

Gift: These natives can be thrust into challenging situations, where they are called upon to reconcile the contradictory manifestations of Saturn and Uranus. They can facilitate a logical and well-thought-out execution of large-scale innovative plans and projects. They can successfully decode innovative technology solutions to those who are less technologically savvy. These natives work well at finding compromise between opposing factions in society. Astrologer Donna Cunningham, in an article published in the July 6, 2015, issue of *The Mountain Astrologer*, aptly coined individuals with Saturn/Uranus combinations as "grounded eccentrics and sane weirdos." She describes the blending of these energies as someone who is "self-directed and self-motivated" and "wise elders of their tribes."

Shadow: The shadow side of this combination is that these individuals can be prone to anxiety and indecision from continually being pulled into situations where they have strongly different urges. On the one hand, they want to be known as being responsible; however, they have the overwhelming urge to break free from expectations and obligations. It can be difficult for these natives to find inner peace because they feel that new frontiers are out there for them, yet they want to fulfill their responsibilities. They can be fearful and lack confidence to move forward, yet they resent having restrictions. These individuals may not trust that anything in their lives will stay constant.

Uranus/Neptune

Uranus rules intuition, originality, individuality, and the sudden and unexpected.

Neptune rules ideals, creative imagination, transcendence, compassion, and vision.

A Uranus/Neptune combination is similar to having Uranus in the Twelfth House in that these individuals have unusual spiritual interests and uncanny insights into spiritual and hidden realms.

Gift: These individuals are open to higher dimensional realms. They are prone to intuitive insights and psychic impressions, which often sense hidden agendas and underlying trends. These natives can take up causes on behalf of the weak and the underprivileged. These combinations often occur at times when major spiritual and scientific progress is occurring for humanity. A propensity may occur to be overly idealistic.

Shadow: The shadow side of this connection can be confusion and lack of clarity over prevailing and upcoming trends. They may have underlying anxieties connected to fear of the future and fear of the unknown. Strange notions regarding the paranormal and psychic phenomena can be present.

Uranus/Pluto

Uranus rules intuition, originality, individuality, and the sudden and unexpected.

Pluto represents regeneration; transformation; and a compelling, fundamental approach.

The combination of Uranus and Pluto is highly dynamic and can lead to awakenings and experiences that trigger deep trans-

formation and change. These consciousness-expanding instances can result from flashes of intuitive insights or result from outside circumstances that thereafter change the native's life. They have original thinking that leads to technology solutions that assist in healing and involvement in advances that can shape society.

When society experiences Uranus and Pluto in combination, the urge for freedom and reform are awakened, and the Plutonic shadow side, including the urge for more power and extreme violence, is also aroused. These periods have recurred throughout history, instituting change in areas that include civil rights, the women's movement, and uprisings against injustices in society relating to income disparities. Mass movements occurred across the globe during the time periods that this aspect was in effect.

Gift: The gift this combination offers is that of expanded self-awareness. The process of gaining this awareness may not necessarily come at an opportune time given the unexpected attribute of Uranus. Nonetheless, in retrospect, the native will have made great strides toward self-empowerment. Uranus can bring forth the truth, regardless of how deeply it may have been hidden. These natives are reformists of the highest order, with worthy ideals and clear morals.

Shadow: The shadow side of this combination is shock and a radical purging that is difficult to recover from. At its extreme, the connection between Uranus and Pluto can cause drastic upheaval, destruction, and annihilation.

Uranus/Chiron

Uranus rules intuition, originality, individuality, and the sudden and unexpected.

When society experiences Uranus and Pluto in combination, the urge for freedom and reform is awakened. Mass movements have occurred across the globe during the time periods that this aspect was in effect, instituting change in areas that include civil rights, the women's movement, and injustices relating to income disparities.

Chiron represents core wounds and the desire to overcome them, and healing.

Uranus in combination with Chiron helps the native to free themselves from self-imposed limitations and buried traumas. Uranus is symbolized by a lightning bolt, which breaks up obstacles and reveals a deeper level of the truth. These natives benefit from innovative healing modalities, including those that stimulate the body's chi, or the body's electrical and energy systems.

Gift: Chiron represents the urge to become whole and heal the Self. When combined with Uranus, the native can gain insights into their subconscious patterns at the hand of unexpected circumstances. Uranus sharpens one's intuitive faculties, and "a-ha" moments can occur where they get glimpses into patterns related to their core wounding.

Shadow: These natives are sensitive to any kind of judgment and criticism. They feel they have a right to be who they are, although they may not realize that underlying wounding exists that they are not aware of. They can be closed off emotionally as an avoidance tactic for unconscious blocks and fears.

Uranus/Eris

Uranus rules intuition, originality, individuality, and the sudden and unexpected.

Eris represents the determination to remove limitations that impede the soul's evolution.

Gift: Uranian individuality is a distinct asset when looking to overcome the conditioning that is imposed by the collective or parental and family influences. These natives can draw on their inherent originality for manifesting solutions that can benefit society.

Shadow: Rebelliousness to the extreme can be counterproductive when looking to make successful and lasting changes to society. The outlier side of Eris can be inordinately accentuated and lead to isolation and disappointment.

Uranus/North Node

Uranus rules intuition, originality, individuality, and the sudden and unexpected.

The North Node represents future direction, soul guidance, and fulfillment.

The North Node emphasizes the importance for the native to develop the attributes represented by Uranus. These include thinking outside of the box and the ability to embrace diverse groups of humanity.

Gift: The North Node sign, placement, and interactions with other planetary bodies give clues to one's destiny and life path. Uranus indicates that the native benefits from staying attuned to changing times and new waves of thought as well as to cutting-edge technology solutions and innovations. Uranus honors individuality and respects the unique contributions each person brings

to the planet. These natives fulfill their purpose through being a unifier for humanity rather than through being a divider.

Shadow: The shadow side of this connection can indicate an individual whose extreme desire for freedom conflicts with the social order. Their nonconformist and rebellious tendencies can become an obstacle for them and ultimately alienate those who can further their purpose.

Uranus/South Node

Uranus rules intuition, originality, individuality, and the sudden and unexpected.

The South Node represents familiarity, gratification, and the path of least resistance.

The combination of Uranus and the South Node can indicate an individual who places a great deal of emphasis on their personal freedom. They can have difficulty conforming to rules and regulations, which they will need to integrate with their North Node sign and placement.

Gift: An individual with a Uranus/South Node combination is an independent thinker who knows themselves. They are not likely to compromise their integrity and prefer to be straightforward and upright. They accept others for who they are and are not likely to be judgmental.

Shadow: The shadow side of this placement is an individual who is uncooperative, irresponsible, and rebellious. They are used to getting their own way and will be dis-

> Uranian individuality is a distinct asset when looking to overcome the conditioning that is imposed by the collective or parental and family influences.

ruptive and even obnoxious until they get what they want.

Uranus/Ascendant

Uranus rules intuition, originality, individuality, and the sudden and unexpected.

The Ascendant represents one's approach, orientation, and the window through which one sees the world.

Gift: These are highly intuitive and unique individuals who have a pulse on the latest and greatest, whether it be style, what's trending, or innovative solutions. They know who they are and what they want. These natives usually live unusual and interesting lives.

Shadow: These natives can have eccentric behaviors that disrupt the social order and further alienate those they want to embrace. Stress and anxiety can plague these natives. They are hyperactive and have difficulty focusing.

Uranus/Midheaven (MC)

Uranus rules intuition, originality, individuality, and the sudden and unexpected.

The Midheaven (MC) represents image, outer aspirations, and career orientation.

With Uranus at the top of the chart, a strong drive is present to be respected for one's unique contributions and innovations. These natives are straightforward in their dealings with the public.

Gift: Individuals with Uranus connected to the Midheaven can be trailblazers in their field. They are noticed by higher-ups and influential members of society for bringing innovative solutions and new ideas to their profession. They are trendsetters in the social sphere.

Shadow: In spite of their innovative ideas and the value they can offer to their careers, these natives can be disruptive and irresponsible, qualities that outweigh the benefits they offer. As a result, they may not be favored by those in authority. Their unreliable and recalcitrant actions can be judged by society with this placement of Uranus. Sudden changes in reputation and professional standing can occur.

NEPTUNE

Neptune's discovery in 1846 was followed by its swift ingress into Pisces and Conjunction with Jupiter. The era of Neptune in Pisces between 1848 and 1862 witnessed an intersection between several radical idealistic movements involving gender, religion, and race.

Neptune, along with Uranus and Pluto, symbolizes collective forces that constantly prompt change (and hopefully growth) in our consciousness, according to astrologer Stephen Arroyo. Neptune is a higher octave of Venus and thus, in its purest expression, signifies universal love as well as dreams, intuition, inspiration, otherworldliness, mysticism, and spirituality.

Neptune rules high ideals, an active creative imagination, and psychic and spiritual visions. The Neptune archetype of oceanic oneness with all of creation is an apt description for this otherworldly energy that can attain high ideals by virtue of possessing inherent inspiration and openness to the universal flow of love and creative energy.

Neptune can also represent a fog that clouds our vision and gives an unrealistic and illusory take on things. Discernment, ruled by Mercury-ruled Virgo, the sign opposite Pisces, is exactly the energy that is most often needed for its balance.

Neptune, the Roman god of the sea, lends his namesake planet the mystical influence of the unknowable deep.

Neptune was the Roman version of the Greek god Poseidon. As the god of the sea and all waters, the Neptune archetype takes one out of the earthly plane to a place that is unbounded. The sea is unbounded and deep. The sea flows and has a natural rhythm. The sea smooths out rough edges and makes them smooth, as it does with stones, shells, and bones that wash up on the shore.

Individuals with a prominent Neptune placement can be uncomfortable in mundane reality, as if these souls remember life on other planes of existence. Neptune touches into the collective unconscious, the vast merging of dreams, fears, and disappointments. Like water, Neptune can't be tightly held. Neptune is the whisper of fog that gently touches one's cheek.

Gift: Mystical inclinations and inspirations are some of the positive expressions of Neptunian energies with the planet's "urge to merge" with the Infinite. At its best, it can expand one's connection with what was previously thought possible. It can open the individual to other realms that include creative art forms, music, poetry, and dance. The Neptunian archetype is spiritual in its essential nature, with an innate understanding of the power of love and compassion.

Shadow: Neptune's shadow gives way to irrational ideas, negative fantasy, distorted half truths, and fear. Neptune can blur the boundaries between what is real and what is simply a wishful ideal, thereby sowing confusion, idealization, and self-deception. Because of its idealistic orientation, in its shadow state Neptune can cause false expectations, which can ultimately lead to forsakenness. A poorly aspected Neptune can lead to addictive behavior patterns as well. A "woe is me" martyr syndrome can be lurking in the shadows when Neptune is in a difficult aspect with the luminaries or with the ruler of the Ascendant. Fogginess, spaciness, and a failure to act as a result of confusion or lack of clarity is the lower expression of Neptune.

NEPTUNE IN THE SIGNS

Neptune takes about 184 years to travel around each of the signs of the Zodiac. Neptune spends about 13 years in each sign. Neptune is the furthest planet from the Sun now that Pluto has been designated as a dwarf planet.

Neptune's sign position is more generational than personal. Neptune's sign position can show how creative, mystical, inspirational, spiritual, and cultural expressions manifest through the characteristics of each sign. Neptune is the planet of dreams, and the sign location will indicate the type of dreams that each generation may be most drawn to.

The dates connected to Neptune in each sign are approximate. Although Neptune spends generally 13 years in each sign, Neptune will retrograde to the previous sign at the beginning of its journey in a sign. Similarly, near the completion of its journey in a sign, Neptune will move forward into the next sign and then retrograde back again.

Neptune in Aries
(1861–1875; 2025–2039)

Neptune in the sign of new beginnings produces a generation that is motivated to initiate and energize spiritual ideals that fit the changing times. Individuals from this period of time may stand out as brave and courageous and be willing to fight for their dreams and visions. They may be seeking to redefine their identity in light of the oneness and vastness of the greater universe.

Gift: Individuals with this placement will fight for their dreams and visions. Inspiration is their guidepost. These are the crusaders. Avant-garde, revolutionary leaders can emerge who inspire others with their vision for an ideal society, where each person can fully develop their gifts and talents.

Shadow: The shadow side of this placement is that individuals will fight for selfish gains at the expense of the rest of society. Delusions can cloud one's vision, and they can be fighting on the basis of disinformation and results that are not likely to be plausible.

> Neptune's sign position can show how creative, mystical, inspirational, spiritual, and cultural expressions manifest through the characteristics of each sign.

Neptune in Taurus
(1874–1889; 2039–2052)

The Neptune in Venus-ruled Taurus generation brings forth practical ideals that are related to material resources. Preservation of Earth's natural resources is at the top of its mind.

Gift: Neptune in Taurus generates visionaries who formulate practical solutions that support Earth and its inhabitants, preserve natural resources, and even out discrepancies between the haves and the have-nots.

Shadow: The shadow sides of Neptune in Taurus include deceptive practices regarding the allocation of material resources, issues around toxic substances buried in the earth and floating around in the oceans, and the extinction of species as a result of the inappropriate use of toxic chemicals and pollutants in the environment.

Neptune in Gemini (1887–1902)

Characteristic of the Uranus in Mercury-ruled Gemini generation are those who develop the creative, intuitive, and higher-dimensional attributes of the mind. Telepathic communication modalities are nurtured, and the image-generating faculties of the mind are explored.

Gift: Higher dimensions of the mind are explored, and new modes of communication are discovered based upon insights from visionaries with Neptune in Gemini. Much is achieved in the realm of space travel and discoveries regarding maintaining life forms given alternate atmospheres in space.

Natives with Neptune in Leo belong to a generation with strong ideals connected to love and romance. This is a highly creative group with varied talents in the artistic, film, musical, and performing arts fields.

forth new ways of generating ample sustenance for feeding and nurturing Earth's populations. Natives from this generation are tuned in to alternate dimensions, and many have well-developed psychic and mediumistic tendencies.

Shadow: The shadow sides of Neptune in Cancer can be misguided psychic impressions that create delusional behavior patterns, codependent family ties where outsiders are excluded, and false ideas and misguided ideals that pertain to nationalism and belonging.

Neptune in Leo (1914–1929)

The Neptune in Leo generation loves pomp and circumstance. The arts flourish, and entertainment has its place in smoothing out the rough edges. Remember the Roaring Twenties?

Gift: Natives with Neptune in Leo belong to a generation with strong ideals connected to love and romance. This is a highly creative group with varied talents in the artistic, film, musical, and performing arts fields. A fresh appreciation for entertainment and fun is present.

Shadow: The shadow side of this placement can be a preoccupation with the dream world and with ideas that are too far outside the realm of possibility.

Shadow: The other side of the entertainment bubble of the Roaring Twenties was the Great Depression. The shadow side of this placement is a disregard for the practical concerns of life and unwise stock market speculations.

Neptune in Cancer (1901–1916)

The Neptune in Cancer generation brings focus back to the home turf. Ideals related to family values are redefined based upon current lifestyles and child-rearing practices. Neptune is well placed in Cancer, which is the sign of exaltation for Neptune.

Neptune in Virgo (1928–1943)

Neptune is not well placed in Virgo, the sign opposite Pisces. Neptune has free-flowing, creative, and imaginative attributes, whereas Virgo is detail-oriented and analytic. The Neptune in Virgo generation grew up during the Great Depression with adverse material circumstances. Ideals of discernment were necessary for survival.

Gift: Visionaries from the Neptune in Cancer generation can tune in to and bring

Gift: The gift that Neptune in Virgo offered this generation was an idealism surrounding self-care and the care of those in need regarding health and nutrition. Systems and services were instituted that helped care for the needs of children, the elderly, and the less fortunate. Ideals surrounding employment and health care were put into place that were useful and had a practical application.

Shadow: The shadow side of this placement includes a deceptive belief that necessity outweighs discernment. Toxic chemicals were added to food, water, and the environment that supported material gain rather than the health and well-being of individuals.

Neptune in Libra (1942–1957)

Neptune in Venus-ruled Libra highlighted the ideals of partnership and cooperation. The postwar generation centered around finding peace and harmony after an upheaval of the family structure and news of death and destruction. Psychedelics, recreational drugs, and meditation opened new doorways to other dimensions and alternative beliefs in spirituality and consciousness.

Gift: Neptune in Libra held high principles for relationship potential and helped further ideals of balance between participants in a relationship and between the sexes in general. Movements evolved over issues of fairness, justice, and harmony, including women's liberation and antiwar movements. New art and music forms evolved at the behest of these natives. Leisure activities and lifestyle changes resulted from individuals who were looking to find balance from the difficult postwar era.

Shadow: Less than probable ideals regarding relationships surfaced as movies and television became more prominent in people's lives. Romantic expectations that were difficult to attain triggered an increase in divorces and separations. Recreational drug use became a panacea for the discontent and changing lifestyles that people were experiencing.

Neptune in Scorpio (1955–1970)

The Neptune in Scorpio generation brought forward an unveiling of life's deeper mysteries. Sexual ecstasy became a sought-after ideal, propelling sensationalism and sexual liberation.

Gift: The gift from Neptune in Scorpio centered around more attention being paid to deep-rooted psychological issues and treatments. People felt the significance of understanding each other and the importance of addressing issues that can foster change and transformation. Visionaries expounded on the meaning of life, which fostered investigations into life's mysteries and experimentation with sex, drugs, metaphysics, and the occult.

> The gift from Neptune in Scorpio centered around more attention being paid to deep-rooted psychological issues and treatments.

Shadow: Sex, drugs, and rock and roll could be used for avoidance and escapism from daily life chores and practical considerations. These natives have a strong desire by nature that can overshadow them at times. Addictive behaviors can result. The desire to merge and ideals of sexual unions can result in codependent behavior patterns, including possessiveness and jealousies.

Neptune in Sagittarius (1970–1984)

The Neptune in Sagittarius generation is highly idealistic and spiritually oriented. They are philosophical and adventurous. A keen interest in cultural traditions serves to expand cuisines around the world and have an influence on fashion and home décor. New Age practices with international origins became more available.

Gift: Individuals with Neptune in Sagittarius are highly spiritual and value having a philosophy in life that gives comfort in challenging times. These are natural visionaries who idealize freedom, justice, and honesty. They are optimistic and generous.

Shadow: The shadow side of this placement shows up in speculative ventures. Deceptive advertising and shadowy salespeople can egg these folks on to make investments and buy into other speculative ventures that don't work out well. Their adventurous nature coupled with an optimistic view of mankind can be used against them. Aimless wandering can result from a lack of focus. A fanatical adherence to misguided beliefs and self-described religious prophets can also occur.

Neptune in Capricorn (1984–1998)

The Neptune in Capricorn generation brought forth ideals of economic sovereignty and material well-being. Neptune is debilitated in Capricorn due to its exaltation in Cancer, the sign opposite Capricorn, where ideals are formulated around one's family and inner life rather than around ambition and material gain.

Gift: These natives take a realistic approach toward manifesting their dreams and visions. Neptune in Capricorn natives are able to take advantage of the practical, ambitious, and realistic aspects of Saturn as they frame their ideals. They are especially interested in attaining prosperity and achieving fame and success. These natives are thoughtful, resourceful, and focused.

Shadow: The shadow side of Neptune in Capricorn is a focus on material attainment to the exclusion of emotional fulfilment that can be derived from pursuing ideals that are directly related to human interactions. Their personal dreams focus on material happiness rather than connecting with transcendent and spiritual realms. Faith can be lacking when the harsh realities of life pose challenging situations.

Neptune in Aquarius (1998–2012)

The Neptune in Aquarius generation is highly altruistic. They are natural humanitarians with strong ideals that are connected to helping others and bringing diverse groups of people together. Each person's individuality is valued without inappropriate judgment or undue criticism.

Gift: The gifts derived from this placement are the lofty humanitarian ideals put forth by these individuals. Futuristic in their orientation, advancements in technology, health care, and space exploration are likely. They seek to unveil the truth and bring diverse groups of people together. Scientific investigations in genetics and technology advancements focused on social media are highlighted.

Shadow: The shadow side of Neptune in Aquarius is an individual who is detached, aloof, and self-centered. Their dream of the cold, hard truth can exclude human warmth and empathy. These natives can be blindly altruistic and lose track of current circumstances and the more mundane aspects of human suffering. They can also lack responsibility for their own day-to-day activities.

The Neptune in Aquarius generation is highly altruistic. They are natural humanitarians with strong ideals connected to helping others and bringing diverse groups of people together. Futuristic in their orientation, advancements in technology, health care, and space exploration are likely.

Neptune in Pisces (2011–2026)

Neptune is at home in Pisces, and as a result, characteristics of this generation will amplify the characteristics of Neptune. These include ideals that center on compassion, empathy, the arts, and spirituality as well as a heightened interest in metaphysics and all things mystical.

Gift: Neptune in Pisces brings an outpouring of compassion and empathy and an awareness of Universal Oneness. The spiritual values of love, peace, faith, devotion, and trust are highlighted. This placement of Neptune has the ability to see the value of coming together. These individuals are tuned in to the collective, and they understand that one person's suffering affects everyone. Natives with this placement can easily tap into their dreams, and they have fertile and active imaginations that they can apply to their creative pursuits.

Shadow: These individuals have escapist tendencies. Elements of reality can be too intense for these sensitive beings. Addictions can occur as a means of escape when life is coming up short from the ideal envisioned by them. Disillusionment and forsakenness are part of the shadow side of this placement. These individuals may learn that they cannot always control events; however, through invoking faith and trust in the divine, they can get through difficult situations.

NEPTUNE IN THE HOUSES

Neptune's position by house indicates the area of life where the individual may be idealistic. It can signify which of life's areas can be affected by dreams, premonitions, and deeper intuitive insights. Similarly, the house position shows the areas in which a person is likely to be unrealistic and prone to delusion. The native can attach spirituality to the areas of life ruled by that particular house.

Neptune in the First House

The First House rules appearance, health, general temperament, and sense of self. The First House defines you and the image you project to others.

Natives with Neptune in the First House are strongly affected by this placement. They are highly sensitive and receive strong sensations regarding their environment. They need more peace and tranquility in their everyday lives than most people.

Gift: Neptune in the First House is highly impressionable and intuitive. Some individuals with this placement have an etheric or mysterious feel to them, a unearthly sensibility that is intriguing to others. They are likely to be mystically inclined and possess psychic or clairvoyant abilities. Often, these natives have artistic or musical talents, depending on the sign placement and planetary combinations of Neptune.

Shadow: Mundane objectives can be challenging for these natives. They prefer a more spiritual or esoteric atmosphere. Highly sensitive, they can pick up negative energies easily, especially when they are in a vulnerable state. A challenge for those with a prominent Neptune placement is staying true to themselves in spite of a desire to be everything to everyone. It is

> Neptune in the First House is … likely to be mystically inclined and possess psychic or clairvoyant abilities.

important for them to maintain clear and consistent boundaries since they are so easily influenced.

Neptune in the Second House

The Second House is connected with finances, values, material possessions, talents, and resources. The Second House represents the value we give to ourselves and, in turn, that which we possess.

Individuals with Neptune in the Second House are idealistic about money matters and material possessions. They have an aesthetic appreciation of the finer things and may have a tendency to be overly trusting of others in financial dealings.

Gift: Neptune in the Second House generally bestows artistic or musical talents. These natives have a highly refined aesthetic sensibility. Often, human values are more important to them than material objects. They can rely on hunches and intuition in their financial dealings. They trust that they will have what they need, and many times, they do. They often donate to humanitarian and spiritual causes.

Shadow: The shadow side of this placement is that the native can be so overly idealistic and trusting that they are open to deceptive influences. Money issues can develop due to not paying adequate attention to details in financial interactions. Their financial dreams and visions can be impractical and difficult to attain, thereby causing them disappointment and frustration.

Neptune in the Third House

The Third House is connected with ideas, communication, siblings, neighbors, and short journeys.

Neptune in a house governed by Mercury can be highly intuitive and often telepathic. Visual imagery skills are likely to be well developed. These natives can have connections with mass media and marketing.

Gift: Natives with a Third-House Neptune placement can put others at ease with their engaging communication style. They are good listeners and display a presence when communicating, indicating to others that they intuitively understand them. Highly intuitive, they can be channels for inspired ideas and can receive information from higher realms.

Shadow: The shadow side of this placement is that the native can tune out and miss important details. They can be dreamy and spacey, especially when they are not interested in the subject matter. They may not be good at sticking to schedules and showing up to places on time. They can be absentminded and prone to misunderstandings.

Neptune in the Fourth House

The Fourth House is about the home, family, genetic inheritance, foundational stability, innermost feelings, later life, and the end of matters.

Neptune in the Cancer-ruled Fourth House gives the individual a caring disposition that gives comfort to family members as well as to those whom they consider part of their extended family. They are prone to idealize their family, their parents, and their family heritage.

Gift: Unconditional love and a deeply caring disposition are characteristics of an individual with Neptune in the Fourth House. Human principles are more important to them than formalities or material considerations. Peace and tranquility are important to these natives. Vibra-

Neptune in the Fourth House gives the individual a caring disposition that gives comfort to family members and to those they consider part of their extended family.

tionally sensitive, these natives are soothed by living near bodies of water and comfortable in pastoral environments.

Shadow: Natives with Neptune in the Fourth House are challenged to see their childhood in a realistic light. The past can be idealized as the good old days despite challenges and difficult times, which can lead to continuous dissatisfaction with the present. These natives choose to be in denial over their past rather than deal with deep-rooted emotional issues.

Neptune in the Fifth House

The Fifth House rules creative self-expression, children, love, passion, romance, playfulness, and joy.

Natives with Neptune in Leo's Fifth House are imaginative and highly creative. Combining the imagination and the fantasy orientation of Neptune with Leo's creative and expressive abilities yields a highly talented individual with a keen flair for theater and other forms of entertainment.

Gift: These natives are enthusiastic, warm, charming, and delightful to all ages. Children and adults alike respond to their talents and creative abilities, and they are able to help those with disabilities and special needs. Aside from being great entertainers, these individuals are ardent romanticists.

Shadow: Neptune in the Fifth House individuals can have idealistic romantic expectations that can be shattered in the light of day. Their love life can involve a lot of fantasy and be weak on realistic expectations. These natives can also romanticize the capabilities of their children. They can be secretive and deceptive in their romantic ventures.

Neptune in the Sixth House

The Sixth House governs daily routines, acts of service, the work-life balance, health, due diligence, pet care, coworkers, and employees.

The Sixth House belongs to Mercury-ruled Virgo, which inclines these natives to dedicated service and the care of others. Their desire to help others can have a spiritual aspect to it and can include various forms of spiritual healing.

Gift: The native brings forth the gift of dedicated selfless service. They are idealistic in their desire to make life easier for others and for themselves. They have high standards around their work ethic, which can border on self-sacrifice unless they initiate boundaries for themselves. Many have healing abilities, telepathic communication with animals and plants, and a strong intuitive sensibility regarding health and the nutritional needs of themselves and others.

Shadow: The shadow side of Neptune in the Sixth House can indicate difficulty with

maintaining a schedule or routine and avoidance of day-to-day responsibilities. Steady employment may be difficult to sustain unless the native is able to find work that is compatible with the nature of this placement. Health issues can be difficult to diagnose since Neptune can bring confusion. These natives are likely to be more sensitive to drugs, alcohol, and substances that can produce allergies. The Sixth House is a health house, and the body may have more difficulty in ridding itself of toxins when Neptune is placed here.

Neptune in the Seventh House

The Seventh House rules close personal relationships, agreements, and compromises.

Neptune in the Seventh House, a placement traditionally ruled by Libra, can be idealized in their partners and the concept of partnership. These natives can see the highest spiritual attributes in the other person and then become disappointed when other aspects of the personality show up.

Gift: The gift of this placement is a strong intuitive awareness of others. These individuals speak to the soul of others, which can help others become more connected to their true selves. When they don't have expectations, these natives can read others' intentions. This ability bestows upon natives with this placement the ability to be good mediators and negotiators. They may be drawn to those with artistic and musical talents.

Shadow: The shadow side of this placement is the inability to set realistic expectations of partners and close personal relationships. When the rose-colored glasses come off, disappointment and resentment occurs. These natives can get involved with shady characters due to a lack of discernment and misplaced dreams and wishes.

An avoidance of commitment can occur given that these individuals may not always set clear boundaries.

Neptune in the Eighth House

The Eighth House rules joint ventures, intimacy, sex, death, transformation, and psychic dimensions.

Neptune in Pluto's house of transformation can give the native strong psychic and mediumistic abilities. A strong interest in psychic phenomena is likely. Confusion and deception where other people's finances are involved can occur.

Gift: Neptune in the Eighth House can give the native unique psychic and intuitive gifts. Individuals with this placement can have a strong desire to merge with another. A sexual union is one way to fulfill the desire to merge, especially when coupled with tantric or spiritual rituals. Shared belongings can also fulfill the desire for a union: what's yours is mine, and what's mine is yours. Natives with this placement can receive strong psychic impressions, which includes communication with souls in other dimensions.

Shadow: The shadow side of Neptune in the Eighth House can indicate deep sexual yearnings that lead to indiscriminate sexual encounters, with subsequent health or psychological issues. The shadow can also play out as deception in financial dealings, with the Eighth House ruling other people's finances, taxes, inheritances, and insurances. A blurring of boundaries with shared finances and inheritances can occur. These natives may keep fuzzy financial records or completely ignore financial responsibilities.

Neptune in the Ninth House

The Ninth House rules higher education, long-term goals, foreign travel, publicity, adventures, religion, and philosophical and ethical pursuits.

Natives with a Ninth House Neptune are spiritually and metaphysically oriented. These individuals are likely interested in pursuing studies in religion, spirituality, philosophy, art, and mysticism in diverse cultures.

Neptune in Sagittarius's Ninth House natives are great visionaries. The rest of the natal chart will indicate the likelihood of manifesting these visions. Imagination and faith run strong with these individuals.

Gift: Natives with a Ninth-House Neptune placement are spiritually and metaphysically oriented. The Ninth House also rules higher education, philosophy, publishing, and travel. These individuals are likely to be interested in pursuing studies in fields related to religion, spirituality, philosophy, art, and mysticism related to diverse cultures. These natives are able to adapt a philosophic perspective where faith and trust in a higher power can bring them peace and comfort when they are experiencing challenging times.

Shadow: The shadow side of a Ninth-House Neptune placement can be blind faith when dreams and visions are not substantiated by realistic assessments. The Ninth-House influence can lead the individual to be living in the projected future rather than in the present. These natives can be prone to disillusionment when belief systems that they are following don't pan out the way they initially thought. Fanaticism is also possible. Misunderstandings with relatives connected to a partner can occur.

Neptune in the Tenth House

The Tenth House rules public achievements, reputation, authority, and prestige.

A Neptune in the Tenth House placement can be a visionary in their field, where they have a sixth sense regarding upcoming trends and the needs of society. They can achieve recognition in a career related to the arts, theater, music, healing, and spirituality.

Gift: Individuals with Neptune in the Tenth House are highly imaginative and acutely intuitive when it comes to tuning in to the subconscious murmurings of the collective. They are therefore able to foresee trends, styles, and fashions and act upon them. They are likely to be strongly visually oriented, and this ability can manifest through art forms and the media. A desire is present to help those who are less fortunate, so they can have some connections to healing professions or charitable organizations.

Shadow: The shadow side of this placement is confusion over career choices and difficulty in landing in what the native believes is their destined occupation. Their expectations can be unrealistic, or the native may vacillate or be irresponsible in sticking to a specific path. Parental input in early childhood or a lack of self-worth can be sources of their confusion in adult life. Escapist tendencies or those that involve drugs, alcohol, or other forms of addiction will be picked up by those in authority or by the public.

Neptune in the Eleventh House

The Eleventh House rules friends, hopes, wishes, groups, and a sense of belonging in the world.

Neptune in the Eleventh House of hopes and wishes offers these individuals a strong faith for attaining their cherished ideals and visions. They likely to have altruistic humanitarian views.

> Natives with an Eleventh-House Neptune placement can gain inspiration from friends or group affiliations that assist them in formulating their dreams.

Gift: Natives with an Eleventh-House Neptune placement can gain inspiration from friends or group affiliations that assist them in formulating their dreams. They are likely to have spiritually oriented or creatively inclined friends with whom they feel a strong kinship. Group associations can include those connected to spirituality, humanitarian causes, and addiction rehabilitation and counseling. These natives are strongly compassionate and care about helping the underdogs.

Shadow: The shadow side of this placement can show up as a lack of social discrimination and friendships that can be deceptive and unreliable. It may be difficult for them to sustain clear boundaries with friends, whereby the native often feels taken advantage of or otherwise disappointed. This placement of Neptune can lead to the improbable pursuit of their hopes and dreams, which is likely due to an unrealistic assessment of what is involved or from seeking support from those who cannot be helpful.

Neptune in the Twelfth House

The Twelfth House rules secrets, unconscious patterns, karma, closure, institutions, connections with higher sources, enlightenment, and undoing.

An apt description of Neptune in the Twelfth House by Paramahansa Yogananda is this: "I am no longer the wave of consciousness thinking itself separated from the sea of cosmic consciousness. I am the ocean of Spirit that has become the wave of human life."

Gift: Natives with a Twelfth-House Neptune placement are very sensitive to psychic impressions, underlying vibrations, and motivations. They can be adept at picking up on what is not seen or what others may miss. The gift they derive from this ability is an awareness of what is needed in order to elevate the consciousness of individuals and the collective. They are able to translate their impressions into artistic expressions and provide healing and spiritual assistance to those in need.

Shadow: The shadow side of this placement is an inability to successfully function in society due to extreme sensitivity and possibly a desire to avoid the harsh realities of life. These natives often need time alone so that they can process the inundation of energies that they are constantly receiving. They can benefit from using tools and modalities that protect them from absorbing so many discordant vibrations.

NEPTUNE COMBINATIONS

Neptune/Sun

Neptune rules ideals, creative imagination, transcendence, compassion, and vision.

The Sun indicates purpose, self-expression, creative life force, and conscious will.

The Neptunian influence brings added grace and sensitivity to the Sun's self-expression and conscious will. The higher dimensional orientation of Neptune brings a desire to exceed worldly ambition and constraints of the ego and help others who are less fortunate. They seek to enrich their lives through characteristic expressions that are ruled by Neptune that include art, music, photography, theater, spirituality, psychic phenomena, and healing.

Gift: They can have deep-rooted compassion and regard for mankind that is attributed to a Sun/Neptune combination. These natives feel Universal Oneness, which can extend to include all living things. They are highly sensitive to the suffering of others and are often regarded as empathic. The combination of the Sun and Neptune gives a highly refined nature that tunes in to the subtleties of the senses. A softness in their eyes can have a mesmerizing effect on others, perhaps due to their lack of brusqueness or the smoothness of their moves, as if they don't want to offend or hurt anyone. They excel in any talents and expressions that make use of their sensitivity and refinement, which includes those talents that are dependent on well-developed senses, all five of them, and includes sixth-sense expressions.

Shadow: These natives love to embrace fantasy, which isn't to say that their perceptions don't have a kernel of truth in them. They need to figure out how much

A Sun/Neptune combination can bring deep-rooted compassion. These natives feel the Universal Oneness which can extend to include all living things. Highly sensitive to the suffering of others, they are often regarded as empathic.

of this is real and how much of it is playing on their hopes and wishes and their unrealistic expectations or assessments. They can be easily led astray due to their innocent and trusting nature. It can seem at times that they are living in another dimension besides here on Earth. They can have memories of a more ideal existence, which can lead to disappointment and even depression when the realities of an ordinary existence with others who are less sensitive and aware hit home. The shadow side of a Sun/Neptune combination boils down to frustration and disappointment that can ensue from either setting unrealistic expectations or losing one's sense of self or one's self-identity in order to please or help others. The tendency to sacrifice cannot be at one's own expense.

Neptune/Moon

Neptune rules ideals, creative imagination, transcendence, compassion, and vision.

The Moon rules the soul, core instincts, the personality, and subconscious conditioning.

Neptune sensitizes an already sensitive Moon with heightened compassion and strong emotional empathy for all living things. They feel the discomfort of others as well as their joy. Neptune brings idealism and spirituality to the native's conscious awareness. These natives are naturally attuned to meditation and contacting higher realms of consciousness.

Gift: Fanciful Neptune enhances the imagination and responsiveness to sensory input, enriching musical, artistic, theatrical, and photographic talents for these natives. Their tastes are super refined, which contributes to their culinary gifts. They are particularly sensitive to subtleties of tone in both visual and musical realms. These natives are psychically attuned to the emotions of others as well as to environmental stimuli. The Moon/Neptune combination sees and relates to the best in others and can inspire them to be their best selves.

Shadow: Emotions can be subject to illusions and fantastical assumptions. A need to sacrifice can be attributed to unconscious feelings of not doing enough, as if an ideal exists that can never be reached. Neptune adds confusion to emotional issues. Self-pity and martyrdom can ensue as a result of their overly sensitive nature. Escapism is too often a viable option to experiencing the pain that they would otherwise feel. These natives can have a strong reaction to toxic substances due to the sensitivity of their constitution.

Neptune/Mercury

Neptune rules ideals, creative imagination, transcendence, compassion, and vision.

Mercury rules communication, mental processes, and the logical mind.

Mercury in combination with Neptune can endow the native with a highly creative and vivid imagination. They have a highly developed sixth sense that can pick up information from the ethers, both consciously and subconsciously.

Gift: This combination can contribute to inspirational thinking that can motivate others through their ability to logically communicate high-minded ideals and concepts. The combination lends itself to a mind prone to magical thinking with an affinity for the arts, music, and poetry. They are visionaries and often receive information through visions and imagery. These natives are not limited to logical thinking and can get impressions that others may miss. They can often see into motives and behavior patterns due to the subtleties that they pick up. As a result, they often excel in theater due to their ability to pick up on innuendos.

Shadow: This sensitive thinker can get easily confused when picking up impressions from others and from the environment. Difficulty focusing can occur. The truth can be mutable and unclear. Others can have an undue influence on their thinking due to a tendency to pick up on their thoughts and beliefs. These natives can be elusive and deceptive. They can live in their own fantasy world, where they lose track of reality.

Neptune/Venus

Neptune rules ideals, creative imagination, transcendence, compassion, and vision.

Venus represents love, relationships, beauty, values, comfort, and material resources.

Neptune is the higher octave of Venus. Venus is the planet of love, relationships, beauty, values, comfort, money, and material resources. Neptune rules our dreams and visions. Venus is exalted in the sign of Neptune-ruled Pisces, which lends itself to the highest and purest form of spiritual love.

Gift: Unconditional, pure love is a beautiful gift that natives with this combination can experience in their life. People are often elevated in the company of this individual due to their unique ability to relate to the highest and best in them. A romantic at heart, they have a knack for helping others feel special. These natives are aesthetically sensitive and perceptive. Their vivid imagination and refined sensitivity incline these natives toward music, photography, and mystically inspired art. They excel at perceiving the subtleties of artistic expression. Their heightened sensory awareness gives them an edge in any creative expression, whether it entails the visual arts, cooking, music, or the performing arts.

Shadow: Yearning for something or someone that doesn't exist is typical of the shadow side of this combination. This individual can be always looking for the perfect life, the perfect relationship, the perfect love, only to be disappointed once reality sets in. When expectations run haywire, they become set up for frustration and disappointment since their expectations are often not met. These natives can lose themselves in others, where they give up any semblance of personal boundary and dedicate themselves to another's expectations and happiness. The result is an emptiness when their sacrificial gestures are not returned in kind.

Neptune/Mars

Neptune rules ideals, creative imagination, transcendence, compassion, and vision.

Mars rules assertiveness, energy, drive, and courage.

The combination of Mars and Neptune produces individuals who are generally helpful and artistically inclined. Often found in healing and service professions, these natives are intuitive and very good at inspiring others.

The combination of Mars and Neptune is comparable to having Mars in Pisces. These individuals are inspiring, generally helpful, and artistically or musically inclined.

Gift: Individuals with Mars and Neptune in combination are helpful and can often be found in healing and service professions. These natives are intuitive and very good at inspiring others. It is natural for them to want to find a higher meaning in their action. They have a talent for creative visualization that is an asset in creative endeavors.

Shadow: Neptune can dilute the forcefulness of Mars, which can be a detriment in competitive situations or situations that require focus. The natures of these two planetary energies are very different from each other: Mars is highly directed, and Neptune is not. Confusion over desires and actions that lead to accomplishments are likely.

Goals may be more fanciful than realistic. Setbacks can lead to disillusionment, whereby the native loses intention or abandons any inspiration to keep on going.

Neptune/Jupiter

Neptune rules ideals, creative imagination, transcendence, compassion, and vision.

Jupiter represents the higher mind, greater truths, expansiveness, hope, and optimism.

A Jupiter/Neptune combination can open pathways to the celestial realms, expanding access to the individual's highest visions and dreams. On the other hand, the Neptunian influence can also dissolve boundaries, and when Jupiter combines with Neptune, the result can expand collective illusions, delusions, and deception. Neptune is visionary but is also potentially delusional.

Gift: The combination of Jupiter and Neptune opens the native to the possibility for miracles. They are inclined to transcend and connect with the spirit and the field of all possibilities and creativity. These individuals seek internal peace regardless of external conditions. This combination can bring an outpouring of compassion and an increase in spiritual and metaphysical interests. They are charitable, sympathetic, humanitarian, highly visionary, and imaginative. This planetary combination can indicate a transcendent breakthrough with access to divine realms or a spectacular blunder prompted by deception and fantasy.

Shadow: Jupiter tends to "think big," and it is not unlikely for Jupiter to expand the amorphous borders of reality and think too big at times. Individuals with this combination can lack discernment and be charitable and too trusting to the undeserving. They need frequent reality checks whenever speculating or investing their time and money. Jupiter expands Neptune's ability to absorb and hold toxins. Natives with this combination need to be mindful of toxic fumes and other environmental factors. It is likely that they are super sensitive to certain medications, drugs, and alcohol, which all come under the influence of Neptune.

Neptune/Saturn

Neptune rules ideals, creative imagination, transcendence, compassion, and vision.

Saturn rules responsibility, adjustments to limitations, sustainability, and structure.

Saturn is tasked with creating resilient and sustainable formats and structures, whereas Neptune dissolves boundaries and borders so that merging occurs with the unbounded. Saturn rules the material world, and Neptune rules the transcendent. Saturn rules fears, and Neptune rules trust.

> The shadow side of a Saturn/Neptune combination is a fear that the rug will be pulled out from underneath them.

Gift: Saturn can bring focus, structure, and organization to one's dreams and visions. These natives are able to successfully balance realistic expectations with faith and trust that their dreams can manifest. They have a belief that anything is possible. They are practical dreamers and visionaries who can achieve their dreams with grit, discipline, focus, vision, creativity, and a lot of trust. These natives are often seekers on a path to higher consciousness. They understand the basic laws of nature, including the law of cause and effect.

Shadow: The shadow side of a Saturn/Neptune combination is a fear that the rug will be pulled out from underneath

them. These natives can feel ungrounded and that they cannot fully depend on or trust anything or anyone in this world. It can be very difficult for these individuals to fully let go and trust. Instead, they can overperform for fear that they are not doing enough or underperform with an attitude of "why bother?" They are prone to frequent episodes of depression and bouts of forsakenness. They have an underlying feeling of dissatisfaction with everyday life but lack the focus or will to do anything about it.

Neptune/Uranus

Neptune rules ideals, creative imagination, transcendence, compassion, and vision.

Uranus rules intuition, originality, individuality, and the sudden and unexpected.

A Neptune/Uranus combination is similar to having Uranus in the Twelfth House in that these individuals have unusual spiritual interests and uncanny insights into spiritual and hidden realms.

Gift: These individuals are open to higher dimensional realms. They are prone to intuitive insights and psychic impressions, which often sense hidden agendas and underlying trends. These natives can take up causes on behalf of the weak and the underprivileged. These combinations often occur at times when major spiritual and scientific progress is occurring for humanity. A propensity may occur to be overly idealistic.

Shadow: The shadow side of this connection can be confusion and lack of clarity over prevailing and upcoming trends.

The gift of a Neptune/Chiron combination is an innate understanding of the power of faith, unconditional love, and prayer. An individual with this combination may tend to be a daydreamer and can have problems with addiction.

They may have underlying anxieties connected to fear of the future and fear of the unknown. Strange notions regarding the paranormal and psychic phenomena can be present.

Neptune/Pluto

Neptune rules ideals, creative imagination, transcendence, compassion, and vision.

Pluto represents regeneration; transformation; and a compelling, fundamental approach.

Neptune/Pluto combinations are generational in nature. Often, this combination can affect world karma and the destiny of the collective more than one's individual life. These natives can feel drawn to bring-

ing a new and higher level of consciousness to humanity.

Gift: The gift of this combination is a belief that universal love can heal the woes of the world. Natives have faith in the divine and a belief in the salvation of humanity.

Shadow: The shadow side of this combination is a belief that spiritual regeneration is hopeless and that individuals are victims to corrupt political, social, and religious institutions.

Neptune/Chiron

Neptune rules ideals, creative imagination, transcendence, compassion, and vision.

Chiron represents core wounds and the desire to overcome them, and healing.

A Neptune/Chiron combination can indicate that the native has issues surrounding their self-worth that need healing. They likely need to learn to value themselves and set boundaries so that others don't take advantage of them.

Gift: The gift of a Neptune/Chiron combination is an innate understanding of the power of faith, unconditional love, and prayer. Meditation practices can help these natives achieve peace of mind. Dance, music, art, dream analysis, and drama are vehicles that can help these individuals process emotional discomfort and get in touch with deeper emotional blocks.

Shadow: The shadow side of this placement is a tendency to be a daydreamer and not a doer. Avoidance tactics can be deeply rooted in their psyche, and these natives have a penchant for glossing over deep-rooted emotional issues in favor of lofty, and often unrealistic, dreams. Individuals with this combination can have problems with addiction caused by core wounds that occurred in their early years. Chiron will create discomfort until the native chooses to address this wounding.

Neptune/Eris

Neptune rules ideals, creative imagination, transcendence, compassion, and vision.

Eris represents the determination to remove limitations that impede the soul's evolution.

Gift: The native can successfully utilize transcendental practices in order to reinforce their evolutionary journey. Music, sound therapy, and color therapy are other practices that they can draw upon as supportive to their quest to resonate with their inner selves.

Shadow: False illusions can color natives' perceptions, sending them on a mission for naught. Disillusionment can thereby temper their otherwise lofty intentions to assist members of society who need help.

Neptune/North Node

Neptune rules ideals, creative imagination, transcendence, compassion, and vision.

The North Node represents future direction, soul guidance, and fulfillment.

The North Node emphasizes the importance for the native to develop the attributes represented by Neptune, which can include incorporating a spiritual practice in their lives and applying a more trusting attitude to their affairs.

Gift: The gift of a North Node/Neptune combination can be that the native has a spiritual or more universally oriented mission. These natives have psychic and intuitive abilities that assist them in fulfilling their destiny. They can benefit from following their hunches, which will put them in the right place at the right time.

Shadow: The shadow side of this placement is that the native can be drawn into seductive and potentially deceptive activities. They are attracted to the mysterious, which can put the individual into dangerous situations. These individuals can be blindsided by a desire to please and end up in perilous situations.

Neptune/South Node

Neptune rules ideals, creative imagination, transcendence, compassion, and vision.

The South Node represents familiarity, gratification, and the path of least resistance.

The combination of Neptune and the South Node indicates that the native is comfortable with a spiritually or artistically oriented lifestyle.

Gift: Individuals with a Neptune/South Node combination can bring forward sensitivity, a strong intuition, and the likelihood of spiritual leanings that they can incorporate on their current path. They are compassionate and care about those in less fortunate circumstances. These natives can have artistic, musical, or dramatic abilities.

Shadow: These natives may have engaged in deceptive practices in the past, which may incline them toward secretive and clandestine activities. They can be prone to fantasy schemes and unrealistic visions that lead them to an unfortunate outcome. They can lack discernment and follow paths that look or sound good on the surface but lead down a rabbit hole.

Neptune/Ascendant

Neptune rules ideals, creative imagination, transcendence, compassion, and vision.

The Ascendant represents one's approach, orientation, and the window through which one sees the world.

Gift: The combination of Neptune with the Ascendant enhances the native's psychic and intuitive capabilities. They are inexplicably guided by inspirations and hunches and can often be an enigma to themselves and others. They possess a mysterious and alluring magnetism that is captivating to those they encounter. These natives are highly imaginative, and their visionary abilities can be channeled into artistic, dramatic, and musical talents.

> The combination of Neptune with the Ascendant enhances the native's psychic and intuitive capabilities.

Shadow: The shadow side of this placement is an elusiveness that is hard to pin down. These natives can have a difficult time coping with the mundane realities of life. They may not feel that they are at home on planet Earth, which hinders them from partaking in earthly activities that can bring them satisfaction.

Neptune/Midheaven (MC)

Neptune rules ideals, creative imagination, transcendence, compassion, and vision.

The Midheaven (MC) represents image, outer aspirations, and career orientation.

With Neptune at the top of the chart, a kinship with professions occurs that makes use of the native's imaginative, aesthetic, and spiritual inclinations. These natives may not excel in positions that are highly regimented and require a practical and disciplined methodology.

Gift: Individuals with a strong Neptune/Midheaven connection can inspire large groups of people with their uplifting views and the hypnotic effect they can have on an audience. It is an excellent combination for someone involved in the creative arts, music, entertainment, and the expansion of consciousness.

Shadow: The shadow side of this combination is that the native has to be careful not to get involved in intrigues and scandals, as public humiliation is possible. Personal and private affairs are not so likely to be kept private, especially if they include a clandestine or off-color aspect.

PLUTO

Pluto was held as the ninth planet from the Sun when first discovered by Clyde Tombaugh in 1930. Pluto is believed to consist of a rocky core surrounded by a layer of water and ice. The planet, located in the Kuiper Belt, is relatively small, with a highly eccentric orbit that is inclined at 17 degrees, much greater than other planetary orbits that surround the Sun. As a result, Pluto spends part of its time inside the orbit of Neptune. Pluto has an orbital period of 247.686 years.

After more than seven decades, Pluto's status as a planet was questioned after several objects of similar size were also discovered in the Kuiper Belt. Eventually, the discovery of Eris in 2005, which was 27 percent more massive than Pluto, led to

Though distant Pluto was reclassified as a dwarf planet in 2005, the new designation hasn't lessened its importance to our star charts. Pluto is a catalyst for bringing unconscious material to the surface and seeks to uncover our not-yet-discovered talents and true identity.

Pluto's reclassification as a dwarf planet in 2006.

Pluto was named after the Roman god of the Underworld, who ruled over everything that was buried under Earth's surface, including the dead. Pluto's job was to divide what was worthwhile, which of the dead would head to the Elysian fields, and which souls would go to hell. Pluto also rules over precious metals that are buried under the Earth.

Pluto is a catalyst for bringing unconscious material to the surface. Pluto seeks to uncover the part of ourselves that lives deep in our unconscious along with our not-yet-discovered and true identities.

"Pluto's role is to make you live according to who you truly are," says Christopher Renstrom of *Astrology Hub's Weekly Horoscope*. "Pluto is the planet of ordeals—it demands that we face or fight for things that matter on a very, very deep level. But in addition to ordeals, Pluto also encourages the transformations that arise from the ordeals we go through. If you choose to take on the current ordeals in your life with your full heart and your entire soul, you will be transformed, resulting in a rebirth and a new lease on your life."

Pluto is the planet of transformation. Pluto activates the life force in us that needs to be raised and released from entrapments. Pluto reveals self-oriented patterns, ego-oriented traits, fears, and self-doubts that have outlived their purpose. Pluto can breathe new life into deadened parts of the soul and foster a renewed evolutionary purpose.

Pluto also rules obsession, compulsion, jealousy, manipulation, and control. Pluto's gift is self-empowerment, and its shadow is self-serving power at the expense of others. Pluto can be slow and relentless in the process of uncovering the truth. The nature of Pluto is to release and free up energy. Hence, Pluto is associated with atomic explosions, energy production, and nuclear power.

Astrologer Dane Rudyhar saw Pluto as the way to experience a profound deep dive into what is seated in our psyche, especially the fears that prevent us from embracing what is truly ours to do.

The Pluto archetype represents power and empowerment.

Gift: Pluto is a gift if we heed her call and do the necessary inner work. Pluto is the part of us that can squarely face difficult truths and persistently hold the intention to resolve anything preventing us from a full empowerment of the soul. Pluto can heal and transform our physical, emotional, mental, and spiritual bodies with a relentless desire that emanates from deep within our core.

Shadow: Pluto will insist upon transformation and bring discomfort until we feel that no other choice exists but to surrender and change. Pluto can bring out the shadow side of whatever signs, houses, or planetary bodies it touches. Pluto deconstructs the symbolism of the sign that it is moving through. When Pluto is at play, coming alive and shedding one's skin can feel like dying.

Pluto in the Signs

Pluto's orbit is extremely eccentric, wildly off the ecliptic and sometimes closer to the Sun than Neptune, spending between 14 and 31 years in a sign. When Pluto was discovered in 1930, fascism was rising in the world, and the power of atomic energy was becoming known.

Pluto's sign position is more generational than personal. Pluto's sign position can show how power, transformation, regeneration, forced change, and research manifest through the characteristics of each sign. Pluto is the planet of death and rebirth. The sign location will indicate the type of changes that each generation may be most drawn to.

> Pluto is the planet of death and rebirth. The sign location will indicate the type of changes that each generation may be most drawn to.

The dates connected to Pluto in each sign are approximate. Although Pluto spends generally between 14 and 31 years in each sign, Pluto will retrograde to the previous sign at the beginning of its journey in a sign. Similarly, near the completion of its journey in a sign, Pluto will move forward into the next sign and then retrograde back again.

Pluto spends the least amount of time in Libra and Scorpio due to its elliptical orbit.

Pluto in Aries (1822–1853)

Pluto in Aries, a sign associated with courage, passion, initiative, violence, and assertion, depicts a generation that includes the American pioneer. Revolutionary movements were also initiated in Europe. Many gun manufacturers coincidentally appeared during this time frame.

Gift: Motivated, clear, and energized, these natives withstood many obstacles and hardships in order to establish a new life.

Shadow: The shadow side of this generational energy includes the genocide of the Native Americans and increased tension around the enslavement of Africans.

Pluto in Taurus (1851–1884)

Pluto in Venus-ruled Taurus can be associated with materialism, resources, and land. Great economic expansion took place during this period.

Gift: The Industrial Revolution occurred during this time period, and factories began to appear in order to promote efficiency in the production of goods. Banking acts were passed, and the New York Stock Exchange opened. In 1863, Abraham Lincoln's Emancipation Proclamation freed slaves from being the property of slaveowners.

Shadow: Divisions in wealth began to appear during this generation that were associated with the peak of the Industrial Revolution. Splits formed, with extreme wealth of tycoons on one side and extreme poverty resulting from low wages and substandard living conditions at the other end of the spectrum. Monopolies began to be formed, which exacerbated the divisiveness.

Pluto in Gemini (1882–1914)

Pluto in Mercury-ruled Gemini had a major effect on mass communications and mass media.

Gift: This was a period of new ideas and inventions and the expansion of previously discovered modes of technology. The automobile, telephone, radio, and phonograph were among the significant developments of this generation.

Shadow: The shadow side of this generation evolves from the dualistic nature of new ideas and advancements in technology and includes extremes of greed and ruthless behaviors.

Pluto in Cancer (1912–1939)

The Pluto in Cancer generation endured two world wars as well as the rise of fascistic leaders. Nationalism prevailed in many parts of the world and gave rise to extreme sentiments, triggering world wars during this generation.

Gift: Food shortages initiated industrialized solutions in the food industry that expanded the ability to feed people in times of shortages. The family unit was strengthened and appreciated. People began to form communities that included extended family when separated from their birth families due to war or immigration. Patriotism strengthened.

Shadow: The shadow side of this placement was the distortion of the love of one's country into the extremism of nationalistic tribalism and ultimately fascism in the two world wars. Manipulation and exploitation of the masses occurred through food deprivation and starvation in order to gain power and control.

Pluto in Leo (1937–1958)

Characteristics of the Pluto in Leo generation are such themes as the fascination with power, charismatic leadership, and authoritarian politics. Power is held by those who have a flair for attracting the masses. Hitler rose to power during this period. Following World War II, society changed, and a strong desire for individual expression arose as the nuclear family fragmented.

Televisions became commonplace in homes by the end of this generation, and enjoyment and even laughter became more easily available. A massive explosion in

The gift from a Pluto in Leo placement is warm, charismatic leadership ability. Individuals with this placement are confident, strong-willed, loyal, and talented, with a flair for the dramatic.

birth rates occurred following World War II, producing the Baby Boomers.

Gift: The gift from a Pluto in Leo placement is warm, charismatic leadership. Natives are confident, strong-willed, and loyal. Individuals with this placement are talented and have a flair for the dramatic. Creative self-expression, romance, and the need for fun and entertainment are deeply held desires and often quite necessary for these individuals. Creative endeavors assist them in transforming negative emotions by channeling their energy into productive outlets.

Shadow: The shadow sides of this placement are false pride and a sense of entitlement. These natives lack humility, are self-centered and egotistical, and can be bullies. Transformation occurs for them when they go to extremes of ego aggrandizement and control and circumstances

trigger a downfall from power. These natives can want to live through their children if they have not developed their own talents and abilities. Again, challenges can evolve that instigate life-changing soul-searching and growth.

Pluto in Virgo (1956–1972)

The Pluto in Mercury-ruled Virgo generation became obsessed with making sense out of wartime and the postwar reaction that ensued. Their aim became categorizing, organizing, and constructing rules of service duty, stewardship, and employment. Early computer programs, calculators, beginnings of the internet, and ATM machines came into being. Medicare and Medicaid were established during this time, and environmental organizations such as Greenpeace came into being. Sexual morality became a theme as a result of the discerning orientation of Virgo during this period.

Gift: Pluto in Virgo is highly organized and fancies making order out of information, people, and standards of behavior. They are practical and want to make their day-to-day life as efficient as possible. These natives are humble and are not inclined to be egotistical when it comes to making changes either for the sake of efficiency or as an act of service to a cause they believe in. They can bring forward stringent nutritional and healthcare practices when required. Physical injury or chronic illness can be triggers for profound lifestyle changes.

Shadow: The shadow side of this placement is all work and no play, thereby leaving the native unfulfilled and overextended. Health issues can ensue as a result of stress and exhaustion, and subsequent transformation and life changes can be the outcome. Too much categorization and pigeonholing can contribute to inefficiency in work environments, whereby a big-picture perspective is lost. Dehumanization can occur where everyone is expendable. A tendency to be overly critical can occur.

Pluto in Libra (1971–1984)

The Pluto in Venus-ruled Libra generation placed an emphasis on relationships, equal rights, and justice. New concepts of marriage developed, and this period contributed to increases in divorce, including the legalization of no-fault divorce. The antiwar movement was prevalent during this generation and was popularized by artists, musicians, and entertainers.

Gift: Gifts from the placement of Pluto in Libra include a focus on developing fulfilling personal relationships. As a result, these natives are willing to go through various iterations of changes and self-examination in order to achieve this goal. The sharing of responsibilities in partnerships takes precedence over sexual identity roles that were prevalent in earlier generations. Personal empowerment comes through compromise and cooperation rather than through having power over another.

Medicare and Medicaid were established during this time, and environmental organizations such as Greenpeace came into being.

Shadow: The shadow side of this placement is a gnawing dissatisfaction in close business and personal connections. Outer circumstances can cause the native to look inward and take ownership of their role in interpersonal relations. It can take time for them to realize that the path to fulfillment is not through power over another in relationships. These individuals can have legal encounters that are troublesome in their lives. Disruptive urges to go against the legal system and get away with deviant behaviors are possible.

Pluto in Scorpio (1983–1995)

The Pluto in Scorpio generation has been characterized by sociologists as the millennials. Pluto-ruled Scorpio governs sex, death, transformation, determination, and the occult. Plutonian themes during these years encompassed those of nuclear proliferation and include the Chernobyl nuclear power plant disaster; the AIDS epidemic, which killed millions; and dark themes in entertainment, music, art, and literature that depict sex, violence, and the occult.

Gift: Pluto in Scorpio natives have an ardent desire to embrace transformation and change, which can follow the exploration of human desires and the darkest impulses. They are often fearless, determined, and intense, which, when applied toward evolutionary growth, can be enormously productive. These individuals understand power and how the right use of power can be a force for good.

Shadow: Compulsive, obsessive, and fanatical behavior patterns are likely ramifications of the shadow side of Pluto in Scorpio. These behaviors are likely to have themes of sex, control, death, jealousy, possessiveness, rage, danger, and the supernatural. These natives can drive themselves to the edge or beyond before they seek spiritual guidance and counseling or before dire necessity causes them to regenerate.

The Pluto in Sagittarius generation brings a fresh perspective to the planet, an expansive view that includes the integration of various world cultures, a spiritual reorientation that applies to all peoples, and the freedom for each person to be themselves. With an idealism that they harbor for humanity, they are able to hold their visions for the future and make changes accordingly.

Pluto in Sagittarius
(1748–1762; 1995–2008)

The Pluto in Sagittarius generation brings a fresh perspective to the planet. This generation has an expansive view that includes the integration of various world cultures, a spiritual reorientation that applies to all peoples, and the freedom for each person to be themselves. This generation also witnessed changes in how people acquire knowledge and distribute information. The digitization of information, the dot-com boom, and the onset of social media characterize this time frame.

Gift: The gift from a Pluto in Sagittarius placement is the idealism that they harbor for humanity. Their beliefs are strong, and they are able to hold their visions for the future and make changes accordingly.

Truth is important to these natives, and they seek to integrate a higher truth that we are all human, we are all different, and each person's differences make up the whole.

Shadow: The shadow side of this placement is the polarization of religious beliefs and cultural differences. Extremism, fundamentalism, and divisiveness result from tunnel vision that is set on resisting change. Old ideologies are held on to, and their inability to transform their thinking leaves these individuals frozen in time. The expansive view of Pluto in Sagittarius can neglect important details for the sake of the big picture. These individuals can become distracted and overlook essential elements that are necessary to make decisions that allow them to achieve their vision.

Pluto in Capricorn
(1762–1778; 2008–2024)

The Pluto in Capricorn generation is likely to institute extreme changes in government, banking, and corporate structures. Capricorn relates to banking, investments, capitalism, infrastructure, management, the status quo, and plutocrats who exploit the masses. Changes in banking and investments due to digital currencies are reflective of this generation. In 2008, when Pluto entered Capricorn, the global financial crisis occurred.

Gift: Pluto in Capricorn offers the gift of perseverance. The influence of Saturn provides these natives with the staying power to see through changes that they deem necessary. This placement of Pluto provides a reality check to current ideologies, methodologies, laws, rules, and regulations. This influence evaluates whether they are efficient and will be sustainable so that they can pass the test of time. This placement will seek out weaknesses in structures and infrastructures so that they can be made more resilient.

Shadow: The shadow side of this placement is where control is kept at the top, with a top-down approach that subjugates the masses. Discrepancies in wages, living conditions, and opportunities increase due to disproportionate allocations. Ambitions run rampant without consideration of the greater good. Plutocracies seek more and more power at the expense of the masses.

Pluto in Aquarius
(1777–1798; 2023–2044)

If Pluto in Capricorn is characterized by a top-down approach, where rules are determined by a select few, Pluto in Aquarius is invested in the democratic distribution of power. Everyone counts, and all of humanity is important. Consensual participation and decision making takes precedence in this generation. New scientific discoveries are likely in health care and environmental cleanup. Significant changes involving genetic technologies that have a profound effect on life-threatening illnesses are likely. Advances in laser therapies are also likely during this period.

Previously, Pluto entered Aquarius just following the birth of the U.S. Constitution when the prevailing mood was equal justice for all. On July 14, 1789, mobs in France stormed the Bastille, initiating the French Revolution with the outcry of "Equality, Liberty, and Fraternity."

Gift: Combining the innovative impetus of Uranus-ruled Aquarius with Plutonian determination brings a strong momentum to break through restrictions of the past and create new, original, and innovative structures. A strong ability to focus on goals and objectives is present. Expect original ideas, a strong need for personal freedom, and the tearing down of structures that are divisive. The truth is important to Aquarius. Transparency in business, government, politics, and major institutions will likely be issues that come to the fore. Individuals with this placement will be free-spirited, honest to a fault, and highly individualized.

Shadow: The shadow sides of Pluto in Aquarius are likely to be revolutionary movements that seek to tear down businesses, governments, and institutions using whatever means they can, sometimes at the expense of human values. Rebellious actors with little regard for law and order are likely to become more commonplace. These behaviors may not result in desired changes until innovative alternatives are brought to the fore.

Pluto in Pisces
(1798–1823; 2043–2068)

Pluto's previous journey through Pisces was at a time that marked a high point in the arts. Pisces is a romantic sign. Venus is exalted in Pisces. A rebirth in romanticism is likely to occur during Pluto's next sojourn in Pisces. The spiritually oriented influence of Neptune may bring forth spiritual leaders who emphasize principles of oneness. The transformative influence of Pluto combined with Pisces's compassion and empathy will likely make great progress in dissolving barriers between cultures, races, social classes, and outer-dimensional entities. Advanced healing practices are likely to further incorporate color, sound, aromatherapy, and energy.

Gift: Gifts from Pluto in Pisces individuals will include a refined artistic sensitivity and expanded aesthetic sensibility. An awakened compassion for those who are less fortunate will spur advances in regulations and laws that will provide more opportunities for those in unfortunate situations. These individuals are imaginative and highly intuitive, with well-developed psychic abilities.

Shadow: Self-destructive behavior patterns can result from an increase in depression and the forsakenness that results from unmet fantasies and expectations that are common when Neptune blurs the boundaries between reality and the imagination. Neptune rules drugs and mind-altering substances, and when combined with the compulsiveness that is so common with Pluto, addictive behavior patterns can result. Pluto in Pisces can increase escapist tendencies.

PLUTO IN THE HOUSES

Pluto is a catalyst for bringing unconscious material to the surface. The house place-ment of Pluto in the natal chart will give a view into the area of life where the native will be less in control. Issues such as those centered around betrayal, control, obsession, paranoia, rage, and loss are likely. As a result, these individuals may be challenged to search for deeper meanings in the area associated with Pluto's placement.

Pluto in the First House

The First House rules appearance, health, general temperament, and sense of self. The First House defines you and the image you project to others.

Pluto in Mars's First House is strongly placed. Mars is considered to be the higher octave of Mars, so instead of rushing headlong into a new situation, Pluto analyzes first and then carefully slithers into a new situation. These natives exude an intensity that is coupled with an intriguing charm and an aura of confidence and power.

Gift: The gift of this placement is steadfast determination and a highly developed sense of personal power. These natives probe beneath the surface and are able to keenly evaluate the hidden motives of others. They tune in to the undercurrents surrounding situations that escape most people. This placement of Pluto is excellent for fields that involve scientific or medical analysis, surveillance, and occult phenomena. These individuals generally have a strong will, which can be directed toward significant healing and accomplishment when directed positively. They have a great capacity to regenerate themselves once they perceive that transformation is necessary for their survival or well-being.

Shadow: This placement of Pluto can be a double-edged sword in that the individual's willpower and determination can be used toward a negative end if they so desire. Obsessive and compulsive behaviors are likely. These natives don't tend to do anything halfway, and if they are gripped by a negative impulse, it can be difficult for them to exert self-control. The sign placement and planetary combinations at play will determine how this energy can manifest. Suspicion and paranoia are likely as shadow elements of this placement, especially when the native lacks a strong self-image and self-confidence.

Pluto in the Second House

The Second House is connected with finances, values, material possessions, talents, and resources. The Second House represents the value we give to ourselves and, in turn, that which we possess.

The Second House is the house of values, material resources, and self-worth, and Pluto in this position may cause the native to go through periods of economic crisis before they reevaluate their real value and feel entitled to their due compensation. Talents are also ruled by the Second House, and challenging circumstances can occur that bring to light their previously uncovered talents and abilities. With this placement, the native can be more interested in material possessions that have an intrinsic value rather than unnecessary or extraneous things.

Gift: Pluto in the Second House can bring great determination for acquiring financial resources. In general, determination and a methodical and steadfast approach to situations are two of the abilities that these individuals bring to a situation. They are highly resourceful and have the ability to regenerate a condition or solve a problem that appears to be hopeless. These natives are good strategists, and their analytic abilities can assist them in both problem solving and spotting a good deal. This placement can bring wealth when combined with Jupiter, as is the case with Bill Gates.

Pluto in Mars's First House is strongly placed, gifting a steadfast determination and a highly developed sense of personal power.

Shadow: The downside of this placement can be a tendency to be greedy and to place too much value on money and ownership at the expense of human connection, which would lead to their emotional fulfillment. Material possessions and money can be used as control mechanisms over others. They can use uncouth, illegal, and subversive means to obtain money and material possessions.

Pluto in the Third House

The Third House is connected with ideas, communication, siblings, neighbors, and short journeys.

Pluto in a house ruled by Mercury can give these natives a penchant for analytic and focused thinking. They are able to communicate convincingly, as if they project themselves into the other person's mind, and they know exactly how to present the information. These natives don't like to mince words.

Gift: It can take individuals with this placement a while to figure out how to be effective communicators, but once they do, they can be quite masterful. They have the ability to understand the motivations of others even better than others understand themselves. They have penetrating minds that seek to get to the core of issues and make excellent problem solvers. They excel in situations that require a steadfast focus and good analytical abilities. They can generally be trusted to keep a secret.

Shadow: The shadow side of this placement is that these natives can be overly opinionated and can have beliefs based more on bias than on fact. Control issues can evolve that are related to siblings or neighbors. It is not unlikely that they would be accused of scheming and plotting behind their backs. Sibling rivalry can be strong with these natives. Mental stress can result from obsessive thinking. Stress-reduction techniques can benefit these individuals by lessening the circular thinking patterns that keep them in their minds.

> Their passion and focus can be a motivation to others. When they are engaged in helping those in need, the powerful sensitivity these natives offer is very healing.

Pluto in the Fourth House

The Fourth House is about the home, family, genetic inheritance, foundational stability, innermost feelings, later life, and the end of matters.

Pluto in the Fourth House can indicate a native with strong interests in home and family. They can be willing to go to extremes to protect and take care of their families, an experience that results in further empowering them.

Gift: Individuals with a Fourth-House Pluto placement can be highly resourceful in finding ways to care for their family members. They can have a keen sensibility for understanding and providing for the needs of each person, even during difficult times or when they are pulled away from home for other activities. These natives can see the potential in properties and heirlooms and bring them back to life. They have a knack for choosing investment properties that can lead to financial gain.

Shadow: The shadow side of this placement can be skeletons in the closet that the native avoids dealing with until circumstances unleash an eruption that forces them to do so. Pluto in the Fourth House individuals can be involved in power struggles in the home or with family members. They can be overly possessive, abusive, and controlling, which alienates family members and disrupts the peace. Issues can occur involving the care of parents in later life that cause interruptions in the native's lifestyle.

Pluto in the Fifth House

The Fifth House rules creative self-expression, children, love, passion, romance, playfulness, and joy.

Natives with Pluto in Leo's Fifth House transform themselves through love and romance, their creativity, or their children. These areas touch their hearts, and the power of love gives them the motivation they need to make changes for a happier life. The Fifth House rules joy, and it is this joy that they seek.

Gift: Natives with Pluto in the Fifth House can be passionately romantic and demonstrative about love. This passion can be further sublimated into creative expression, which can include artistic endeavors, theater, and children. They are talented performers who can take on the essence of the roles they are playing. Their passion and intensity are captivating to any audience.

Shadow: The shadow side of a Pluto in the Fifth House placement is an out-of-control ego that seeks aggrandizement at any cost. Gambling and speculation can become obsessive addictions that cause major financial losses. An obsession with sex is also possible with this placement. These natives can live through their children when they don't have the confidence or courage to develop their own natural talents and abilities. This can lead to resentments and ultimately create distance between them.

Natives with Pluto in the Fifth House can be passionately romantic and demonstrative about love. Their captivating passion can be further sublimated into creative expression.

Pluto in the Sixth House

The Sixth House governs daily routines, acts of service, the work-life balance, health, due diligence, pet care, coworkers, and employees.

The Sixth House belongs to Virgo, a house placement that gains fulfillment through acts of service as well as from their day-to-day routines. When Pluto is positioned in the Sixth House, the native can find their personal power through helping others in need and from sticking with regimens long enough to gain benefit from them.

Gift: Pluto adds passion and determination to the areas that a house encompasses. When Pluto is located in the Sixth House, the native can work tirelessly to accomplish tasks required of them. They excel at taking charge and strategically approaching the job at hand. Their analytical orientation as-

sists them in prioritizing each facet of a project and then generating a timeline for its completion. Their passion and focus can be a motivation to others. When they are engaged in helping those in need, the powerful sensitivity these natives offer is very healing. Individuals with this placement have an edge on their own health problems by utilizing their ability to penetrate beneath the surface of issues they encounter. Their research skills combined with their determination to follow a steady regimen can help them to overcome problems and transform negative habit patterns.

Shadow: These individuals can get involved in power struggles and one-upmanship with their coworkers or hired help. It is not beneath them to engage in workplace intrigues. Bad habits can lead to health problems, and these natives can push the envelope before they decide to

Pluto in the Eighth House of transformation is focused on whatever is hidden or beneath the surface—life's secrets and mysteries, including sex, death, birth, magic, and an awareness of subtle dimensional realities. These natives can be deeply affected by the death of loved ones, which can ultimately open doorways into the afterlife.

take charge of their health and make changes. Endurance, which is characteristic of this placement, can work to the native's disadvantage. They can allow a negative situation, a bad habit, or a painful health condition to exist for far too long before taking remedial steps.

Pluto in the Seventh House

The Seventh House rules close personal relationships, agreements, and compromises.

Pluto in the natural home of Libra brings passion and intensity to close relationships. These natives can sense their partner's needs and motivations. Close connections can be an impetus for change and growth

in their lives. The concept of finding a soul mate is an important quest for them. Disappointments in this area can be harsh for these individuals. They need to periodically take a step back in order to gain a clearer perspective on their strong personal connections. This placement can bring about legal challenges since the Seventh House rules open enemies.

Gift: The gift that Pluto in the Seventh House offers is that these individuals will seek a relationship that will help them grow. They can be vigilant about healing blocks and problems that arise in their partnerships and in close personal and business relationships. These individuals will do whatever it takes to make a partnership work if they are motivated to do so. They are intense, passionate, charismatic, and like to feel that they are fully involved in central key aspects of the relationship. They are attracted to strong and powerful individuals with whom they are on an equal footing.

Shadow: The shadow side of this placement can entail a need to control the other person when they are in close business or personal relationships. A boatload of sensitivity, occasional paranoia, and jealousy can lead to unpleasant and unequivocal negative behaviors that include rage, retaliation, contentiousness, and revenge. Often, these natives seek an airtight relationship, whereas their prospective or current partners may need more personal freedom in their close connections.

Pluto in the Eighth House

The Eighth House rules joint ventures, intimacy, sex, death, transformation, and psychic dimensions.

Pluto in the house of transformation is well placed and focused on whatever is hidden or beneath the surface. Human motivations and life's secrets and mysteries, including sex, death, birth, magic, and an awareness of subtle dimensional realities, are all in the purview of this placement. These natives can be deeply affected by the death of loved ones, which can ultimately open doorways into the afterlife.

Gift: Since these natives operate in the realm of the less obvious, they can be helpful to others who are experiencing challenges and those in crisis. They draw upon their sharpened perceptive capabilities, akin to a sixth sense, and good analysis techniques to come up with solutions. Their diagnostic aptitudes can assist them in healing professions. These natives can be comfortable with passion, intimacy, and intense experiences with others. An Eighth-House Pluto placement can assist in sniffing out good investment possibilities.

Shadow: The shadow side of an Eighth-House Pluto placement is a power struggle with money and material resources. Deep-seated control issues can arise in situations that include legacies, inheritances, sexual intimacy, and their partner's resources. These natives can be highly manipulative and underhanded when dealing with joint finances, taxes, insurances, and inheritances. Sexual intimacy may not be truly satisfying to them until they release fears of losing control or other blockages that they may have buried deep in their subconscious.

Pluto in the Ninth House

The Ninth House rules higher education, long-term goals, foreign travel, publicity, adventures, religion, and philosophical and ethical pursuits.

Pluto in the home of Sagittarius will motivate the native to pursue a philosophy of life that they can abide by. They can be seekers of higher consciousness and follow a path of mastery to become adept.

Advanced education can fulfill their desire to become an expert in a particular field. Whatever their path, the native is empowered through having a mission that they feel is elevating and that helps them to see their place in the world. These natives can also be inspired to make changes that transform existing educational, religious, and political systems.

Gift: Natives with a Ninth-House Pluto placement can have profound insights into various world cultures. Archaeology, world history, religion, and the interplay of civilizations can be areas of interest for them. Persuasive at conveying their knowledge and beliefs, these natives can excel in fields such as education and politics and be advocates for cultural organizations and human rights. They are captivating speakers and lecturers and are often able to inspire others through media and literature. The Ninth House rules publishing, which can include using all modes of communication to get knowledge, beliefs, and opinions across to large groups of people.

Shadow: The shadow side of this placement is that these natives can get extremely attached to their opinions and beliefs. Bigotry and religious fanaticism can result. Spiritual pride can become a means of exploiting others. These natives can use spirituality and religious fervor as a way of thinking that they are superior to others.

Pluto in the Tenth House

The Tenth House rules public achievements, reputation, authority, and prestige.

Pluto in the Tenth House combines the planetary characteristics of Pluto and Saturn. These individuals are determined, ambitious, and steadfast in whatever they desire to achieve. They can pull out all the stops in order to gain notoriety and success. Once they do achieve recognition for their achievements, they will attempt to hold on to their control at all costs.

Gift: Individuals with Pluto in the Tenth House have an unwavering focus coupled with a strong sense of commitment and responsibility. They will go to great lengths to become successful in their chosen profession. Status and reputation are important to them, and they can be diligent in keeping both intact. These natives can seek to make changes in social structures that they consider to be outdated. They can successfully contribute to reforming their professional field and possibly make important contributions to the world. They are charismatic and charming and have a pulse on what is fashionable and popular. They instinctively know how to work a room.

Shadow: These natives don't like to be challenged in their rise to success and like it even less once they are at the top of their game. They will fight off their adversaries and can stoop to underhanded tactics if they deem it necessary. In truth, they can get an adrenaline rush from throwing off their competition. Empathy may not live in their bones. They can be harsh and ruthless when their pride or ego is at stake.

Pluto in the Eleventh House

The Eleventh House rules friends, hopes, wishes, groups, and a sense of belonging in the world.

Pluto in the Eleventh House natives can be dedicated proponents of social change and transformation. These are serious humanitarians and can often be found in

professions that seek to achieve scientific and humanitarian advances.

Gift: Individuals with this Pluto placement can be successful and dynamic group leaders. They have a penetrating insight into group undercurrents and can successfully let each member of the group have their voice be heard. These individuals choose their friends carefully and are willing to put in the effort to resolve issues that may arise. They will help their dearest friends through life challenges and any crisis they should encounter. They are likely to have powerful and influential friends and group associations. Some may be associated with healing and other esoteric practices that seek to elevate human awareness.

> Pluto in the Eleventh House natives ... are serious humanitarians and can often be found in professions that seek to achieve scientific and humanitarian advances.

Shadow: The shadow side of this placement is a delicate and strong ego that does not respect the rights of others. They may have to learn cooperation through challenging and difficult situations that occur in social settings or through friendships. Power struggles and control issues can arise in friendships or with group associations. These challenges may be more prevalent prior to the native developing a strong sense of their own identity and beliefs.

Pluto in the Twelfth House

The Twelfth House rules secrets, unconscious patterns, karma, closure, institutions, connections with higher sources, enlightenment, and undoing.

Pluto in the Twelfth House individuals have a strong drive to illuminate unconscious murmurings that show themselves in fits and starts. They can sense that they need to get in touch with buried aspects of themselves, which can lead them to seek assistance through psychology or many of the occult sciences. Life challenges can lead these individuals to further accept their own power, an aspect of themselves that they may have previously been afraid to acknowledge and embrace.

Gift: These natives can have profound psychic insights that tune in to underlying motivations, thoughts, and feelings of others. They strongly pick up on trends in the collective unconscious, which can awaken a deep desire to improve the circumstances of those who are less fortunate. The combination of their exceedingly compassionate nature with highly developed intuitive powers often leads these natives into fields where they can help others. These natives respond well to solitude, meditative techniques, and healing modalities that draw their attention inward and allow aspects of their unconscious to rise to the surface. They need time away from the intensity of helping and analyzing others in order to process their desires and needs.

Shadow: The strong determination of Pluto can work against the native when they put themselves at risk, sometimes when engaged in situations that they perceive as helping others. The Twelfth House is also the house of self-undoing. It is called that because unconscious motivations that are not acknowledged can become hidden drivers that subject the native to seeking challenges that push their limits. These unconscious impulses can be undermining to the native's health and well-being and attract negative energies and secret enemies.

PLUTO COMBINATIONS

Pluto/Sun

Pluto represents regeneration; transformation; and a compelling, fundamental approach.

Pluto in the Twelfth House individuals can have profound psychic insights and strongly pick up on trends in the collective unconscious. Their compassionate nature and intuitive powers often lead them into fields where they can help others.

The Sun indicates purpose, self-expression, creative life force, and conscious will.

Investigative Pluto combines with the illuminating Sun, and you can be sure that an individual with this combination does not see anything at face value. They have a laser focus and persistence that gets to the bottom line sooner rather than later. This is a combination that will go all in, with no halfway. They do not stick their toe into the water.

These natives like to hold their cards close to their hearts. They don't like to expose their vulnerabilities for fear that it will lessen their power and reduce their ability to control a situation. They are as intense about controlling themselves as they are about controlling their environment. These natives often have a fascination with the dark side of life and all that is considered taboo, as if it unleashes a challenge for them to have power over the hidden and potentially uncontrollable.

Gift: This native believes in the ability to change, transform, and regenerate, which can give an innate healing ability and an all-around desire to grow and evolve. Keen perceptive abilities allow this native to see below the surface and get to the root of an issue. The person is a natural at taking adverse situations and using them for self-empowerment. These individuals go through many periods of self-transformation and self-renewal. They are capable of brilliant and profound insights, which gives them a great deal of power and strength.

Shadow: The shadow side of a Sun and Pluto combination can see the world through the lens of control and power. Sometimes in their life, they might have to make serious decisions as to whether they want to take the high road or give in to ego-driven impulses that go against their own well-being as well as that of others. Their desires are strong and often obsessive, overshadowing common sense and egging them on toward what can become self-destructive behavior. Their desire for intensity can lead them to seek the challenge of going right to the edge. A lot can be going on below the surface with these individuals, which can include jealousies, deep-rooted vulnerabilities, paranoia, and a nagging suspicion of others' motives. Getting in touch with and facing these darker patterns can begin the transformation process, where the native can ultimately relieve their gnawing discomfort and release the creative energy held within.

Pluto/Moon

Pluto represents regeneration; transformation; and a compelling, fundamental approach.

The Moon rules the soul, core instincts, the personality, and subconscious conditioning.

Pluto combining with the Moon brings emotional intensity. Their feelings are keenly felt, which is perhaps the trigger that leads them to want to take a deep dive into understanding their subconscious makeup. A desire is present to be in control of their feelings rather than having their emotions be a dominating influence over them.

Gift: These natives are willing to delve into their emotional discomfort and figure out its root cause. They believe in peeling back the layers to get to the crux of an issue. Self-empowerment is their goal, and they have an innate understanding of the right use of power. They are natural therapists and healers, helping others figure out what is motivating them. They have the courage and determination to overcome obstacles. They believe in transformation, and they are not limited to cultivating their inner lives. They do not hesitate to improve their outer environment with renovations and makeovers.

> As much as these natives want to have some control over their feelings, their strong desire by nature can lead them to self-destructive actions.

Shadow: Huge emotional fluctuations can occur due to the intensity of their emotions. As much as these natives want to have some control over their feelings, their strong desire by nature can lead them to self-destructive actions. Obsessive and compulsive behaviors can be daunting to these natives, making it difficult for them to find inner peace. The shadow side of a Moon/Pluto combination manifests as suspicion, jealousy, out-of-control anxiety, and trepidation.

Pluto/Mercury

Pluto represents regeneration; transformation; and a compelling, fundamental approach.

Mercury rules communication, mental processes, and the logical mind.

The combination of Mercury and Pluto results in a laser-focused mind that is capable of high levels of concentration and deep analysis.

Gift: Natives with a Mercury/Pluto combination have remarkable investigative abilities and can gain insights that uncover information that others miss. Their skill set includes the ability to probe and comprehend hidden material and evidence, making them good detectives, medical practitioners, and therapists. These individuals are strategic and persuasive thinkers who can get to the bottom of an issue and convince others with their persuasive communication skills. They make good strategists due to their ability to evaluate all angles of an issue. They are well equipped to do jobs that others may lack the focus, patience, and analytical skills to attempt.

Shadow: Natives with a Mercury/Pluto combination can have an obsessive mind that can't let go and move on. Their thought process can get caught up in looping, whereby the same thoughts keep returning over and over, spiraling into circular thinking patterns that stem from unconscious fears and self-limiting beliefs. Their strategic reasoning ability can embrace underhanded schemes, especially when they are overwhelmed by out-of-

When Venus and Pluto connect, there is a desire to transform and be transformed through love. There is a strong desire to connect and merge at all levels, physically, emotionally, mentally, and spiritually.

control desires. They can use force or pressure to get others to conform to their way of thinking. They can have a tendency to manipulate the truth.

Pluto/Venus

Pluto represents regeneration; transformation; and a compelling, fundamental approach.

Venus represents love, relationships, beauty, values, comfort, and material resources.

When Venus and Pluto connect, a desire occurs to transform and be transformed through love. Emotional intensity and passion in their connections occur, whether they be romantic, personal, or social. Transformation can occur either through conscious effort based upon not having their needs met or through outer events that the native feels that they don't have control over.

Individuals with this combination will likely experience intense emotional deaths and rebirths at some point, which will mark a major turning point in their life.

Gift: These natives are passionate and ardent partners and lovers. This planetary connection can indicate the capacity for regenerating a relationship to a highly spiritual level. They can feel that the relationship was destined and part of a cosmic plan. A strong desire occurs to connect and merge at all levels—physically, emotionally, mentally, and spiritually—yielding an airtight relationship and union. These natives can be artistically talented, which is passionately expressed through their artistic milieu. In each case, the artwork will be captivating and absorb onlookers.

Shadow: The shadow side of a Venus/Pluto combination occurs when emotions and passions get out of control and trigger compulsive behavior patterns. Usual triggers include jealousy, possessiveness, sexual desire, and control of financial and material resources. Sometimes, the shadow side will manifest as the need to find passion at any cost. These natives can create experiences for the sole sake of creating a stir. These natives are not beyond playing games to get a rise out their significant other or people close to them. These natives can be fascinated and ultimately obsessed by the unknown and the forbidden. They can be inordinately stimulated and involved in sexual passion and indulgence. Clandestine encounters appeal to them.

> The combination of Jupiter and Pluto can generate the desire for the attainment of personal empowerment.

Pluto/Mars

Pluto represents regeneration; transformation; and a compelling, fundamental approach.

Mars rules assertiveness, energy, drive, and courage.

Mars and Pluto are a power-packed duo, where Pluto is the higher octave of Mars. These planetary energies can be explosive together or, when used consciously, can be highly energetic and productive. Similar to Mars in Scorpio, the native can be driven, compulsive, and sometimes feel as though they are superhuman, which energetically can be true at times. "Don't stop until you drop" is a motto for these folks.

Gift: The gift that the persistence of this combination bestows is the ability to rise to the task or mission, whatever that mission happens to be at the time. This is a "don't stop until you drop" energy combination, where desire combines with directed actions. This combination has a regenerative quality and can bestow an ability to self-heal when directed accordingly.

Shadow: Passions and desires can be overwhelming, and regret, shame, and serious consequences can occur as a result. An unconscious acting out of inner wounds and held resentments can also occur. Personal affronts can be difficult to release and can fester, thereby triggering misdirected anger and rage. Obsessive behavior patterns, a power-hungry drive for power, control, and domination can occur.

Pluto/Jupiter

Pluto represents regeneration; transformation; and a compelling, fundamental approach.

Jupiter represents the higher mind, greater truths, expansiveness, hope, and optimism.

Jupiter expands and Pluto transforms, making this a power combination that can bring immense inspiration, strong desires, and resourcefulness that can implement change and transformation.

Gift: The combination of Jupiter and Pluto can generate the desire for the attainment of personal empowerment. Natives need to get to the bottom of anything that interferes with growth so that the next phase of change and rebuilding can occur. This desire applies to both identifying and removing internal subconscious blocks as well as to external problem-solving so that progress can continue. These natives demonstrate good judgment that can be applied to any kind of issues before them. They can be persuasive, as they key into underlying motivations and speak to others' subconscious needs and desires. They can harness enthusiasm for growth, change, and evolution, even making this process into an adventure.

Shadow: The shadow side of the Jupiter/Pluto combination is that it can increase the desire for power and control beyond appropriate limits. Jupiter can expand whatever energies it touches, and Pluto, also known as the god of the Underworld, can lead the native down a rabbit hole in search for the taboo, the forbidden, control, and power. Pluto can be extreme, and Jupiter can enhance Pluto's intense, polarized nature. The result can be a tendency to go overboard, compulsive behavior patterns, power struggles, and manipulation. These natives can be inclined to overreach and have an all-or-nothing approach when they would be better served by a more gentle and moderate approach.

The combination of Saturn and Pluto offers the individual the gift of a focused and disciplined approach to undertaking life's challenges and subsequent changes. They have tremendous discipline and display amazing fortitude and perseverance.

Pluto/Saturn

Pluto represents regeneration; transformation; and a compelling, fundamental approach.

Saturn rules responsibility, adjustments to limitations, sustainability, and structure.

The combination of Saturn and Pluto can produce tremendous discipline toward the process of self-regeneration and transformation, or this combination can bring forward the darker side of both energies. Deeply subconscious fears and paranoia may be stimulated. At the social level, when these two planetary bodies meet, events are triggered, including influenza and viral outbreaks, as well as other apocalyptic events that cause mass hysteria.

It is likely that circumstances will contribute to these natives having to reinvent themselves several times over the course of their lives.

Gift: The combination of Saturn and Pluto offers the individual the gift of a focused and disciplined approach to undertaking life's challenges and subsequent changes. They have tremendous discipline and display amazing fortitude and perseverance. These natives are strong in their convictions, and they believe in self-empowerment through transformation and regeneration. They are supportive of helping others take charge of their lives and make changes for their betterment. These individuals can effect subtle yet powerful changes in their own lives and in society.

Shadow: The shadow side of the combination of Saturn and Pluto can bring great fear of the unknown. Subconscious fears that rise up and cause anxiety and panic are possible, making it necessary for the native to ideally pause and take stock of the core issues that can be buried. Paranoia can overshadow social interactions and personal relationships. These natives can be manipulative and self-serving and strategically attempt to control others for fear that others will exert control over them. Obsessive-compulsive behavior patterns are likely. Material goals and ambition can be sought at the expense of anyone or anything that gets in their path.

Pluto/Uranus

Pluto represents regeneration; transformation; and a compelling, fundamental approach.

Uranus rules intuition, originality, individuality, and the sudden and unexpected.

The combination of Uranus and Pluto is highly dynamic and can lead to awakenings and experiences that trigger deep transformation and change. These conscious-ness-expanding instances can result from flashes of intuitive insights or result from outside circumstances that thereafter change the native's life. They have original thinking that leads to technology solutions that assist in healing and involvement in advances that can shape society.

When society experiences Uranus and Pluto in combination, the urge for freedom and reform are awakened, and the Plutonic shadow side, including the urge for more power and extreme violence, is also aroused. These periods have recurred throughout history, instituting change in areas that include civil rights, the women's movement, and uprisings against injustices in society relating to income disparities. Mass movements occurred across the globe during the time periods when this aspect was in effect.

Gift: The gift this combination offers is that of expanded self-awareness. The process of gaining this awareness may not necessarily have come at an opportune time given the unexpected attribute of Uranus. Nonetheless, in retrospect, the native will have made great strides toward self-empowerment. Uranus can bring forth the truth, regardless of how deeply it may have been hidden. These natives are reformists of the highest order, with worthy ideals and clear morals.

Shadow: The shadow side of this combination is shock and a radical purging that is difficult to recover from. At its extreme, the connection between Uranus and Pluto can cause drastic upheaval, destruction, and annihilation.

Pluto/Neptune

Pluto represents regeneration; transformation; and a compelling, fundamental approach.

Neptune rules ideals, creative imagination, transcendence, compassion, and vision.

Pluto/Neptune combinations are generational in nature. Often, this combination can affect world karma and the destiny of the collective more than one's individual life. These natives can feel drawn to bringing a new and higher level of consciousness to humanity.

Gift: The gift of this combination is a belief that universal love can heal the woes of the world. Natives have faith in the divine and a belief in the salvation of humanity.

Shadow: The shadow side of this combination is a belief that spiritual regeneration is hopeless and that individuals are victims to corrupt political, social, and religious institutions.

Pluto/Chiron

Pluto represents regeneration; transformation; and a compelling, fundamental approach.

Chiron represents core wounds and the desire to overcome them, and healing.

Pluto in combination with Chiron adds determination and focus to get to the bottom of whatever issues need to be healed. This can be an incredibly strong combination for a healer who can channel their perceptive insights and analytical skills into helping others. The native likely had to delve into their own unconscious traumas, which empowered them to effectively use their healing capabilities.

Gift: Chiron and Pluto together can result in a high level of desire and sensitivity

that is oriented toward perceiving underlying wounds and subsequently helping others to heal. Having had to come into contact with their own vulnerabilities, these natives develop empathy and compassion toward others.

> Chiron and Pluto together can result in a high level of desire and sensitivity that is oriented toward perceiving underlying wounds and subsequently helping others to heal.

Shadow: Constant irritations, including chronic pain, can be the impetus for resolving core wounds that the native had been previously sweeping under the rug. These individuals may have had unfortunate experiences that include separation and rejection that resulted from a lack of sympathy toward others. They may have taken a callous approach to people with disabilities and those in less fortunate circumstances.

Pluto/Eris

Pluto represents regeneration; transformation; and a compelling, fundamental approach.

Eris represents the determination to remove limitations that impede the soul's evolution.

Gift: Pluto can give a big bump to the drive and determination of Eris, encouraging the native to pull out all the stops to get to the bottom of whatever is interfering with the native becoming their true authentic self. They have laser vision, penetrating falsehoods and anywhere a lack of authenticity exists.

Shadow: The downside of the Pluto and Eris combination is the potential for self-destructive behavior. Unresolved ego issues can undermine good intentions, muddying the waters of what could otherwise be major evolutionary progress.

Pluto in combination with the Ascendent can give the native strong perceptive abilities. These extraordinary problem solvers love a good mystery, which they're bound to solve with great willpower and stamina. They are likely to be magnetic and mysterious at the same time.

Pluto/North Node

Pluto represents regeneration; transformation; and a compelling, fundamental approach.

The North Node represents future direction, soul guidance, and fulfillment.

The North Node emphasizes the importance for the native to develop the attributes represented by Pluto, which include determination, focus, and self-empowerment. It will significantly benefit the individual to be steadfast in unveiling underlying issues that prevent them from following a path that will bring personal fulfillment and self-empowerment. Pluto can also indicate that it can benefit the native to pursue a track in the healing arts, metaphysics, or scientific research.

Gift: Pluto combined with the North Node can bring perceptive abilities that can assist the native in understanding hidden motives and feelings of those who could assist or prevent the native from manifesting aspects of their destiny. Pluto also brings strength and determination that can help them stay on track. These natives instinctively understand the importance of change and transformation when an approach is not working. They can let go of their ego and move on.

Shadow: The shadow side of a Pluto/North Node combination is an obsessive, ego-driven nature that ultimately generates setbacks and unnecessary obstacles for the native. These natives can be their own worst enemy, where they continually undermine their progress.

Pluto/South Node

Pluto represents regeneration; transformation; and a compelling, fundamental approach.

The South Node represents familiarity, gratification, and the path of least resistance.

The combination of Pluto and the South Node can indicate that the native understands the importance of staying on track despite obstacles they may encounter.

Gift: These individuals can have well-developed psychic gifts that they can use to follow a path that will benefit them and bring them the self-empowerment that one receives when they are on the right track for their life's work.

Shadow: The shadow sides of this placement are well-established behavior patterns of underhandedness, manipulation, and power struggles that can be somewhat unconscious; however, they are the first course of behavior for the native. They can feel that it is their right to be abusive and act like a bully as long as it serves their purpose. They may find that they are frequently a victim of circumstance and not understand why.

Pluto/Ascendant

Pluto represents regeneration; transformation; and a compelling, fundamental approach.

The Ascendant represents one's approach, orientation, and the window through which one sees the world.

These natives are deliberate and strategic in their approach to life. They dislike superficiality and nonessentials. They may change their appearance several times over the course of time. They are likely to be magnetic and mysterious at the same time,

emanating a presence that is difficult for others to read.

Gift: Pluto in combination with the Ascendant can give the native such strong perceptive abilities that they observe reality in terms of energy and vibrations. It is as if they have an X-ray vision that sees what others miss. When combined with the analytical abilities of Pluto, these natives are extraordinary problem solvers and researchers. They love a good mystery, which, sooner or later, they are likely to solve. They have great willpower and stamina that can be used to follow through on their desired endeavors, which can include self-healing and regeneration.

Shadow: The shadow side of this placement is an obstinate and secretive individual who is overly suspicious of everyone's motives and situations in general. They cannot go with the flow and relinquish control for the greater good. It is all about being in control and a pervasive fear of the unknown should they lose control.

Pluto/Midheaven (MC)

Pluto represents regeneration; transformation; and a compelling, fundamental approach.

The Midheaven (MC) represents image, outer aspirations, and career orientation.

Pluto at the top of the chart brings a strong determination to succeed and attain social status and prominence.

Gift: These natives have the willpower and fortitude to achieve the desired professional ambitions and notoriety. They are likely to embark on several approaches to attain their goal, intuitively knowing when to change direction or up the ante when they sense stagnation. They are adept at foreshadowing obstacles and perceiving possible future trends that enhance their potential for success. These natives can do well in politics and in areas connected to science, research, and healing.

Shadow: The shadow side of this placement is a power-hungry individual who will do whatever it takes to get to the top. Devious methodologies, underhanded actions, and manipulation are all part of their bailiwick. Politically, this combination can produce a tyrannical leader.

Chiron

Chiron orbits between Saturn and Uranus and is the link between Saturn, the last of the original planets that represented traditional astrology, and Uranus, the planet that connects us to the mysteries and infinite possibilities of the heavens. As the bridge between Saturn and Uranus, Chiron begs the question: What does it take to evolve from Saturn's material limitations to Uranus's freedom and liberation?

Chiron is the archetype of the wounded healer. Chiron is also known as the Rainbow Bridge, which connects one realm, the material, third-dimensional realm, to another, the realm where anything is possible, the realm of true liberation.

Moving into new and higher dimensions can require that one step outside of their comfort zone. One may feel out of place and vulnerable. The Chiron energy further examines what makes one uncomfortable. What is revealed as layers are peeled back in the process of soul searching? Do

family patterns exist that were inherited or absorbed that are not helpful in furthering one's growth and development?

Duality, and the reconciliation of duality, is the essence of Chiron. Chiron is the combination of a half-man, half-horse centaur. The process of integrating the disparaging combination of a being that is half human and half animal is symbolic for integrating the contradictory aspects of the psyche. Ultimately, Chiron's purpose is to restore wholeness through the integration of one's animal nature and one's spiritual nature. When an individual can recognize that what is considered positive and what is considered negative can all be found within themselves, they are no longer triggered by division. They can witness all of humanity in themselves and in others.

The mythology of Chiron powerfully illustrates how one's core wound can later become one's greatest gift. According to

The planetoid Chiron was named for the wise centaur adopted and raised by Apollo and Artemis. Chiron represents the integration of challenging wounds, often wounds that occurred in early childhood and are buried deep within the subconscious.

myth, Chiron was rejected at birth by his mother, who could not reconcile his appearance as half human and half animal. Chiron's primal wound is one of rejection for being who he is, for his true nature. Eventually, Chiron was adopted by the Sun God, Apollo, who then taught him the arts of healing, prophecy, and astrology. These teachings, combined with Chiron's intrinsic connection to the animal spirit world, helped him become the greatest healer and teacher of his time.

Chiron became known as the wounded healer when, in a battle between man and the centaurs, he was shot in the hoof with a poisoned arrow. In spite of his great knowledge and skill, he was unable to heal himself and thus asked the gods to end his life. His request was granted, and he was taken into the heavens, creating the constellation of the Centaur.

Chiron represents the integration of challenging wounds, often wounds that occurred in early childhood that are buried deep within the subconscious. Once conscious awareness is brought to the realization that these uncomfortable, difficult experiences were actually preparations for greater achievements, great healing occurs that can be shared with others if so desired, hence the archetype of the wounded teacher/healer.

A blog post by Astrohealer from November 14, 2020, says, "Etymologically speaking, the word 'chaos' means 'abyss, that which gapes wide open.' The same concept is carried over in 'Chiron' which is etymologically related to the Greek 'surgeon,' the person who cuts and opens (in order to heal)… Chiron can also represent various forms of crossing and bridging."

Chiron's wound can be deeply rooted in the past, which requires a lot of digging and cutting open in order to bring this wound to the surface. Chiron's location in the chart gives clues as to the areas of life, house placement, and energetic manifestation—sign placement—of where healing is needed. Chiron can show areas where the individual may not have conformed to the status quo, meaning that the primal wound may have been triggered by a rejection or by not being accepted for being different, as was the case for Chiron's appearance at birth. Chiron stirs up feelings of abandonment, rejection, shame, inadequacy, and irrelevance.

Julie Dembowski in her blog post of April 7, 2022, "Defining Chiron," says, "My recent work has been pointing more and more to the isolating way we're thinking of Chiron. It hurts! It's over there! It's tricky to understand, to access! We'd rather not think about it, probably because *Chiron in healed form asks us to be thoroughly responsible for ourselves*—and most of us would rather leave a little room for excuses, blame, and a wee bit of slack—and I don't blame anyone for that."

Chiron has an exaggerated elliptical orbit, meaning that Chiron can spend as little as 1.5 years in the signs Virgo and Libra, and as long as eight years in Aries. Chiron returns to its exact placement at birth on the average of every 50.7 years. The Chiron return that occurs at this time is often when one can peel back the layers in order to expose aspects of primal wounding. The Chiron return also marks an opportunity for self-empowerment through realizations that occur during this significant period.

CHIRON IN THE SIGNS

Chiron in Aries

Chiron in Aries, the first sign of the Zodiac and the place where the focus is on the development of the Self, is motivated, clear, and energized; these natives can have the opportunity to get in touch with places in their subconscious that have prevented or interfered with their pioneering spirit and uniqueness. An Aries seeks to develop their identity. Just as the Sun is exalted in Aries, where the "I am" presence can shine and individuality can assert itself, deep wounding can occur where the native does not feel that they have the right to be themselves. Outside influences, including parental norms imposed during childhood and societal conditioning, have challenged these souls to express who they rightfully are. Chiron in Aries will seek to heal the expression of their true individuality.

Gift: Chiron in Aries is about taking responsibility for one's true existence. It is about being present, with all the wounds, pain, and shame that come with it. The gift that ensues from this placement is to be able to be oneself, notwithstanding the fear, guilt, and shame. These natives receive the gift of self-realization and self-empowerment. They receive the gift of strength of purpose and a solid identity.

> Chiron in Aries is about taking responsibility for one's true existence. It is about being present, with all the wounds, pain, and shame that come with it.

They know themselves. They have learned that they do not have to be someone they are not; they simply have to accept who they are. The gift that these individuals receive from Chiron in Aries is that they have the courage to resist being homogenized into mainstream culture. They can stand without fear as their own person, true to themselves.

Shadow: The shadow side of this placement can have several manifestations prior to when the incremental healings take place. These include dialogues in one's mind that reflect statements such as "I am not enough" and "I don't fit in." They tend to under the radar and not express their opinions and beliefs. They may feel the need to continually prove themselves so that they are liked by everyone. These natives are likely to feel that they are not seen or heard. The wounding can also manifest itself in behavior patterns through a tendency to hurt themselves or through other forms of self-destructive activities and abuses.

CHIRON IN TAURUS

Chiron in Venus-ruled Taurus can indicate that issues surrounding self-worth are present. These natives will strive to heal the subconscious blocks that cause the native to not value themselves. They will strive to develop a value system that resonates with their current level of self-awareness. Chiron in Taurus is interested in rebuilding something new once they heal their blockages.

Gift: Taurus rules all that is valued, and these natives are likely to pursue a quest in order to redefine what is most important to them. As a Fixed Earth sign, they are likely to be concerned with material values; with the Venus rulership of this

house, financial resources and cultural artifacts are likely to be included. These natives can make great contributions to culture. They are preservers of values and Earth's resources.

Shadow: The shadow side of this placement can manifest as an indulgent sensuality that compensates for issues around self-worth. Greed and a great emphasis on money and material possessions can be symptoms of deeper issues with Chiron in Taurus. These individuals can have core issues from their upbringing, where they were demeaned and continually criticized for some lack which they may or may not have had.

CHIRON IN GEMINI

Chiron in Mercury-ruled Gemini can indicate that challenges are present in areas connected with communication or learning. They feel that they are not heard when they speak even though they have something important to say. They are continually misunderstood. Learning disabilities or speech impediments are possible. Core wounds can result from issues around their upbringing, where no one was interested in what they had to say, constant comparisons to siblings and relatives, or problems in early education or delayed learning that resulted from physical impediments or other circumstances.

Gift: The gift of this placement is that these natives have a natural ability to help others through the power of their words. These natives may have learned through their challenges how to redirect their negative thoughts and focus on positive affirmations. Reframing negative self-talk is an important aspect of their healing process. Techniques that focus on mindfulness and using alternate methods of communication, such as art therapy or music therapy, can help to release the gifts they have deep inside.

Shadow: The shadow side of this placement is that these individuals do not feel that they can express their innermost self. When they do, they are not heard. This deep frustration can manifest as extreme shyness, stage fright when in a group, and extreme anxiety whenever attention is on them to say something. This placement can manifest as the native having a loss for words or not being able to say what they mean. They feel that they can't fit in with others or are constantly comparing themselves to others.

CHIRON IN CANCER

Individuals with Chiron in Cancer can have wounds centered around feeling loved, nurtured, and supported. They may compensate for these feelings by forming codependent relationships or through eating disorders and psychosomatic illnesses. They may need constant validation and approval from others.

Gift: The gift from a Chiron in Cancer placement is that these natives can be of great help in social service fields working with underprivileged groups and disadvantaged children. They are highly empathic and sensitive to the needs of others. By getting in touch with their wounding, they realize that the bottom line is that they must learn to love themselves. They realize that everything they need comes from within. Once they are self-empowered, they will attract what they need from others.

Shadow: The shadow side of this placement manifests itself when the individual seeks unattainable partners who won't commit. The native can be noncommittal

The gift from a Chiron in Cancer placement is that these highly empathetic natives can be of great help in social service fields working with underprivileged groups and disadvantaged children.

when pursued by others for fear of getting hurt. Another manifestation can play out as digestive issues and eating disorders.

CHIRON IN LEO

Chiron in the sign ruled by the Sun may have issues around expressing themselves. They can have a strong need to be the center of attention, yet they are somehow always in the background or are not receiving the accolades or adoration they deserve.

Gift: Chiron in Leo is well placed for a public figure who seeks to unveil Chiron's gifts. Chiron in Leo is associated with self-expression and talent. If core wounds need to be identified and healed, Chiron's placement in sunny Leo is more apt to shine the light on them. These natives will often acknowledge that they are talented;

however, they may not believe in their talents until repeatedly proving to themselves that they are. It is not uncommon for celebrities and famous people to have this Chiron placement.

Shadow: Individuals with Chiron in Leo feel that they are constantly ignored. This placement indicates that core wounds can be connected to self-esteem. These issues can manifest themselves as someone who is always offended. They may feel that they are not getting the credit they deserve and can harbor a "how dare you" attitude. A fear is present of being unremarkable or average, which is compensated for by always having to prove themselves. The shadow side of this placement can manifest as someone who always avoids being in the spotlight since they believe that they are unworthy. Instead, they may assist others, including their children, in being successful.

> The Chiron in Virgo wound is displayed when the individual continually seeks perfection; they feel that something is wrong with them when their idea of perfection is not attained.

CHIRON IN VIRGO

Mercury-ruled Virgo is highly analytical and continually searches for perfection. The Chiron in Virgo wound is displayed when the individual continually seeks perfection; they feel that something is wrong with them when their idea of perfection is not attained. These individuals are never satisfied because deep inside, they believe that they are not up to the task. Their quest is learning to be human and not a machine. Chiron spends comparatively less time in Virgo and Libra due to the nature of its orbit.

Gift: Individuals with Chiron in Virgo strive to do well, and yet, through that striving,

they encounter personal pain and frustration. As they develop perspective and learn to set realistic expectations of what is possible, they become highly skilled at helping others to improve their lives. They have a keen organizational sensibility and can excel at logically assessing a task's worthiness and timeline. This placement can be successful in healthcare fields. They realize the value of diligence when seeking to overcome illnesses and health-related issues.

Shadow: The shadow side of Chiron in Virgo is their black-and-white thinking. No middle ground exists. No shades of gray. Their analyses are mental in nature and lack perspective, compassion, and heart. These natives can have core wounds stemming back to feeling that they never measured up and hence, never received love. Parents may have been hypercritical, or the native perceived them to be so. Individuals with Chiron in Virgo can have highly sensitive digestive issues. Virgo rules the intestines, which is also an area where food allergies can manifest.

CHIRON IN LIBRA

Chiron in Venus-ruled Libra can indicate core issues connecting to others in a deep and meaningful way. Attempts to relate may have been thwarted either through outright rejection or as a result of overprotective parents who never allowed the child significant opportunities to relate to other children. Chiron spends comparatively less time in Virgo and Libra due to the nature of its orbit.

Gift: Natives with Chiron in Libra have a deep desire to connect with others, which is the gift of this placement. They seek to understand how they impact one another. These individuals want to get it right, so they keep engaging even though their relationships can be very painful. They continually learn more about themselves through their interactions with others. The frustrations they encounter are the driving force for a deep dive into their wounding. These natives can offer wisdom to others with their interpersonal relationships. They understand the quest for harmony.

Shadow: Rejections and repeated situations of being the odd one out in social situations are likely to be expressions of this wounding. Self-sabotage can take the form of extreme sensitivity, jealousy, possessiveness, and constant criticism of partners because they are not who you want them to be. These individuals can often give far more than they receive or hold back on giving completely. In any case, they are searching for the right balance. Libra rules balance and equality, and it is through inequality that Chiron will point out wounding.

Chiron in Scorpio natives love to solve a good mystery with their well-developed probing skills. Having explored boundaries and uncomfortable truths themselves, they can become powerful counselors, healers, and shamans.

CHIRON IN SCORPIO

Chiron in Pluto-ruled Scorpio natives are driven by a deep desire to heal discomforts in their life. They have a knack for uncovering what is buried in the untapped resources of the subconscious. Self-transformation is a central theme for these individuals.

Gift: Chiron in Scorpio natives love to solve a good mystery. They have well-developed probing skills that gain tremendous satisfaction from getting down to the bottom of an issue. Highly determined,

these individuals know what they want and have the resolve to dedicate themselves to getting it. They are highly resourceful. Chiron enhances Pluto's urge to transform and gives these individuals an edge on changing whatever is not working. They are not only capable of finding solutions; they can easily let go of whatever wasn't working to begin with. Having done the work themselves, these individuals are formidable counselors and healers.

Shadow: The shadow side of this placement is that the native may have had to go through pain and great discontent prior to acknowledging the need to delve deep in order to get to the uncomfortable truth. Pluto likes to stretch and push out to the brink before turning back. It is through this exploration of boundaries and potentially of the darker sides of life that they can become such powerful healers and shamans.

CHIRON IN SAGITTARIUS

Chiron in Sagittarius individuals are constantly seeking the meaning of life. They seek a belief system that they can count on. They are seekers and adventurers. Wounding can occur through disillusionment in a religion or philosophy that doesn't continue to satisfy, leaving them to feel disconnected. Perhaps childhood upbringing required that the native strictly adhere to a religious or spiritual practice that is later meaningless to them.

> The shadow side of a Chiron in Sagittarius placement is the belief that the grass is always greener somewhere else.

Gift: Life can be a great adventure to those born with Chiron in Sagittarius. Such is the great gift of this placement. They gain revelations from each new experience. They subsequently can uplift others through their ever-expanding perspective. They seek to break boundaries and expand limitations. They believe in the power of positive thinking.

Shadow: The shadow side of a Chiron in Sagittarius placement is the belief that the grass is always greener somewhere else. Others are better off than they are. Rather than find their power and feeling of place in the world from deep within, they are often looking outwardly to find the answers. It is not uncommon for the shadow side of this placement to manifest as al-ways looking to the future rather than taking charge of each issue that comes up in the present moment, which would enhance self-empowerment.

CHIRON IN CAPRICORN

Chiron in Capricorn natives are diligent and efficient toward their healing process once they get on track with what needs to be done. Their approach is logical and efficient. Through experiences of not being recognized for their achievements, these natives are motivated to search for a deeper meaning to their lives. This search can lead them to connecting to their inner value, which subsequently triggers outer recognition and improvement in their social status.

Gift: Chiron in Capricorn offers the gift of perseverance despite adversities. They are survivors. Status and achievement are important to them, and through oppositional elements and necessary modifications, these natives find their calling. Fulfillment lies in their ability to align with the path that they believe they are the most qualified to follow and that reflects their inner talents and gifts. Their self-empowerment allows them to help others find their true path to success.

Shadow: The shadow side of this placement is that the native is forced to achieve, yet in spite of their achievements, they lack inner fulfillment. Initially, the burden for the native to be a high achiever came from external circumstances, which can include parental or societal pressure that was either real or simply perceived by the native to be so. Because their heart was not on the path they chose, they experienced a lack of recognition, or their achievements went unnoticed. As a result, these natives can give up or sublimate their discontent and feelings of failure into activities where they are more in control.

CHIRON IN AQUARIUS

Chiron in Uranus-ruled Aquarius is humanitarian, original, and highly idealistic. Trials and tribulations may have resulted from disappointments in friendships or through feeling left out of group activities. As a result, these individuals had to come to terms with their individuality.

Gift: Individuals with Chiron in Aquarius can help those who identify as outsiders find their unique talents and abilities. They are proponents of personal freedom and individuality, where the ideal means that each person is marching to their own rhythm. They have a talent for helping others find their place in a group or community. Realistic goal setting is another gift that an individual with Chiron in Aquarius may have learned to master over time.

Shadow: Chiron in Aquarius can indicate that the native has to become more realistic in determining their cherished hopes and wishes. Their overly idealistic and trusting nature may have led to disappointments and sorrow, which the native can choose to wallow in, or they can choose to reevaluate, knowing that they are deserving. The combination of realistic expectations and soul searching can ultimately help them manifest their wishes. Individuals with this placement can choose to be hermits and withdraw from society or choose a path that is so eccentric that others have difficulty relating to them.

Chiron in Pisces brings the ability to connect at a deep level with others and heal themselves through helping others. The ability to identify with another is so strong that these individuals become the other person for an instant, ultimately identifying with the solution.

CHIRON IN PISCES

Individuals with Chiron in Pisces can feel that their mission in life is to heal others. Combining the compassionate, empathetic nature of Chiron with the healing orientation of Pisces can give these natives a profound level of sensitivity to the plight of others. Some can have an ailment that becomes part of their healing journey and further impacts their compassionate nature.

Gift: The gift that Chiron in Pisces brings is the ability to connect at a deep level with others. These individuals can heal themselves through helping others. Their ability to identify with others is so strong that they become the other person for an instant, feeling their plight and ultimately identifying with the solution. Chiron in Pisces natives are frequently involved in healing and in philanthropic activities. They are likely to have musical and artistic talents.

Shadow: Natives with Chiron in Pisces placements can feel that they were dealt an unfair hand in life. Their lot is one of misfortune and sadness. Their highly empathic disposition picks up on everyone's suffering, including that of the collective. They can be martyrs to the core, with deep wounding where they believe that they do not deserve joy and happiness. Individuals with this placement can engage in escapist behaviors and addictions.

CHIRON IN THE HOUSES

The house position of Chiron reveals the area of life that dominates the native's wounding and the gifts that will be revealed as a result of the healing. Chiron's location identifies the issues that can motivate growth.

CHIRON IN THE FIRST HOUSE

The First House rules appearance, health, general temperament, and sense of self. The First House defines you and the image you project to others.

Chiron is strong in the First House, which can affect the individual in a couple of ways. These individuals are continually reminded of their wound, which interferes with the full expression of who they are deep inside. They are on a continual journey of self-discovery. They are also super sensitive to what others need and are likely to have healing abilities.

Gift: These natives have learned self-love and self-respect through their trials and tribulations. They see the warning signs whenever they dip into feelings of self-doubt or when they get back into patterns of appeasing others. They pause long enough to come back to themselves and reestablish who they are. Those with a Chiron in the First House placement are natural healers. Challenges and difficult times they experienced have awakened their compassion and empathy for the suffering of others. They are insightful counselors who can be successful in helping others empower themselves. These natives can assume a Chironic role, which can include that of teacher, mentor, or healer.

Shadow: Individuals with Chiron in the First House can have an obvious wound that affects their appearance or the manner in which they project themselves. The First House segment of their chart rules early childhood, and this wounding can be one that these natives have to carry throughout their lives. The shadow side of this placement can manifest as an individual who is constantly sacrificing their own needs for those of another. They are pleasers, always looking to receive validation from others. With this placement, it can be difficult to find meaning in life.

CHIRON IN THE SECOND HOUSE

The Second House is connected with finances, values, material possessions, talents, and resources. The Second House represents the value we give to ourselves and, in turn, that which we possess.

One's possessions or material resources can assume more importance than the individual's sense of self-worth. A lack of financial security may have led these natives down a path whereby they discovered hidden talents and abilities that they did not know they had. This placement begets these questions: What matters most to the individual? How does the individual take care of their basic needs?

Gift: Chiron in the Second House natives have done tremendous soul searching regarding their values and what is important to them. Fluctuations in finances or material losses may have guided these natives to a reevaluation of what matters. Material possessions may not have been as important as they were led to believe. These individuals can help the materially underprivileged redefine what is important to them. They can be successful in helping others find ways to support and develop their talents and abilities.

> The shadow of Chiron in the Second house is that these natives may believe that their values are the only true values.

Shadow: The shadow of Chiron in the Second house is that these natives may believe that their values are the only true values. They can have talents and abilities that are disregarded as unimportant because they do not fulfill society's ideology of what is important. The shadow can also manifest as money and material possessions becoming more important than human values that could bring emotional fulfillment to the individual.

CHIRON IN THE THIRD HOUSE

The Third House is connected with ideas, communication, siblings, neighbors, and short journeys.

Chiron in a house governed by Mercury can predispose these natives to wounding that affects their ability to successfully communicate. These individuals feel misunderstood or not heard. Difficulties can arise from issues surrounding information processing or from a physical disability related to communication. Sibling relationships, or lack thereof, can assume importance in the individual's life with this placement.

Gift: Knowledge is power to an individual with Chiron in the Third House. These natives may strive to master a particular subject in order to develop the confidence to speak or otherwise communicate about it. Technology can assist in getting one's point across. Small accomplishments add up, contributing to an overall comfort level that they can then share with others who feel that they are not heard.

Shadow: Self-expression was likely thwarted in early childhood, and these individuals don't know how to express themselves without a tinge of anger or frustration and have a tremendous fear of rebuke. As a child, an understanding may have been present that "children should be seen and not heard." As an adult, the shadow of this placement can manifest as an avoidance of meaningful communication or as a need to create an uncomfortable or hostile environment before blurting out what they want to express.

CHIRON IN THE FOURTH HOUSE

The Fourth House is about the home, family, genetic inheritance, foundational stability, innermost feelings, later life, and the end of matters.

Chiron in the Cancer-ruled Fourth House can indicate that the native may need to separate themselves from their past. Family traumas or other unhappy mem-

Individuals with Chiron in the Fifth House discover themselves through creative talents or through participating in the lives of children. They know how to stir hearts and enliven the atmosphere via art, music, or entertainment or simply through their openhearted and charming personalities.

ories can require acknowledgment and subsequent forgiveness so that they can move forward. Self-worth issues can result from a parent who was emotionally or physically unavailable. These natives may have issues connected to belonging, of not feeling comfortable or at home anywhere.

Gift: The gift from this placement is a strong sense of empathy whereby these natives can help others coming from similar circumstances. They can become great caretakers, having developed compassion for those without a secure family life or without a home. A deep appreciation of family and an expanded awareness of the Self can develop from the native delving into their ancestry and cultural traditions.

Shadow: Individuals with Chiron in the Fourth House can overidentify with their family heritage and cultural upbringing to the extent that they lose track of their unique gifts and desires. The shadow side can manifest as dependence on family and a refusal to grow up and become independent. Childhood hurts can leave a scar such that these natives can forgo family ties completely in order to avoid getting hurt. Genetic wounding has possibly been carried down through generations so that these individuals blindly participate in the same patterns. Addictions can be genetically inherited.

CHIRON IN THE FIFTH HOUSE

The Fifth House rules creative self-expression, children, love, passion, romance, playfulness, and joy.

Chiron in the Fifth House can indicate a damaged inner child who doesn't know how to play or express themselves creatively. They very likely have creative talents that require persistent trial and error prior to having the confidence to master their craft. They discover themselves through their creative talents or through raising or participating in the lives of children.

Gift: The gift of a Chiron in the Fifth House placement is knowing how to stir the hearts of others. Through creative self-expression via art, music, or entertainment or simply through their open-hearted and charming personality, they know how to enliven the atmosphere. Children, whether their own or those belonging to someone else, will play an important role in their lives. These natives can become mentors to children.

Shadow: The shadow side of this placement can be a false pride and inflated ego. These individuals can avoid facing past hurt by taking an overly aggressive stance in social situations. They insist on being the center of attention for fear of being ignored. They can bully others for fear of being bullied themselves. Fear of betrayal can lead them to betray first. They are afraid to love. These natives can have issues surrounding sexual expression, where they can be controlled by sexual exploits or stay away from sexual activity as a result of prior wounding.

CHIRON IN THE SIXTH HOUSE

The Sixth House governs daily routines, acts of service, the work-life balance, health, due diligence, pet care, coworkers, and employees.

Chiron in the Sixth House natives understand either innately or through hardship and trial and error the principle of daily maintenance and how it can make one's life easier. These individuals can identify with their jobs and see their occupations as an extension of themselves.

Gift: The gift of a Chiron in the Sixth House placement is a fastidious approach to resolving health-related issues. These natives can seek out solutions and stay on track until they see progress in their quest. An innate understanding is present of the value of maintenance in all areas of life. Day-to-day consistency is a tool for making life easier. They can share their organizational skills to help others become empowered and release stress caused by overwhelm. These natives can have healing abilities.

Shadow: The shadow side of Chiron in the Sixth House can show up as a health-related problem. More information on the nature of their health vulnerability can be gleaned from Chiron's sign placement. They can have psychosomatic illnesses or use their health as an avoidance mechanism for participating in activities that they are not comfortable with. Individuals with this placement can avoid any activity that involves repetition and consistency for fear of losing part of themselves. They may have a subconscious memory of being forced to do activities that they did not want to do.

CHIRON IN THE SEVENTH HOUSE

The Seventh House rules close personal relationships, agreements, and compromises.

Chiron in Venus-ruled Libra's house can indicate troubles relating to close personal connections, especially when relating intimately to another. In spite of the native's strong desire to be in a partnership, relationships prove to be too painful.

Chiron in Pluto's house of transformation can indicate major changes in one's life that contributed to the self-empowerment of the native. Near-death experiences or the death of loved ones may have impacted their lives and expanded their psychic ability to help others through major transitions in their lives.

Gift: The gift of this placement is that the individual with Chiron in Libra has a deep desire to connect with others. They seek to understand how they impact another. These individuals want to get it right, so they keep engaging even though their relationships can be very painful. They continually learn more about themselves through their interactions with others. The frustrations they encounter are the driving force for a deep dive into their wounding. These natives can offer wisdom to others with their interpersonal relationships. These individuals understand the search for harmony, which comes from a relationship based upon fairness and personal responsibility, where each person works toward developing self-awareness rather than blaming the other.

Shadow: The shadow side of this placement can manifest as an avoidance of close

relationships, as an overdependence on a partner, and as self-sabotage, whereby the native selects a partner who is unavailable. The deep emotions that arise from a close connection are frightening to the native. Deep-rooted issues are touched upon, and the native would rather avoid or undermine relationships than dig into issues that are connected to possible rejection or fears around not being in control.

CHIRON IN THE EIGHTH HOUSE

The Eighth House rules joint ventures, intimacy, sex, death, transformation, and psychic dimensions.

Chiron in Pluto's house of transformation can indicate major changes in one's life that contributed to the self-empowerment of the native. Near-death experiences or the death of loved ones may have impacted their lives and expanded their psychic abilities.

Gift: The gift of this placement is the ability to help others through major transitions in their lives, which can include birth, death, life-threatening illnesses, addictions, and traumas. They are used to drama and intense emotions, and through these experiences, they unveil their inner strength and chip away at their own wounding. They deeply experience many aspects of life—the good, the bad, and the ugly—and through these involvements, they unveil their strength and power. They may develop an interest in chakra healing, kundalini energy, and tantric yoga practices.

Shadow: The shadow of this placement is the engagement of self-destructive behaviors, where the individual is driven to go to extremes so that they can test limits and prove their power. The shadow side is when they go overboard. These natives may have to come to terms with their strong desire by nature. The shadow of feeling powerless can lead these individuals to want to control and manipulate others. Jealousy and greed can lead to destructive behaviors. Possible issues with inheritances or divorce settlements can point out core issues that the native has not dealt with.

CHIRON IN THE NINTH HOUSE

The Ninth House rules higher education, long-term goals, foreign travel, publicity, adventures, religion, and philosophical and ethical pursuits.

Chiron in the Ninth House natives are often interested in philosophy and spirituality. They seek to find an overriding belief system that they can count on to carry them through difficult times. The Ninth House brings an abiding perspective to life.

Gift: The gift of Chiron in the Ninth House is that these individuals can bring their soul's higher purpose into their everyday life. They are able to live their beliefs. They feel the omnipresent support of the Universe and can draw on this support as needed. They can offer inspiration to others. These are the people who can walk their talk.

Shadow: The shadow side of a Ninth-House Chiron placement is that these natives wander aimlessly from one belief system to another. They seek a teacher or guru that will help improve their lives; however, these teachings never seem to really resonate with them. They strive to make sense out of life and often end up feeling depressed. These individuals can become eternal students or seekers. They

> The gift of Chiron in the Ninth House is that … [t]hey feel the omnipresent support of the Universe and can draw on this support as needed.

are seekers who don't find the fulfillment they seek because their answers ultimately come from within.

CHIRON IN THE TENTH HOUSE

The Tenth House rules public achievements, reputation, authority, and prestige.

Chiron in Capricorn's Tenth House is focused on reputation, achievement, social status, and authority. Woundedness can easily play out for these natives. Their need for recognition, acknowledgment, appreciation, and respect is strong, and situations can arise that threaten these deep-seated needs, encouraging these natives to dig into subconscious memories.

Gift: Recognition from one's achievements is a such a strong motivation that it becomes an impetus to resolve issues around not receiving acknowledgment, recognition, or respect as a child from their family or at school. These natives become good mentors to others and help them to achieve balance between their personal and social interests. The gift from having done the inner work expresses itself as self-empowerment from manifesting their true purpose in a practical way on Earth. The Tenth House is the natural home of Capricorn, which is ruled by Saturn. Practical results, balanced ambition, and steadfast achievement are all possible as gifts from this placement.

Shadow: The shadow side of this placement can be when the native uses their authority to control others as compensation for not feeling in control of their own life.

Natives of Chiron in the Twelfth House, traditionally called the "house of undoing," are likely to be highly empathic and compassionate to the suffering of others. Very tuned into undercurrents, they can feel another's pain and become powerful healers themselves.

Gift: The gift of this placement is that these natives can come to terms with their uniqueness and individuality. Through helping others accept their differences, they become more comfortable with who they are. These natives excel as group mentors who help others to be comfortable with themselves. They set an example of someone who is content to be in their own skin. Through self-acceptance, these natives become good friends to others. They cease looking for approval and can establish friendships based upon sharing. These natives can become advocates for social change.

Shadow: The shadow side of this placement is that these natives become determined to be different. They overcompensate for their fear of rejection or their desire to not be left out by pushing others away. They become the rebels, although they are rebellious in ways that do not bring others along with them. They may seek to impose their ideals upon others. The shadow side can also manifest as obsessive conformity for fear of expressing any part of themselves that could be deemed unacceptable.

Another possibility is that the native refuses to take on any position of authority. They don't try to succeed for fear of ridicule and rejection. On the other hand, they can pour a huge amount of energy into their career and neglect their own needs.

CHIRON IN THE ELEVENTH HOUSE

The Eleventh House rules friends, hopes, wishes, groups, and a sense of belonging in the world.

Chiron in the Eleventh House natives can feel like they are on the outside looking in. Their childhood may have been characterized by feeling left out. Being different plagues them, and they try really hard to fit in. Friendships and social acceptance are important to these individuals. This challenge can lead to searching deeper into childhood memories until finally coming to a place of peace with being themselves.

CHIRON IN THE TWELFTH HOUSE

The Twelfth House rules secrets, unconscious patterns, karma, closure, institutions, connections with higher sources, enlightenment, and undoing.

Chiron in the Twelfth House natives are likely to be highly empathic and compassionate to the suffering of others. They may have subtle memories of suffering that they once experienced. These memories have been stuffed away into the depths of the unconscious. The Twelfth-House placement can carry a deep desire to be free of blind spots. At the highest level, these natives seek enlightenment or peace in the here and now.

Gift: The gift of a Twelfth-House Chiron placement is the desire to be free of subconscious baggage. These natives can create situations unconsciously that force them to face their fears and buried traumas. The Twelfth House is traditionally called the house of undoing. The native accentuates the energy of that planetary body until whatever is hidden becomes obvious and subsequently healed and self-empowered. These natives can become powerful healers themselves. They are very tuned in to undercurrents and can feel another's pain. This empathic nature can help others in emotional and physical distress.

Shadow: The shadow side of this placement is the reluctance to delve into their subconscious motives. These natives can work hard to keep their wounds hidden from any conscious unraveling. The constant discomfort they feel is preferable to feeling the pain of any buried trauma. These individuals are martyrs, and their wounds become an essential part of who they are.

CHIRON COMBINATIONS

Planetary contacts to Chiron indicate energies that provide support to Chiron's quest for healing and self-empowerment.

CHIRON/SUN

Chiron represents core wounds and the desire to overcome them, and healing.

The Sun indicates purpose, self-expression, creative life force, and conscious will.

The combination of the Sun and Chiron yields a powerful combination that can influence the native in several ways. The purposeful rays of the Sun can combine with the healing nature of Chiron and deliver a soulful urge to bring healing to the planet. The individual's strong desire to heal may be the result of having had to wrestle with deep wounding to their self-esteem and confidence after a debilitated upbringing, whereby they had to struggle to assert themselves. They can then become a coach to help others develop confidence so that they can ultimately shine. Through helping others, these natives can develop the confidence that they needed all along. The wounded healer archetype is powerful and very real and tells the Chiron's story of crossing the bridge from the material to the spiritual realms.

The Sun conjunct with Chiron represents the instinct of the human spirit to manifest itself and leave something immaterial behind. Our spirit-seeking manifestation represents our "gift to the world." The Sun is our individuality, what makes us unique, our divine mission in this lifetime. The Sun conjunct with Chiron is the compelling drive to push beyond your existing boundaries to find your true zone of genius. The process of learning about your true self, the process of becoming who you are meant to be, cannot be an easy one, hence the wound.

Gift: The Sun brings hope and confidence to the native to delve into the deeper recesses of their psyche that are hampering their ability to shine. The Sun brings perpetual light to issues and to the psychological wounds that the native must overcome in order to express the creativity that wells up inside of them. The power of this combination is the strength and courage that is inherent in the Sun when coupled with Chiron's drive to heal nagging discomforts and vulnerabilities that are preventing the full flourishing of the individual's growth and evolution.

Shadow: These natives may have a lifelong challenge to find out who they are at their core. A deep wounding to the ego has occurred. Who am I? Why am I here? They have difficulty in being themselves. Their lack of purpose can be daunting. With Chiron in combination with the Sun, they have the drive to find out. A perpetual glimmer from the Sun's rays gives them a chance to find the inner meaning to their struggle. They have the power to transform from seeing themselves as empty and lonely to wanting to express their inner light in spite of their acknowledged vulnerabilities.

> The power of this combination is the strength and courage that is inherent in the Sun when coupled with Chiron's drive to heal nagging discomforts and vulnerabilities....

CHIRON/MOON

Chiron represents core wounds and the desire to overcome them, and healing.

The Moon rules the soul, core instincts, the personality, and subconscious conditioning.

The combination of the Moon and Chiron can indicate an individual who instinctively uses their healing abilities. These individuals are extremely sensitive, and their sensitivity senses emotional blocks that interfere with full self-empowerment and the development of consciousness.

Gift: Natives with a Moon/Chiron combination can be very powerful healers. Their attunement to their own soul urges and their awareness of the power of emotions when channeled positively as a tool for manifestation are gifts that they can share with others. They can be an example of someone who has been through major emotional crises and came out at the other end—i.e., the wounded healer archetype. Their acute sensitivity and heightened compassion for the suffering of others align them to practices that involve one of the many forms of healing.

Shadow: Deep-rooted problems can exist that are connected to issues around giving and receiving nurturance. The native may have been denied the encouragement and support that they needed to feel safe in their upbringing. In any case, they are coming from a position of lack. As a result, their strongly emotional nature is continually seeking compensation for the emptiness within from sources that are never giving them the fulfillment they crave.

CHIRON/MERCURY

Chiron represents core wounds and the desire to overcome them, and healing.

Mercury rules communication, mental processes, and the logical mind.

These individuals may be unconscious of how they project themselves mentally when speaking and otherwise communicating, learning, or teaching until a situation arises that triggers them. They then can become aware of their deficiencies or social skills. Analyzing the root cause of what is behind why they were triggered in the first place is a sign of healing that can be under the influence of Chiron.

Gift: Unexplained bouts of anxiety, stress, or depression can cause the native to delve deeper into their unconscious patterns and ultimately release memories from childhood or delve into inherited family patterns. The gift that ensues is expanded awareness of the initial problem or a medical solution that ultimately diminishes the discomfort they initially experienced. This individual can help others who might be experiencing similar issues if they so choose. These natives can choose to rewire their thinking patterns through positive affirmations, various forms of therapies, and fastidious conscious awareness of their disempowering thoughts. These individuals can use voice, sounds, thoughts, and language for healing purposes.

Shadow: The shadow side of this combination of Mercury and Chiron can indicate that the cognitive functioning of the native has been diminished or overpowered by one's subconscious wounding or sensitivity. Similarly, discomfort can occur in social situations or when speaking in public, which can be explored. A well of mental creativity may not yet be unleashed due to the resistance to explore the psyche. Pain can occur from not having their voice heard.

CHIRON/VENUS

Chiron represents core wounds and the desire to overcome them, and healing.

Venus represents love, relationships, beauty, values, comfort, and material resources.

Combinations between Venus and Chiron involve getting in touch with how the individual expresses love and healing obstacles that prevent the full expression of love. The individual can have old relationship traumas that require healing. This

Combinations between Venus and Chiron involve getting in touch with how the individual expresses love and healing obstacles that prevent the full expression of love. This individual can use what they gleaned from their own healing to help others, particularly women, with relationship issues and self-worth.

combination can lead to the healing and to questioning values and self-worth.

Gift: Long-term subconscious blocks that have prevented fulfilling love relationships are released. Inherited genetic patterns are sought and revealed, giving way to a conscious awareness of those patterns that have caused disappointment or lack of relationships. Awareness is brought to views and attitudes surrounding money, finances, and material resources. Values are redefined, where those imparted to the native from their upbringing are replaced by ones more suitable to their beliefs and ideals. This individual can use what they gleaned from their own healing to help others, particularly women, with relationship issues and self-worth.

Shadow: The native keeps encountering the same relationship issues over and over again. Issues occur involving the principle of attraction in both relationships and financial matters. Areas of the physical body connected with Venus may be more vulnerable and be in need of healing. Issues can occur with gender identity that need attention.

CHIRON/MARS

Chiron represents core wounds and the desire to overcome them, and healing.

Mars rules assertiveness, energy, drive, and courage.

The combination of Mars and Chiron can indicate that deep wounding is likely regarding any of the following: aggression, anger, sexuality, courage, or the ability to fulfill desires.

Gift: Discomfort in any of the areas ruled by Mars, which include lack of assertiveness, uncontrolled anger, sexual disfunction, the inability to fulfill desires, and abusive behavior, can lead the native to probe into their subconscious motivations. Releasing primal wounds in any of the above areas can bring newfound comfort and conscious awareness to the native. Post-healing, the native can help others heal their wounds.

Shadow: Perpetuating negative behavior patterns associated with Mars without engaging in soul-searching and the subsequent healing keeps the native in their wounds.

CHIRON/JUPITER

Chiron represents core wounds and the desire to overcome them, and healing.

Jupiter represents the higher mind, greater truths, expansiveness, hope, and optimism.

Jupiter in combination with Chiron can relate to a need to overcome a wounding related to faith and trust in a positive outcome. Fear is present that the rug can get pulled out at any time that causes deep-rooted, subconscious distrust of the divine.

Gift: These natives hold a strong belief in the power of healing. They can have a personal philosophy where they have gained mystical wisdom connected to their own wounding and subsequent healing. They have found a perspective with which they can integrate their negative experiences and reestablish stasis. These natives can profess ethical and ideological convictions around helping others. Themes that might interest them from a societal point of view include the involvement with solutions for those connected to banishment, ridicule, and unfortunate life circumstances, especially in early childhood. Judgment of others is kept in check through a realization that everyone has positive and negative traits and that with the proper training and opportunity, negative behaviors can be healed. They believe in redemption of the soul through faith and knowledge. As luck would have it, Jupiter can bring to awareness, through situations and personal interactions, places where hurt and pain is ready to be released and healed.

> Jupiter in combination with Chiron can relate to a need to overcome a wounding related to faith and trust in a positive outcome.

Shadow: The shadow side of a Jupiter/Chiron combination can manifest as a quest to find meaning in life. These individuals can get lost in the discomfort of the pointless turmoil of life, placing their faith and trust in one school of thought after another. As seekers, they may chase after various gurus and teachers, never finding peace or a sense of well-being, reinforcing their distrust of some promise for healing and reinforcing a belief in suffering and pain. Their early worldview may have been built upon the concept of terminal suffering and pain, and the native has struggled to put their early life experiences into perspective. These natives may not be open to seeking help, preferring to indulge their pain.

CHIRON/SATURN

Chiron represents core wounds and the desire to overcome them, and healing.

Saturn rules responsibility, adjustments to limitations, sustainability, and structure.

The combination of Saturn and Chiron can indicate core wounds connected with authority figures. These natives can take a disciplined approach to their own healing and the healing of others.

Gift: Natives with a Saturn/Chiron combination can be influential in creating structures and programs for healing and the development of higher consciousness. They can apply discipline and focus for their own healing. These natives are likely to prefer following organized, established programs for healing and expanding their consciousness. They can be advocates for humanitarian causes and will often assist in contributing to their successful outcome.

Shadow: These natives may have a domineering, critical parent who undermined their confidence and self-worth. They can be prone to feelings of guilt and, in extreme cases, feel guilty for their own exis-

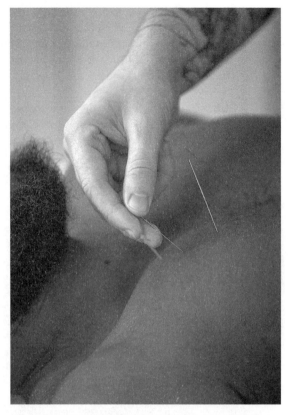

Uranus in combination with Chiron helps the native to free themselves from self-imposed limitations and buried traumas. They benefit from innovative healing modalities, including those that stimulate the body's chi or electrical and energy systems.

tence. They can be hard on themselves, never feeling that they are doing enough.

CHIRON/URANUS

Chiron represents core wounds and the desire to overcome them, and healing.

Uranus rules intuition, originality, individuality, and the sudden and unexpected.   .

Uranus in combination with Chiron helps the native to free themselves from self-imposed limitations and buried traumas. Uranus is symbolized by a lightning bolt, which breaks up obstacles and reveals a deeper level of the truth. These natives benefit from innovative healing modalities, including those that stimulate the body's chi, or the body's electrical and energy systems.

Gift: Chiron represents the urge to become whole and heal the Self. When combined with Uranus, the native can gain insights into their subconscious patterns at the hand of unexpected circumstances. Uranus sharpens one's intuitive faculties, and "a-ha" moments can occur, where they get glimpses into patterns related to their core wounding.

Shadow: These natives are sensitive to any kind of judgment and criticism. They feel they have a right to be who they are, although they may not realize that underlying wounding exists that they are not aware of. They can be closed off emotionally as an avoidance tactic for unconscious blocks and fears.

CHIRON/NEPTUNE

Chiron represents core wounds and the desire to overcome them, and healing.

Neptune rules ideals, creative imagination, transcendence, compassion, and vision.

A Chiron/Neptune combination can indicate that the native has issues surrounding their self-worth that need healing. They likely need to learn to value themselves and set boundaries so that others don't take advantage of them.

Gift: The gift of a Chiron/Neptune combination is an innate understanding of the power of faith, unconditional love, and prayer. Meditation practices can help these natives achieve peace of mind. Dance, music, art, dream analysis, and drama are

vehicles that can help these individuals process emotional discomfort and get in touch with deeper emotional blocks.

Shadow: The shadow side of this placement is a tendency to be a daydreamer and not a doer. Avoidance tactics can be deeply rooted in their psyche, and these natives have a penchant for glossing over deep-rooted emotional issues in favor of lofty, and often unrealistic, dreams. Individuals with this combination can have problems with addiction that are caused by core wounds that occurred in their early years. Chiron will create discomfort until the native chooses to address this wounding.

CHIRON/PLUTO

Chiron represents core wounds and the desire to overcome them, and healing.

Pluto represents regeneration; transformation; and a compelling, fundamental approach.

Pluto in combination with Chiron adds determination and focus to get to the bottom of whatever issues need to be healed. This can be an incredibly strong combination for a healer who can channel their perceptive insights and analytical skills into helping others. The native likely had to delve into their own unconscious traumas, which empowered them to effectively use their healing capabilities.

Gift: Chiron and Pluto together can result in a high level of desire and sensitivity that is oriented toward perceiving underlying wounds and subsequently helping others to heal. Having had to come into contact with their own vulnerabilities, these natives develop empathy and compassion toward others.

Shadow: Constant irritations, including chronic pain, can be the impetus for resolving core wounds that the native had been previously sweeping under the rug. These individuals may have unfortunate experiences that include separation and rejection that resulted from a lack of sympathy toward others. They may have taken a callous approach to people with disabilities and those in less fortunate circumstances.

CHIRON/ERIS

Chiron represents core wounds and the desire to overcome them, and healing.

Eris represents the determination to remove limitations that impede the soul's evolution.

Gift: A strong desire to heal genetic, societal, and familiar patterning can propel this individual through trials and tribulations that eventually lead to a rebirth of the soul. They are examples of those who express themselves clearly, authentically, and in a way that challenges those around them.

Shadow: These folks can get caught up in the process of healing themselves and run into obstacles at every turn, which tests their determination and the purity of their intent. They may have to resolve issues that revolve around the theme of rejection.

CHIRON/NORTH NODE

Chiron represents core wounds and the desire to overcome them, and healing.

The North Node represents future direction, soul guidance, and fulfillment.

The North Node emphasizes the importance for the native to develop the attributes represented by Chiron, which include delving into the unconscious, healing, and teaching. It will benefit the individual to be steadfast in unveiling underlying issues that prevent them from following a path that will bring personal fulfillment and self-empowerment. Chiron can also indicate that it can benefit the native to pursue a track in the healing arts.

Gift: Chiron combined with the North Node supports these natives in embracing self-empowerment and taking responsibility for their issues rather than casting blame on others. They may find that they are continually having to confront wounding from times past so that they can move forward with their destiny. The issues they confront likely have a fated quality to them, leading them down an ultimate path to self-fulfillment and self-discovery.

Shadow: The shadow side of a Chiron/ North Node combination is the lack of fulfillment that comes from the feeling that something more is out there in life. Unprocessed hurts, wounds, and blows to their self-esteem are continually haunting these individuals. They can be their own worst enemy, where they continually undermine their progress due to deep-rooted issues that have been swept under the rug.

> The North Node emphasizes the importance for the native to develop the attributes represented by Chiron, which include delving into the unconscious, healing, and teaching.

CHIRON/SOUTH NODE

Chiron represents core wounds and the desire to overcome them, and healing.

Chiron in combination with the Midheaven is a powerful placement, with individuals who are not seeking power for power's sake. They have processed many of their deepest wounds and gained personal empowerment as a result.

The South Node represents familiarity, gratification, and the path of least resistance.

The combination of Chiron and the South Node can indicate that the native has had experience with overcoming issues that plague them and possible disabilities in the past and that they can bring the desire for self-empowerment and healing to current situations.

Gift: These individuals can assume responsibility for their conscious and unconscious issues, which helps them to continue to move forward on their path. They can have healing abilities, where they can help others. They have attained a level of self-awareness in the past.

Shadow: The shadow side of this placement is that a strong memory connected to a past life can be holding the native back from developing their destiny in this lifetime. They may need to pay more attention to their North Node sign and house placement and develop the attributes that are thereby indicated.

CHIRON/ASCENDANT

Chiron represents core wounds and the desire to overcome them, and healing.

The Ascendant represents one's approach, orientation, and the window through which one sees the world.

These individuals can be natural healers, counselors, teachers, or mentors. They are likely to be predisposed toward a life of service.

Gift: Chiron in combination with the Ascendant can give the native strong healing abilities. Self-awareness is important to these individuals. These natives take responsibility for what they put out in the world. They are charismatic, and because they have processed much of their subconscious issues, they excel as healers, spiritual mentors, and teachers.

Shadow: The shadow side of this placement is when the ego gets in the way and their healing ability ceases to flow. Their healing gifts can be used to control those they seek to heal. They can become overly invested in playing the role of a guru.

CHIRON/MIDHEAVEN (MC)

Chiron represents core wounds and the desire to overcome them, and healing.

The Midheaven (MC) represents image, outer aspirations, and career orientation.

Chiron in combination with the Midheaven is a powerful placement. These natives have either encompassed their personal power or have not. Parental influence may have noticed something special about them and subsequently pressured them to follow a path that the native never fully embraced or refuted. Planetary transits, including the Saturn return, the Uranus Opposition, and the Chiron return, may have to transpire before these natives fully embrace their power and healing ability with this placement.

Gift: Individuals with this placement are not seeking power for power's sake. They have processed many of their deepest wounds and gained personal empowerment as a result. They are not trying to prove anything. They are motivated to help others become empowered as a healer, mentor, spiritual teacher, or practioner. These individuals are highly charismatic. They realize that the mastery of power is a sacred gift.

Shadow: The shadow side of this placement can manifest as confusion regarding the use of their power. Family expectations can play an important role with these natives. The Midheaven axis intersects with the chart's nadir, or the Fourth-House cusp that rules family. As a result of family pressure, these natives can have an aversion to power and seek to avoid any position of authority. They may feel that they do not fit in anywhere.

The Nodes of the Moon

The nodes of the Moon are not planetary bodies; they are considered to be shadow planets. They don't have a physical mass or an existence. Similar to the concept of a black hole, they are highly magnetic, mathematical points that cause gravitational pull. The Lunar Nodes are highly impactful points in the birth chart, and significant attention was paid to them centuries prior to the discovery of Uranus, Neptune, and Pluto. They were known as the Dragon's Head and the Dragon's Tail by Arabic and European astrologers. In Vedic astrology, the North Node is called Rahu and the South Node is called Ketu, and these two points are considered to be as important as the other traditional planets.

The Lunar Nodes are the two points where the Moon's orbital path crosses the ecliptic. The ecliptic is the Sun's apparent path through the sky when observed from Earth. We have two Lunar Nodes, the North Node and the South Node, which are always opposite each other. The North Node crosses the ecliptic heading toward the North Pole of Earth, and the South Node crosses the ecliptic heading toward the South Pole of Earth.

The Lunar Nodes are the only astrological bodies that move backward. Because of their backward movement, the Lunar Nodes are associated with the past. They are an indicator of the integration of an individual's past karma and actions with their future destiny. The North and South Nodes form an axis in the birth chart that describes an individual's talents and gifts, those that they are born with and those that they will benefit from developing.

The nodes of the Moon spend about a year and a half in each sign before retrograding into the previous sign.

The nodes tell us about our deep desires in this lifetime as well as what we need to heal from the past. The nodes are indicators of the spiritual meaning of one's life. The

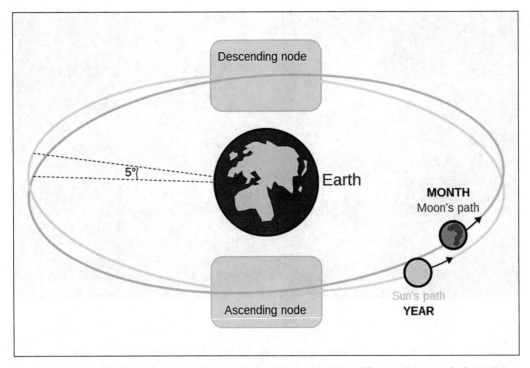

The Lunar Nodes are the two points where the Moon's orbital path crosses the ecliptic. They were known as the Dragon's Head and the Dragon's Tail by Arabic and European astrologers.

North Node is the direction we're headed in life, whereas the South Node represents a deep-seated habit that may not be furthering our growth. The South Node tends to operate on automatic pilot and indicates the skills, experiences, and qualities that have already been developed. The North Node represents a less familiar, more demanding path, yet one that will support and further our growth and development.

The South Node also represents unfinished business from the past. Conjunctions and challenging aspects to the South Node from other planetary bodies can provide clues regarding unfinished business so that pitfalls can be avoided while moving forward.

Differing opinions exist between astrologers regarding correlations between planetary influences and the nodes in astrology. The North Node can have a connotation connecting it to spiritual growth, and the expansive influence of Jupiter and the South Node is related to Saturn, whereby the karmic influence of past lives is brought forward to be balanced in this life.

The Lunar Nodes are related to solar and lunar eclipses. When an eclipse takes place, it is because a shadow is cast over either the Sun or the Moon. The shadow is either the North or South Node, which lines up with either the Full Moon or the New Moon when an eclipse occurs.

When the Moon comes between the Sun and Earth, the shadow of the Moon falling on Earth leads the North Node.

NORTH NODE AND SOUTH NODE POLARITIES IN THE SIGNS

The North and South Nodes always reside in opposing signs, so a resonance and balance always occurs that is derived from integrating the qualities of one sign to enhance the fulfillment of the opposite sign. The nodes complete each other. Ideally, the individual can find ways to use the gifts and talents that they have already developed from the South Node to support the development of their North Node talents and gifts. The individual is urged to focus on the North Node and to face any challenges that may ensue. The North Node is guiding one toward their ultimate destiny and fulfillment, and it may take faith and trust to move forward into unknown territory rather than stay stuck in the familiar.

> Ideally, the individual can find ways to use the gifts and talents that they have already developed from the South Node to support the development of their North Node talents and gifts.

Neither polarity exists in a vacuum; what matters is the integration between the two with a focus on the North Node, using what has preferably been learned from the South Node placement.

NORTH NODE AND SOUTH NODE POLARITIES IN THE HOUSES

The North and South Nodes always reside in opposing houses, so a resonance and balance always occurs that is derived from integrating the qualities of the opposing houses in the same way that the qualities of the opposing signs are integrated. The nodes complete each other. Ideally, the individual can find ways to use the gifts and talents that they have already developed from the South Node to support the development of their North Node talents and gifts.

THE NODAL RETURN

When the nodes return to the same sign and degree of birth, an individual naturally moves in the direction of their destiny. Fated events and fated relationships can occur at these times that help the individual embrace their North Node destiny. Nodal returns occur at approximately these ages: 18, 37, 55, and 74.

THE ARIES AND LIBRA POLARITY AND THE FIRST-HOUSE AND SEVENTH-HOUSE POLARITY

The polarity between Aries and Libra and the First House and Seventh House is about finding the balance between the Self and the Not Self. Aries (First House) is fiery and active and symbolizes consciousness in the subjective mode. Libra (Seventh House) is an Air sign that focuses awareness on the individual's relationship with others. When the Lunar Nodes reside along this axis, a transference of priority will occur between the subjective, individually oriented mode of Aries (First House) to the socially oriented, relationship-oriented Libra (Seventh House) and vice versa.

Gift: The gift from having the nodes in Aries and Libra or the First-House and Seventh-House polarity is that the native brings a well-developed sense of themselves into their relationships. They are self-reliant, self-empowered, and independent. Relationships, personal and business, are empowering and fulfilling to all participants.

Shadow: The shadow side of the Aries/Libra or First-House/Seventh-House nodal polarity manifests in unsatisfying personal and business relationships. Ongoing issues and imbalances occur around issues of giving and receiving and between independence and codependence.

Aries North Node/Libra South Node; First House North Node/Seventh House South Node

The individual is challenged to act on their own instincts and have the courage to rely on their own convictions. Codependency can be an issue here with the South Node in Libra or in the Seventh House. These individuals run the risk of relying too much on the opinions and assistance of others. They can depend on others to fulfill their needs rather than seek to be independent, which is the key to their spiritual development. Courage is an attribute that benefits these natives. Times may occur in their life when they have to muster the courage and conviction to follow a path that is unfamiliar to them. Venturing forward will bring great rewards and fulfillment. Patterns that include the desire to continually please others or the need for steady help from others can hinder their self-development.

Libra North Node/Aries South Node; Seventh House North Node/First House South Node

An Aries or First-House South Node placement challenges the native to let go of a "go it alone" way of being. They are not an island unto themselves. They have to let others into their world. Teamwork and alliances are on the agenda for their growth and development. Cooperation and compromise are their path to spiritual growth and development. The South Node in Aries or the Seventh House can find it difficult to let others into their lives. Their knee-jerk reaction can be that of competitiveness or argumentativeness. These natives can bring forward the gifts they received from developing themselves in the past to a balanced relationship, where each person is self-empowered.

THE TAURUS AND SCORPIO POLARITY AND THE SECOND-HOUSE AND EIGHTH-HOUSE POLARITY

The Taurus and Scorpio polarity as well as the Second-House and Eighth-House polarity is the axis of resources and what we value. Taurus (Second House) is about what's mine, and Scorpio (Eighth House) is about what's ours or what's yours. Taurus (Second House) is self-reliant and has a well-developed sense of self-worth. Scorpio (Eighth House) can be emotionally and physically dependent on other people.

Taurus (Second House) is sensual and enjoys the comforts of life. The Taurean influence desires material and emotional security. The Scorpio (Eighth House) influence seeks to unveil whatever is hidden and beneath the surface. Their desire to discover hidden truths often means that they have to let go of whatever is no longer serving then. Change and radical transformation can ensue. Self-empowerment for a Scorpio can mean letting go of non-essential material baggage and psychological attachments. Scorpios want to free themselves of anything that is controlling them. Tauruses move slowly, and uprooting themselves for the sake of change is not necessarily appealing to them.

Gift: The gift of the Taurus/Scorpio and Second-House/Eighth-House polarities is the balance between comfort, ease, and security and change, regeneration, and renewal, whereby the native can let go of whatever is bogging them down and interfering with their growth and progress. A healthy balance occurs between self-sufficiency and depending on others. Intimacy is mutually fulfilling, coming from a foundation of self-worth and self-awareness. Scorpio and the Eighth House desire surrendering to another from a place of love; however, it is only when the Taurean need for safety and security is fulfilled that these individuals can truly surrender to another or to the shifts that they deem necessary in order to further their growth.

Shadow: The shadow side of this placement manifests as overdependence on others emotionally and materially as a substitute for developing one's talents and abilities. Lethargy, fear of change, and a lack of self-esteem interfere with the native's growth and development. As a result, these individuals can seek to control and manipulate others. Power struggles are abundant, and they are substituted for healthy interchanges based upon mutual self-respect and recognition.

Taurus desires material and emotional security. Scorpio seeks to unveil whatever is hidden and beneath the surface. Self-empowerment for a Scorpio can mean letting go of non-essential material baggage and psychological attachments.

Taurus North Node/Scorpio South Node; Second House North Node/Eighth House South Node

An individual with the North Node in Taurus or in the Second House is encouraged to find satisfaction from the simple pleasures in life. These natives feel secure and safe when they have a strong material base. The influence of the South Node in Scorpio or in the Eighth House can bring forward a subconscious influence of always being in a state of crisis or on the edge. Building a solid foundation that the native can rely upon is of the utmost importance. Developing gifts, talents, and abilities contributes to the native's self-worth and develops an inner feeling of security that is not dependent solely on material resources and cannot be easily controlled or manipulated by another. The South Node in Scorpio or in the Eighth House can have an instinctual suspicion of others. Control and manipulation may be a lingering unconscious memory, and the individual benefits from practical pursuits that bring tangible results and stability. A straightforward, down-to-earth approach gives these individuals the safety and security they need to make positive changes in their lives.

Scorpio North Node/Taurus South Node; Eighth House North Node/Second House South Node

An individual with the North Node in Scorpio or in the Eighth House benefits from the awareness that true safety and security evolves from self-mastery and self-empowerment. Life requires adapting to change and transformation. No other way exists to avoid getting stuck in patterns that are not life-supporting. These individuals benefit from stepping out of their comfort zone and reevaluating their material needs and beliefs regarding security. Open-hearted sharing can bring rewards and fulfillment. Sharing talents and abilities in order to help others in times of crisis can bring great fulfillment to these natives and further their spiritual development.

THE GEMINI AND SAGITTARIUS POLARITY AND THE THIRD-HOUSE AND NINTH-HOUSE POLARITY

The Gemini/Sagittarius and the Third-House/Ninth-House polarities are both on an axis of information, knowledge, communication, travel, movement, and law.

The Gemini nodal influence, which includes the Third House, processes information from a logical, fact-based perspective. The Sagittarius nodal influence, which includes a nodal placement in the Ninth House, moves the Gemini theme to a more abstract level that includes conceptualizing an overall perspective and philosophy. The Gemini/Third-House placement is intellectual, with varied interests. Sagittarius and the Ninth-House node seek to explore different points of view and concepts. The Third House and Gemini nodes are associated with people from their immediate environment, including neighbors, acquaintances, siblings, and extended family. The Ninth-House and Sagittarius node placements are associated with foreigners and varied cultures. Gemini is connected to short trips and local travel, and Sagittarius is associated with long journeys. The Ninth-House Sagittarian nodal

influence creates visionaries who expand the boundaries of daily life.

Gift: The gift from a nodal placement that spans either the Gemini/Sagittarius or the Third-House/Ninth-House axis is the ability to formulate and communicate an overall perspective from an abundance of varied facts on multiple issues. These natives make excellent writers and teachers. They have the unique ability to interact with people from wide-ranging and diverse backgrounds. They can take logical steps to manifest their dreams and visions. These are individuals with an open mind and the curiosity to see the adventure in learning. The truth is important to them, and they arrive at conclusions using logic and objectivity.

Shadow: The shadow side of this nodal axis is bigotry and the inability to expand their perspective to be inclusive of diverse cultures, philosophies, and ideas. Blind belief and propaganda can override logical thinking. These natives can have disabilities that affect their communication skills. Their attention span can be an issue due to their inability to focus. These natives can be disinterested in learning because they don't believe that they have the ability to understand new ideas or concepts.

Gemini North Node/Sagittarius South Node; Third House North Node/Ninth House South Node

The Gemini/Sagittarius and the Third-House/Ninth-House axis is the axis of knowledge. This axis rules how we process information and how we make sense of the world. Gemini and Sagittarius have different approaches to knowledge and systems of knowledge that include education, religion, customs, and lifestyle. Gemini North Node and North Node in the Third House natives' greatest asset is their ability to communicate. They are curious learners

Natives with Cancer/Capricorn nodal placement have a strong sense of responsibility combined with a deep desire to help and care for others. They do well working for larger social structures and public service institutions that serve humanity.

and love to share what they know with others. They can share their quick wit with an overriding perspective that can make a point that is easily understood. Freedom is important to these natives, and they may have to curtail their wandering lust in order to connect with their immediate environment and the people around them. Practical skills and details are important with this North Node placement.

Sagittarius North Node/Gemini South Node; Ninth House North Node/Third House South Node

The North Node in either Sagittarius or in the Ninth House denote an open-minded individual who has a strong desire to accumulate and share knowledge. This placement can indicate that the native is challenged to be honest in all situations and develop a strong inner faith that supports them in their quest to pursue their

destiny. These natives can follow a path for their spiritual growth that includes a lifelong search for wisdom, knowledge, and a philosophy of life that they can abide by. Evolutionary growth is furthered through the exploration of new horizons through travel or via dreams and visions. To support their path, these natives can incorporate their accumulated knowledge and communication skills.

THE CANCER AND CAPRICORN POLARITY AND THE FOURTH-HOUSE AND TENTH-HOUSE POLARITY

The Cancer/Capricorn and the Fourth-House/Tenth-House polarity brings together the best of both a responsible and caring nature. Practicality, responsibility, and building workable and sustainable structures and guidelines are all characteristics of Capricorn and the Tenth House.

Heightened sensitivity and a deeply caring nature describe Cancerian/Fourth-House traits. The unification of this polarity is integrating human values with rules and regulations. It is the integration of family needs with a personal desire to be successful in the outer world. It is about integrating social responsibilities with family responsibilities. Capricorn is the strict father who provides materially for the family, and Cancer is the warm and gentle mother who cares for the household. The blending of all of the above polarities is the genius of balancing either of the juxtapositions of the nodes.

Gift: The gift offered by a nodal placement along the Cancer/Capricorn or Fourth-House/Tenth-House axis is that these natives have a strong sense of responsibility combined with a deep desire to help and care for others. They do well in working for larger social structures and public-service institutions that serve humanity. They have a healthy respect for tradition and ancestral roots. The practical and efficient nature of Capricorn and the Tenth House can bring sustainable solutions to fulfilling the needs of those who require extra care and assistance.

Shadow: The shadow of the nodal placement along the Cancer/Capricorn or the Fourth-House/Tenth-House axis is anxiety and overwhelm from being the go-to person who has to take care of everyone's needs. They can feel taken advantage of and powerless to move out of their role as the assumed caregiver. These individuals can be overly possessive, dependent, and insecure and have a great need for self-acceptance. Ambition and a desire for social prestige and power can usurp family responsibilities and those in the home. These individuals can be overly serious and restricted emotionally.

Cancer North Node/Capricorn South Node; Fourth House North Node/Tenth House South Node

North Node in Cancer and Fourth-House individuals are very supportive to the needs of others. How they can best fulfill those needs is a dynamic at play for these natives. Respect for tradition and a love of family are characteristics that are indicated by this placement. They are gentle and caring. They can use the practicality and efficiency learned from the South Node placement in Capricorn or in the Tenth House to find solutions for those in need. The South Node in Capricorn and in the Tenth House can be power-driven and ambitious where the needs of the system are more important than the needs of loved ones and those who are vulnerable.

Capricorn North Node/Cancer South Node; Tenth House North Node/Fourth House South Node

Individuals with the North Node in Capricorn or in the Tenth House are likely to be ambitious with a keen desire for success, recognition, respect, and status. It serves them to develop a strong work ethic and a conscientious nature that strives to make the best use of their abilities. The South Node in Cancer or in the Fourth House can indicate a highly emotional individual who puts caring for others ahead of developing their talents and abilities and bringing them forward out into the world. The line of least resistance may be to stay home rather than to go out into the world. Safety and security are likely to be strong tendencies. With this placement, the native is challenged to leave the safety and protection of the nest and acknowledge their vulnerabilities and move through them with the tenacity and diligence that the North Node in Capricorn or in the Tenth House will support.

THE LEO AND AQUARIUS POLARITY AND THE FIFTH-HOUSE AND ELEVENTH-HOUSE POLARITY

The Leo (Fifth-House) and Aquarius (Eleventh-House) polarity is about using the warmth and charisma of Leo to reach out to others. They are on a mission guided by the Aquarian and Eleventh-House dynamic in order to bring groups of people together for a common cause. These can be disparate individuals from diverse backgrounds who come together through the leadership and organizational ability of the Leo energy for a common cause. This polarity is also represented by the dramatic orientation of Leo and the objective positioning of Aquarius. Combining these seemingly different approaches to a situation is the challenge of this nodal axis.

Gift: The gift of a nodal placement that combines the Leo/Aquarius or Fifth-House/Eleventh-House dynamics and characteristics is heartfelt objectivity, where the individual can honor their uniqueness and at the same time give equal weight to everyone else's talents and gifts. Great benefits can be brought to all situations through the ability to combine the courage, creativity, leadership, and organizational talents of Leo and the Fifth House with the nonjudgmental, objective, innovative, and humanitarian traits of Aquarius and the Eleventh House. The Fixity of both signs makes this a powerful axis that can be beneficial to all populations, including children who fall under the domain of Leo. A great synthesis can occur that unites people, and they can have some good Leo, Fifth-House fun while they are doing so.

Shadow: The shadow side of this Leo (Fifth-House)/Aquarius (Eleventh-House) axis is too much ego that needs to exert its power and one-upmanship over others.

The Leo/Aquarius polarity harnesses the warmth and charisma of Leo to reach out to others. They are on a mission guided by the Aquarian dynamic to bring together disparate individuals from diverse backgrounds for a common cause.

They are not able to relinquish being the center of attention and put a damper on any group endeavor through their emotional outbursts and need for attention. The shadow can also manifest as cold-heartedness and severe objectivity when a more creative and fun-oriented approach would better serve the situation and everyone involved. The futuristic and outside-the-box approach can be *too* outside the box and not be supportive of everyone's goals and objectives.

Leo North Node/Aquarius South Node; Fifth House North Node/Eleventh House South Node

The Leo placement gives one a warm, playful, heartfelt energy. This placement of either a Leo North Node or a Fifth-House North Node is on a mission to follow their heart and be spontaneous. These natives may have to get used to being more in the limelight. The Aquarius or Eleventh-House North Node positions may not be accustomed to being a focus of attention. "Live and let live" is a motto that the Leo soul can resonate with, and luckily, the influence of the South Node in either Aquarius or the Eleventh House brings honesty and objectivity to the mix. These natives are challenged to connect with their inner child and have fun. Leo is a sign of courage, and the extra oomph can combine with the Aquarian desire to benefit humanity and reach a wider audience.

Aquarius North Node/Leo South Node; Eleventh House North Node/Fifth House South Node

The Aquarius or Eleventh-House nodal position is vested in using their skills for the benefit of humanity. These individuals are forward-thinking and inventive. They enjoy challenging the status quo through their innovative and somewhat eccentric behavior. Cultivating friendships and participating in group associations further their growth and ultimate fulfillment. They are challenged to shift away from a "me first" approach to relationships, where each person is recognized for their contributions. Combining the warmth and charm of Leo with the desire to reach out to diverse groups of people and bring them together is in line with their spiritual growth.

THE VIRGO AND PISCES POLARITY AND THE SIXTH-HOUSE AND TWELFTH-HOUSE POLARITY

The Virgo/Pisces and the Sixth-House/Twelfth-House polarity is balancing the practical logic and daily task orientation of Virgo and the Sixth House with the expansive oneness and compassion of Pisces and the Twelfth House. The Virgoan/Sixth-House orientation is service oriented and keeps its nose to the grindstone, whereas the Piscean/Twelfth-House orientation is searching all the realms and picking up impressions, with an extra eye for those who are in need. The integration of these two dynamics can bring practical solutions that can help the underprivileged or infirmed. Virgo is highly discerning and detail-oriented, whereas Pisces is feeling-oriented and can sense trends and tune in to underlying vibrations. Both energies are service-oriented and want to help others. They go about in different ways that can blend to bring practical, analytical, heartfelt solutions that will make the world a better place.

Gift: The gift of the Virgo/Pisces and Sixth-House/Twelfth-House nodal polarity is the ability to focus on physical reality in order to further spiritual growth. These individuals can take full advantage of the physical, mental, and spiritual interconnection that affects health, stress, and all-around peace of mind. Balancing this polarity brings humility and ego purification through spiritual practice and empathy. These natives are attuned to human suffering and are willing to take the appropriate steps find practical solutions. They understand that progress and protection of the most vulnerable are achieved through a series of orderly changes. This axis can sense when existing structures are no longer working due to the Piscean/Twelfth-House sensitivity to undercurrents and trends and seek to initiate new structures that better suit the prevailing needs.

Shadow: The shadow side of the Virgo/Pisces or Sixth-House/Twelfth-House nodal placement includes escapist tendencies with an aversion to practical, mundane tasks. These natives may be prone to addictions. The other side of the coin is a native who is a workaholic without paying attention to their health and spiritual development. Perfectionist tendencies can preclude compassion and empathy for others. Behind-the-scenes manipulation and intrigue can occur.

Virgo North Node/Pisces South Node; Sixth House North Node/Twelfth House South Node

North Node in Virgo or Sixth-House individuals are highly duty-oriented and disciplined. They are logical, analytical, practical, and realistic. Their destiny is connected to undertaking a healthy, practical approach to life. The South Node in Pisces or the Twelfth House gives these natives a vivid imagination; however, a tendency occurs to prefer the dream state over day-to-day mainte-nance. The Piscean tendency to be easily dis-tracted means that these individuals will benefit from clear goals and a strong, detailed structure to support those goals. Perfecting their craft brings personal fulfillment and supports fulfilling their destiny.

> These natives are attuned to human suffering and are willing to take the appropriate steps to find practical solutions.

Pisces North Node/Virgo South Node; Twelfth House North Node/Sixth House South Node

These compassionate souls with a Pisces or Twelfth-House North Node placement seek to support people in need and improve living conditions for those who are less fortunate. They can be artistically or musically inclined and have an interest in healing and possibly metaphysics. These natives benefit from developing their abilities in these areas, which can lead to the ultimate fulfillment of their destiny. It is important for them to develop faith and trust, even when it appears that the perfectionist tendencies acquired by their Virgo or Sixth-House placement puts undue pressure on them. They can get caught up in mundane affairs and too many details and lose track of the big picture that they are seeking to initiate. The gift of these placements is that they can bring their innate ability to create a practical plan to manifest in esoteric and lofty ideals.

NODES COMBINATIONS

North Node/Sun

The North Node represents future direction, soul guidance, and fulfillment.

The Sun indicates purpose, self-expression, creative life force, and conscious will.

The North Node emphasizes the importance for the native to develop the attributes represented by the Sun. This suggests that worldly success, recognition, and a life filled with purpose and creative self-expression are part of the destiny that the native will be drawn to fulfill.

Gift: The native is aligned and consciously aware of their purpose and what brings them happiness and fulfillment. A higher force has stirred them in a direction that may be different from the one they initially followed, as if circumstances showed up at the right time and place to influence important life choices. Once on the path that brings fulfillment, a sense of being on auto-pilot and going along for the ride occurs.

Those with a Sun and South Node connection have likely achieved a high level of success in the past. They know what it feels like to be on the right path, which can be applied to any new direction they pursue.

Those with a Sun and South Node connection have likely achieved a high level of success in the past, although they have the urge to find a new direction. They have an inherent self-confidence that can carry them into new realms of experience and fulfillment.

Gift: Individuals with this combination know how to be successful. They know what it feels like to know when they are on the right path. This inherent knowing can be applied to whichever new direction resonates with them to pursue. They are at a definite advantage having the wherewithal to put themselves out into the world. The key is for them to stay attuned to when it is time for them to move on to something new that aligns to the soul's growth and evolution.

Shadow: These natives can be so connected to the past due to accolades bestowed upon them for their achievements in the early part of their lives that it is difficult for them to pursue other avenues of expression. Whatever had worked before is no longer satisfying or is not coming together as easily as before. It is not as easy to be in the limelight as it once was. Bragging and self-aggrandizement may not be received well by those they are looking to impress. The old self needs to be brought up to the present day and find a new future self in order to feel good about themselves.

Shadow: The individual's ego or sense of identity isn't aligned with the direction that will most benefit them to pursue. A disconnect occurs between how the ego values the urges of the true self, perhaps as a result of imposed restrictions from their upbringing or from societal norms. The struggle that ensues is feeling out of place or never fully satisfied in spite of achievements, material comfort, and recognition. An underlying nagging feeling can occur for these natives that they need to take a chance, follow their heartfelt urges, and do what makes them happy.

SOUTH NODE/SUN

The South Node represents familiarity, gratification, and the path of least resistance.

The Sun indicates purpose, self-expression, creative life force, and conscious will.

NORTH NODE/MOON

The North Node represents future direction, soul guidance, and fulfillment.

The Moon rules the soul, core instincts, the personality, and subconscious conditioning.

Individuals with a North Node/Moon connection have a deep, intuitive urge to embark upon the path indicated by the sign and placement of their North Node.

Gift: As karma would have it, these natives have an advantage in that they emotionally connect to the path of destiny that lies before them. They can feel comfortable that they are on the right path, and they instinctively know when they wobble away from it. They have the know-how needed to take advantage of trends and attain popularity. Sales, marketing, public relations, advertising, entertainment, and politics are areas that they can excel in, depending on the sign and placement of the Moon and the North Node.

Shadow: These individuals have a nagging feeling that something more is out there for them, that they don't fit in with what they are doing and the direction they are going in. They feel out of place, as if something is missing from their lives. They can be overly attached to parental or societal expectations that have led them to pursue avenues that they were never fully aligned to.

SOUTH MODE/MOON

The South Node represents familiarity, gratification, and the path of least resistance.

The Moon rules the soul, core instincts, the personality, and subconscious conditioning.

Natives with a Moon/South Node connection may feel that they have to redo something they have done previously. They may, by happenstance, find themselves in a field that is very familiar to them.

Gift: The gift of the South Node is using skills that have been developed in the past and bringing them forward to incorporate them into the destiny indicated by the sign and placement of the North Node. With the Moon associated with the South Node, gifts that can be gleaned include a warm, generous personality that is nurturing. They have a knack for connecting with the public and instinctively know how to sense and take advantage of whatever is trending.

Shadow: These natives can have strong emotional ties to the past. It may be very difficult for them to break away from expectations instilled upon them from early childhood. They may feel bound to enter into a field associated with family, like a family business or a field with deep roots to their ancestral lineage. Fulfilling these expectations is likely to bring them dubious satisfaction. They can have deep-rooted, subconscious habits and emotional patterns that no longer serve them. A lack of emotional fulfillment can plague them, and they can feel that they don't receive the nurturing and support they need. They can have feelings of isolation and aloneness.

> With the Moon associated with the South Node, gifts that can be gleaned include a warm, generous personality that is nurturing.

NORTH NODE/MERCURY

The North Node represents future direction, soul guidance, and fulfillment.

Mercury rules communication, mental processes, and the logical mind.

When Mercury connects with the North Node, the native's mental capacity has added potential in the areas represented by the North Node sign and house placement. A strong emphasis can be placed on the intellect and further developing the intellect, communication modalities, and other Mercurial talents.

Gift: The native may possess a versatile mind that is quick, witty, and adaptable with their destiny linked to fulfilling aspects of their Mercurial skills: speaking, comedy, writing, research, teaching, or public relations. They may feel that they have a gift for languages. An ease in communicating is present that can lead to career and personal fulfillment.

Shadow: These natives can fall into a trap of dispersing an inadvertent amount of energy gabbing and pursuing social media at the expense of a more constructive use of the talents and abilities they may have.

SOUTH NODE/MERCURY

The South Node represents familiarity, gratification, and the path of least resistance.

Mercury rules communication, mental processes, and the logical mind.

The native has well-developed mental faculties that are intuitive and skilled in various forms of communication. In Vedic astrology, this combination is indicative of a spiritual thinker.

Gift: Individuals with a Mercury/South Node connection may have been precocious as children and young adults. They have a well-developed communication style that is easy for others to understand. They can be super dexterous in their movement or with their hands, contributing to skillfulness in dance, gymnastics,

or areas involving craftmanship. Languages are easy for them to learn.

Shadow: These natives can have communication barriers that can be overcome such as learning disabilities or dyslexia. They can also be restless and prone to stress and anxiety due to a highly sensitive nervous system.

NORTH NODE/VENUS

The North Node represents future direction, soul guidance, and fulfillment.

Venus represents love, relationships, beauty, values, comfort, and material resources.

These individuals may be attractive and sensitive but are not able to sustain a suitable relationship until they consciously learn how to be in a relationship and make it work. They may find little value in money and material resources.

Gift: A Venus/North Node connection indicates that relationships are or will be important to these individuals. Love and significant relationships of all types may be a central theme that will impact them. They may feel intuitively destined to one day meet their soulmate. Their charm and charisma increase as they age. Others may be instinctively drawn to them, and it may turn out that these are destined connections.

Shadow: These natives can use their magnetism and charm to deceive and manipulate others. They can continually engage in frivolous relationships without any intent to develop a deeper connection or commitment. They can be spendthrifts.

SOUTH NODE/VENUS

The South Node represents familiarity, gratification, and the path of least resistance.

Venus represents love, relationships, beauty, values, comfort, and material resources.

Relationships are familiar territory for these individuals. Situations will deter these natives from forming superficial relations that don't further their growth and development.

Gift: Natives are naturally magnetic, graceful, and charming and have a knack for putting others at ease. They are experienced in interacting in social situations. Connecting with others comes naturally to them. These natives may have to learn the true meaning of love. They may have taken for granted people who loved them in the past. These individuals likely have artistic or musical talents that were previously developed. These abilities may show up at a young age.

Shadow: The shadow side of the Venus/South Node connection is that these individuals may need to become more independent. A pattern of codependence can occur that feeds into their relationship patterns. Unconscious motivations affect the individual.

A Venus/North Node connection indicates that love and significant relationships of all types may be a central theme that will impact them. Others may be instinctively drawn to them.

NORTH NODE/MARS

The North Node represents future direction, soul guidance, and fulfillment.

Mars rules assertiveness, energy, drive, and courage.

Gift: Strength and courage are assets for these individuals. They have the drive and stamina to get fully involved in life and take on situations that can at first glance appear daunting and require a stick-to-it, energetic approach. They can surprise themselves and others with the ease with which they can accomplish these types of activities and gain further cooperation and support. They can pursue various types of adventures from which they can gain notice.

Shadow: For the sake of getting notice and attention, these individuals can overdo bravery and courage and take on self-destructive activities. Their ambition can be overly ego-driven and come off as excessive to those they are wanting to impress. They can lack sensitivity to others as well as to situations around them.

SOUTH NODE/MARS

The South Node represents familiarity, gratification, and the path of least resistance.

Mars rules assertiveness, energy, drive, and courage.

These natives can be too familiar with an aggressive and competitive approach to situations that others find overwhelming. They are naturally courageous and will fight for what they want. Once they learn to integrate these traits into a more harmonious and diplomatic approach, they will find that their success yields appreciation from others.

Gift: Natives with this combination of Mars with the South Node are not afraid to lend a hand in situations and activities that require courage, strength, and fortitude. They can be naturally energetic and enthusiastic, although they can have a tendency to be overly impulsive if not kept in check. They are willing to fight for their beliefs and pursue causes that are at the forefront of innovation. These are the original pioneers. Tactics and strategy come naturally to them.

Shadow: Anger and sexual energy can be mired in the past or old habits. These natives may need to learn to walk away from a fight or take time out before initiating any kind of hasty action that won't ultimately benefit them. This combination can also imply a lack of assertiveness based upon unsuccessful endeavors from the past. Overcompensation can ensue, and the native can become fearful and phobic about ever taking the initiative. Repressed Mars energy can show up as negative, aggressive patterns or behavioral issues.

NORTH NODE/JUPITER

The North Node represents future direction, soul guidance, and fulfillment.

Jupiter represents the higher mind, greater truths, expansiveness, hope, and optimism.

The North Node emphasizes the importance for the native to develop the attributes represented by Jupiter. This suggests that a philosophy of life that assists the native in fostering faith and trust will be beneficial.

Gift: Jupiter in combination with the North Node can bring a life theme chock full of opportunities and good fortune. They may be known for their positive attitude and easygoing nature. Their generosity, high moral standard, and benevolence to all peoples open doors for them, leading to circumstances and people that support their causes. These people are frequently in the right place at the right time. They feel the support of nature, which becomes a guidepost for them and affirms that they are on the right path.

Shadow: The individual's social views and values may not support their path of destiny. They can be overly judgmental of others and limit themselves from interactions and opportunities that they could benefit from. Wanderlust can keep these individuals from staying in one place, where their fate would like them to be. They can take too much for granted and miss out on opportunities that require follow-through. Blind optimism can lead them down a less advantageous path. Overindulgence and greed can be tendencies that prevent these natives from taking advantage of opportune breaks and prospects.

SOUTH NODE/JUPITER

The South Node represents familiarity, gratification, and the path of least resistance.

Jupiter represents the higher mind, greater truths, expansiveness, hope, and optimism.

The combination of Jupiter and the South Node bestows a deep-rooted sensibility that luck is on their side. They likely come from deeply spiritual roots and have earned good karma. These natives are innately easygoing and generous.

The combination of Jupiter and the South Node bestows a deep-rooted sensibility that luck is on their side. They likely come from deeply spiritual roots and have earned good karma that they can bring forward in this life.

Gift: These natives are innately easygoing and generous. They have a life philosophy that carries them forward through difficult circumstances. It is easy for them to put their experiences in perspective, and they are able to help others by providing an alternate and more expansive point of view. They are naturally attuned to people of other cultures and able to integrate cultural experiences into their current life path.

Shadow: The shadow side of the Jupiter/South Node combination is a lack of determination and stick-to-it-ness. They are used to receiving life's bounties on a silver platter and do not have the wherewithal to forge their path when circumstances are tough. They can have an inflated view of themselves that is not in alignment with their capabilities.

NORTH NODE/SATURN

The North Node represents future direction, soul guidance, and fulfillment.

Saturn rules responsibility, adjustments to limitations, sustainability, and structure.

The North Node emphasizes the importance for the native to develop the attributes represented by Saturn, which include discipline, focus, and responsibilities to accomplish their heartfelt desires.

Gift: These natives have an opportunity to develop mastery in this lifetime. Through discipline and responsibility, they are able to attain their destined path. These individuals are focused on overcoming challenges and obstacles in their path. They benefit from staying on a straight and narrow track and embracing a resolute moral code. They benefit from adhering to protocols regarding timing and formalities.

Shadow: Natives with a Saturn/North Node combination can have a pessimistic attitude and may resist challenges before them. They can tend to hold on to the past and resist moving forward when letting go of the past is precisely what is needed and required.

SOUTH NODE/SATURN

The South Node represents familiarity, gratification, and the path of least resistance.

Saturn rules responsibility, adjustments to limitations, sustainability, and structure.

The combination of Saturn and the South Node can indicate that the native is familiar with limitations and able to handle responsibilities. They are likely to prefer solitude and a humble lifestyle.

> Discipline and self-mastery are a given for these individuals. They are capable of working in isolation and may have had to learn to be self-reliant.

Gift: Discipline and self-mastery are a given for these individuals. They are capable of working in isolation and may have had to learn to be self-reliant. These are traits that they can carry forward in achieving their current ambitions.

Shadow: These individuals can have rigid personalities that are not comfortable relating to others. They can be cold and calculating and may have issues trusting others. These natives may want to embrace attributes that contribute to a flourishing society that include cooperation and interdependence.

NORTH NODE/URANUS

The North Node represents future direction, soul guidance, and fulfillment.

Uranus rules intuition, originality, individuality, and the sudden and unexpected.

The North Node emphasizes the importance for the native to develop the attributes represented by Uranus. These include thinking outside of the box and the ability to embrace diverse groups of humanity.

Gift: The North Node sign, placement, and interactions with other planetary bodies give clues to one's destiny and life path. Uranus indicates that the native benefits from staying attuned to changing times and new waves of thought as well as to cutting-edge technology solutions and innovations. Uranus honors individuality and respects the unique contributions each person brings to the planet. These natives fulfill their purpose through being a unifier for humanity rather than through being a divider.

Shadow: The shadow side of this connection can indicate an individual whose extreme desire for freedom conflicts with the social order. Their nonconformist and rebellious tendencies can become an obstacle for them and ultimately alienate those who can further their purpose.

SOUTH NODE/URANUS

The South Node represents familiarity, gratification, and the path of least resistance.

Uranus rules intuition, originality, individuality, and the sudden and unexpected.

The combination of Uranus and the South Node can indicate an individual who places a great deal of emphasis on their personal freedom. They can have difficulty conforming to rules and regulations, which they will need to integrate with their North Node sign and placement.

Gift: An individual with a Uranus/South Node combination is an independent thinker who knows themselves. They are not likely to compromise their integrity and prefer to be straightforward and upright. They accept others for who they are and are not likely to be judgmental.

Shadow: The shadow side of this placement is an individual who is uncooperative, irresponsible, and rebellious. They are used to getting their own way and will be disruptive and even obnoxious until they get what they want.

NORTH NODE/NEPTUNE

The North Node represents future direction, soul guidance, and fulfillment.

Neptune rules ideals, creative imagination, transcendence, compassion, and vision.

The North Node emphasizes the importance for the native to develop the attrib-

utes represented by Neptune, which can include incorporating a spiritual practice in their lives and applying a more trusting attitude to their affairs.

Gift: The gift of a North Node/Neptune combination can be that the native has a spiritual or more universally oriented mission. These natives have psychic and intuitive abilities that assist them in fulfilling their destiny. They can benefit from following their hunches, which will put them in the right place at the right time.

Shadow: The shadow side of this placement is that the native can be drawn into seductive and potentially deceptive activities. They are attracted to the mysterious, which can put the individual into dangerous situations. These individuals can be blindsided by a desire to please and end up in perilous situations.

SOUTH NODE/NEPTUNE

The South Node represents familiarity, gratification, and the path of least resistance.

Neptune rules ideals, creative imagination, transcendence, compassion, and vision.

The combination of Neptune and the South Node indicates that the native is comfortable with a spiritually or artistically oriented lifestyle.

Gift: Individuals with a Neptune/South Node combination can bring forward sensitivity, a strong intuition, and the likelihood of spiritual leanings that they can incorporate on their current path. They are compassionate and care about those in less fortunate circumstances. These natives can have artistic, musical, or dramatic abilities.

Individuals with a Neptune/South Node combination are comfortable with a spiritually or artistically oriented lifestyle. They are compassionate and care about those in less fortunate circumstances.

utes represented by Pluto, which include determination, focus, and self-empowerment. It will significantly benefit the individual to be steadfast in unveiling underlying issues that prevent them from following a path that will bring personal fulfillment and self-empowerment. Pluto can also indicate that it can benefit the native to pursue a track in the healing arts, metaphysics, or scientific research.

Gift: Pluto combined with the North Node can bring perceptive abilities that can assist the native in understanding hidden motives and feelings of those who could assist or prevent the native from manifesting aspects of their destiny. Pluto also brings strength and determination that can help them stay on track. These natives instinctively understand the importance of change and transformation when an approach is not working. They can let go of their ego and move on.

Shadow: These natives may have engaged in deceptive practices in the past, which may incline them toward secretive and clandestine activities. They can be prone to fantasy schemes and unrealistic visions that lead them to an unfortunate outcome. They can lack discernment and follow paths that look or sound good on the surface but lead down a rabbit hole.

Shadow: The shadow side of a Pluto/North Node combination is an obsessive, ego-driven nature that ultimately generates setbacks and unnecessary obstacles for the native. These natives can be their own worst enemy, where they continually undermine their progress.

NORTH NODE/PLUTO

The North Node represents future direction, soul guidance, and fulfillment.

Pluto represents regeneration; transformation; and a compelling, fundamental approach.

The North Node emphasizes the importance for the native to develop the attrib-

SOUTH NODE/PLUTO

The South Node represents familiarity, gratification, and the path of least resistance.

Pluto represents regeneration; transformation; and a compelling, fundamental approach.

The combination of Pluto and the South Node can indicate that the native understands the importance of staying on track despite obstacles they may encounter.

Gift: These individuals can have well-developed psychic gifts that they can use to follow a path that will benefit them and bring them the self-empowerment that one receives when they are on the right track for their life's work.

Shadow: The shadow sides of this placement are well-established behavior patterns of underhandedness, manipulation, and power struggles that can be somewhat unconscious; however, they are the first course of behavior for the native. They can feel that it is their right to be abusive and act like a bully as long as it serves their purpose. They may find that they are frequently a victim of circumstance and not understand why.

NORTH NODE/CHIRON

The North Node represents future direction, soul guidance, and fulfillment.

Chiron represents core wounds and the desire to overcome them, and healing.

The North Node emphasizes the importance for the native to develop the attributes represented by Chiron, which include delving into the unconscious, healing, and teaching. It will benefit the individual to be steadfast in unveiling underlying issues that prevent them from following a path that will bring personal fulfillment and self-empowerment. Chiron can also indicate that it can benefit the native to pursue a track in the healing arts.

Gift: Chiron combined with the North Node supports these natives in embracing

> Chiron combined with the North Node supports these natives in embracing self-empowerment and taking responsibility for their issues rather than casting blame on others.

self-empowerment and taking responsibility for their issues rather than casting blame on others. They may find that they are continually having to confront wounding from times past so that they can move forward with their destiny. The issues they confront likely have a fated quality to them, leading them down an ultimate path to self-fulfillment and self-discovery.

Shadow: The shadow side of a Chiron/North Node combination is the lack of fulfillment that comes from the feeling that something more is out there in life. Unprocessed hurts, wounds, and blows to their self-esteem are continually haunting these individuals. They can be their own worst enemy, where they continually undermine their progress due to deep-rooted issues that have been swept under the rug.

SOUTH NODE/CHIRON

The South Node represents familiarity, gratification, and the path of least resistance.

Chiron represents core wounds and the desire to overcome them, and healing.

The combination of Chiron and the South Node can indicate that the native has had experience with overcoming issues that plague them and possible disabilities in the past and that they can bring the desire for self-empowerment and healing to current situations.

Gift: These individuals can assume responsibility for their conscious and unconscious issues, which helps them to continue to move forward on their path. They can have healing abilities, where they can help others. They have attained a level of self-awareness in the past.

Shadow: The shadow side of this placement is that a strong memory connected to a past life can be holding the native back from developing their destiny in this lifetime. They may need to pay more attention to their North Node sign and house placement and develop the attributes that are thereby indicated.

NORTH NODE/ERIS

The North Node represents future direction, soul guidance, and fulfillment.

Eris represents the determination to remove limitations that impede the soul's evolution.

Gift: This individual will have destiny on their side when it comes to fostering major evolutionary change at both personal and societal levels, depending upon the house positioning of Eris and the nodes. They may not fully enter their stride until they have incorporated the wisdom from the South Node house placement.

Shadow: The shadow side of this combination comes from not integrating the wisdom from the South Node house placement.

SOUTH NODE/ERIS

The South Node represents familiarity, gratification, and the path of least resistance.

Eris represents the determination to remove limitations that impede the soul's evolution.

Gift: These natives may be on a mission to manifest fairness and justice. Familiar with issues of inequality in personal relationships, they will diligently strive to express their authentic nature. Eris will be in Aries until 2048, expanding the likelihood that a Libra South Node could be in the mix.

Shadow: Codependency can characterize the native's close relationships, thereby creating stress and disfunction. Self-sabotaging patterns can interfere with attempts to fulfill their destiny.

The Kuiper Belt Dwarf Planets

The Kuiper Belt is a region filled with icy bodies lying in outer space beyond Neptune. The Kuiper Belt wasn't discovered until 1992. Since then, astronomers have discovered several Kuiper Belt Objects and dwarf planets within the region. It is possible that the Kuiper Belt contains as many as 200 dwarf planets.

Pluto was the first true Kuiper Belt Object (KBO), although scientists didn't recognize it as such until other KBOs were discovered. Pluto was reclassified as a dwarf planet in 2006. In order to be classified as a full-scale planet, a planetary body has to orbit the Sun, it must have enough gravity to force it into a spherical shape, and it must be large enough that its gravity has cleared any objects of similar size from being near its orbit. Pluto does not fulfill the last requirement but is covered in the chapter "The Outer Planets" due to its prominence in astrology interpretation.

Although Pluto's reclassification to dwarf planet may be seen in some ways as a de-

motion, its return to its true Kuiper Belt family means exactly the opposite. Pluto has returned to its true galactic position. It has more in common with Sedna and its 12,000-year orbit than it does with Neptune. Pluto has been recast as a gateway to our galactic selves. Therefore, Pluto has increased in significance in charts rather than becoming less important, as some might imagine.

Sedna, a KBO that's about three-quarters the size of Pluto, was discovered in 2004. Sedna takes about 10,500 years to make a single orbit due to its distance from the Sun. Sedna is the Goddess of the Sea or the Mistress of the Sea.

Eris was discovered in 2005. Eris has been called Pluto's feminine twin and the sister to Mars, giving it a reputation as the female warrioress goddess. Eris is bigger and brighter than Pluto. Eris orbits the Sun approximately once every 580 years.

Two more dwarf planets, Haumea and Makemake, were discovered within a few

Since the Kuiper Belt's discovery in 1992, astronomers have discovered several Kuiper Belt objects and dwarf planets within the region. Pluto, the first true Kuiper Belt Object (KBO) discovered, may share its home with as many as 200 dwarf planets.

months of each other in the Kuiper Belt. Both dwarf planets have a profound connection to nature and Earth activism. Haumea is the more philosophical and Makemake the more activist of the two.

Haumea, named after the goddess of fertility and childbirth in Hawaiian mythology, was discovered on December 28, 2004. Haumea is the third-largest known dwarf planet in the Kuiper Belt.

When astronomer Mike Brown discovered Haumea, it was the brightest object in the Kuiper Belt. It was also the oddest. It was shaped like a cigar, composed of a rock core and a thin ice surface, and it was spinning extremely fast, completing rotation every four hours. It takes 283 years to orbit around the Sun, around 35 years longer than Pluto's orbit of 248 years, but Haumea's orbit is more elliptical, so it travels much further from Earth than Pluto does.

Makemake, discovered on March 31, 2005, is likely to be the second-largest Kuiper Belt Object. Makemake comes inside of the orbit of Pluto at its closest point to Earth. Makemake's overall orbit is 306 years, compared to Pluto's orbit, which is 248 years. Makemake is attributed to environmental activism, named after the creator and fertility god Makemake.

In 2006, Eris and the largest asteroid, Ceres, were also classified as dwarf planets, although Ceres lies between Mars and Jupiter rather than in the Kuiper Belt. Previously, Ceres was described as an asteroid.

The three dwarf planets—Haumea, Eris, and Makemake—were discovered one after the other, further expanding our solar system beyond its previous boundaries.

The Kuiper Belt Objects are creating a shift beyond the spiritual concepts of transcendent Neptune and transformational Pluto toward a galactic consciousness. Humans are becoming agents of cocreativity with universal forces. In this galactic consciousness, time and space are relative, and conscious awareness spans many dimensions simultaneously.

ERIS

Even though Eris is the largest dwarf planet, it wasn't used in chart interpretations for several years following its discovery. Information gleaned regarding Eris is based upon ancient myths and stories that have come down through history.

Eris's name was chosen by a team of scientists at Caltech. Its assigned name evokes myths that subsequently led to the initial astrological interpretations of this dwarf planet. According to the *Planet Waves* blog by Eric Francis, "One of Eris's discoverers, Chad Trujillo, said that the discovery team agreed that it was the perfect name to give a major discovery at this time in history because the world is in such madness...."

According to legend, Eris wasn't invited to a wedding that all of the other gods and goddesses on Olympus were invited to. She decided to create mischief by throwing a golden apple into the celebration with an inscription reading that it was for the fairest. It was not a surprise that Venus (Aphrodite), Athena, and Hera all claimed the title, each flaunting their own gifts. Zeus didn't want to make the decision himself and assigned the choice to a mortal, who ultimately chose Aphrodite after promises were made by each of the goddesses. Her promise was to present him with the beautiful and loving Helen. Later, the mortal married Helen of Troy, and this ultimately caused a war between Troy and Greece known as the Trojan War.

Eris thereby was awarded the title the Goddess of Discord.

Eris is also said to be the sister of Mars, the God of War, whom she accompanied into battle, supporting her reputation as the warrioress goddess.

According to Beth Turnage in *Astrology Explored*, "Eris, the black winged goddess of Strife is a portion of the Sumerian goddess Innana. Innana could be wily and cunning. She was a powerful warrior, who drove a war chariot, drawn by lions. Innana ruled as a goddess during the dawn of human civilization and not only represented strength in battle, but also: She endowed the people of Sumer with gifts that inspired and insured their growth as a people and a culture."

Expanded interpretations of Eris's attributes are becoming more accepted as it is further observed in natal charts and by transit. While Eris may be the catalyst, the chaos is not necessarily of its making. Eris reveals what is hidden in the system that is not in alignment with evolution. Eris signifies breaking through what is too small for you. Eris represents discovering who you are to your core and then adapting aspects of your life to the new you. A struggle may ensue. The act of breaking through old paradigms can be difficult at times.

Discord, strife, and chaos enter our lives so that we can find ways to make changes in order to find more harmony. It puts us in touch with our deepest passions and desires, and its warrior nature helps us fight to bring them to fruition based upon its placement and connections to other planets in the chart.

Eris represents a feminine warrior energy that fights for the soul. When it was first

According to legend, Eris wasn't invited to a wedding that all of the other gods and goddesses on Olympus were invited to. She became the Goddess of Discord after mischievously tossing a golden apple into the celebration with an inscription reading that it was for the fairest.

discovered, it was called Planet X, for which it garnered the nickname Xena, after the television show by the same name. Eris, the warrioress goddess, forces one to act upon their most deeply held values. She demands conviction in that fight, regardless of the upheld beliefs of the collective.

Eris is likened to Pluto in that Eris is the Goddess of Transformation and Pluto is the God of Transformation. Just like Pluto, Eris challenges and pushes our buttons when change is needed. It brings discord only when it knows that it's time for a greater harmony to be born. Both dwarf planets relate to the unconscious; to those areas where we have been strongly influenced by the collective; and, more personally, to our parental upbringing and close personal relationships.

As the warrioress goddess, Eris's link to the feminine principle was reinforced by the observation of trends occurring during Conjunctions of Chiron and Eris during the early 1970s. According to astrologer Eric Francis, a key characteristic of this period was that the feminine movement was becoming a self-aware entity, whereby women have at least the same potential as men and are entitled to the same rights and privileges.

Eris moves very slowly around the Sun; therefore, several generations will have Eris in the same sign. The dwarf planet takes 556 years to orbit the Sun. Eris will be in Aries from 1926 until 2048. When in Aries, Eris shows courage and is willing to fight for its deepest held beliefs. The placement gives it an edge in being a pioneer, breaking out of predefined roles. In Aries, Eris can fight for its beliefs and its soul's purpose.

Gift: In the birth chart, Eris can indicate the area of life where one is willing to be different in order to follow one's deepest beliefs. Eris represents the area of the chart where the individual is empowered to take charge over a difficult area of their life. An empowered Eris follows the calling of its unique imprint. It is secure in its sense of self and does not succumb to the beliefs and mores of society. Eris signifies breaking out of imposed structures and belief patterns that are no longer appropriate or that are limiting further growth and evolution of the soul.

> Eris in the First House individuals project a strong sense of who they are at their core or, at least, who they are at this point in their growth and evolution.

Shadow: The shadow side of Eris is rebellious and competitive but often to no avail since the discord created is overdone and disproportionate for the task at hand. Its placement can also indicate areas where we can get caught up in strife or where we are blamed or accept blame, as was the case in the mythology of Eris triggering the Trojan War. Without courage or conviction, the individual can feel that they are treading water or walking on a hamster wheel and not making significant evolutionary progress.

ERIS IN THE HOUSES

Eris in the First House

The First House rules appearance, health, general temperament, and sense of self. The First House defines you and the image you project to others.

Gift: Eris in the First House individuals project a strong sense of who they are at their core or, at least, who they are at this point in their growth and evolution. As they continue to grow and peel back layers, revealing more of who they are, the projection of themselves that they passionately project can shift. They possess the passion and determination to take a stand for the beliefs that they identify with.

Shadow: Too much ego and arrogance can get intertwined with their passion for reflecting their deeply held core beliefs. The discord they create can become counterproductive to the goals they are wanting to achieve. Rather than being an instrument for growth, the native can experience pain and loss.

Eris in the Second House

The Second House is connected with finances, values, material possessions, talents, and resources. The Second House represents the value we give to ourselves and, in turn, that which we possess.

Gift: Beliefs in how to preserve and value Earth's resources can trigger societal awareness and shifting. Their values regarding wealth, sharing of resources, and what is important can be different from the traditional views of society and can shed light on important ways to better utilize Earth's resources.

Shadow: These natives can fight to hold on to their personal wealth and resources. Their wealth can be used to create divisiveness and strife rather than as a tool to help those who are less fortunate.

A Fifth-House Eris can successfully apply creativity to express the truth of who they are at their core. Their artistic and dramatic style is strong and passionate.

Eris in the Third House

The Third House is connected with ideas, communication, siblings, neighbors, and short journeys.

Gift: These individuals have the courage and fortitude to express their unique ideas in spite of societal pressure to follow conventional thinking. They can use their communication skills to ardently get their points of view across to members of society.

Shadow: Arrogance, anger, and ego can get in the way of communicating less orthodox ideas to society. Their ardently held beliefs are not communicated in a way that is heard.

Eris in the Fourth House

The Fourth House is about the home, family, genetic inheritance, foundational stability, innermost feelings, later life, and the end of matters.

Gift: A strong inner awareness of the true meaning of stability and family values may conflict with many members of society; however, these natives have the drive and passion to bring forth comfort and harmony in their home. They have the drive and determination to unravel genetic inheritances in order to bring forth more physical and mental harmony for themselves and future generations.

Shadow: In the struggle against injustice and oppression, these individuals can lose sight of their goal to create a more satisfying home environment. They can get into power struggles with household members, causing strife and discord.

Eris in the Fifth House

The Fifth House rules creative self-expression, children, love, passion, romance, playfulness, and joy.

Gift: A Fifth-House Eris placement can successfully apply creativity to express the truth of who they are at their core. These creative modalities can help to bring aspects of themselves to their conscious awareness and then convey their revelations to society. Their artistic and dramatic style is strong and passionate.

Shadow: These natives can get caught up in being bullies in order to demand attention. Childish behavior and too much pride can interfere with the message that these individuals are wanting to convey.

Eris in the Sixth House

The Sixth House governs daily routines, acts of service, the work-life balance, health, due diligence, pet care, coworkers, and employees.

Gift: The placement of Eris in the Sixth House can motivate the research and the practical application of healthcare solutions that resonate with and support the native as well as society. These methods may not be condoned by the traditional medical establishment, although the native will be relentless in their pursuit of health-giving results. These individuals can create harmonious workplace environments where each person can express their unique contributions.

Shadow: Illness can result when the individual doesn't resonate to their true nature.

Eris in the Seventh House

The Seventh House rules close personal relationships, agreements, and compromises.

Gift: A Seventh-House placement of Eris can strive to find unique ways to model personal and business relationships so that each individual can resonate to their own true self and not conform to the imposed mandates of society. They will not tire in their quest of manifesting satisfying and harmonious partnerships.

Shadow: The constant focus on continuing to be true to one's beliefs and true nature can rule out compromise in those matters that can create peace and harmony in relationships. These natives can be too strong and not be discerning on the best ways to achieve their goals for a successful relationship.

Eris in the Eighth House

The Eighth House rules joint ventures, intimacy, sex, death, transformation, and psychic dimensions.

Gift: Eris in the house ruled by Scorpio in the natural Zodiac ups the ante on the need to get to the bottom of matters.

These natives can be excellent researchers, not giving up until they reach a goal that resonates with them. Matters pertaining to sex, birth, and death may be a strong focus, with the native seeking ways to elevate these life events to new ways of consideration.

Shadow: These natives can lack the sensitivity, respect, and discernment necessary to maneuver in the areas ruled by the Eighth House, which include sex, death, birth, and their partner's resources. They may feel limitations in these areas that don't resonate to their core beliefs; however, they may be too forceful and impatient to work with others.

Eris in the Ninth House

The Ninth House rules higher education, long-term goals, foreign travel, publicity, adventures, religion, and philosophical and ethical pursuits.

Gift: These natives will pursue studies and seek to expand upon conventionally accepted belief systems, especially those related to religion, spirituality, and philosophy. Travel to remote locations and studies of lesser-known cultures can contribute to their expanded perspective, which they are ardently intent upon sharing with others.

Shadow: These natives can get overzealous in their beliefs and attempt to foster their belief systems upon others, even if they are not appropriate for them. A cultish side exists to these individuals, where they may either become rebellious members of a cult or create their own,

> Eris in the house ruled by Scorpio in the natural Zodiac natives can be excellent researchers, not giving up until they reach a goal that resonates with them.

projecting that they are the one who has the keys to the kingdom.

Eris in the Tenth House

The Tenth House rules public achievements, reputation, authority, and prestige.

Gift: Eris's desire to elevate the status of the underdog and those who are less privileged can inspire these natives to attain public or influential status so that they can effect change and transformation in society. These natives will fight for those who are less fortunate.

Shadow: Impetuousness, strife, and discord in the public arena can lead to public disdain, and their message will be lost on deaf ears.

Eris in the Eleventh House

The Eleventh House rules friends, hopes, wishes, groups, and a sense of belonging in the world.

Gift: These natives are inclined to form groups and organizations that will promote the betterment of outliers in society. Their innate wisdom for respecting the soul urges of others can lead to satisfying connections and friendships. Friendships based upon the mutual respect of each individual's uniqueness can foster evolutionary growth for both participants.

Shadow: Feelings of being an outsider can prevent successful participation in groups and organizations where the native could make important contributions. Similarly, unwarranted competition with members of groups or organizations can lead to the native not being accepted in situations where their input could be valuable.

Eris in the Twelfth House

The Twelfth House rules secrets, unconscious patterns, karma, closure, institutions, connections with higher sources, enlightenment, and undoing.

Gift: Natives with Eris in the Twelfth House can fiercely pursue a path to enlightenment. They have the impetus to release unconscious patterns that are holding them back and fostering limitations on their soul's growth. They can work in institutions and hospitals to help less fortunate members of society improve their sense of worth. They have the ability to contact higher realms and share the information they glean to help others.

Shadow: In their attempt to alleviate karma, they can be creating more karma. The Twelfth House is also the house of undoing, meaning that unconscious behavior patterns can create more karma for the native. In this case, it would be unconsciously creating strife and discord when not warranted, which can make these individuals' lives more difficult.

ERIS COMBINATIONS

Eris/Sun

Eris represents the determination to remove limitations that impede the soul's evolution.

The Sun indicates purpose, self-expression, creative life force, and conscious will.

Gift: When Eris combines with the Sun, the native is on a mission to express their authenticity in all aspects of their lives. They are aligned to the discovery of their true soul's calling and mission in life. They are likely to assist others in finding their true purpose as well.

Shadow: These individuals get caught up in ego identification with their mission to find authenticity in their own lives and in society. They flaunt their beliefs with arrogance, which ultimately creates divisiveness. Their efforts are unproductive and discordant.

Eris/Moon

Eris represents the determination to remove limitations that impede the soul's evolution.

The Moon rules the soul, core instincts, the personality, and subconscious conditioning.

Gift: These natives have an innate gift for spotting phoniness and inauthenticity. They strive to uncover false belief systems and subconscious programming that resulted from society and parental conditioning. They desire to help others unveil their true selves.

Shadow: Subconscious competitiveness and a propensity to create strife and discord can characterize these natives in situations when they consciously want to improve their lives and the lives of those around them. They can be abrasive.

Eris/Mercury

Eris represents the determination to remove limitations that impede the soul's evolution.

Mercury rules communication, mental processes, and the logical mind.

Gift: These natives make great spokespeople for enlightening others on the disparaging influences of the collective unconscious. They can express their own stories in an effective manner that helps others.

Shadow: The communication style of these natives serves to alienate others, so they don't hear or receive what the native wants to convey. They can be on a mission that is ineffective.

Eris/Venus

Eris represents the determination to remove limitations that impede the soul's evolution.

When Eris combines with the Sun, the native is on a mission to express their authenticity in all aspects of their lives. They are aligned to the discovery of their true soul's calling and mission in life.

Venus represents love, relationships, beauty, values, comfort, and material resources.

Gift: These natives attract to themselves like-minded souls that accompany them on their journey to their next level of evolution. They seek to find purity and authenticity in their relationships.

Shadow: Their exceedingly strong competitive nature can cause these individuals to seek love for the sake of love. Their lack of discernment can send them barking up the wrong tree. They are inclined to create strife and discord in social situations, whereby they become an outcast, without the comraderie they desire.

Eris/Mars

Eris represents the determination to remove limitations that impede the soul's evolution.

Mars rules assertiveness, energy, drive, and courage.

Gift: Combining the energies of Mars and Eris, mythically known as brother and sister, warrior and warrioress, is a force to be reckoned with when the goal is generating change. This combination can focus in on what is inauthentic and unfair where the betterment of society is at stake.

Shadow: These natives can lose track of what they are fighting for. Personal issues can overshadow the purity of their quest.

Eris/Jupiter

Eris represents the determination to remove limitations that impede the soul's evolution.

Jupiter represents the higher mind, greater truths, expansiveness, hope, and optimism.

Gift: Expansive Jupiter can lend perspective to Eris's quests and assist the native in ascertaining beneficial outcomes in their personal and societal ventures.

Shadow: Jupiter has been known to overdo, and when these two energies combine, the process for attaining their desired result can be fraught with too much fight and determination.

Eris/Saturn

Eris represents the determination to remove limitations that impede the soul's evolution.

Saturn rules responsibility, adjustments to limitations, sustainability, and structure.

Gift: Saturn can add structure to Eris's intentions so that social change can follow a step-by-step approach to reach their desired outcome. Saturn also adds patience

and perseverance, which can tone down the impetuous nature of Eris.

Shadow: Limitations and setbacks can throw a monkey wrench into plans and actions undertaken by the native. The native may have to do more soul searching before ascertaining a successful outcome.

Eris/Uranus

Eris represents the determination to remove limitations that impede the soul's evolution.

Uranus rules intuition, originality, individuality, and the sudden and unexpected.

Gift: Uranian individuality is a distinct asset when looking to overcome the conditioning that is imposed by the collective or parental and family influences. These natives can draw on their inherent originality for manifesting solutions that can benefit society.

Shadow: Rebelliousness to the extreme can be counterproductive when looking to make successful and lasting changes to society. The outlier side of Eris can be inordinately accentuated and lead to isolation and disappointment.

Eris/Neptune

Eris represents the determination to remove limitations that impede the soul's evolution.

Neptune rules ideals, creative imagination, transcendence, compassion, and vision.

Gift: The native can successfully utilize transcendental practices in order to reinforce their evolutionary journey. Music, sound therapy, and color therapy are other

> Saturn can add structure to Eris's intentions so that social change can follow a step-by-step approach to reach their desired outcome.

practices that they can draw upon as supportive to their quest to resonate with their inner selves.

Shadow: False illusions can color natives' perceptions, sending them on a mission for naught. Disillusionment can thereby temper their otherwise lofty intentions to assist members of society who need help.

Eris/Pluto

Eris represents the determination to remove limitations that impede the soul's evolution.

Pluto represents regeneration; transformation; and a compelling, fundamental approach.

Gift: Pluto can give a big bump to the drive and determination of Eris, encouraging the native to pull out all the stops to get to the bottom of whatever is interfering with the native becoming their true authentic self. They have laser vision, penetrating falsehoods and anywhere authenticity is lacking.

Shadow: The downside of the Pluto and Eris combination is the potential for self-destructive behavior. Unresolved ego issues can undermine good intentions, muddying the waters of what could otherwise be major evolutionary progress.

Eris/Chiron

Eris represents the determination to remove limitations that impede the soul's evolution.

Chiron represents core wounds and the desire to overcome them, and healing.

Gift: A strong desire to heal genetic, societal, and familiar patterning can propel this individual through trials and tribulations that eventually lead to a rebirth of the soul. They are examples of those who express themselves clearly, authentically, and in a way that challenges those around them.

Shadow: These folks can get caught up in the process of healing themselves and run into obstacles at every turn, which tests their determination and the purity of their intent. They may have to resolve issues that revolve around the theme of rejection.

Eris/North Node

Eris represents the determination to remove limitations that impede the soul's evolution.

The North Node represents future direction, soul guidance, and fulfillment.

Gift: This individual will have destiny on their side when it comes to fostering major evolutionary change at both personal and societal levels depending upon the house positioning of Eris and the nodes. They may not fully enter their stride until they have incorporated the wisdom from the South Node house placement.

Shadow: The shadow side of this combination comes from not integrating the wisdom from the South Node house placement.

Eris/South Node

Eris represents the determination to remove limitations that impede the soul's evolution.

The South Node represents familiarity, gratification, and the path of least resistance.

Gift: These natives may be on a mission to manifest fairness and justice. Familiar with issues of inequality in personal relationships, they will diligently strive to express their authentic nature. Eris will be in Aries until 2048, expanding the likelihood that a Libra South Node could be in the mix.

The South Node represents familiarity, gratification, and the path of least resistance. Eris represents the determination to remove limitations that impede the soul's evolution. These natives may be on a mission to manifest fairness and justice.

Shadow: Codependency can characterize the native's close relationships, thereby creating stress and disfunction. Self-sabotaging patterns can interfere with attempts to fulfill their destiny.

SEDNA

Dwarf planet Sedna moves slowly. Pluto takes 248 years to orbit the Sun, while Sedna takes a massive 12,000 years.

According to astrologer Barbara Schermer in her article titled "Goddess for Our Time" in the April/May 2009 issue of *The Mountain Astrologer*, on the evening of November 13, 2003, astronomer Mike Brown and his team, using a new imaging technique, began to identify planetlike bodies. This resulted in the detection of

the body that Brown submitted to the International Astronomical Union. Brown and his team reasoned: "Our newly discovered object is the coldest, most distant place known in the solar system, so we feel it is appropriate to name it in honor of Sedna, the Inuit Goddess of the sea, who is thought to live at the bottom of the frigid Arctic Ocean."

Sedna is the Inuit goddess who rules over the bounty of the sea. According to myth, when Sedna was young, she refused to marry and comply with the cultural ways of her tribe. She eventually married, although it turns out that she married a bird that was disguised as a handsome, enigmatic man. This husband could only feed her fish since he was a bird. When her father visited and saw her plight, he killed her bird-man husband, and he and Sedna fled from the island in his kayak. A fierce storm arose, and in an attempt to save his own life, the father threw Sedna overboard into the cold Arctic Sea. She attempted to hold on, but her father severed her fingers. Sedna fell to the bottom of the sea and was transformed into a goddess. Her severed fingers became dolphins and whales. As a goddess, she ensured that the Inuits were fed, clothed, and housed from the depths of the ocean.

Sedna awakens several principles as a feminine archetype. She discovered a higher consciousness and a new purpose after her deep dive into her own being. In spite of her situation, Sedna stands for avoiding the mindset of seeing herself as a victim. Rather, she kept an open heart, presumably playing the drums and singing in order to keep herself alive.

Sedna represents the experience of stepping beyond culturally approved roles, surrendering and eventually reforming into a

Sedna, the Inuit Goddess who rules over the bounty of the sea, represents the experience of stepping beyond culturally approved roles, surrendering, and an eventual reformation into a divine form.

divine form. She stands for making choices and sticking to them. Sedna is also seen as a protector of the environment.

Sedna can indicate in a chart where an individual may have become frozen inside due to a lack of protection and nurturing and where and how the letting go of frozen aspects of emotions can occur.

SEDNA IN THE SIGNS

Given her irregular orbit, Sedna is now nearing us, relatively speaking. Sedna will be closest to Earth in the year 2076 in the sign of Cancer.

Little information is available regarding Sedna moving through the signs of Aries and Taurus and even less information regarding Sedna in Gemini. Barbara Schermer has done quite a bit of research in this area through her examination of the charts of prominent individuals making contributions to society as well as events taking place during these periods.

In the above-mentioned article in *The Mountain Astrologer*, Barbara Schermer offers the following information on sign placement. Some discrepancy has occurred regarding the ingress of Sedna in the signs below. According to Alan Clay, first published by *The Astrological Journal* in 2010 and the Astrological Association of Great Britain in 2019, the dates are shown in italics below.

Sedna in Aries (1867–1968): "A look at the data suggested that Sedna appearing in the charts of births and events in fiery Aries signifies inspiration, motivation, even the incitement of outrage; therefore, the label 'Catalysts' seemed apt."

Sedna in Taurus (1968–2010; *1965–2024*): "With Sedna in earthy Taurus, determination and problem-solving are apparent, so I have chosen to call those having this placement the 'Manifestors.'"

Sedna in Gemini (2024–2068): Sufficient information is not available to provide adequate information regarding this placement; however, according to Alan Clay, "We're currently in what we're calling a digital revolution, the Sedna in Taurus phase. And with Sedna's entry into Gemini in 2024, it is likely that this will morph more into a consciousness revolution...." We see that Sedna is Gemini is going to be all about the rise of "Artificial Intelligence," which will inevitably promote a consciousness, and spiritual, revolution.

SEDNA IN THE HOUSES

Sedna's placement in the houses can indicate where the individual needs to be cut loose from traditional roles. Sedna is at home in the frozen depths. The house placement can show the areas where exploration into the deep unconscious must take place. Decisions come from exploring the depths of one's feelings in order to determine what feels right.

Gift: Having an open heart, which brings a transcendent peace.

Shadow: Victimization, alienation, unrelenting trauma, and suffering can occur in the areas ruled by the house placement of Sedna.

HAUMEA

Haumea is connected with how an individual sustains themselves and how we sustain our species. Haumea is activating a galactic consciousness connected with sustainability.

When we allow ourselves time to connect deeply with what nourishes us, we lose our fear that we will ever have to do without and that nourishment will not be there when we need it.

Astrologer Philip Sedgwick suggests on his website that Haumea gives a soulful confidence and unshakeable personal inner knowing, restoring a rock-solid integrity. Its negative expression may include being insecure, dramatic, and attention seeking and using the energy of others to its own benefit (nonpaid volunteers, fans, devotees).

Haumea represents the area in the astrology chart where the individual pays attention to their connection to nature and to life. It may manifest itself in an individual having some part to play regarding fertility, regeneration, or coming back to life through some kind of emergent technology, natural medicine, sacred ceremony, or similar.

MAKEMAKE

Makemake was named for the creator god of a small, isolated volcanic island in the Pacific Ocean known as Rapa Nui or Easter Island. Although the island may appear insignificant, its history has interested scholars throughout the years. Of particular interest is its location in the Pacific along with the unusual culture of Easter Island, with its large, carved stone heads. The Birdman myth and tradition has also drawn significant attention.

According to astrologer Henry Seltzer, founder and CEO of Time Passages Software, the archetype of the Birdman myth relates back to the meaning of Makemake in the chart. The archetype connects to inwardly tuning in to the depths of the psyche in order to obtain a more passive and feminist form of received wisdom that can be merged with the outer-oriented male warrior energy.

The myth goes as follows: Tribal elders selected a Birdman each year who would compete with other candidates in a dangerous journey involving climbing huge cliffs, swimming in dangerous waters, and returning with the first bird egg of the season. The triumphant Birdman would then meditate in a hut, and after a year, he would bring his visions back to the culture. Visualizations and the power of positive thinking are all examples of an active Makemake placement.

Makemake was named for the Creator God of Rapa Nui, also known as Easter Island. Images of Makemake and the birdmen of his cult are carved in petroglyphs on the island.

Astrologer Philip Sedgwick believes that the position of Rapa Nui bears a direct relationship to the Galactic Center. It's thought that the original Polynesian people arrived in their canoes around 380 C.E., having navigated their way by the stars thousands of miles across the deep ocean. Sedgwick further adds that according to the mythology of Rapa Nui, Makemake, known as the creator of humanity and the god of fertility, was the chief god of the Birdman cult. Images of Birdman are carved in petroglyphs on the island and worshipped in the form of sea birds.

Sedgwick sees Makemake as having the courage to face the peril of the spiritual journey, as symbolized by the ritual "race" through shark-infested waters and up sheer cliffs to find the egg, which symbolizes rebirth or initiation and spiritual renewal.

Modern-day interpretation also connects the dwarf planet to environmental activism based upon the neglect of Earth's natural resources and cultural values. Advanced civilization has used and abused the beauty, glory, and richness of the resources that Earth has given us. On the global level, Makemake represents the damage to culture and the environment that result from modern values that cling to an attachment to wealth and status, which is believed to be superior to a more integrated and sustainable way of life.

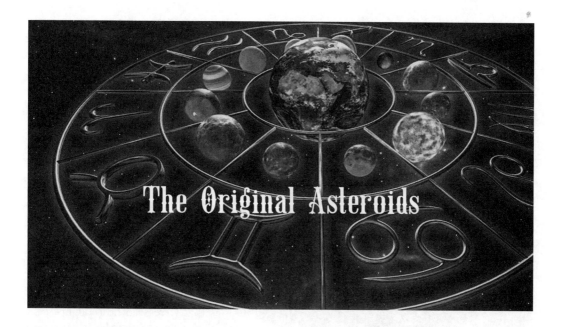

The Original Asteroids

The first wave of feminism was initiated with the discovery of four asteroids at the beginning of the 19th century: Ceres, Juno, Vesta, and Pallas Athena.

When these feminine asteroids were then included in an ephemeris in the early 1970s, it coincided with an upsurge in the rise of consciousness in women. Previously, only the Moon and Venus represented feminine archetypes, whereas all of the other planets were representative of male archetypes.

These four original asteroids lie between the inner and more personal planetary bodies—Mercury, Venus, and Mars—which pertain to the individual, and the social planets, which include Jupiter and Saturn. The social planets represent our society, culture, religion, and economy.

Asteroids are bits of rock floating in space. Tens of thousands of them exist, mostly found in the Main Asteroid Belt between Mars and Jupiter. Beyond the original four

asteroids, their use by astrologers has become increasingly popular.

Demetra George in her iconic book *The Asteroid Goddesses* played a major role in enlivening the four archetypes of feminine wisdom represented by Ceres, Juno, Vesta, and Pallas Athena, each offering a particular type of wisdom.

Each asteroid goddess has a somewhat glib meaning: Ceres is the mother, Juno the wife, Vesta the guardian of the sacred flame, and Pallas Athena the wise one. Digging deeper, the truer meaning of these asteroid goddesses is revealed, replacing the false stories that the Greek and Roman cultures laid over the ancient matriarchal mythologies.

CERES

Ceres, previously an asteroid, is now classified as a dwarf planet. After Ceres's discovery in 1801, it was classified as a planet

Depicted in this first century fresco alongside her son Bacchus, Ceres was the Roman goddess of agriculture, grain, and fertility. She represents the depth of motherly love as well as issues in the parent–child relationship.

more personal, human aspects and galactic consciousness.

Ceres's connection with Pluto through her mythical daughter, Persephone, accentuates her connection to the mystery of deep transformation through attuning to natural cycles. When Persephone was presumably abducted by Pluto, Ceres had to recover from grief and loss.

Ceres represents the depth of motherly love as well as the grief, loss, and response to the abduction of whomever we love most. She also represents issues in the parent–child relationship.

A concept introduced by astrologer Alan Clay is that Ceres can be thought of as the higher octave of the Moon, "meaning that the emotional security of the Moon is transmuted to a sustenance and nurturing of our spiritual security and sense of place on planet Earth with Ceres."

Clay continues: "This is very similar to Sedna, except that Sedna operates on a far vaster scale, so we may find that Sedna is the higher octave of Ceres—where the spiritual security and sense of place on Earth with Ceres is transmuted into transpersonal nurturing of our spirituality and sense of place in the revolutionary cycle with Sedna."

Ceres represents the nourishment needed to make life worth living.

until the 1850s when it was reclassified as an asteroid. In 2006, when Ceres was declared a dwarf planet, the feminine movement shifted gears, with women moving beyond demands for equality and choosing instead to step into leadership roles.

Ceres is the largest body in the asteroid belt that lies between Mars and Jupiter and, accordingly, it entertains a great presence. Ceres accounts for approximately one-third the size of the entire asteroid belt.

A curious connection has occurred between the planets Pluto and Ceres. Astronomers found that they are made from similar material and may have been born in the same realm. Somehow, Ceres was pulled into a closer orbit and now sits between Mars and Jupiter in the Main Asteroid Belt, creating a bridge between the

JUNO

Juno is commonly represented as the energy of intimate relationships or the commitment-in-relationships asteroid. Juno is connected to the aspects of a relationship that are concerned with sharing and appropriate boundaries with another person. Juno is connected with making the most out of a relationship. Juno will also indicate where issues can arise if the individual is not treated with respect and fairness. The Juno archetype can assist in finding ways to honor both personal purpose and connection through commitment, equality, and loyalty.

The shadow side of Juno can be similar to several versions of the mythology and include power struggles, jealousy, or manipulation. Juno was often represented as a jealous wife. Her influence goes far beyond that.

The mythology and archetype of Juno have a few interpretations, some of which have evolved over time. In Greek mythology, Juno is Hera, and Zeus is her counterpart. In Roman mythology, they are Juno and Jupiter. As Queen of the Gods, one may assume that Juno was incredibly powerful and had an ideal, goddesslike relationship with the beneficent Jupiter. While her archetypal energy is quite compelling, it carries along with it many gifts and shadows along with a great deal of learning potential.

Several myths exist about the marriage between Juno, or Hera, and Jupiter, or Zeus. In one of these myths, the goddess was deceived by the Zeus/Jupiter admirer who was entranced by her and ultimately raped her. Out of shame and obligation, Hera agreed to marry him and completely commit to the relationship.

Another mythical rendition says that the pair was married in secret, and this secret was held for 300 years. The reason the secret was held for that long was because it took all those years for the Hellenistic people to convert to monogamy, which is the type of marriage and commitment that

Pictured here with husband Jupiter, Juno was the queen of the Roman pantheon. Juno's placement in a chart reveals the motivations for being in a relationship as well as core wounds related to attachment.

Juno represents. In the honeymoon phase of their marriage, a lot of love and passion actually existed between them. This quote from *The Iliad* shows this: "Never has such desire for goddess or woman flooded and overwhelmed my heart. Never have I felt such love, such sweet desire as fills me now for you," said Zeus to his wife. As time went on, however, Zeus flaunted his lovers and illegitimate children. Hera remained faithful.

As a result, the asteroid Juno indicates commitment and jealousy rather than love. The theme of withdrawal is also present since Hera would frequently withdraw to her special spot in order to cope with her displeasure. She would withdraw and hide for hundreds of years sometimes, yet she always came back. Zeus would go to great lengths to draw her out of her hiding even though he had no intention of giving her the love that she so desired and deserved.

In early Rome, Juno's temple was where money was made; she was referred to as Juno Moneta, the protector of funds.

Juno's sign position colors the type of energy one's commitment embodies as well as the kind of things that are worthy of commitment. Juno's house placement represents the area of focus where one is likely to commit.

Juno's placement in a chart reveals the motivations for being in a relationship as well as the core wounds related to attachment.

VESTA

Vesta was the Roman goddess of the hearth fire. According to Cicero, Vesta represented the vital force at the root of the life of the community. The priestesses guarded the sacred fire. The Vesta archetype represents the spark of fertility and the sexual and fertilizing power of the goddess.

Vesta reminds us that we must keep that sacred fire burning. One's needs and wants matter; they are alive, boundless, and eternal. Vesta represents the capacity to be open to one's own sacred nature, to see oneself as divine, and to connect with the creative force of divinity in everyone.

Vesta is also a strong indicator for career or calling. It represents an area of life where an individual is passionately drawn. Its position in the chart is a powerful indicator for what an individual must do in order to keep their inner flame shining brightly. Vesta indicates the areas in which the individual has a vested interest, where passion occurs. It points to one's most revered values.

The shadow aspect of Vesta can produce a feeling of submission, where the individual is working to keep someone else's flame alive.

Vesta's sign position will indicate how the individual expresses their ability to keep their sacred flame alive.

PALLAS ATHENA

Pallas Athena, the daughter of Zeus, is the archetype of the wise one. Pallas Athena is a point in the astrology chart that is associated with a type of intelligence that is related to perception and the ability to see patterns and the interrelationship of concepts. It has an ability to link, unify, and bring pieces together.

As a mythological goddess, Pallas Athena was born from the head of Zeus as an emanation of his mind and as a fully formed feminine warrior. She is portrayed in early images as clad in armor, holding a spear and shield. The shield is protective, not only as a physical barrier against vulnerability to attack but also as using intelligence as a strategy for defense. She is strong-willed and can act on her own knowledge and wisdom, although it is said that she prefers artful diplomacy over conflict. She is ready to fight if need be.

Pallas Athena was also honored as a goddess of healing. Her ability to see patterns also allows her to see the parts that don't fit or where imbalances occur in the physical. Legend indicates that Pallas Athena miraculously healed through the power of her mind. Her statue stands on the Acropolis next to that of Hygeia, the Goddess of Health.

The astrological Pallas Athena is a unifier and a defender of social justice. Pallas

Athena invites the integration of dualities. It prefers using wisdom as a solution for expressing nonjudgmental solutions to situations created by opposing forces.

The shadow side of Pallas Athena manifests as a victim mentality. The individual can be prone to righteous indignation, withdrawal, and even self-sabotage due to judgments over alternative viewpoints. Pallas Athena's issues can express themselves as an imbalance in the masculine and feminine aspects of the Self.

The sign placement and influences from planetary combinations reflect the individual's ability to perceive patterns that constitute the whole. The house position indicates the area in the individual's life where this is most likely to occur.

GLOSSARY

Ascendant (Asc)—The Ascendant represents one's approach, orientation, and the window through which one sees the world.

Benefics—Traditional astrology describes Venus and Jupiter as benefics, meaning that they are fortunate and will generally provide favorable results in the chart.

Chiron—Chiron represents core wounds and the desire to overcome them, healing.

Eighth House—The Eight House rules joint ventures, intimacy, sex, death, transformation, psychic dimensions.

Eleventh House—The Eleventh House rules friends, hopes, wishes, groups, sense of belonging in the world.

Eris—Eris represents the determination to remove limitations that impede the soul's evolution.

Fifth House—The Fifth House rules creative self-expression, children, love, passion, romance, playfulness, and joy.

First House—The First House rules appearance, health, general temperament and sense of self. The First House defines you and the image you project to others.

Forth House—The Fourth House is about the home, family, genetic inheritance, foundational stability, innermost feelings, later life and the end of matters.

Jupiter—Jupiter represents the higher mind, greater truths, expansiveness, hope and optimism.

Mars—Mars rules assertiveness, energy, drive and courage.

Mercury—Mercury rules communication, mental processes and the logical mind.

Midheaven (MC)—The Midheaven represents image, outer aspirations and career orientation.

Moon—The Moon rules the Soul, core instincts, the personality and subconscious conditioning.

Neptune—Neptune rules ideals, creative imagination, transcendence, compassion and vision.

Ninth House—The Ninth House rules higher education, long term goals, foreign travel, publicity, adventures, religion, philosophical and ethical pursuits.

North Node—The North Node represents future direction, soul guidance and fulfillment.

Pluto—Pluto represents regeneration, transformation, a compelling, fundamental approach.

Saturn—Saturn rules responsibility, adjustments to limitations, sustainability, and structure.

Second House—The Second House is connected with finances, values, material possessions, talents and resources. The Second House represents the value we give to ourselves and, in turn, that which we possess.

Seventh House—The Seventh House rules close personal relationships, agreements, compromises.

Shadow—Identifying the shadow aspects in oneís psyche and bringing these patterns to the forefront of consciousness is highly important in manifesting the gifts that the placement offers.

Sixth House—The Sixth House governs daily routines, acts of service, the work/life balance, health, due diligence, care of pets, coworkers, and employees. The body you are born with is governed by the First House, whereby choices made over time create the body governed by the Sixth House.

South Node—The South Node represents familiarity, gratification and the path of least resistance.

Sun—The Sun indicates purpose, self-expression, creative life force and conscious will.

Tenth House—The Tenth House rules public achievements, reputation, authority, prestige.

Third House—The Third House relates to ideas, communication, siblings, neighbors, short journeys.

Twelfth House—The Twelfth House rules secrets, unconscious patterns, karmà, closure, institutions, connection with higher sources, enlightenment, undoing.

Uranus—Uranus rules intuition, originality, individuality and the sudden and unexpected.

Venus—Venus represents love, relationships, beauty, values, comfort, and material resources.

FURTHER READING

"31 Most Inspiring Paramahansa Yogananda Quotes (2023)." Unico Things, January 1, 2023. http://www.unicothings.com/parama hansa-yogananda-quotes/.

Arroyo, Stephen, *Karma & Transformation: The Inner Dimensions of the Birth Chart,* 2nd edition, CRCS Publications, 1992, p. 72.

Artley, Malvin. Capricorn_22 letter from Subscriber. Email dated January 17, 2022. http://www.malvinartley.com/subscriber-archives.

Bailey, Alice A., *Esoteric Astrology,* 1st edition, Lucis Publishing Companies, 2012, p. 148.

Clay, Alan. "Sedna Consciousness—The Soul's Path of Destiny," *The Astrological Journal,* April 1, 2019.

Demboski, Julie. "Defining Chiron." Julie Demboski's ASTROLOGY, April 7, 2022. https://juliedemboski.com/2022/04/07/defining-chiron/.

Forrest, Stephen, *The Inner Sky: How to Make More Fulfilling Choices for a More Fulfilling Life,* reprint, Seven Paws Press, 2012.

Francis, Eric. "Eris Notebook: Dancing with Discord." Planet Waves, November 10, 2020. https://planetwaves.net/eris-notebook-danc ing-with-discord.

Myss, Carolyn. "When You Bring Your Shadow into the Light, It No Longer Has Power over You." Caroline Myss, August 22, 2017. http://www.myss.com/bring-shadow-light-no-longer-power/.

Ottewell, Guy. Earth Sky, January 7, 2022. http://www.earthsky.org/author/guyottewell.

Rudd, Richard, *The Art of Contemplation: Gentle Path to Wholeness and Prosperity,* Gene Keys Publishing, 2018.

"Warren G. Bennis Quote." AZ quotes. Accessed January 25, 2023. https://www.azquotes.com/quote/23976.

INDEX

Note: (ill.) indicates photos and illustrations